AGRARIAN QUESTIONS
Essays in Appreciation of T.J. Byres

AGRARIAN QUESTIONS
Essays in Appreciation of T.J. Byres

edited by

Henry Bernstein and Tom Brass

FRANK CASS
LONDON • PORTLAND, OR

First published in 1996 in Great Britain by
FRANK CASS & CO. LTD.
Newbury House, 900 Eastern Avenue, London IG2 7HH England

and in the United States of America by
FRANK CASS
c/o ISBS, 5804 N.E. Hassalo Street, Portland, Oregon 97213-3644

Transferred to Digital Printing 2004

British Library Cataloguing in Publication Data

A catalogue record for this book is available from
the British Library

ISBN 0–7146–4774–8 (hardback)
0–7146–4332–7 (paperback)

Library of Congress Cataloging in Publication Data

A catalog record for this book is available from
the Library of Congress

This group of studies first appeared in a Special Issue on
'Agrarian Questions: Essays in Appreciation of T.J. Byres'
of The Journal of Peasant Studies,
Vol.24, Nos.1 & 2, October 1996/January 1997, published by Frank Cass & Co. Ltd.

Contents

A Publisher's Appreciation

FRANK CASS

I am very pleased to contribute a short personal note to this much deserved volume dedicated to Terry Byres, to mark his sixtieth birthday and his many scholarly achievements. His international reputation has been largely made by his contribution to the academic study and debate of peasant societies and agrarian problems, and as the distinguished founder of, first, the *Journal of Development Studies* (1964) and then, as now, the founder editor of the *Journal of Peasant Studies* (1973).

After working for three years in the newly opened Economist Bookshop, from 1949 to 1952, and having published my first title, a reprint of George Unwin's classic *Economic Organisation in the Sixteenth and Seventeenth Centuries* in 1957, I occupied premises in Woburn Walk, Euston, from 1959 to 1966, which combined my early publishing activities together with a shop carrying a stock of old and out of print books on the social sciences. The clientele were mainly academics and students searching for out of print books in that era before widespread reprints and the introduction of photocopying. During this period Frank Cass published some hundred reprints a year, following suggestions by academics and often incorporating additional material by scholars. We also published some new books, developing a serious academic list that concentrated then, as now, on the social sciences.

I got to know Terry well in those early days, following his move to London in 1962. He was a frequent and most welcome visitor, and we talked of our ideas and visions for our futures. Mine was to develop a serious independent publishing house, his to be able to play a part in the processes of knowledge and education, to understand and deal with problems of underdevelopment.

Terry was always offering help and practical advice. He brought in and introduced to me numerous colleagues, all with interesting ideas, and many of them, under Terry's genial aegis, became our early authors, editors and journal contributors. At the time that the first issue of our first journal (*Middle Eastern Studies*) was about to appear in 1964, Terry dropped in one day and said that he wanted to discuss a matter of some importance: 'Frank, how would you like to publish a new journal in an emerging subject area?'. 'Yes', I replied immediately, 'I would like to publish your journal. What's it on?'. My knowledge as a journal publisher of two month's experience and my respect for Terry were all that were necessary to agree to proceed with this project.

The *Journal of Development Studies* was an immediate success, to be emulated subsequently by that of the *Journal of Peasant Studies*. The formation of *JPS* and its context are described in Terry's introductory essay to the *Twenty Volume Index of the Journal, 1973–1993* that he produced with Henry Bernstein and Tom Brass.

The two journals are a testament to Terry Byres' exceptional commitment to his chosen field of study. Both benefited by his support of younger academics, discovering, helping and guiding their progress, providing them often with their first opportunity of publication. He encouraged many overseas academics and helped them with their important first opportunity to publish internationally. This demonstrated values that I shared. He initiated special issues in book form to allow for a more in-depth study of an important topic. He worked closely and well with our own house editors, particularly the first, Jim Muir, now the distinguished BBC Middle East correspondent (failing which Jim would have made a serious rival to his idol, John Cleese) and, since 1985, with our current editor, Lydia Linford, whose support and skills Terry much appreciates. It says much for Terry that his friendships and loyalties endure.

Since Frank Cass moved its offices into the suburbs in 1966, my meetings with Terry have been less frequent but just as enjoyable. These meetings, typically culminating with a meal at an Indian restaurant, always provide me with an opportunity to enjoy Terry's vivid and humorous commentary on the subjects close to his heart: the currents of intellectual life (including the latest 'scandals' and 'outrages' of academics and their institutions), new discoveries of fine malt whiskies and where and how they are made, the ups and downs of soccer yesterday and today, the food we are eating and its ranking in the comparative standards of Indian cuisine.

I am delighted to be able to publish this volume of appreciation. The papers by his distinguished peers address more fully the signficance of his scholarship and its many contributions. This foreword enables me to thank Terry for providing the model from which the Cass journal publishing programme has developed, and the *Journal of Peasant Studies* for setting and maintaining the standards of quality we aspire to for all our journals.

Questioning the Agrarians:
The Work of T.J. Byres

HENRY BERNSTEIN and TOM BRASS

T.J. (Terry) Byres, the founder and moving spirit of the *Journal of Peasant Studies*, celebrates his sixtieth birthday on 6 October 1996. As his fellow editors of the Journal, we felt that a collection of papers by some of his personal friends (as well as intellectual comrades) would provide a fitting appreciation of his achievements to date. We have divided the labour of this introduction between us: Henry Bernstein first sketches the man and the milieux; Tom Brass summarises and locates central themes of Byres' intellectual work; we then jointly introduce the papers in the volume.

THE MAN AND THE MILIEUX

To venture a portrait of Terry Byres, however modest in scope, is both presumptuous and risky. One hopes that one day he will write the memoir of the places, times, processes and influences of his intellectual career, and the rich cast of characters he has engaged with along the way.

Terry was born into the working class of Aberdeen where his childhood and school days were framed by the Depression of the 1930s, the Second World War and post-war austerity. Not least among his incomparable fund of anecdotes and stories are those of this first period of his life, when widespread poverty and economic insecurity were confronted by a vibrant class culture defiant of established authority and respectability and ingenious in outwitting its rules and guardians. One surmises that many of Terry's characteristic traits carry the imprint of that milieu: combativeness without aggression, generosity and honesty, an instinctive antipathy to all forms of pretension and arrogance – all wrapped in the sardonic humour and salty speech of its rich oral tradition.

After various primary schools, Terry attended Robert Gordon's College

Henry Bernstein is at the Department of Development Studies, School of Oriental and African Studies, University of London, Thornhaugh Street, Russell Square, London WC1H OXG, UK, and Tom Brass is at the Faculty of Social and Political Sciences, University of Cambridge, Free School Lane, Cambridge CB2 3RQ, UK.

in Aberdeen from 1948 to 1954, as a Foundation Scholar. The great legacy of the Scottish 'academy' (secondary or high school), in one of the centres of the Scottish Enlightenment, provided stimulus and opportunity to a working-class youth of the city eager for knowledge. As an undergraduate at the University of Aberdeen, Terry won prizes in Latin as well as in Economic History and Political Economy, graduating with First Class Honours in Economics in 1958. After a frustrating year as a research student at Cambridge, he registered at the University of Glasgow where he gained a B.Litt. in 1962 with a dissertation on 'The Scottish Economy During the Great Depression, 1873–1896, with Special Reference to the Heavy Industries of the South-West' (see Byres [1967a]). Two years in Glasgow added experience and appreciation of another locale of Scottish life and culture, quite distinct from that of his native Aberdeen.

Issues of industrialisation, and the master disciplines of Political Economy and Economic History, provided central threads in Terry's subsequent work. They were also central to the terrain of the leading British Marxist scholars of Terry's formative intellectual period: Maurice Dobb and Ronald Meek in Political Economy, Christopher Hill, Rodney Hilton, Eric Hobsbawm and Edward Thompson in Economic and Social History. The milieu of British communist intellectual life, and the prominence within it of several generations of exceptionally gifted political economists and historians, thus provided another key influence on the vision and agenda of the young T.J. Byres. Perhaps Dobb's example proved the most pertinent. Dobb ('a political economist of quite remarkable breadth and power' – Byres [1995d: 563]) combined theoretical and historical investigation of economic development in the transition to capitalism in Western Europe, in the experience of the Soviet Union, and in relation to accumulation and planning in postcolonial countries. Of these India was of particular interest to Dobb and other British communist intellectuals of the time: it was by far the largest of Britain's former colonies with a long and dynamic history of anti-imperialist struggle; it had a well-established Communist Party and progressive intelligentsia; its independent government was committed to industrialisation and economic transformation in which planning and state economic management were expected to exercise a leading role.

Having completed his B.Litt. at Glasgow, Terry Byres moved to the School of Oriental and African Studies (SOAS) at the University of London, as a Research Fellow in 1962, where he now embarked on the study of economic development in the Third World. Appointed Lecturer in Economics at SOAS in 1964, he spent the first year of his new tenure in India, whence derived his subsequent commitment to that country, and deep affinity with its left intelligentsia whose projects, aspirations, struggles and achievements constitute a further, central, and enduring milieu shaping his preoccupations and activity [*Byres*, 1995d: 565]. He took to India as to a second home, with a passion for its history, the comradeship of those he encountered and worked with, the political and intellectual challenges of its problems and prospects of economic development. He also discovered a passion for its cuisine, and was startled and thrilled to hear words in Hindi that he knew from the speech of his father, who was of 'tinker' (Romany) origin.

In the 1960s, then, Terry directed his attention to the relatively new field of development economics, to which he brought his knowledge of the classical political economy of accumulation and growth and strong grounding in economic history. His early publications focused on the experience and issues of economic planning in India [*Byres*, 1966a; 1966b; 1967b; 1969b], subsequently extended in work on the role of foreign aid in the macroeconomics of development [*Byres*, 1972c; 1972d]. His vitality and vision were responsible for establishing the *Journal of Development Studies* (JDS) in 1964, a pioneering journal of its time (thereby also making his mark on the history of Frank Cass: *JDS* was one of the first journals published by Cass which now has a portfolio of some 50 academic journals). Terry declined the invitation to succeed Professor Edith Penrose, his colleague at SOAS, as Managing Editor of JDS in 1967, but continued as a member of its Editorial Advisory Board and Reviews Editor until 1973, when he resigned to establish the *Journal of Peasant Studies* (JPS).

In retrospect, the founding of *JPS* seems a natural step in Terry's trajectory from the early 1960s and the intellectual milieu in which it occurred. Terry's fascination with the agrarian question in India started with some articles given him by S.C. Gupta in 1963 and the issues they raised [*Byres*, 1995d: 566]. Then there was the new dimension of India's agrarian question generated by the inception of the Green Revolution in the latter part of the 1960s, and its effects. An early and prescient article on 'The Dialectic of India's Green Revolution' [*Byres*, 1972a] was followed by a series of important analyses [*Byres*, 1980a; 1981a; 1982a; *Byres et al.*, 1983; *Byres and Crow*, 1988d]. At the same time, from the beginning of his work on India, Terry has been consistently concerned with the implications of agrarian structure and change for economic transformation more generally, and above all industrialisation. This central intellectual agenda encompasses issues of technical change, forms of agrarian property relations and labour regimes, the agricultural surplus and accumulation, the class relations, politics and policies that shape processes and outcomes – pursued within a comparative framework informed by the exceptional range of his reading [*Byres*, 1972g; 1974; 1977b; 1979; 1982b; 1986a; 1991a; 1995d; 1996b).

A notable feature of the 1960s was the impact of several major works on peasantry [*Byres*, 1994g] that modified or challenged the Marxist classics on the agrarian question in different ways, stimulating the tasks of rethinking, restating or extending its problematic in relation to both the historiography and contemporary significance of agrarian transitions. The charged intellectual milieu of the 1960s and 1970s – of new Marxist and neo-Marxist currents as well as their contestation by other approaches (the influence of Chayanov, rediscoveries of Weber, neo-populism) – led to the 'Peasants Seminar' at the University of London. First convened by Terry Byres and Charles Curwen in January 1972 (it continued to run until 1988), it 'quickly revealed a neglected set of issues, a host of unresolved questions, a ferment of ideas, and a burning contemporary relevance ... If the challenge were to be faced, then it seemed that there was a strong case for the discipline and focus of a journal' [*Byres*, 1994g: 3].

JPS first appeared in October 1973, under the joint editorship of Terry Byres, Charles Curwen and Teodor Shanin. Teodor Shanin withdrew in 1975, and virtually exclusive responsibility for the Journal rested on Terry's efforts from its inception to when he was joined by Henry Bernstein in 1985 and Tom Brass in 1990. It must be very rare in the annals of scholarly journals, that a quarterly publication of such substance and compass was driven by the intellectual vision, energy and effectiveness of one person.

Together with a potent and evolving intellectual agenda, the 'nutrient source' (to use a favourite metaphor of Terry's) of his continuous engagement with India and Indian comrades, the currents and mixed fortunes of Marxist intellectual work in recent decades, and the project of JPS as a unique medium of international scholarship and debate in agrarian political economy, another key milieu of Terry's activity is that of SOAS.

A critical sociological and cultural history of SOAS would be of great intrinsic interest, and Terry would be among the most appropriate candidates for that task. Suffice it to say that when he joined the School, it was dominated by the attitudes, practices and indeed personnel of its imperial and colonial provenance, and long continued to be so, though not without tension and contestation. A number of younger left academics were pushed out of SOAS in one way or another, a particularly notorious example being Biplab Das Gupta, a good friend of Terry's. Of a distinctive group of Scottish leftists at SOAS, Alec Gordon and Jack Gray left the School, Malcolm Caldwell was constantly harassed (until his murder in Cambodia in 1978), Bill Warren, another close friend and combative sparring partner of Terry's, held on until his tragic death in 1978. Bill Warren shared with Terry a tenacity, an ability to forge and pursue his own agenda without fear or favour of the established authority of the School, and willingness to confront the latter's machinations.

It was 20 years before Terry was promoted to a Senior Lectureship at

SOAS in 1984, during which time he had published a series of substantial, creative and important papers, his reputation and influence had grown commensurately, he had established the *Journal of Development Studies* and then the *Journal of Peasant Studies*, and had been approached with offers of senior appointments elsewhere.

In 1988 he became Acting Head of the Economics section of the combined Department of Economic and Political Studies, and when that devolved into two separate entities in 1990, was first Head of the new Economics Department from 1990 to 1994. During his tenure, the staff in Economics expanded considerably with a number of imaginative appointments of both established and younger academics (both categories including former students of Terry's), to constitute one of the strongest and most interesting centres of progressive scholarship, not least in the political economy of development, anywhere. The building of this new Department of Economics is another testimony to his commitment, energy, strong sense of responsibility and discipline, attention to detail and indeed management skills – which combine to make him so effective.

After the long hiatus before his promotion to Senior Lecturer, subsequent and fitting elevation was more rapid: Terry became Reader in 1990 and then Professor of Political Economy in the University of London in 1992. It is a matter of deep satisfaction to him to occupy a position with the title of his beloved Political Economy (on which he insisted), and to others that official recognition of his contributions was thus conferred, however belatedly as Meghnad (Lord) Desai pointed out at Terry's Inaugural Lecture.

The period as Head of Department, and the seriousness with which he undertook its tasks, inevitably, and severely, constrained Terry's research and writing activities, although first priority continued to be given to the work of *JPS*, as always. This did not, however, prevent him from organising a major conference on 'The State and Development Planning in India' in 1989, which brought together a galaxy of Indian scholars and led to the publication of a landmark collection of papers [*Byres,* 1994a]. A sabbatical year in 1994–95 generated the manuscript of his first monograph [*Byres,* 1996b; discussed in the paper by Bernstein in this volume]. The release of his astonishing energy from the demands of the Headship is also manifested in the preparation of a second edition of Byres [1994a], to which he is contributing a substantial essay on the period 1989–96 (which marks India's exposure to the blast of liberalisation and structural adjustment), editing and contributing to another major forthcoming collection on *The Indian Economy: Major Debates Since Independence,* and completing, with Graham Dyer (former student, comrade, and fellow Scot), a book on *The Logic of Peasant Agriculture.* And there are those (including the present author) exerting pressure on him to extend the detailed treatment of his comparative political economy of agrarian transitions [*Byres*, 1986a; 1991a; 1996b].

To those who enjoy the stimulation and warmth of his friendship, and to the many others able to benefit from the richness of his writing, it is gratifying that he is in the full flow of intellectual production with no sign of losing momentum. That richness of his work draws on the influences and challenges of the milieux that have been indicated, combined and developed through a distinctive agenda and commitment, to which this sketch can not do justice. It has not conveyed, for example, the full scope of his intellectual curiosity and appetite for history, further exemplified in two other landmark collections that Terry animated, and which first appeared in *JPS*, on *Sharecropping and Sharecroppers* [*Byres*, 1983b] and *Feudalism and Non-European Societies* [*Byres and Mukhia*, 1985a]. It has not touched on the nomination of personal, and various, delights in the corpus of his writing – for this author they include the enthusiasm for Scottish peasant song, of which Terry is practitioner as well as historian [*Byres*, 1976a], the incomparable essay on Charan Singh which concentrates more insight, analytical muscle, and sheer vitality of the dialectic than many shelves of books on such topics [*Byres*, 1988a], and the incisive critique, both impassioned and cultured, of the Eurocentrism of Blackwell's *Dictionary of Marxist Thought* [*Byres*, 1984b].

The intellectual contributions are there for people to read and assess for themselves, and will continue to flow from his active spirit. Of the person who produced them from such engagement with his milieux and times, only one thing need be added. For this writer, Terry Byres is one of nature's true democrats in his relations with others: it is this that pervades his warmth and generosity, his passions, honesty and adherence to principle, which in turn fuel and direct his intellectual dynamism, ideological clarity, and engagement.

QUESTIONING THE AGRARIANS: SOME KEY THEMES

In a series of incisive, wide-ranging and politically symptomatic interventions over the last 30 years, T.J. Byres has contributed to debates about the political economy of development that have covered the central and interrelated theoretical areas of the agrarian question: the presence/absence of a marketed surplus for industrialisation (see especially Byres [1974]), the impact on the latter issue of the invverse relationship and populist notions of 'urban bias' (see especially Byres [1972g; 1974; 1979; 1988a]), the role in industrialisation of agrarian transition(s) generally (see especially Byres [1977b; 1983b; 1985a; 1991a; 1991d; 1996b]), and the contribution to the latter process(es) of planning [*Byres*, 1966a; 1966b; 1967b; 1969b; 1994a; 1994e]. All these contributions have been informed in turn by an insistence on the presence, occurrence and significance for capitalist accumulation of peasant differentiation, class formation and class struggle (see especially Byres [1981a; 1986b; 1988b; 1991a]).

It is noteworthy that Byres first made and then sustained his views about the agrarian question in what was becoming an increasingly unfavourable intellectual and academic climate.[1] This was a time when, at the end of the 'development decade' of the 1960s, the long dominant peasant-as-cultural-'other' approach of anthropology had been joined by the more rigorous peasant-as-economic-'other' approach associated with the work of Chayanov.[2] Following the availability in English translation of the latter text [*Chayanov*, 1966], its populism began to influence the debate about the centrality to development strategy of peasant economy.[3] Widely anthologised and highly influential, Byres' arguments about the political and economic impact on development theory of 'urban bias' and the resurgence of agrarian populism have been vindicated, as the case of new farmers' movements in India and elsewhere confirms.[4]

It is perhaps because of the intrinsic tensions in populist/neo-classical economics, and how they were exposed, that the debate about development in general and its applicability to the peasantry has shifted during the last decade, away from economics and once more towards culture. In contrast to the agrarian question of Marxism, therefore, which focuses on the way peasant *economy* changes, the agrarian myth of populism now seeks to recuperate peasant essentialism by shifting the focus on to the way in which peasant *culture* (= the root of 'otherness'/'difference') remains the same. Varieties of currently fashionable environmentalism, postmodernism, feminism and conservatism have all combined with populism first to identify and then to celebrate the innateness of peasant cultural identity in the ('post-colonial') Third World.[5] Together with ex-Marxists who have joined the ranks of the *pentiti* ('the repentant ones'), those who fuel this kind of reaction now devote much of their time to the formulation of warnings about the impossibility of progress, the end of development in general and largescale industrialisation in particular, and thus the inevitable demise of Marxist political economy.

In an important sense, the contributions by Byres to the debate about the significance of a marketed surplus, his criticisms of populism, and his examination of the different paths of transition all constitute a discourse about development that has been informed centrally and consistently by the interrelated concerns of a Marxist political economy. The lack of economic development is linked by him to a failure to generate resources for industrialisation, which in turn derives from a failure to solve (or, in the case of populism, perhaps even to pose) the agrarian question. Moreover, in the discourse of a Marxist political economy the agrarian question is not just about a transition to capitalism but also (and more importantly) about the possibility of socialism.[6] Since many aspects of agrarian question are covered in the contributions to this volume, in this section it is intended to outline briefly the importance of just three of his interventions: the marketed surplus, populism, and agrarian transition(s).

Agrarian Question I: The Marketed Surplus

Many of the theoretical and political components that subsequently assume importance in his formulation of the agrarian question can be traced back to the issue of the marketed surplus, which for Byres is at the centre of any debate about how less developed countries industrialise.[7] From the 1960s onwards Third World industrialisation has been the issue confronting not just economists but all those interested in development, and in this regard Byres' concerns as an economist are not unusual.[8] What was and remains distinctive about his approach, however, is an insistence that the issue of industrialisation is one that cannot be formulated by development economics, much less by economics alone, or indeed by a politically-unspecific (= uncommitted) political economy; much rather, it is one that can be posed only in terms of a Marxist political economy.[9]

The significance of a marketed surplus for a Marxist political economy, and more particularly for the successful resolution (or otherwise) of the agrarian question, is not difficult to discern. Since for Marxism industrialisation is the *sine qua non* of economic development, the main question for Byres [1974] is how in a context of underdevelopment the resources for accumulation are to be mobilised from within what remains an economically backward agriculture. For this reason, he argues, both the desirability and objectives of any land reform programme should be assessed by the needs of industry, which in turn requires that its beneficiaries should increase output but not consume this, ensuring thereby that a *net* marketed surplus is produced for and delivered to industry.[10] Whether or not (and by whom) such a surplus is transferred is a matter of class relations and struggle: depending on the historical context, therefore, this will involve rich peasants at some conjunctures and collectives at others.

A crucial aspect of this emphasis by Byres on the marketed surplus has been the wider issue of the inter-sectoral terms of trade between industry and agriculture. Even where/when pre-capitalist obstacles to the delivery of a marketed surplus have been eliminated, and a capitalist agriculture has developed, Byres argues, there is no certainty that the market mechanism will of itself ensure favourable terms of trade for industry. This is because in such circumstances a class of agrarian capitalists will now be powerful enough to exercise effective *political* pressure on (or through) the state to maintain the terms of trade in favour of agriculture, a situation which he accurately describes as 'rural bias incarnate'. As the example of Charan Singh in Western UP during the 1960s, and subsequently that of the new farmers' movements which emerged in the Green revolution areas of India during the 1980s confirm, this is exactly what occurred following the development of a capitalist agriculture in such contexts.[11]

Agrarian Question II: Populism

It is precisely the centrality to debates about resolution/non-resolution of the agrarian question of the presence/absence of marketed surplus that has brought Byres into intellectual and political collision with populism generally, and two influential neo-populists (Michael Lipton, Charan Singh) in particular.[12] Unlike Byres, for whom the principal object of a capitalist land reform is the economic provision for industry of a net marketed surplus, populists such as Lipton and Charan Singh have emphasised the production and retention within agriculture of a gross marketed surplus that raises consumption in rural areas but does not necessarily generate industrialisation. Because capital is scarce relative to labour, Lipton and other like-minded populists argue, underdeveloped countries must eschew large-scale industrialisation for the foreseeable future in favour of small-scale labour-intensive artisan and peasant production.[13]

As peasant smallholding is efficient, populists maintain, family farms can thus produce enough to meet food requirements of the rural sector, in this way solving the social problem of rural poverty. However, such a view is confronted with a rather obvious difficulty in that land reforms have manifestly failed to eradicate rural poverty in underdeveloped countries. Since they regard the peasantry as economically undifferentiated, and economic contradictions consequently occur not within sectors and thus within classes but rather between sectors and between classes, populists have an explanation for this failure. That the peasantry throughout the Third World remains poor is therefore attributed by both Lipton and Charan Singh not to the effects of capitalist accumulation (depeasantisation, proletarianisation) but rather to the presence of 'urban bias', or the belief that resource flows/allocations to and policy decisions emanating from the town/city always and automatically discriminate against agriculture.[14]

Not only does Byres [1979: 220ff.] challenge the central tenet of this populism (that in the Third World undifferentiated smallholders are economically the most efficient producers) but he also successfully questions the evidence presented by Lipton [1977a] in support of his main arguments for the existence of 'urban bias' [1979; 218ff., 223ff., 227ff.]:

that rural producers everywhere are heavily taxed in relation to urban counterparts, and further that they are all victims of an enduringly unfavourable inter-sectoral terms of trade which – being state-designed and thus urban-friendly – is therefore persistently manipulated against agriculture (price distortions and policies; high farm input prices coupled with low output prices, and so forth).[15] Opposed not just to landlordism and finance capital but also to socialism and collectivisation, contemporary populism is in fact class-specific, its denials notwithstanding: in developing countries it is, as Byres shows, the ideological viewpoint of the rich and middle peasantry.[16]

Agrarian Question III: Transition(s)

Much of Byres most recent work [1991a; 1996b] has focused on the different ways in which a marketed surplus is generated, and the correspondingly diverse historical Asian paths (Japan, South Korea, Taiwan) followed by the process of agrarian transition.[17] Taking his point of departure from the classical texts (Marx [1976], Lenin [1964], Kautsky [1988]), Byres considers the agrarian question in terms of its historical antecedents in Europe: the English path, where the decline of feudalism is accompanied by the emergence of capitalist farming, class struggle and class formation (depeasantisation/proletarianisation); the French path, in which serfdom disappears as a result of successful class struggle waged 'from below' by peasants against the landlord class; and the Prussian path, or 'capitalism from above', a process whereby an impoverished peasantry is subordinated by and becomes the workforce of a landlord class that engages directly in capitalist farming.[18] By contrast, where a landlord class is either weak or non-existent, there occurs a process of 'capitalism from below'; in the case of the American path, therefore, the persistence of family farming is attributed both to the relative absence of wage labour and to state policy protecting smallholders against the effects of overproduction.[19]

In contrast to many non-Marxist texts which see Japanese, South Korean and/or Taiwanese industrialisation as a democratic model for the whole of Asia, Byres questions the extent to which the post-1945 land reforms in these contexts actually corresponds to these much-vaunted instances of 'capitalism from below', arguing that pre-war class dominance by landlords in Japan itself and Japanese colonisation of Korea and Taiwan supports the opposite path: a process of 'capitalism from above', albeit qualified by the absence of capitalist relations in the countryside, the significant surplus-extracting role of the Japanese, South Korean and Taiwanese state (from the peasantry in the form of taxation), and the uniqueness in Japan of the landlord class itself.[20] In the cases of Korea and Taiwan, agrarian transition was linked to colonial rule by Japan during the first half of this century, and in particular the cheap rice policy of the colonial state. The economic growth generally and especially the industrialisation which took place in all three Asian contexts, however, was premised on terms of trade that were against agriculture.

THE PAPERS

Many of the theoretical and political issues central to Byres' work on the agrarian question are addressed by the contributions to this volume. The first, by Henry Bernstein, provides a critical appreciation of Byres' project on the comparative political economy of agrarian transitions, first sketched in a seminal conference paper [*Byres*, 1986a] and further developed in a full theoretical and historical exploration of the Prussian and American paths of transition [*Byres*, 1996b]. Bernstein's discussion raises a number of substantive and methodological issues, briefly illustrated in relation to the accounts of Prussia/Germany and the USA in particular. These issues include the 'world historical' timing of various (completed) agrarian transitions; how the uneven and combined development of capitalism on a world scale changes the conditions and prospects of agrarian transitions in social formations where they have not (yet) occurred; relations between the economics and politics of the agrarian question; and indeed issues of the completion of agrarian transition and what the resolution of the agrarian question means to different social forces in different places at different times. The discussion of such issues seeks to build on, complement, and extend the achievements of Byres' comparative political economy to date.

The paper by Massoud Karshenas likewise builds on Byres' work, in particular his critique of the influential neo-populist notion of 'urban bias' (see above). Karshenas begins with a meticulous critique of a recent and massive World Bank Study on 'the political economy of agricultural pricing policy', that exposes its theoretical, methodological and empirical defects – in relation to its neo-classical analytical framework of allocative efficiency *and* its neo-liberal ideological agenda. The approach and findings of the World Bank Study are contested by an alternative explanation of intersectoral resource flows in the experience of five important Asian countries, namely China, India, Iran, Japan and Taiwan. These case studies show that dynamic economies in non-agricultural sectors and the efficiency of resource use in agriculture (largely neglected by the proponents of urban bias) are key to understanding historic patterns of intersectoral resource flows and particular trajectories of economic development.

Complementing the macroeconomic focus of Karshenas' paper, that by Graham Dyer offers a rigorous survey and assessment of another longstanding debate on which T.J. Byres has made his mark, namely that concerning the inverse relationship between farm size and productivity, and its policy implications for land reform. In a systematic review of the methodological procedures, empirical evidence and conceptual assumptions structuring neo-classical claims about the inverse relationship in Indian agriculture, Dyer argues that it is not superior entrepreneurship or land fertility but the class relationships and exploitation that underlie them which explain why poor peasant smallholdings in an economically backward agriculture intensify cultivation. Following the introduction of new (Green Revolution) technology in India, and state induced peasant co-operativisation in Egypt, the inverse relation breaks down in dynamic agricultural contexts as capitalist relations and forces of production come to predominate.

The paper by Gary Tiedemann on 'Communist Revolution and Peasant Mobilisation in the Hinterland of North China' shifts the focus from economics to political sociology (the political and ideological practices [and their social bases] of historically and socially differentiated peasantries have also long been an important theme within Byres' political economy of agrarian questions, and the object of many articles published in JPS). Drawing on a rich, and growing, detailed historical literature, Tiedemann explores the failure of communist mobilisation of the peasantry in the 1920s in the hinterland of the North China plain, with its distinctive history of state weakness, social turbulence and collective violence. In the 1920s it was warlordism rather than landlordism that compounded the harsh pressures on peasant existence, that in turn generated fierce resistance by local self-defence organisations in ways that defy received notions of peasant 'moral economy' as well as simplistic expectations of class action. Tiedemann suggests that Party cadres learned the lessons of the setbacks of the 1920s, so that after the Japanese invasion of 1937 they were able to create policies and forms of organisation in the countryside of North China that were much more effective and, of course, made a crucial contribution to the subsequent success of the Chinese revolution.

In his contribution, Tom Brass presents a critique of agrarian populism – also an important focus of Byres' own work – and examines the fictional composition of agrarian populist 'community' (= utopia) and its 'other' (= dystopia) as this structures three literary/filmic texts in the realm of 'popular culture' over a 50 year period: *Caesar's Column* (1890) by Ignatius Donnelly, *The Journey of My Brother Alexei to the Land of Peasant Utopia* (1920) by A.V. Chayanov, and the 1937 film directed by Frank Capra of the novel *Lost Horizon* (1933) by James Hilton. In each case the discourse-against reveals the dystopic of agrarian populism to consist of urban contexts in which large-scale technified production generates strife between finance capital and proletariat that threatens to culminate in socialism. By contrast, the discourse-for of agrarian populism identifies its fictional utopia as harmonious, rural and orientalist, a place where small-scale producers (artisans, peasants) predominate and from which both finance capital and proletariat have been banished.

The paper by Jairus Banaji develops a theme of central importance in the political economy of modern capitalist agriculture, namely the nature and growth of contemporary agribusiness, not least in the context of globalisation of capital. Drawing on research undertaken for trade unions in the food industries of Bombay, Banaji first outlines the impact of global capitalist competition on the food industry in India, and in particular how subsidiaries of multinational corporations (such as Brooke Bond, Cadbury Schweppes, British American Tobacco) have from the early 1990s onwards restructured production in order to enhance, maintain or restore profitability worldwide. In India, following economic and financial liberalisation, a major effect of inward investment by agribusiness in search of cheap labour and new markets has been diversification into food processing, the rapid growth of contract farming, and an offensive against working class unionisation as part of the project of deregulation.

Prabhat Patnaik's paper is also concerned with the international conditions of economic development, cast within a more formal macroeconomic framework and linking with some of the issues of Karshenas' paper (both acknowledge the importance of Kalecki's work to understanding the dynamics of economic transformation). Patnaik's analysis considers how the character of agricultural and industrial sectors within an economy, and their interrelations, are mediated by the international trade regime. Dependence on agricultural exports, even when used to finance manufacturing imports, will result in economic contraction in 'agriculture-constrained' economies, even if export performance is assessed positively on other criteria. This argument, as that of Karshenas, contributes to illuminating the basic flaws of neo-liberal policy prescription in the era of structural adjustment.

The costs of the current neo-liberal orthodoxy are also highlighted in the final paper by Peter Nolan, in the context of 'transitional' economies. Nolan contrasts economic progress in China (growth in output, decline in poverty but increased inequality) and regress in Russia (poor economic performance, decline in national income and net national product, increased poverty and inequality), against the lack of political progress in both countries: formal democratisation offset by gangsterism and authoritarianism in Russia, absence of democracy and human rights abuses in China. The differences in economic fortunes are attributed to the combined impact in Russia of rapid economic liberalisation with the destruction of a strong nation state, and the project in China of careful movement towards a state guided market economy, harnessing entrepreneurial energies within a collectivist framework made possible by political stability and coherence.

NOTES

1. This contention is perhaps nowhere better illustrated than in the political trajectory of a sister publication, *The Journal of Development Studies*. What used to be an interesting and politically heterogeneous forum for the discussion of a wide variety of approaches to the issue of development has now become a publication in which many complex development issues are reduced to mathematical formulae. One result of this change is that *The Journal of Development Studies* now reads much like an in-house publication of the World Bank, with politics to match.

2. For examples of the peasant-as-cultural-'other' approach of anthropology, see among many others the classical texts by Redfield [1956] and Wolf [1966].

3. For examples of the peasant-as-economic-'other' approach, see Wharton [1970], Lipton [1974; 1977a], Shanin [1972], Sahlins [1972], Malinowski and de la Fuente [1982], Richards [1985], and Plattner [1989]. Like other interventions in debates about the peasantry during the 'development decade', it was its politics as much as anything that made Chayanovian analysis so acceptable once again in the 1970s and 1980s, particularly amongst economists and sociologists working for international food and development agencies. Based on the peasant family farm and small-scale technology, Chayanovian theory presented the possibility of agricultural production without having substantially to reform the existing agrarian structure. In other words, it entailed neither rural property redistribution nor collectivisation, and as such was not merely compatible with capitalism but would also not lead to socialism. Moreover, since even a rise in output from smallholding agriculture was never going to be large enough to feed domestic populations, let alone export food to other markets, this kind of policy was also extremely favourable to food-exporting metropolitan capitalist countries.

4. Of the many examples which it is possible to cite regarding the different kinds of influence exercised by Byres' writings on populism and urban bias, two will suffice. First, the acknowledgement of Byres' influence by the author of another important text on populism [*Kitching*, 1982: ix]. And second, the rapid sale at a CPI (Communist Party of India) stall on the Bankipur Road in Patna of copies of a pirated pamphlet version [*Byres*, 1988c] of Byres' article on Charan Singh (an episode witnessed in India during January 1990 by Tom Brass, a fellow editor of the *Journal of Peasant Studies*).

5. The list of texts which, under the influence of currently fashionable postmodern theory, in one way or another end up denying the possibility/desirability of socio-economic development is now very long, and would include the following: Guha [1982–89], Laclau [1985], Shiva [1988], Scott [1990], Pieterse [1992], Escobar and Alvarez [1992], Prakash [1992] Latouche [1993], and Booth [1994]. That an overlap exists between the populist Thirdworldism of the European 'new' right (on which see, for example, Bodemann [1986], Ferraresi [1987], Taguieff [1994], Sacchi [1994] and Biehl [1995]) and the essentialist view of peasant/'popular' culture which structures much postmodern theory about development is also equally clear, not least because each attributes underdevelopment in the Third World to an innate, socio-economically ineradicable and culturally empowering 'difference'/ 'otherness' [*Brass*, forthcoming]. As Byres himself might put it, there is all too often an inverse relationship between intellectual achievement/relevance and intellectual fashion.

6. Precisely when the objective of a transition to socialism becomes necessary, and is therefore to be raised by Marxists in terms of the practice it entails, is of course a matter of continuing debate. For some the mere presence of capitalism is itself sufficient, whereas for others it is necessary that a capitalist transition be fully accomplished. This in turn raises other questions: whether it is necessary that a capitalist transition be effected in the narrower context of agriculture or at the wider level of the social formation. It is the latter conceptualisation to which Byres [1991a: 3–4, 12] adheres.

7. See Byres [1991a: 6] for a more recent reaffirmation of this point.

8. In what came to be known as the 'development decade' of the 1960s, there was a widespread concern among non-Marxist intellectuals generally and economists in particular about the implications for 'political stability' of an economically backward agriculture in the Third World, not least because of fears that food scarcities occasioned by population growth would fuel revolution (and apprehension by seemingly confirmed by the events in Cuba during 1959). This concern led to a consideration of the ways in which Third World peasant agriculture might be modernised so as to generate food surpluses, which resulted in among other things the installation of the Green revolution. It is not without significance, therefore, that the opening address to the 1965 Conference on Subsistence and Peasant Economics was given by John D. Rockefeller [1970], and that the focus of most of the published contributions [Wharton, 1970] was on issues largely unconnected with a Marxist concept of the agrarian question. Much of the discussion in the 1965 Conference concerned the ways in which peasant farming might be modernised so as to increase food output, which would in turn enhance consumption among the rural poor, thereby preventing famine/starvation in the rural Third World and hence the possibility of revolution by the rural poor. It should be noted, however, that non-Marxist economists have long had a similar interest in the potential for and impact of Indian peasant mobilisation. In his 1940 Presidential Address (on the theme of 'The Peasant and Politics') to the Conference of the Indian Society of Agricultural Economics, Malcolm Darling [1940: 7, 8, 9] noted:

> Man, said Aristotle, is a political animal. This may be true of urban man, perhaps even of western man, but it is certainly not true of the Indian peasant. On the contrary he is essentially a non-political animal. He has always "let the legions thunder past" and plunged in work again, in the work of wrestling for daily bread with a despotic and capricious nature. But great changes are taking place ... The [1914–18] war released forces which are spreading all over India, and their effect upon the peasant has been to set him thinking about his rights instead of his obligations. Three years ago, too, he was given the vote. This may prove to be a momentous change in his political history. [...] How dangerous a situation ... can be when the peasant asserts his rights and the landlord relies for the defence of his interests upon hereditary right rather than upon service to his tenants and the community is shown by what happened in Europe after the [1914–18] war. In Roumania the landlord was deprived of nearly 12 million acres in return for an almost nominal compensation. In Poland he also lost much of his land and was only partially compensated, and in Russia he lost everything. In all three countries this was done by the party in power to gain the political allegiance of the peasant, in the first two to avoid revolution in the last to confirm it. In India the rapid increase in population is already putting the tenant at a disadvantage, and if we are to avoid serious disturbance, of which there are already ominous signs, he will have to be increasingly protected. But it is not easy to say how this can best be done and the problem is essentially one for politician and economist to consider together.

9 On the continuing importance of a specifically Marxist political economy, see for example, Byres [1994e: 5; 1995d].

10. On this point see Byres [1974: 244–5], where he observes that although land reform would indeed generate an increase in output, the latter would for the most part be consumed within the agricultural sector. While gross marketed surplus would increase, therefore, a net marketed surplus would not.

11. For explicit references by Charan Singh to the exercise of such power on behalf of rich peasants, see Byres [1988a: 158]. On the emergence in India of new farmers' movements, see the contributions to Brass [1995]. It is a matter of regret that another text revisiting 'urban bias' [Varshney, 1993] fails to acknowledge Byres' contribution (while confirming its accuracy).

12. It is noteworthy that, unlike many ex-/non-/anti-Marxists who now demonise Marxism and deem it unworthy of intellectual consideration, Byres has always treated the ideas of political opponents with respect, even when disagreeing strongly with them. This is true not only of non-Marxist economists generally (on which see Byres [1995d]) but also of his many

exchanges on the subject of neo-populism, in particular those with the neo-classical economist Michael Lipton (Byres [1974; 1979], Lipton [1974; 1977a]) and about the Indian politician Charan Singh [Byres, 1988a]. In characteristically generous mode, therefore, Byres [1979: 211] has described Lipton as 'one of [the] most influential members [of the Institute of Development Studies at Sussex University] and one of its most formidable intellects'. 'No one', Byres [1979: 210] observes, 'today puts the neo-populist case more persuasively, more ingeniously, with an astonishing array of arguments, or more passionately, and ... reaches both the professional economist and a far larger audience than those who are capable of writing only in jargon'. Equally, when writing about the Russian neo-populist A.V. Chayanov, Byres [1994g: 7] notes that: 'if much of [the] attention to Chayanov (and his legacy) has been critical, then that is a recognition of, and a response to, the power and distinctiveness of his writing and his considerable contemporary appeal'. Much the same applies in the case of Charan Singh, another neo-populist with whose politics Byres disagrees fundamentally. Indeed, chiding those who scoff at the idea of Singh as an intellectual or dismiss Singh's ideas as unimportant, Byres [1988a: 139–41, 163, 165–6, 176–8, 180] has defended both the intellectual status of Singh himself and the importance of Singh's ideas, insisting rightly that – political and theoretical disagreements notwithstanding – these merit serious consideration. (It scarcely seems necessary to point out that in an important sense this approach is entirely in keeping with present academic trends: whereas Marxists tend to deny ideological plurality in theory but to implement it in practice, non-/anti-Marxists generally and postmodernists in particular advocate plurality in theory but invariably deny this in practice.)

13. For the views of Charan Singh regarding the economic superiority of peasant smallholding (= the debate about the inverse relationship), see Byres [1988a: 175–6, and especially 176–8]. In keeping with the classical tradition of populism generally (and its Russian and North American variants in particular), both Lipton and Charan Singh express hostility to industrialisation, not least because large-scale capitalism and technology will undermine peasant proprietorship and also entail an increased reliance on wage labour [Byres, 1988a; 173–6, 178–9]. The sub-text to the latter concern is also a familiar one: the populist fear of the uncontrollable 'mob-in-the-streets', or a proletariat that will usher in socialism.

14. 'Urban bias and its underpinning class analysis', Byres [1979: 236] concludes, 'simply serve to conceal the true class antagonisms and to divert attention away from the class struggle which is actually taking place'. Significantly, the mobilising slogan ('Today, India's villages are the colony of the city') adopted by the followers of Charan Singh in 1979 not only contains echoes of 'urban bias' [Byres, 1988a: 162, 179] but is similar in this respect to the one ('Bharat versus India') subsequently popularised by Sharad Joshi, leader of the farmers' movement in Maharashtra (on which, see Brass [1995]).

15. For the success of the political struggle waged by Charan Singh on the one hand against the compulsory procurement by the state of a marketable surplus from rich peasants (except at high foodgrain prices acceptable to the latter), and on the other against the imposition of land taxes (opposition by him to which was formulated in 'what would later be termed "urban bias"'), see Byres [1988a: 156ff., 159–61, 170ff.]. Significantly, the work of Lipton is cited by Charan Singh in support of his own views, and although Lipton makes no reference to the views of Charan Singh, as Byres [1988a: 168–9] notes in passing '[h]e might well have done so, in detail and with favour' since 'Charan Singh had been expounding [Lipton's] arguments in extenso, with skill and with passion, for some 40 years before this'.

16. For the anti-landlordism of Charan Singh, and his antagonism towards moneylenders, see Byres [1988a: 142–3, 147ff., 170ff.]. Although he acted in the interests of both middle and rich peasants, Charan Singh – himself of rich peasant origin – represented mainly this latter stratum of the peasantry, one that was undergoing a transition to capitalist farming [Byres, 1988a: 146, 147, 152–3, 153ff., 162, 166–8]. For Charan Singh's opposition not just to socialism and collectivisation but also to including poor peasants and agricultural labourers as beneficiaries of any land redistribution, see Byres [1988a: 172–3]. Although Lipton [1977b] has denied that he is opposed to socialism, and attempts to distance himself from other populists/neo-populists, Byres [1979: 234] argues persuasively that this is rhetorical. Such a view is borne out by the fact that the version of socialism which Lipton [1991] finds

the most congenial is none other than 'analytical Marxism', a thinly-disguised variant of neo-classical economic theory not dissimilar to his own.

17. The necessarily abbreviated account which follows is based only on Byres [1991a: 3–76], and cannot but fail to do justice to the richness and complexity of Byres' own analysis of the multiple paths of agrarian transition. For an historically and contextually complementary account of agrarian transition, see Bernstein [1994].

18. For the English, Prussian and French paths of agrarian transition, see Byres [1991a: 13ff., 22ff., 34ff.].

19. For the American path, see Byres [1991a: 27ff.]. 'It is essential to recall', notes Byres [1991a: 32], 'that the agrarian question in the sense of whether agriculture will make the necessary contribution to capitalist industrialisation was triumphantly resolved in the United States.'

20. For the Japanese, South Korean and Taiwanese paths, together with the nature of their interconnectedness, see Byres [1991a: 41ff., 50ff.]. As a result of the resource transfer (mainly labour-power) from agricultural to non-agricultural production during the Tokugawa period, which both increased the industrial reserve army of labour and simultaneously enhanced the productivity of labour-power retained in agriculture, it has been argued by Nakamura [1966: Ch.7] that in Japan agricultural growth rates during the Meiji era were actually much higher than previously thought (an increase hidden by the fact that peasant farmers underreported crop yield so as to avoid taxation). On the possibility of replicating the South Korean/Taiwanese path throughout Asian social formations, Byres [1991a: 58–9] comments:

> Elsewhere in Asia, where capitalist paths are being attempted, either landlord classes continue powerful (as, say, Pakistan), or survive in somewhat weakened but by no means inconsequential form (as, say, in India). Pervasively, unlike South Korea and Taiwan, highly differentiated and significantly differentiating peasantries are to be found ... It seems likely that the prospects for capitalist agrarian transition elsewhere in Asia ... will more fruitfully be sought in the careful investigation of landlord classes and of the processes of differentiation at work, than in the probably unique features of the South Korean/Taiwanese path. That is to be stressed.

REFERENCES

(a) *T.J. Byres: A Select Bibliography*

Byres, T.J., 1966a, 'The Political Economy of Indian Planning', *Journal of Development Studies*, Vol.2, No.2.

Byres, T.J., 1966b, 'Indian Planning on the Eve of the Fourth Five-Year Plan', *World Today*, Vol.23, No.3.

Byres, T.J., 1967a, 'Entrepreneurship in the Scottish Heavy Industries, 1870–1900', in P. Payne (ed.), *Studies in Scottish Business History*, London: Frank Cass

Byres, T.J., 1967b, 'Does Indian Planning Face a Crisis?', *Venture*, Vol.19, No.4.

Byres, T.J., 1969a, 'Thor, Adam Smith, Marx – and Myrdal?', *Asian Review*, Vol.2, No.3.

Byres, T.J., 1969b, 'Economic Planning in India', *Venture*, Vol.21. No.8.

Byres, T.J., 1972a, 'The Dialectic of India's Green Revolution', *South Asian Review*, Vol.5, No.2.

Byres, T.J., 1972b, 'Economists in Kandy', *South Asian Review*, Vol.5, No.3.

Byres, T.J., 1972c, 'From What Types of Government Should Poor Countries Accept What Kinds of Aid?', *Bulletin of the Institute of Development Studies*, Vol.4, Nos.2–3.

Byres, T.J. (ed.), 1972d, *Foreign Resources and Economic Development: A Symposium on the Report of the Pearson Commission*, London: Frank Cass.

Byres, T.J., 1972e, 'Introduction', in Byres [1972d].

Byres, T.J., 1972f, 'The White Man's Burden in a Neo-Colonial Setting', in Byres [1972d].

Byres, T.J., 1972g, 'Industrialisation, the Peasantry and the Economic Debate in Post-Independence India', in A.V. Bhuleshkar (ed.), *Towards Socialist Transformation of the Indian Economy*, Bombay: Popular Prakashan.

Byres, T.J., 1974, 'Land Reform, Industrialisation and the Marketed Surplus in India: An Essay on the Power of Rural Bias', in D. Lehmann (ed.), *Agrarian Reform and Agrarian Reformism*, London: Faber & Faber.

Byres, T.J., 1976a, 'Scottish Peasants and Their Song', *Journal of Peasant Studies*, Vol.3, No.2.

Byres, T.J., and P. Nolan, *Inequality: India and China Compared, 1950–1970*, Milton Keynes: Open University Press.

Byre, T.J., 1977a, 'Introduction' to A. Mitra, *Calcutta Diary*, London: Frank Cass.

Byres, T.J., 1977b, 'Agrarian Transition and the Agrarian Question', *Journal of Peasant Studies*, Vol.4, No.3.

Byres, T.J., 1979, 'Of Neo-Populist Pipe-Dreams: Daedalus in the Third World and the Myth of Urban Bias', *Journal of Peasant Studies*, Vol.6, No.2.

Byres, T.J., 1980a, 'The Green Revolution's Second Phase', *Journal of Peasant Studies*, Vol.7, No.2.

Byres, T.J., 1980b, 'Peasants as Unfinished History', *Economic and Political Weekly*, Vol.15, No.31.

Byres, T.J., 1981a, 'The New Technology, Class Formation and Class Action in the Indian Countryside', *Journal of Peasant Studies*, Vol.8, No.4.

Byres, T.J., 1981b, 'Of Slumbering Academics and Peasants' Sons: Perspectives on the Peasantry of the Northeast of Scotland', *Journal of Peasant Studies*, Vol.9, No.1.

Byres, T.J., 1982a, 'The Political Economy Technological Innovation in Indian Agriculture', in R.S. Anderson, P.R. Brass, E. Levy and B.R. Morrison (eds.), *Science, Politics and the Agricultural Revolution in Asia*, Boulder, CO: Westview Press.

Byres, T.J., 1982b, 'India: Capitalist Industrialisation or Structural Stasis?', in M. Bienefeld and M. Godfrey (eds.), *The Struggle for Development: National Strategies in an International Context*, New York: John Wiley & Sons.

Byres, T.J., 1982c, 'Agrarian Transition and the Agrarian Question', in J. Harriss (ed.), *Rural Development*, London: Hutchinson University Library.

Byres, T.J., Crow, B. and M.-W. Ho, 1983a, *The Green Revolution in India*, Milton Keynes: Open University Press.

Byres, T.J. (ed.), 1983b, *Sharecropping and Sharecroppers*, London: Frank Cass

Byres, T.J., 1983c, 'Historical Perspectives on Sharecropping', in Byres [1983b].

Byres, T.J., 1984a, 'Amiya Bagchi and the Political Economy of Underdevelopment', *Social Scientist*, No.132.

Byres, T.J., 1984b, 'Eurocentric Marxism and the Third World: A View from the Academy in the Anglophone Metropolis', *Economic and Political Weekly*, Vol.19, No.13.

Byres, T.J. and H. Mukhia (ed.), 1985a, *Feudalism and Non-European Societies*, London: Frank Cass.

Byres, T.J., 1985b, 'Modes of Production and Non-European Pre-Colonial Societies', in 1985a.

Byres, T.J., 1986a, 'The Agrarian Question, Forms of Capitalist Agrarian Transition and the State: An Essay with Reference to Asia', *Social Scientist*, Nos.162–3.

Byres, T.J., 1986b, 'The Agrarian Question and Differentiation of the Peasantry', Foreword to A. Rahman, *Peasants and Classes*, London: Zed Books.

Byres, T.J., 1987, 'Sukhamoy Chakravarty on Marxist Economics and Contemporary Developing Economies: Some Comments', *Cambridge Journal of Economics*, Vol.11, No.2.

Byres, T.J., 1988a, 'Charan Singh (1902–87): An Assessment', *Journal of Peasant Studies*, Vol.15, No.2.

Byres, T.J., 1988b, 'A Chicago View of the Indian State: An Oriental Grin without an Oriental Cat and Political Economy without Classes', *Journal of Commonwealth and Comparative Politics*, Vol.26, No.3.

Byres, T.J., 1988c, *Charan Singh (1902–87): An Assessment*, Patna: People's Book House (a reprint of Byres [1988a]).

Byres, T..J. and B. Crow, 1988d, 'New Technology and New Masters for the Indian Countryside', in B. Crow, M. Thorpe *et al.*, *Survival and Change in the Third World*, Oxford: Polity Press.

Byres, T.J., 1989a, 'Krishi Prashna o Krishakder Bibhajan ("The Agrarian Question and Differentiation of the Peasantry")', in A. Rahman, *Krishi Prashna, Aitihasik Rush Bitarka ebam Tritiya Bishwa ta Prasangikata (The Agrarian Question, the Historic Russian*

Controversy and its Relevance to the Third World), Dhaka, Bangladesh: University Press Limited (Bengali translation of Byres [1986b]).

Byres, T.J., 1989b, 'The New Technology, Class Formation and Class Action in the Indian Countryside', in H. Alavi and J. Harriss (eds.), *Sociology of 'Developing Societies': South Asia*, London: Macmillan (a reprint of Byres [1981a]).

Byres, T.J., 1989c, 'Charan Singh: Madhyam Vo Dhani Kisano Ki Chinta' ('Charan Singh: Strong Concern for Rich and Middle Peasants'), *Sancha*, Vol.1, No.11 (Hindi translation of Byres 1988a]).

Byres, T.J., 1990, 'A Note on T.V. Sathyamurthy, "Indian Peasant Historiography: A Critical Perspective on Ranajit Guha's Work"', *Journal of Peasant Studies*, Vol.18, No.1.

Byres, T.J., 1991a, 'The Agrarian Question and Differing Forms of Capitalist Transition: An Essay with Reference to Asia', in J. Breman and S. Mundle (eds.), *Rural Transformation in Asia*, Delhi: Oxford University Press.

Byres, T.J., 1991b, 'South Asian Economic Development', in R.H. Taylor (ed.), *Handbooks to the Modern World: Asia and the Pacific – Volume 2*, New York: Facts on File.

Byres, T.J., 1991c, 'Foreword', to A. Sinha, *Against the Few: Struggles of India's Rural Poor*, London: Zed Press.

Byres, T.J., 1991d, 'The Agrarian Question' and 'Peasantry', in T. Bottomore *et al.*, *Dictionary of Marxist Thought*, Oxford: Blackwell.

Byres, T.J., 1993, 'Charan Singh (1902–87): An Assessment', in D. Arnold and P. Robb (eds.), *Institutions and Ideologies: A SOAS South Asian Reader*, Richmond, Surrey: Curzon Press (an abridged version of Byres [1988a]).

Byres, T.J. (ed.), 1994a, *The State and Development Planning in India*, Delhi: Oxford University Press.

Byres, T.J., 1994b, 'Preface', to Byres [1994a].

Byres, T.J., 1994c, 'In Memoriam: Krishna Bharadwaj and Sukhamoy Chakravarty', in Byres [1994a].

Byres, T.J., 1994d, 'Introduction: Context and Background', in Byres [1994a]

Byres, T.J., 1994e, 'State, Class and Development Planning in India', in 1994a.

Byres, T.J., Bernstein, H. and T. Brass (eds.), 1994f, *The Journal of Peasant Studies: A Twenty Volume Index*, London: Frank Cass.

Byres, T.J., 1994g, 'The Journal of Peasant Studies: Its Origins and Some Reflections on the First Twenty Years', in Byres [1994c].

Byres, T.J., 1995a, 'Preface' to T. Brass (ed.), *New Farmers' Movements in India*, London: Frank Cass.

Byres, T.J., 1995b, *Political Economy, the Agrarian Question and the Comparative Method*: London: SOAS (Inaugural Lecture delivered at SOAS on 27 October 1994).

Byres, T.J., 1995c, 'Political Economy, the Agrarian Question and the Comparative Method', *Economic and Political Weekly*, Vol.30, No.10.

Byres, T.J., 1995d, 'Political Economy, the Agrarian Question and the Comparative Method', *Journal of Peasant Studies*, Vol.22, No.4.

Byres, T.J., 1996a, 'The Need for the Comparative Method in the Social Sciences, its Clarifying Power and Some Problems: An Essay with the Agrarian Question in India in Mind', in A. Bhaduri, N. Chandra, K. Krishnaji, D. Nayyar, P. Patnaik and K. Raj (eds.), *Economics as Ideology and Experience: Essays in Honour of Ashok Mitra*, London: Frank Cass.

Byres, T.J., 1996b, *Capitalism from Above and Capitalism from Below: An Essay in Comparative Political Economy*, London: Macmillan.

(b) *Other References*

Bernstein, H., 1994, 'Agrarian Classes in Capitalist Development', in L. Sklair (ed.), *Capitalism and Development*, London: Routledge.

Biehl, J., 1995, '"Ecology" and the Modernisation of Fascism in the German Ultra-Right', in Staudenmaier and Biehl [1995].

Bodemann, Y.M., 1986, 'The Green Party and the New Nationalism in the Federal Republic of Germany', in R. Miliband *et al.*, (eds.), *Socialist Register 1985/86*, London: The Merlin Press.

Booth, D. (ed,), 1994, *Rethinking Social Development*, Harlow: Longman Scientific & Technical.

Brass, T. (ed.), 1995, *New Farmers' Movements in India*, London: Frank Cass.

Brass, T., forthcoming, 'From Alienation to (Dis-)Empowerment: The Agrarian Myth in the Discourse of Populism and the Political Right', in T. Brass (ed.), *Peasants and Populism*, London: Frank Cass.

Chayanov, A.V., 1966, *The Theory of Peasant Economy* (edited by Daniel Thorner, Basile Kerblay and R.E.F. Smith), Homewood, IL: The American Economic Association.

Darling, M.L., 1940, 'Presidential Address', *Proceedings of the First Conference Held at Delhi, February 24th and 25th, 1940*, Bombay: The Indian Society of Agricultural Economics.

Escobar, A. and S.E. Alvarez (eds.), 1992, *The Making of Social Movements in Latin America: Identity, Strategy and Democracy*, Boulder, CO: Westview Press.

Ferraresi, F., 1987, 'Julius Evola: Tradition, Reaction, and the Radical Right', *Archives Européennes de Sociologie*, Vol.28, No.1.

Guha, R. (ed.), 1982-89, *Subaltern Studies I–VI*, Delhi: Oxford University Press.

Kautsky, K., 1988, *The Agrarian Question*, 2 vols., London: Zwan Publications.

Kitching, G.N., 1982, *Development and Underdevelopment in Historical Perspective*, London: Routledge.

Laclau, E., 1985, 'New Social Movements and the Plurality of the Social', in D. Slater (ed.), *New Social Movements and the State in Latin America*, Amsterdam: CEDLA.

Latouche, S., 1993, *In the Wake of the Affluent Society: An Exploration of Post-Development*, London: Zed Press.

Lenin, V.I., 1964, 'The Development of Capitalism in Russia', *Collected Works*, Vol.3, Moscow: Foreign Languages Publishing House.

Lipton, M., 1974, 'Towards a Theory of Land Reform', in D. Lehmann (ed.), *Agrarian Reform and Agrarian Reformism*, London: Faber & Faber.

Lipton, M., 1977a, *Why Poor People Stay Poor: A Study of Urban Bias in World Development*, London: Temple Smith.

Lipton, M., 1977b, 'On Not Being Against Socialism', *Journal of Peasant Studies*, Vol.5, No.1.

Lipton, M., 1991, 'Agriculture, Rural People, the State and the Surplus in Some Asian Countries: Thoughts on Some Implications of Three Recent Approaches in Social Science', in J. Breman and S. Mundle (eds,), *Rural Transformation in Asia*, Delhi: Oxford University Press.

Malinowski, B., and J. de la Fuente, 1982, *Malinowski in Mexico: The Economics of a Mexican Market System*, London: Routledge & Kegan Paul.

Marx, K., 1976, *Capital – Volume 1*, Harmondsworth: Penguin Books.

Nakamura, J.I., 1966, *Agricultural Production and the Economic Development of Japan 1873-1922*, Princeton, NJ: Princeton University Press.

Pieterse, J.N. (ed.), 1992, *Emancipations, Modern and Postmodern*, a Special Issue of *Development and Change*, Vol.23, No.3.

Plattner, S. (ed.), 1989, *Economic Anthropology*, Stanford, CA: Stanford University Press.

Prakash, G., 1992, 'The History and Historiography of Rural Labourers in Colonial India', in G. Prakash (ed.), *The World of the Rural Labourer in Colonial India*, Delhi: Oxford University Press.

Redfield, R., 1956, *Peasant Society and Culture: An Anthropological Approach to Civilisation*, Chicago, IL: University of Chicago Press.

Richards, P., 1985, *Indigenous Agricultural Revolution*, London: Hutchinson.

Rockefeller, J.D., 1970, 'The Challenge of Population and Food', in Wharton [1970].

Sahlins, M., 1972, *Stone Age Economics*, Chicago, IL: Aldine Atherton Inc.

Sacchi, F., 1994, 'The Italian New Right', *Telos*, Nos.98–9.

Scott, J.C., 1990, *Domination and the Arts of Resistance: Hidden Transcripts*, New Haven, CT: Yale University Press.

Shanin, T., 1972, *The Awkward Class*, Oxford: Clarendon Press.

Shiva, V., 1988, *Staying Alive: Women, Ecology and Survival in India*, London: Zed Press.

Staudenmaier, P. and J. Biehl (eds.), 1995, *Ecofascism: Lessons from the German Experience*, Edinburgh: AK Press.

Taguieff, P.-A., 1994, 'Origins and Metamorphoses of the New Right', *Telos*, Nos.98–9.

Varshney, A., 1993, 'Self-Limited Empowerment: Democracy, Economic Development and

Rural India', in A. Varshney (ed.), *Beyond Urban Bias,* London: Frank Cass.

Wharton, C.R. (ed.), 1970, *Subsistence Agriculture and Economic Development,* London: Frank Cass.

Wolf, E.R., 1966, *Peasants,* Englewood Cliffs, NJ: Prentice-Hall, Inc.

Agrarian Questions Then and Now

HENRY BERNSTEIN

[A]s the social formation comes to be dominated by industry and by the urban bourgeoisie, there ceases to be an agrarian question with any serious implications [*Byres*, 1991: 12].

[T]he agrarian question is an issue pertaining to capitalism, and not primarily to a period of transition, or 'articulation' between capitalism and pre-capitalist modes of production [*Levin and Neocosmos*, 1989: 243].

The apparent irreconciliability of the two statements cited above prompts some unpacking of meanings of the agrarian question. This is pursued through examining the purposes that inform different meanings, the means used to pursue them, and the analytical and historical coordinates of 'then' and 'now'. The paper builds on the project of T.J. Byres' comparative political economy of agrarian transitions, which it seeks to complement through a primarily conceptual discussion.

AGRARIAN TRANSITION IN THE WORK OF TJ BYRES

The Problematic

The prospects, in contemporary poor countries, are often considered of a limited number of 'paths' of capitalist agrarian transition: a set of paths which have already been traversed successfully in the past. The apparently essential features of these historically traversed paths are identified and are made to constitute the elements of *models* of possible agrarian transition ... It has gradually seemed to me that practice in this respect is defective, and misleading in two important ways. The first is that the paths in question – the 'models' being taken

Henry Bernstein, Department of Development Studies, School of Oriental and African Studies, University of London, London WC1H 0XG. He would like to thank Tom Brass for his comradely advice, and suspects that recent discussions with Mike Morris and Ashwani Saith have infiltrated the argument, responsibility for which, however, is his alone.

to contemporary reality – are too few ... Not only that, but, secondly, the conception of these paths is too stereotyped and too narrow [*Byres*, 1996: 3–4][1].

T.J. Byres has long been concerned with the agrarian question in the development of capitalism and with the economic development of poor countries, and committed to investigation of both areas of study with the analytical tools and methods of Marxist political economy. In recent years these areas of concern have converged explicitly in an intensive study of paths of 'agrarian transition'. This involves a critical (re)reading of classic Marxist theory on the agrarian question; a reconsideration of the historical experiences which furnished its principal points of reference; the expansion of the historical framework in a comparative analysis to reveal the 'substantive diversity' of cases of successful agrarian transition; the use of the findings of this project to illuminate the problems and prospects of economic development in poor countries (above all India, the source of inspiration and special regard throughout Byres' intellectual career).

The groundwork of the project, and its preliminary findings, are contained in Byres' seminal essay on 'The Agrarian Question and Differing Forms of Capitalist Agrarian Transition: An Essay with Reference to Asia' [1991].[2] There he identified several different meanings of the agrarian question in classic Marxism, modified the analytics of the agrarian question with a distinctive formulation of 'agrarian transition', and illustrated the latter in a comparative sketch of six different paths of successful agrarian transition, which are now being explored in greater depth and detail in several subsequent books, of which the first – *Capitalism from Above and Capitalism from Below. An Essay in Comparative Political Economy* [*Byres*, 1996] – focuses on Prussia and the United States. The three meanings of the agrarian question proposed by Byres are as follows.

First, when 'at the end of the nineteenth century, European Marxists investigated the agrarian question, that formulation derived from an explicitly political concern ... how to capture power in countries which continued to have large peasantries' [*Byres*, 1991: 6–7]. That is, capitalist development had generated a growing industrial working class, and the programme of working-class (socialist) parties needed to address strategic alliances with social forces in the countryside where 'the peasant is a very essential factor of the population, production and political power' (*Engels*, 1970: 457).

Byres took Engels' *The Peasant Question in France and Germany* (written in 1894) as the key focus of this 'explicitly political' formulation of the agrarian question, and noted that it contained two important additions to, or modifications of, Marx's analysis. One is that industrialisation in mainland Europe was not *consequent* on a (complete) transformation of agricultural production characterised by the formation of agrarian capital and wage labour as in England, the (necessarily) principal reference point for Marx in *Capital*. At the end of the nineteenth century capitalist transformation of agriculture in this sense was evident only in England itself and in Germany east of the Elbe where its historical trajectory and effects were very different (see below). The other addition/modification is that the peasantries of mainland Europe were subject to new contradictions in their conditions of existence wrought by capitalist development, and that disclosed possibilities of political action and alliances beyond the 'apathy of the French small-holding peasantry' in the mid-nineteenth century, as anatomised by Marx [1970] in *The Eighteenth Brumaire* [*Byres*, 1991: 8].

The second reading of the agrarian question was established by two historic texts published in 1899, Kautsky's *The Agrarian Question* [1988] and Lenin's *The Development of Capitalism in Russia* [1964a]. The key concerns here were the (variant) forms and effects of capitalist development in agriculture, or (somewhat differently) 'the development of agriculture in capitalist society' in the title of the first part of Kautsky's book. Kautsky investigated this primarily in terms of the differences between the development of capitalism in agriculture and industry, while Lenin was concerned to demonstrate 'that capitalism could and actually *was* developing in Russia' [*Byres*, 1991: 9]. Lenin's study was part of the polemics with the narodniks, whose agrarian populism was confronted directly by Lenin's argument of the capitalist class differentiation of the Russian peasantry in Chapter 2 (probably the most enduring and most contested legacy of that work).

Byres derives the third formulation of the agrarian question from the problematic of socialist construction following the Russian revolution of 1917, as presented in Preobrazhensky's *New Economics* (1965, first published 1926). The issue posed here was that of the sources of primary accumulation for the project of socialist industrialisation, which could only be found outside of industry *and* outside of the embryonic socialist economy: in short, by the net transfer of 'surplus' from a peasant agriculture (now freed from landlordism). Preobrazhensky's argument stimulated Byres to reinsert this motif in the investigation of capitalist development, as 'no significant attention had been given, hitherto, as part of the treatment of the agrarian question, to the countryside's role in allowing accumulation to proceed outside of agriculture' [*Byres*, 1991: 11]. Although both 'Kautsky and Lenin were abundantly aware of its significance with respect to capitalist industrialisation ... it did not present itself as being central to the agrarian question' [*ibid*].

This marks the radical core of Byres' reformulation of the agrarian question as *agrarian transition:* the role of agriculture in capitalist industrialisation with *or without* 'the full development of capitalism in the countryside', in the sense of the dominance of capitalist social relations of production (agrarian capital and wage labour). Thus

> We can have a form of agrarian transition, a resolution of the agrarian question in our third sense, such that the agrarian question appears to be resolved in neither the Engels nor the Kautsky–Lenin sense. If, however, the agrarian question is so resolved, in this third sense, in such a way that capitalist industrialisation is permitted to proceed, then, *as the social formation comes to be dominated by industry and by the urban bourgeoisie, there ceases to be an agrarian question* with any serious implications. There is no longer an agrarian question in any substantive sense [*Byres*, 1991: 12, emphasis added].

The purpose of this reformulation, *inter alia*, is to escape the tyranny of the 'English path' (analysed by Marx) in which the transition to a capitalist agrarian order (and its 'agricultural revolution') led to subsequent industrialisation. Not only was the English path exceptional in its historical *circumstances* (as the first transition to capitalist industry) and possibly *its form* (the 'trinity' of capitalist landed property-[tenant] capitalist farmers-agricultural wage workers), but its *'logic '(capitalist* transformation of agriculture as a condition of industrialisation) may be incapable of replication elsewhere, and indeed unnecessary to industrialisation in other circumstances.

The three meanings of the agrarian question thus delineated can be summarised as the problematics of politics, production, and accumulation, which I shall term AQ1, AQ2, and AQ3. They centre respectively on issues of alliances between classes of urban and rural labour (both agricultural wage labour and the poor peasantry) in struggles for democracy and socialism; the development of the productive forces in farming; the contributions of agriculture to primary accumulation for industrialisation – Byres' 'agrarian transition'.

My only comment at this stage, in anticipation of the following discussion, is that separating AQ1 in this way may cause certain difficultes, exposing the investigation of AQ2 and AQ3 to economism. It is useful to distinguish two aspects of the politics of the agrarian question. The first is, in a sense, generic to the methodology of class analysis (hence to the investigation of AQ2 and AQ3): the importance of political class practices and their irreducibility to economic class practices. The second, stemming from Lenin, is that the agrarian question (whether AQ2 or AQ3) has to be viewed in an intrinsically political way in terms of the class dynamics and effects of the manner of its resolution. In this sense, there is the agrarian question of capital and the agrarian question of labour.

In a 'simple analytical framework' appended to Chapter 2 of his book, Byres [1996] introduces more specific concepts for analysing the development of the productive forces, transfers to industry, and intersectoral linkages, as the principal ways in which agriculture can contribute to industrialisation (AQ3). The intensification of farming through technical innovation, and consequent gains in productivity, expresses the most important form of the development of the productive forces (AQ2).[3] The growth of production, especially as a result of technical innovation and productivity growth, increases the 'real' or marketed surplus of agricultural commodities, both 'means of subsistence', notably food ('the physically existing form of variable capital', in Marx's term), and raw materials for manufacturing (an element of constant capital).

For primary accumulation (AQ3) it is not just the mass and rate of growth of agricultural commodities exchanged that is crucial but also their terms of exchange with manufactured commodities: the intersectoral terms of trade. Terms of trade favourable to industry represent a transfer of resources to it from agriculture – precisely as advocated by Preobrazhensky, with pricing policy the obvious instrument of engineering this form of transfer. In addition, again as emphasised by Preobrazhensky, direct taxation of agriculture (as distinct from the indirect taxation effected through pricing policy) yields a financial surplus available to primary accumulation for industrialisation. On the other side of intersectoral trade, agricultural growth stimulates the development of industry by providing an expanding market for manufactured means of production and means of consumption (respectively Marx's Departments I and II of industry). This linkage was stressed by Lenin [1964a] whose *Development of Capitalism in Russia*, it will be recalled, carries the subtitle 'The Process of the Formation of a Home Market for Large-Scale Industry'.[4]

Histories I

The challenge of this problematic of accumulation, including its opening to substantive diversity, is pursued in a comparative overview of seven historical experiences of successful agrarian transition via six paths, respectively those of England, Prussia, the United States, France, Japan, and Taiwan/South Korea (exemplifying the same path). Elsewhere [*Bernstein, 1994: 46–7*] I have summarised Byres' results in a schema structured by key themes of his comparative analysis, namely (i) the nature of agrarian class structure and struggle prior to and during transition, (ii) the characteristic forms of production during transition, (iii) their effects for investment and development of the productive forces in farming, (iv) how they related to industrialisation. That schema need not be reproduced here, where I simply note some of the salient features of four of the paths sketched, with exposition of the Prussian and American paths to follow next.

The *English path* followed the transformation of feudal into capitalist landed property, with the distinctive feature that agrarian capital derived from a different social souce than landed property, namely the differentiation of the (free) peasantry. This generated the class 'trinity' (noted above) and the development of the productive forces in agriculture, through investment by capitalist (tenant) farmers aided by an accomodating class of landed property (so-called 'improving landlords'). Exceptionally, a thoroughly capitalist transformation of agriculture (in the sense of AQ2), both social and technical, *preceded* and contributed to the subsequent (and first) industrial revolution (AQ3).[5]

The *French path* out of feudalism was different: peasant resistance to the seigneurial offensive of the late medieval period did not lead to capitalist agriculture but to a *rentier* landlordism. There was little scope for peasant differentiation, and a tenacious small peasantry, confirmed in its position by the French Revolution and its effects, persisted throughout and beyond nineteenth-century industrialisation. Only in the extensive grain lands of northern France did capitalist farming emerge, from the 1840s. The contributions of agriculture to French industrialisation are not (as yet) specified.

The *Japanese path* in the period following the Meiji restoration (1868) was marked by recurring moments of intense class conflict between a tenant peasantry exposed to increasing exactions in rent and tax and landlords and the state. The latter prevailed to extract levels of surplus that made a significant contribution to Japanese industrialisation. The state and landlords invested in agriculture as well as in industry, stimulating development of the productive forces within highly labour-intensive labour processes in farming and continuing agrarian social relations of precapitalist landed property and a subject peasantry. The level of exaction inhibited any significant differentiation of the peasantry.[6]

The *Taiwanese/South Korean path* originated in the land reforms of the late 1940s. Before 1945 Taiwanese and Korean peasants had borne similar exactions to those in Japan, if anything compounded by Japanese colonial rule (from 1895 in Taiwan and 1910 in Korea) and their role as rice suppliers to Japan. Land reform removed the burden of rent but peasants were then subjected to ruthless state taxation directed to primary accumulation for industrialisation.

All these instances concern agrarian transition as paths out of feudal social relations in northwestern Europe and East Asia, that display strong substantive diversity. The exceptionalism of the English path, and the unspecified contribution of the French path to industrialisation, cast a spotlight on the East Asian experiences, which indeed approximate the extractive logic of Preobrazhensky's model of primary accumulation on the backs of the peasantry. In Japan that logic was effected through the intensification of feudal exploitation, combined with landlord and state investment in agriculture, close management by landlords of tenant production, and a state committed to rapid industrialisation. Taiwan and South Korea after 1945 approach Preobrazhensky's scenario even more closely, with a peasantry now freed from landlordism (as in the USSR after the revolution) and surplus transfer effected by state taxation and pricing policy (as envisaged by Preobrazhensky for the fledgling Soviet state).

Histories II

In his book [1996)] Byres considers the Prussian and American paths of agrarian transition in greater depth and detail, and over a longer time frame, than in the preliminary sketches of his essay [1991]. He selected Prussia and America as they were proposed by Lenin to represent two paths of capitalist transformation of agriculture (beyond Marx's English path): a (reactionary) 'landlord' path driven by the 'internal metamorphosis' of feudal landed property, and a (revolutionary) 'peasant' path that generates classes of agrarian capital and wage labour through social differentiation.[7] Byres' findings provide some surprises, as we shall see.

The story of Prussia starts with German colonisation of Slav lands east of the Elbe from the mid-tenth century onwards, which generated classes of landowners and free peasants in a 'frontier' region that 'was an outlier of feudalism ... part of a feudal social formation but not itself feudal' [1996: 59]. The seigneurial offensive of the fifteenth and sixteenth centuries led to the enserfment of 'one of Europe's freest peasantries' [*Brenner*, 1985: 23] (and by contrast with northwestern Germany). Byres follows Brenner in explaining this outcome east of the Elbe by the relatively weaker social solidarity, hence capacity to resist, of the eastern peasantry, linked to its more individualised ('frontier'-like) organisation of farming. Byres [1996: 87–8] further suggests that peasant differentiation, which Brenner did not explore, may have been an important link between more individualised farming and weaker social solidarity.

The 'second serfdom' thus established the dominant mode of production of the sixteenth and seventeenth centuries, with a correspondence between its relation and forces of production. During the eighteenth century, the final phase of the 'prehistory' of the Prussian transition, the contradictions of the mode of production were manifested in a number of ways. First, the adoption of new and more productive methods of farming – notably of wheat cultivation pioneered in England – was severely constrained by the existing property relations and form of exploitation through labour rent (that favoured the less demanding cultivation of rye). The higher quality and quantity of labour required by new production methods confronted 'the classic dilemma of "shirking", supervision costs and incentives' [1996: 102] of a servile labour regime. Second, and adding pressure to this emergent contradiction, was growing resistance to labour services, especially by stronger peasants. Third, the agrarian structure had increasingly serious effects for the tax revenues and military conscription of the Prussian state as the Junkers continued to absorb both (taxable) peasant land and peasant labour into their (tax-exempt) domains.

Junker power was able to resist pressures for reform of the agrarian system and to prevent any significant differentiation of the peasantry that may have generated agrarian capitalism from below: 'no free market in land or in labour emerged' [1996: 122]. Accordingly, the abolition of serfdom was the result of an external shock (in today's parlance): the invasion and defeat of Prussia by the French armies of Napoleon. This enabled the Prussian state to act on the contradictions outlined above by the Emancipation Edict of 1807, paving the way for the transformation of the Junkers into a class of agrarian capital, albeit one strongly marked by its provenance and the historical circumstances of its 'metamorphosis'. The Prussian state was strongly committed to the reproduction of (a 'reformed') Junker power; the labour regime on Junker estates underwent an uneven transition through forms of tied farm labour that inhibited technical innovation.

Byres' account of the Prussian path ends in 1871 with the creation of the unified German state under Prussian hegemony. The dominance of wage labour and associated development of more modern productive forces in eastern Prussian agriculture that occurred after this date is largely irrelevant, as 'an overall capitalist transition had clearly taken place in the whole Prussian formation' *before* 1871 [1996: 55]. What then was agriculture's contribution to this outcome? Food prices rose between the 1840s and 1870s, with the intersectoral terms of trade favouring agriculture; rather than any transfer from agriculture to industry via taxation, the flow was in the other direction; the technical basis of Junker farming and pauperisation of agricultural labour severely limited rural demand for the products of Department I and Department II industries respectively. The only contribution was to the formation of the urban proletariat by flight from the oppressive conditions of agricultural labour (replaced by increasing labour migration to Junker estates from Austrian Poland and Russia).

In the light of such findings, Byres endorses Lenin's view of the reactionary nature of the Prussian path, but this still leaves a puzzle. For Lenin, Prussia represented a reactionary form of the transition to capitalist agriculture (AQ2). However, in the sense of agrarian transition as formulated by Byres (AQ3), Prussia fails to qualify: 'capitalist industrialisation did proceed ... *in spite of, rather than because of, the contribution of Prussian agriculture*' [1996: 175, my emphasis].

The four chapters of Byres [1996] on America represent a substantial development beyond the historical sketch of the 1991 essay, and also away from Lenin. Two principal paths are analysed, exemplifying sharp regional contrasts: that of slavery succeeded by sharecropping in the South, and that of simple or petty commodity production in the North and West.

Chapter 5 sets the scene of the project of European colonisation and the issues it confronted in establishing control over land and labour. Land was acquired by the cumulative dispossession of indigenous people (American Indians or Native Americans), a process of 'primitive accumulation' traversing three centuries. During the colonial period (seventeenth and eighteenth centuries), 'attempted feudalism', in relation to the ownership and tenure of land thus occupied and securing labour to work it, failed, unlike colonial ventures to the south (Spanish America) and to a lesser degree the north (French Canada), due to successful resistance by settlers on an abundant land frontier. The failure of colonising 'experiments' to solve the labour question through feudal(like) tenancy, (European) indentured labour or the enslavement of indigenous people, underlies the evolution of the distinctive regional paths.

Plantation slavery (with slaves of African origin), the dominant mode of production in the South from the late seventeenth century to 1865, is analysed in Chapter 6, to show that it 'effectively blocked the development of capitalism in the South' [1996: 266] for two principal reasons. The first concerns the labour processes of slave production (and slave resistance within them) which place strong limits on the instruments of production that can be deployed, and on the 'versatility' of slave labour compared with free wage labour (echoing the disadvantages of servile labour noted earlier in the context of eighteenth-century Prussian feudalism). These limits on the productive forces in slave production, as well as the lack of disposable income of slaves, in turn inhibited the development of a market for industrial manufactures. The second principal source of 'specifically retardative effects on the process of national capitalist development' is the 'prebourgeois' nature of the planter class (the words quoted are Genovese's – Byres [1996: 264]. The planters had no interest in using their control of the ante-bellum Southern states to promote industrialisation, and indeed (like their Junker counterparts) used their power to tax commerce and manufacture to support their own agricultural economy. The development of industry, above all industry with a market in free wage labour, would threaten the bases of planter hegemony.

The chapter on slavery also includes a brief section on 'the class of [white] yeoman farmers' in the South, as a potential source of the emergence of capitalist agriculture from below (another analytical parallel with the small minority of free peasants and stronger tenanted peasantry in Prussia). However, the 'yeoman farmers' were an up-country, relatively isolated agrarian formation, engaged in mostly subsistence production, and under the patronage of the planters who shielded them from the penetration of merchant capital, thereby blocking any tendencies to greater commodity production and social differentiation.

Chapter 7 traces the change from slavery to sharecropping, and analyses the nature of the latter. Parallels with Prussia again present themselves. Both the 'second serfdom' and plantation slavery 'had been the response of a dominant class to a chronic labour shortage' [1996: 311]. Both ended after several centuries as the result of military defeat. Immediately after the end of the American Civil War (1864) and abolition of slavery (1865), unsuccessful attempts were made to reorganise plantation production with wage labour. This signalled a switch by Southern landowners to sharecropping as the dominant form of production from the late 1860s to the 1940s.

The core of Byres' analysis of sharecropping is the combination of its form of exploitation and labour processes/productive forces. To maximise their control over the labour process and revenue from share income, Southern landowners (ex-planters) restricted the size of holdings so as to intensify cultivation on them, sought to prevent the access of sharecropping households to off-farm employment and income, and maintained sharecropper insecurity through annual contracts. These measures were combined with landowner supply of means of production and close supervision of the labour process.[8] Exploitation through appropriation of the crop share was reinforced, or intensified, by the extension of credit and resultant sharecropper indebtedness, thus 'interlinked modes of exploitation' that Byres explains [1996: 330–6] with reference to debates in India and the notable contributions of Bharadwaj [1985] and Bhaduri [1973]. The effects for the productive forces are similar to those of Bhaduri's conception of 'semi-feudalism', that is, landowner preference for labour intensification on small farms worked by a dependent and cheap labour force. Southern landowners did introduce technical changes, particularly the use of fertiliser (to offset the declining yields of cotton monoculture) and later tractor ploughing, but these were not sufficient for long-run productivity growth. The adoption of tractor ploughing lagged behind other parts of the USA, and mechanisation was not extended to other cultivation operations and to harvesting. There were 'deeply rooted forces [of exploitation – HB] within the system that prevented, or strongly discouraged, technical change' [1996: 354] – in short, 'the relations of production acted as [a] drag upon the productive forces' [1996: 358].

There was similarly no dynamic towards capitalist farming on the part of 'yeoman farmers' who entered cotton production in the post-bellum period. No longer shielded by planter patronage, they succumbed to domination by mercantile and money-lending capital. The resulting pressures of market interlocking and debt led to many such farmers losing their land and becoming tenants in the 'great upsurge of tenancy' in the South between 1880 and 1900 [1996: 360], with little scope for social differentiation and the emergence of capitalist farming from below.

As might be expected then, sharecropping was able to contribute little more than slavery had to the industrialisation of the South and for more or less the same reasons: post-bellum Southern state governments were controlled by (the same) landowners hostile to economic development that would compete for labour; the limited development of the productive forces in farming and the poverty of sharecroppers restricted the development of the market; the (continuing) immobility of labour under sharecropping inhibited urban migration until the second decade of the twentieth century. Sharecropping ended, and the formation of agrarian capital began in earnest, in the space of a decade in the 1940s and 1950s. Cotton planting expanded as part of the war effort when demand for labour was high, and mechanical harvesters (first patented in 1907) were rapidly adopted to finally displace sharecroppers in the cotton South.

In the course of this exposition of the American South, a number of parallels with the Prussian case has been noted. In his concluding chapter (Chapter 9) Byres assesses the idea of 'the American South as an example of the Prussian path', but rejects it as they were rooted in 'two completely different modes of production', slavery and feudalism [1996: 477]. Moreover, while Prussian feudalism gave way to agrarian capitalism, slavery gave way to sharecropping organised by a 'non-capitalist landlord class' [1996: 323; with the post-bellum South also characterised as 'a backward capitalism' in the title of Chapter 7 and as 'backward capitalism from above' on p.460]. These differences apart, agriculture in neither Prussia nor the American South contributed to capitalist industrialisation, which throws an even greater responsibility on petty commodity production in the American North and West: *the only path of agrarian transition*, in Byres' sense (AQ3), considered in his book.

Chapter 8 registers a significant development of the preliminary sketch in the essay (including shifting the moment of transition forward in time), largely inspired by the remarkable analysis of Post [1995] [*Byres*, 1996: 378]. Byres analyses the transition from 'early' to 'advanced' petty commodity production in three broad phases: the colonial period, the inception of transition from about the 1790s to 1830s, and the accelerated development of 'advanced' petty commodity production thereafter that contributed to industrialisation and the outcome of 'capitalist development from below'. The colonial period saw the initial formation and (geographical) expansion of 'early' petty commodity production, predicated on two processes noted above: dispossession of Native Americans and successful resistance to 'attempted feudalism'. This assured the ample availability of relatively cheap land as the condition of existence of the basic social form of production: independent family farming combined with domestic industry, both largely directed to self-consumption and resistant to the penetration of merchant capital. The largely self-sufficient rural economy grew by demographic and geographical expansion, and extensification of farming, rather than through any marked development of the productive forces.

'Early' petty commodity production as described underwent a transformation between the late eighteenth century and the 1830s. Rising land prices and taxes, that raised the costs of establishing new farms and enlarging existing ones, stimulated the increasing commoditisation of both farming and, after 1820 in the northeast, domestic industry in the countryside through the putting-out system. The distinctive feature of agrarian transition established in this moment of transformation was its *combination* of rapid development of the productive forces in farming (new instruments and techniques of production, specialisation) with the scarcity and high costs of agricultural wage labour. The effects of this combination in advanced petty commodity production, not least technical innovation that *increased labour productivity* as well as yields, were spectacular in the rapid succession of phases of western expansion – the 'agricultural revolution' of the 1840s and 1850s in the Ohio Valley and Great Plains, the post-bellum settlement west of the Mississippi, accompanied by the mechanisation of wheat harvesting and then threshing.

This extraordinary expansion – with its spatial, social and technical correlates – provided the vital stimulus to industrialisation, above all through the massive growth of the 'real' or marketed agricultural surplus and the reciprocal demand for the commodities of Department I and Department II industries.

> The impact of the transformation of the rural class structure on industrialisation in the 1840s and 1850s can be seen directly in the growth of an 'agro-industrial' complex in US industry. The industries producing farm-machinery, tools and supplies, and processing agricultural raw materials (meat packing, leather tanning, canning, flour milling, bailing and so on) were at the centre of the US industrial revolution. Farm implement and machine production alone made up 19.4 per cent of all machine production in 1860, rising to 25.5 per cent

in 1870. Further, these industries experienced important development in their labour-processes (for example, mechanisation of flour milling, the development of the first 'disassembly' line in meat packing, and the use of standardised parts in the construction of reapers) and stimulated technical transformations in other crucial industries [*Post*, 1995: 433].

Byres' verdict on Lenin's formulation of the American path is that Lenin 'was correct with respect to the dynamism he attributed to the agriculture of the (American) North and West; and correct in his interpretation of its implications, with respect to the productive forces and capitalist industrialisation. What he did not anticipate was the remarkable power of advanced petty commodity production to survive' [1996: 435]. Lenin's further consideration of American agriculture in 1915 [*Lenin*, 1964b] led him to confirm his earlier prediction as census data showed a trend towards increasing wage employment in farming. Byres suggests that Lenin got the moment right but the trend wrong: the trend towards agricultural wage employment shown in the 1910 census data was largely reversed by 1920, as 'mechanisation constantly subverted the need for wage labour, and so enabled the continuous existence and reproduction of advanced petty commodity production' [1996: 435].[9]

Some observations on Byres' findings are appropriate at this point. First, he selected Prussia and America as his first cases for more detailed comparison because of their prominence in Lenin's legacy, as noted earlier. However, Byres' problematic of accumulation as he formulates it (AQ3) has a different object than Lenin's problematic (AQ2, and its links with AQ1 – see below). Second, the Prussian path to agrarian capitalism, and its reactionary nature, registers a significant structural difference with the English path: the 'internal metamorphosis' of the Junkers generated a class that *combined* landed property and agrarian capital ('while still exploiting every patrimonial privilege it could keep' – Anderson [1974: 274]). Third, Prussian industrialisation (and its origins) remains a mystery – it proceeded 'in spite of ... the contribution of Prussian agriculture', therefore must have had 'other nutrient sources' [*Byres*, 1996: 175]. The mystery is partly clarified by the historical geography of Prussia. Byres [1996: 57–8] lists the various regions of Prussia, including those territories added to it in the course of its major expansionary thrust from the mid-eighteenth century, a central element in the integration of a number of fragmented political entities that culminated in the unified German state of 1871. The key territorial acquisition for present purposes was that of the Rhine Province in 1815, the heartland of Germany's industrial revolution [*Anderson*, 1974: 272–3]. In short, a search for the contribution of agriculture to the 'nutrient sources' of Prussian industrialisation is not ruled out but would be located in a different 'space' – that of *north-west* rather than north-east Germany. This also suggests, *inter alia*, the centrality of processes of *state formation* (with their own registers of time and space) in the transition to capitalism more generally (see further below).

Prussian industrialisation thus occurred (when it did) only because of the contingent (and timely) incorporation of one of Europe's great industrial growth poles of the nineteenth century, by an expansionist state just starting its belated and reactionary path of transition out of feudalism in its historic heartland: uneven and combined development indeed [*Anderson*, 1974: 236]. Prussia completes the range of the feudal situations (summarised above) selected to test the conception of agrarian transition. Only England and Prussia (and on a regional level, northern France) of these cases experienced the development of capitalist farming before the end of the nineteenth century, but by different paths and with very different results – to the extent that Prussian agriculture failed to satisfy the criterion of agrarian transition as a 'nutrient source' of capitalist industrialisation (AQ3).

This leaves the American North and West, the most spectacular success story of agrarian transition in the nineteenth century, with some highly idiosyncratic features. This transition lacked a feudal provenance. As 'non-commercial family farming' [*Post*, 1982; 1995] or 'early simple commodity production' [*Byres*, 1996] in the colonial north-east had no determinate relation with a class of landed property, nor any internal impulse towards (increased) commoditisation, it took a *non-agrarian class* committed to commodity circulation, market expansion and profit, to engineer the conditions of agrarian transition. That class was merchant capital [*Post*, 1982; 1995: 416–19). In the course of agrarian transition, and thereafter, the social vehicle of economic dynamism in agriculture was petty rather than capitalist commodity production. Finally, the principal contribution of agriculture to American industrialisation was through the 'powerful backward and forward linkages' [*Byres*, 1996: 410] between the two sectors. This bestows an exceptionally 'virtuous' quality on the American path of agrarian transition and its forms of accumulation. Although requiring a 'prehistory' of dispossession of Native Americans, the transition itself exhibits no Preobrazhensky-like logic of extraction, no (more or less) coerced transfers from classes of agrarian labour to primary accumulation for industrialisation central to the East Asian paths of transition.

Histories III

What are the 'lessons' of these historical experiences of agrarian transition/industrialisation for contemporary poor countries? Byres offers some pointed observations on this question. He notes that his book 'is written from the relatively comfortable vantage point of *completed transition*: that is to say, after the dust of history has settled ... The temptation to impose a particular teleology upon the evidence is great', and then asks 'Do these examples of transition help in this respect? Does extended treatment of them help prevent analytical closure?' [1996: 461–2]. That 'the nature of agrarian transition has a decisive influence upon the nature and very possibility of capitalist industrialisation' [1996: 468] is as true for contemporary poor countries as for the historical cases examined. However, the specific trajectories and mechanisms disclosed by the latter do not provide off-the-shelf 'models' for the former.

The English path is 'ruled out' with reference to its 'caricature' in the Permanent Settlement of colonial India [*Byres*, 1991: 60–61)] while the East Asian transitions displayed exceptional features that can not be replicated: 'Ironically, the lessons for contemporary Asian countries seem more likely to come from outside Asia than from those agrarian transitions which have taken place so far within Asia' [1991: 64]. On the other hand, variants of the landlord (Prussian) path may still have some purchase in Latin America and Pakistan [1991: 62–3, 1996: 480–82], and agrarian transition from below (the peasant path) remains a possibility if certain conditions are satisfied: 'a powerful state, with the capacity to move against the social, political and economic power of a strong landlord class', combined with 'sustained struggle by peasants' [1991: 61]. The particular forms of this path can include peasant capitalism and differentiation (Lenin's American path, AQ2, illustrated by the Green Revolution states of northwest India), petty commodity production (the American path of the North and West, AQ3, as analysed by Byres and by Post, 1995), and 'a stubbornly resisting, and surviving, small-peasant economy, as in France' [1991: 61–2, 1996: 479–80, 483].

It seems to me that there are certain ambiguities or slippages here, arising from some conflation of AQ2 and AQ3, and a tendency to extend the term 'agrarian transition' to the trajectories of agrarian structures that coexisted with, traversed ('survived'), or even were transformed during, early industrialisation *without* contributing to its accumulation. In short, there are 'paths' (of change or stasis) of agrarian structure that do *not* qualify as paths of *transition* in the strong sense formulated as AQ3. Examples already given include the Prussian path (a reactionary variant of AQ2), and plantation slavery and sharecropping in the American South that presented obstacles to capitalist industrialisation. Another example is the French agrarian structure of small peasants, just cited, with their capacity of stubborn resistance. If that resistance was to incorporation in capitalist commodity relations and class differentiation, then their 'path' satisfies the criteria of neither AQ2 nor AQ3.

Byres' conclusion in favour of openness – that 'capitalist agrarian transition is protean in its manifest diversity' [1996: 478] – suggests that future history may disclose further surprises. This is something I shall come back to.

THE ANALYTICS OF 'THEN' AND 'NOW'

'Then' and 'now' in the problematic of agrarian transition starts with consideration of the possible relationships, combinations and *sequences* of several distinct analytical moments, and the social forces that promote or hinder their emergence and determine their relative weight. These moments (which, in fact, include elements of AQ2) form three clusters in Byres' framework. The first is (i) the *growth* of agricultural production and productivity (AQ2); the second (AQ3) comprises (ii) the *terms of trade* between agriculture and industry; (iii) the development of agricultural *demand* for industrial products; and (iv) the 'freeing' of agricultural *labour* to join the urban proletariat; the third comprises (v) surplus *appropriation in* agriculture (AQ2), and (vi) surplus *transfer from* agriculture to industrial accumulation (AQ3).[10]

The range of substantive diversity of paths of agrarian transition can be viewed in terms of different combinations of those moments in particular cases, which can be illustrated in order of ascending 'virtue', so to speak. First, the extractive logic of Preobrazhensky serves as a limiting case: it centres on surplus transfer from agriculture (vi), one of the means of which is tight (state) control of the terms of trade (ii), to the point of compulsory requisitions from the peasantry as well as administered prices. In terms of *sequence*, the growth of agricultural productivity (i) and demand for industrial goods (iii) have to await the prior development of industry.[11]

The East Asian cases of transition centred on the two Preobrazhensky-type mechanisms, but surprisingly were able to combine them with the growth of agricultural production and productivity. This reflects the 'most unusual, if not unique' character of the Japanese landlord class, as appropriators of the peasant 'surplus' (v), in its productive (re)investment of rent income in the technical improvement of farming (as well as investing in industry), and, of course, the central role of states that organised surplus transfer from agriculture (via taxation of the peasantry) to industrial accumulation (vi) but also took a keen interest in developing the infrastructure of farming. Points of *sequence* suggested here are that agricultural growth, with its high degree of labour intensity in farming (and presumably in the construction of irrigation and other infrastructure) was not a significant source of demand for industrial goods (iv) during early industrialisation, and that any alleviation of the intensity of exactions from the peasantry, by surplus appropriation and/or transfer, had to await the completion of primary accumulation for industry.

The exceptionally 'virtuous' quality of the American path was already noted, exemplifying the rapid growth of production and productivity through technical innovation in farming (i) and 'powerful backward and forward linkages' between agriculture and industry (i), (iii).[12] There was no surplus appropriation in northern and western agriculture by a class of landed property (v), and no strong mechanisms of surplus transfer at work (vi). Such virtue is further manifested, then, in the *simultaneous* (and 'balanced') development of agriculture and industry.

When these analytical moments are investigated in particular historical cases, their sequence connects with the timing and duration of transitions. *Timing* refers to what I have termed the 'prehistory' of transitions, that provides their initial conditions, and to the (relatively early or late) emergence and combination of key moments during transition. The latter connects with *duration*: the relatively more leisurely or compressed processes and stages of transition from its inception to completion. These distinctions further amplify the substantive diversity of different historical paths of transition. Consider, for example, the trajectories of England and Prussia as two paths of capitalist transformation of agriculture (AQ2). The defeat of the seigneurial reaction in England provided an initial condition for a transition of exceptionally leisurely duration from, say, the fifteenth to eighteenth centuries. The success of the feudal offensive in Prussia, in the second serfdom established by the sixteenth century, 'delayed' the inception of the capitalist transformation of agriculture east of the Elbe until the early nineteenth century. Thereafter, it was relatively rapid, albeit otherwise too 'late' to contribute to Prussian industrialisation (AQ3). Elsewhere, agrarian transitions appear to have been of relatively short duration: from the 1790s to 1830s in the northeastern USA, from the 1870s to the 1920s (?) in Japan, and intensely compressed in Taiwan and South Korea in the 1950s and 1960s.[13]

The analytical moments of Byres' problematic of agrarian transition, and their sequence, help to identify other possible outcomes. One important (negative) instance is when surplus appropriation in agriculture (v) does not translate into surplus transfer to industry (vi), again illustrated by Junker agriculture, both feudal and (later) capitalist, and by slavery and sharecropping in the American South. In the absence of conditions that generate the particularly 'virtuous' character of the (northern) American path, the absence of surplus transfers blocks agrarian transition/ industrialisation. This is illustrated by the inability of the Indian state to tax agrarian property and income, whether of landed property (rent) or of peasant capitalism (profit).[14] Other ways in which the key analytical moments of agrarian transition may be modified include the strategic part that can be played by non-agrarian classes, as merchant capital in the northeastern USA, and by important sources of primary accumulation for industrialisation other than agriculture (see further below).

Of course, the timing and duration of agrarian transitions, together with other aspects of the substantive diversity they display, require explanation through class analysis, including its application to the nature and role of states [*Byres*, 1996: 8; also 1991: 59; 1995: 569]. This is a question of the key social forces that promote or block agrarian transition in specific historical instances (different classes of landed property and, where relevant, agrarian capital and non-agrarian classes of capital, states), and the conditions that give them the capacity to do so (including the trajectories and outcomes of their conflicts with classes of agricultural labour, whether serfs, sharecroppers and other tenants, slaves, or wage workers).

These observations suggest that the substantive diversity of paths of agrarian transition is strongly marked by issues of timing and duration, that register the differential emergence, sequence, weight and combinations of their key analytical moments. This has been illustrated within the framework of Byres' theoretical problematic and its findings. It is now time to note Byres' (almost) exclusively 'internal' forms of explanation, that is, internal in three senses: argument (i) from the *economic logic* of agrarian modes/forms of production (as an articulation of particular class relations of land and labour, labour processes/productive forces, and mode of surplus appropriation), (ii) from the sociological characteristics of specific *agrarian classes*, and (iii) *within* the boundaries of social formations.

This, of course, conforms to much of the expository framework of Marx, Engels, and Lenin, concerning the development of capitalism.[15] In effect, it yields a series of *parallel histories*, the comparative thrust of which is *trans*national rather than *inter*national [*Rosenberg*, 1996: 6], that is to say, comparison between boundaried social formations across time and space, rather than of social formations as *connected* in time and space. To locate agrarian transitions in their international contexts – the times and spaces that social formations share in various ways – is, first, to extend and complement their investigation and explanation beyond their internal dynamics, and, second, to admit the question of how the successful completion of agrarian transition/industrialisation in particular places and times affects the prospects of subsequent transition elsewhere. The first is briefly illustrated here, the second discussed in the section that follows.

Prussian industrialisation, as already shown, is explicable only by the trajectory of Prussian state formation and expansion. This is the object of Anderson's analysis [1974], which explores and *combines*, on one hand, the character of Prussian feudalism, the distinctive features of the Junkers as a class of landed property, and their connections with the institutional development of the Prussian state, and on the other hand, the different stages of inter-dynastic and inter-state contestation that provide the territorial and political contours of the transition from feudalism to capitalism in northern Europe. Prussia emerged from this process as the principal contender for German hegemony over its main rivals, Bavaria and Saxony, by the mid-eighteenth century (the moment when Byres suggests an increasing contradiction between the relations and forces of Junker agriculture started to manifest Prussia's relative economic backwardness). In 1745 'the acquisition of Silesia increased the population of Prussia by 50 per cent at one blow ... endowing it for the first time with a relatively advanced economic region in the East, with a long tradition of urban manufactures (textiles) ... (this was) perhaps the most important and lucrative single addition to any European continental State in the epoch' [*Anderson, 1974:* 266]. And, of course, the acquisition of the Rhine Province in 1815 (above) gave Prussia the locus of the industrial revolution that its agrarian structure east of the Elbe had failed to stimulate.

Beyond this, one should also emphasise that Prussian feudalism was directed to *specialised commodity production* (of grain) *for international trade*, in the period of an increasingly international transition to capitalism.[16] The Prussian trajectory was thus also shaped by the processes and violent fluctuations of international markets (as well as those of state formation with which they were, and are, so closely connected). If this was true of Prussian commercial feudalism within the span of intra-European trade, it applies *a fortiori* to plantation slavery in the New World and its trans-oceanic trade in sugar, tobacco and cotton. For the USA

> it is clear that slave production of cotton was a profitable investment prior to 1860 ... the source of the cotton plantations' profitability was neither the high productivity of slave labour, nor economies of scale achieved under the plantation regime, but the demand for raw cotton by industrialist capitalists in England, and *the complete domination of the world market for raw cotton by the plantations of the American South* ... Northeastern merchants, who facilitated the trade of cotton with the capitalist world market, accumulated mercantile wealth from the circulation of cotton. Cotton, as the major export of the ante-bellum US, also created a favourable balance of trade and sound international credit for American merchants and bankers. *The expansion of commercial slavery provided the basis for both the geographic expansion of merchant capitalist operations (land speculation)* and the importation of money from Europe for merchant-sponsored transportation projects in the 1830s ... *the commodity*

producing character of plantation slavery was a catalyst to capitalist development as long as merchant capital was the major agency for the expansion of commodity production and the deepening of the social division of labour. As merchant capital created the conditions for its (own HB) subordination to industrial capital, by generalising commodity relations in the Northern US, slavery's non-capitalist relations of production became an obstacle to the dominance and expanded reproduction of capitalist production in the US social formation [*Post*, 1982: 31–2, 37, 38, emphasis added].

If 'Prussia presents the classical case in Europe of an *uneven and combined development*' [*Anderson*, 1974: 236], then New World plantation slavery is an even more potent exemplar of the uneven and combined development of capitalism *on a world scale*. Plantation slavery blocked industrialisation in the American South, as Byres shows, but contributed to industrialisation both in Britain *and* in 'the American road to capitalism', as Post's differentiated framework of the timing and spaces of the latter illustrates.[17]

UNEVEN AND COMBINED DEVELOPMENT ON A WORLD SCALE

[I]t is at the international level that the extraordinary drama of modernity rises up to its full height. It is at this level, and this level alone, that we can glimpse the process of the capitalist transformation of humanity *as a whole*: the rise of the West, the engulfing of the non-European world, the globalizing of the sovereign-states system and the world market … [*Rosenberg*, 1996: 5].

The reasons for uneven and combined development on a world scale

lay partly in the historical unevenness of existing human social development … (which) meant that capitalist world development would proceed from many different starting points and in each case find different cultural obstacles to overcome. And this applied in some respects within Europe just as much as outside it. But it was not just a matter of different starting levels … the development of backward societies took place under the pressure of an already existing world market, dominated by more advanced capitalist powers [*ibid.*: 7].

The significance of 'many different starting points' of capitalist development is central to formulating substantive diversity in Byres' comparative investigation, but needs to be complemented by the location of agrarian transitions in the context of uneven and combined development on a world scale – and *its* timing, which brings another angle of vision to bear on issues of 'then' and 'now'. This was illustrated briefly in relation to

Prussia and the American South, and now requires extension to the prospects and problems of agrarian transition in contemporary poor countries. This is evidently an enormous topic, of which the following discussion can only sketch some lines of inquiry and hypothesis.

To map the problematic of agrarian transition, its prospects and problems in contemporary poor counties, onto the framework of uneven and combined development on a world scale, and its periodisation, immediately suggests some central issues. The first necessarily concerns timing. All the successful agrarian transitions analysed by Byres, apart from the East Asian cases, were completed before the end of the nineteenth century. Moreover, all (excluding Taiwan and South Korea) encompassed sources of primary accumulation from territorial expansion, international trade, and/or colonial plunder and surplus extraction, as well as from their own agrarian structures.[18] The transitions of Taiwan and South Korea, the only twentieth-century examples, occurred through a most particular combination of external and internal circumstances (as Byres emphasises), were exceptionally compressed in duration, and appear to have approximated most closely the mechanisms of Preobrazhensky's model, as noted earlier.[19]

For the European colonies of Asia and Africa – created from 'many different starting points' at different moments of an evolving international division of labour, the conjunction of which shaped their trajectories – the question of agrarian transition/industrialisation was delayed until the moment of their independence, mostly from the late 1940s to early 1960s. This connects with a second issue, or set of issues: of how the conditions of industrialisation had changed from those of earlier transitions. When industrialisation was put on the agenda by the nationalist discourses and ambitious development plans of the moment of decolonisation, it would necessarily be denied the opportunities of external sources of primary accumulation enjoyed by the successive generations of earlier industrialisers in Europe, North America, and East Asia,[20] and would confront 'the presence of an already existing world market, dominated by (those) more advanced capitalist powers'.

On the other hand, external sources of industrial accumulation (capital and technology) would be available through foreign investment, both private and public (aid). The conditions, scale, forms and effects of foreign investment, together with the character and effectiveness of 'developmental states', would be major factors in the degrees and types of industrialisation achieved, whether also supported or hindered by agrarian change (or 'bypassing' it[21]). Whatever the outcomes (to date), it seems clear that the intersectoral linkages of agriculture and industry at the core of the ('internalist') problematic of agrarian transition/industrialisation, would now be mediated by the (differential) effects of the circuits of international capital and world markets, for each sector in *any* capitalist economy (central or peripheral).[22]

In short, a century of modern imperialism has extended the determinants of industrialisation far beyond the prospects of agrarian transition in landscapes inhabited exclusively by classes of landed property and agrarian labour. The substantive diversity of forms of agrarian change, of their contributions (or otherwise) to industrial accumulation by relatively 'virtuous' or 'vicious' means (based in the growth of agricultural productivity and dynamic intersectoral linkages, or in more or less coercive transfers), and of degrees and types of industrialisation in the imperialist periphery, prompt a third, connected, issue: which 'contemporary poor countries' are we talking about? A regional answer to this question is indicated in a recent observation by E.J. Hobsbawm [1994: 289, 291] that 'the most dramatic and far-reaching social change of the second half of this century, and the one which cuts us off forever from the world of the past, is the death of the peasantry ... Only three regions of the globe remained essentially dominated by their villages and fields: sub-Saharan Africa, South and continental South-east Asia, and China.'

It is likely that the regions listed (which Hobsbawm 'admits' comprise half the world's population[23]) converge with Byres' 'contemporary poor countries' marked by lack of agrarian transition. If, by his criteria, Latin America, Malaysia and the islands of Southeast Asia, Western Asia and the Maghreb, have not yet undergone comprehensive industrialisation, their patterns of rural emigration and urbanisation today present another stark contrast with the social demography of the historic agrarian transitions. Hobsbawm [1994: 292] continues, that massive exodus from the land

> was only partly due to agricultural progress, at least in the former peasant areas ... the developed industrial countries, with one or two exceptions, also transformed themselves into the major producers of agricultural goods for the world market, and they did so while reducing their actual farming population to a steadily diminishing, and sometimes an absurdly tiny percentage of their people. This was plainly achieved in an extraordinary spurt in capital-intensive productivity per head of the agriculturists ... In the poor regions of the world the agricultural revolution was not absent, through it was patchier ... on the whole, the countries of the Third World, and parts of the (formerly or still socialist) Second World, no longer fed themselves, let alone produced the major exportable food surplus that might be expected from agrarian countries.

These observations coincide with the findings of Harriet Friedmann's remarkable project on 'international food regimes' since 1870, and on the internationalisation/globalisation of the world food economy in the second half of the twentieth century [*Friedmann*, 1978; 1982a; 1982b; 1993; *Friedmann and McMichael*, 1989].[24] This and other work on the international economy of food in the epoch of imperialism provides a fourth set of issues, or focus, concerning the nature of agrarian questions/prospects of agrarian transition today. No attempt is made here to summarise the theoretically sophisticated and historically ramified plan of Friedmann's project that incorporates, *inter alia*, arguments concerning the sources (and costs) of food staples to capitalist industrialisation in different regions of the world economy at different times, and of how international divisions of labour in agricultural production and trade contributed to the formation of the modern state system. I limit myself to culling certain points for present purposes.

The basis of the first international food regime from the 1870s was the massive growth of grain (and livestock/meat) production on the vast internal frontiers of 'settler' states: Argentina, Australia, Canada, and above all the USA.

> Settler agriculture cheapened agricultural commodity production, via the political appropriation and colonization of new lands. Subsequent technical changes, especially merchanized harvesting, adapted settler agriculture to labour shortages. Specialized commodity production ... [was] actively promoted by settler states via land and immigration policy, and the establishment of social infrastructure, mainly railways and credit facilities [*Friedmann and McMichael*, 1989: 101].

Exports, especially of wheat, competed directly with the temperate agriculture of the European homelands of industrial capitalism, by contrast with the complementary tropical agricultural production and exports of Asia and Africa whose colonial subordination and incorporation was completed in the same period. There were thus three distinct zones in the global division of labour in agricultural production and trade, with a key linkage between metropolitan economies and those that became their granaries: 'between goods – and regions – of wage labour and settler agriculture' [*ibid.*].

The first international food regime lasted until 1914, when it was increasingly subverted by the responses of European agrarian interests and states to the crisis induced by imports of cheap grain, by the disruptions of war and the second great depression of the 1930s. Protectionism meant that after 'several decades of war, experimentation and depression, the intensive commercial development of European agriculture finally complemented the industrial structure', while 'settler states introduced direct regulation of agricultural markets to help farmers cope with the collapse of international trade. Price supports and other market controls would eventually be adopted in both Europe and the new nations formed through decolonization' [*ibid*.: 101–2].

The second international food regime after 1945 registered a shift of American grain exports to the countries of Latin American and newly independent Asia and Africa (and later the USSR), a shift spearheaded by food aid policies.

> Aid quickly restructured trade. The United States replaced Europe as the center of international trade. As exchange came to be centered on a dominant source of supply instead of a dominant source of import demand, multiple new import markets were a necessary complement … Aid was the mechanism for overcoming social and national limits to the transformation of self-sufficient agrarian societies into consumers of commercial wheat [*Friedmann*, 1982a: 264].

This shift was partly the result of the continuing nationalist trajectory of European agriculture after 1945, consolidated within the framework of the Common Market/European Community and its Common Agricultural Policy. The post-war international food order started to come apart in the early 1970s for a number of reasons (including the rising costs to the USA of its ever growing grain surpluses, the entry of the EC into export markets, and increasing national self-sufficiency in food production of a number of developing countries, especially in Asia), with an ensuing and endemic anarchy in world grain trade [*ibid*.: 271–82].

The elaboration of the wheat based/wage good regime need not concern us here, in the face of a more recent and potent trend, namely 'the transnational restructuring of agricultural sectors'. This generates agro-food chains 'dominated at both ends by increasingly large *industrial capitals*', and integrated *globally* in ways that undermine 'national agricultures': 'integration occurred first among advanced capitalist countries, then incorporated certain peripheral and even state socialist countries (and marginalized others)' [*Friedmann and McMichael*, 1989: 105, my emphasis].

The first international food regime was marked by competition and the operation of Ricardian comparative advantage in wheat (and meat) production. The second centred on international regulation imposed by American national agriculture, orchestrated in a combination of farm support and strategic export policies and underwritten by the dominance of the US economy and dollar in the long post-war boom. It came under increasing pressure from rival national agricultures that emulated the pattern of national agriculture in the USA to undermine the latter's trade hegemony. While wheat was central to the two international food regimes, and to the cost of wage foods ('the physically existing form of variable

capital') in different places at different times during the period of these
regimes (1870s–1970s), it was marginal to the development of agro-
industry. In the postwar period, the latter centred on the two key agroindustrial complexes of meat and durable (processed) foods, in which rival
national agricultures similarly challenged initial American dominance by
replicating its mechanisms. However, this inter*nationalised* integration of
national agricultures in the patterns of world production and consumption
gave way to increasing *globalisation*. The 'transnational restructuring of
agricultural sectors' is accompanied by growing *private* (corporate), rather
than state or inter-state, global regulation of agricultural production, trade,
processing and consumption: corporations 'are the major agents attempting
to regulate agro-food conditions, that is, to organize stable conditions of
production and consumption which allow them to plan investment, sourcing
of agricultural materials, and marketing' on a global scale [*Friedmann*,
1993: 52].[25]

Again this amplifies how the trajectory of uneven and combined
development on a world scale further breaches the boundaries of national
economies/social formations, *and* also breaches the conventional sectoral
boundaries of agriculture and industry. Is there then still any agrarian
question at the end of the twentieth century? In their different ways,
Hobsbawm's 'death of the peasantry' (and its context) and Friedmann's
periodisation of international, then global, restructuring of agriculture,
appear to imply the death of the agrarian question, and of the possibility of
agrarian transition in any form disclosed by previous history (if not of
industrialisation by other means). One can reinforce this implication with
the hypothesis that the agrarian question of capital has been transcended by
the *generalisation of commodity relations* on the global plane – in the
countryside of South Asia and sub-Saharan Africa as in that of the
industrialised capitalist countries, albeit in different forms and with
different effects.[26]

The End of the Agrarian Question? I

In contemplating the lessons of the first Russian Revolution of 1905–6,
including their implications for his earlier analysis of the development of
capitalism in Russia (see note 9), Lenin took as his reference points the
contrasting paths of capitalist transformation of agriculture of two countries
in which agrarian transition (AQ3) was *already completed* (and whose
industrial power was already challenging that of Britain). His delineation of
the Prussian and American paths was spurred as much by concern with their
political as well as economic effects, *within* the industrial capitalist
formations of Germany and the USA as well as in their trajectories of
transition. This supplies the argument underlying the statement by Levin

and Neocosmos [1989] cited at the head of this essay.[27] To thus retrieve Lenin's concern with AQ1, and to restate its centrality to AQ2 and AQ3, is also to recognise (as above) that 'the primacy of class analysis' [*Byres*, 1996: 8] entails *political class practices* as well as economic class practices, and the irreducibility of the former to the latter. As in other parts of this discussion, I first illustrate this briefly in relation to Prussia/Germany and the USA, with reference to the political trajectory of their transitions *and* its legacy after the completion of transition.

Anderson began his account of Prussian absolutism by noting that the theoretical problems posed by its trajectory (as 'the classical case in Europe of uneven and combined development') 'were specifically raised by Engels, in his famous letter to Bloch in 1890, on the irreducible importance of political, legal and cultural systems in the structure of all historical determination' [1974: 236].[28] The Prussian ascendancy owed much 'to the peculiar cast of the junker class itself' [*ibid.*: 261]. This was a class rooted in the agrarian structure analysed by Byres [1996] but whose social and political character, and role in state building, can not be derived simply from the logic of its manorial production. The Junkers were owners of medium sized commercial farms, and consequently less socially divided than many other European aristocracies; the 'remarkable efficacy' of the Prussian army and civil service 'was a reflection of the unity of the class which staffed them'; 'the Prussian landowning class was more stolidly at one with its state than any other in Europe' [*Anderson*, 1974: 262–5]. In short, the Junkers forged themselves into a formidable class force – in relation to agrarian labour, of course, but also in relation to towns and merchants, to international markets, through the institutional evolution of the apparatuses of the Prussian state, and not least through continuous contestation with rival states. This is what enabled Junker Prussia to acquire its industrial revolution, as it were, by territorial expansion rather than by initiating an agrarian transition in its historic heartland.

Thus some of the co-ordinates of political class practice in Prussia's 'overall capitalist transition', completed before German unification in 1871. Was the social formation then 'dominated by industry and the urban bourgeoisie', with 'no longer an agrarian question in any substantive sense'? The unified German state was established on the eve of the Great Depression of 1873–96, and at the moment of full exposure of European markets to cheap grain imports from the new centres of global wheat production, the significance of which was signalled above [*Friedmann and McMichael*, 1989; also *Djurfeldt*, 1981]. The Junker response and its effects is the object of Gerschenkron's classic work *Bread and Democracy in Germany* [1943; second edition 1966].

That response centred on protectionism, initiated in an alliance with

German industry also threatened by imports in a conjuncture of acute recession, but maintained beyond then in an increasingly tense 'compromise between iron and rye': while industry had experienced a cyclical slump, German grain farming was subject to a *structural crisis* in the face of 'revolutionary changes in the world structure of grain output' [*ibid.*: 45, 47, viii]. Moreover, the cause of the agrarian interest pushed the Junkers into mass politics for the first time, to secure the support of an economically battered peasantry through the ideological appeal of 'agrarian mysticism' [*ibid.*: 17]. Barrington Moore [1966: 448] summarises Gerschenkron's findings that

> the basic elements of Nazi doctrine appear quite distinctly in the Junkers' generally successful efforts, by means of the Agrarian League established in 1894, to win the support of the peasants in non-Junker areas of smaller farms. *Führer* worship, the idea of a corporative state, militarism, anti-Semitism, in a setting closely related to the Nazi distinction between 'predatory' and 'productive' capital, were devices used to appeal to anticapitalist sentiments among the peasantry.

Gerschenkron argues that after military defeat and the failed revolution of 1918 in Germany, the Junkers recuperated their economic and political position, were able to undermine the Weimar Republic and 'to make a signal and sinister contribution to Adolf Hitler's advent to power' – it took another world war to end 'half a millennium of Junker power' [*Gerschenkron*, 1966: viii].

This not only contextualises the urgency of Engels' 'explicitly political concern' with the agrarian question in the industrialised Germany of the early 1890s, but also manifests wider (and connected) issues of (a) the political as well as economic class practices of the agrarian question, (b) the 'concentration of many determinations' (Marx), including those of international forces, of class struggles that effect (or block) agriculture's contributions to industrial accumulation, and (c) appropriate time frames (the 'then' and 'now') of analysis. Gerschenkron's analysis, written during the war against fascism, was explicitly political in its concern with democracy, *and* was also informed by the centrality of the price of bread (both literally and metaphorically) to industrial accumulation. In sum, the dominance of industry, an economic moment, and that of the urban bourgeoisie, a political moment, are neither synonymous nor simultaneous. Rosenberg [1996: 11] characterises Germany after 1871 as a 'society whose own peculiar pattern of combined development had crystallized a strong military-aristocratic definition of the state and a politically weak bourgeoisie', while Anderson [1974: 278] remarked that the new German state 'was now a capitalist apparatus, over-determined by its feudal ancestry'. The Prussian class of agrarian capital of such distinctive feudal ancestry continued to imprint its political force on both German and international events long after 1871.[29]

The politics of the agrarian question can be illustrated similarly in the American context, both during its transition and thereafter. By the 1840s, emergent industrial capital (especially in agro-industry), linked to the growth of agrarian petty commodity production, 'transformed the *geographic* expansion of slavery into an obstacle to the development of capitalism' [*Post*, 1982: 37, my emphasis]. The immediate context was the desire of southern planters to establish plantation slavery in the new territories conquered from Mexico in 1845: it was the need for geographical expansion of both fledgling American capitalism and long established plantation slavery at that *time* that generated contestation over the agrarian forms to be established in that *space*.

The 'economic contradiction between the necessary conditions for the expansion of slavery and capitalism in the 1840s and 1850s determined, *in the last instance*, the *political* class struggles that culminated in the Civil War of 1861–5' [*ibid.*: 49, my emphasis]. With 'in the last instance' and 'political class struggles' (recalling Engels' letter to Bloch, cited by Anderson [1974]), Post serves notice that the Civil War was no simple clash of two economic 'logics'. First, the abolition of slavery after the war was *contingent* – a 'measure forced upon the industrial bourgeoisie by military exigencies and the struggle of the slaves' [*ibid.*: 51]. Second, 'the direct economic impact of the war on industrial capitalism was secondary to the war's *political* effects on capitalist development through the remainder of the nineteenth century' [*ibid.*: 50, original emphasis]. And, third, what of the replacement of slavery by sharecropping, the economic 'logic' and effects of which were as antithetical to industrialisation as those of slavery, as Byres [1996] shows (see also Angelo [1995]? The answer of Post [1982: 51] is that while 'sharecropping did pose definite limits to the transformation of the labour process, it did not have plantation slavery's geographically imperialist tendencies, which had posed an obstacle to the Western expansion of petty commodity production'.[30]

A useful illustration of the politics of the agrarian question in the industrial USA, likewise linking a number of the substantive themes of this discussion, can be drawn from the conjunctures of the interwar and postwar periods. As we saw earlier, Friedmann argues that the defensive politics/ policies of the 1930s shaped an American national agriculture, that then provided the means of a strategic offensive on world markets after 1945. In the USA 'the Depression for agriculture really began in the 1920s' [*Mann and Dickinson*, 1980: 305], manifested in the impact of overproduction, falling agricultural commodity prices, and the falling value of farm assets, on an *agrarian petty bourgeoisie* that had borrowed heavily to invest in expanded production – a familiar contradiction in the agriculture of the industrialised capitalist countries to this day.[31] Just as topical are the types of policies eventually conceded by the US state, in the New Deal of the 1930s, to the political demands of the agrarian petty bourgeoisie and its organisation in the 'farm lobby': support prices, storage and disposal of surpluses, farm income stabilisation [*ibid.*: 305–10].

In modern capitalism, the 'agrarian interest' is not exhausted by farmers (petty bourgeois or capitalist) but also comprises the weight of corporate agribusiness which may both 'dominate' farmers and support certain conditions of their reproduction, politically and ideologically as well as economically. The economic foundation of the link between farmers and agroindustrial capital in the political constitution of 'the agrarian interest' is, of course, the forms of vertical integration of the former in the circuits of the latter.[32] The American grain farmers at the base of the two international food regimes combined with corporate capital upstream and downstream of farming in a powerful political coalition, that meshed with US strategic interests after the war to produce and export surpluses to developing countries – the key realignment of the second international food regime compared with the first.

These rather different examples from Prussia/Germany and the USA illustrate the salience of the issues of AQ1, both during and after agrarian transition, and suggest that the completion of transition/'dominance of industry' does not spell the end of the agrarian question 'in any substantive sense'. However, as we saw, there is another, specifically world historical, sense of the end of the agrarian question, signalled by the forms and stages of internationalisation/globalisation of capital, which has to be taken seriously. This manifests a perverse inversion, an effect hardly unfamiliar in the uneven and combined development of capitalism on a world scale: that the prospects of agrarian transition in contemporary poor countries (or the poorest, as above) that require such transition for industrialisation and economic development, are eliminated by their forms of integration in the capitalist world economy at the end of the twentieth century – in short, the end of the agrarian question *without its resolution*.

The End of the Agrarian Question? II

The bare statement of the end of the agrarian question in the latter sense – the elimination of any prospects of agrarian transition as a route to comprehensive industrialisation in contemporary poor countries – may add 'world system' determinism to other dangers of 'analytical closure'. The danger is familiar from the analytics of dependency theory: that any economic growth and social change in the periphery that falls short of attaining the model of an advanced capitalist economy, thereby fails to qualify as 'proper' or 'real' development. This resonates an idealised or otherwise abstracted model of the advanced economy;[33] empirically, its logic of residual categorisation obscures the massive diversity of the social formations of the periphery, their differential trajectories of capitalist development and what explains them.

On the other hand, the analysis of the global dynamics of capital, and its stage of modern imperialism, generates issues which must inform consideration of all three agrarian questions, without predetermining their answers. First, there is the evident and necessary set of issues concerning how the articulation (and 'performance') of national economies (the formation and functioning of domestic markets, intersectoral linkages, forms and rates of accumulation, the role and effectiveness of state economic management) is shaped by their location in the world economy. This will (always) reveal very different (if not fixed) effects at the centres and peripheries of imperialism *and* within them.

Second, not only will any prospective agrarian transition not replicate the historic paths of transition, but is unlikely to replicate their *mechanisms* (the weight, combinations and sequences of their key analytical moments). This suggests the need for an expanded and modified problematic of agrarian transition/industrialisation in the periphery of contemporary imperialism, a reformulation of its *analytics*. This would entail the investigation for particular social formations of three analytically distinct processes, and their interrelations: (a) location within capitalist world economy and its effects, (b) patterns of agrarian structure and change, (c) forms and degrees of industrialisation. Of course, there is no presumption that reformulating the analytics of agrarian transition in the ways suggested would disclose any uniformity of prospects (nor 'paths') for the social formations of the periphery, whether positive or negative, but it would help identify important differences between them beyond a comparison limited to the immediate forms (and 'internal' logics) of their agrarian structures.

CONCLUSION: THREE AGRARIAN QUESTIONS

If Byres' comparative political economy of agrarian transition has enjoyed the privilege of considering 'completed transition', then I have been privileged by the fruits of his intellectual labour, and the agenda it has enriched, in trying to clarify my own thinking through this essay. The difficulties and problems I have noted are the marks of intellectual struggle, and in an important sense belong to all of us committed to advancing the Marxist understanding of the agrarian question. T.J. Byres confronts the need 'to transcend the sanctity of usage' [1996: 12] at a moment in history when Marxism, 'capital's antagonistic offspring', has to generate means 'to cope with the shifting grounds of struggle' [*Post*, 1996: 16]. He continues to be a beacon of light in our collective project.

By way of conclusion, a different juxtaposition of the three agrarian questions can be suggested. Just as Byres demonstrates the possibility of agrarian transition with or without the capitalist transformation of agriculture (AQ2), one can now pose the salience of AQ1 and AQ2 with or without agrarian transition. The agrarian question of the problematic of transition is, in effect, the *agrarian question of capital*, as remarked above, and specifically of industrial capital. Indeed, this is the reason why the thesis of the end of the agrarian question, as resolved for capital on the global plane of contemporary imperialism, has to be taken seriously. Lenin's designation of the Prussian and American paths fused AQ1 and AQ2, in a concern with the political effects of their distinctive economic trajectories and class coordinates, in particular their effects for *democracy* in Russia after the first revolution. In short, Lenin posed the *agrarian question of the working masses*, both proletarian *and* poor peasant.

This understanding makes certain things clearer, for example, the concern in the Soviet industrialisation debate of the 1920s with the politics of the worker-peasant alliance, and its bearing on the constraints of 'socialist primitive accumulation'. More widely, it explains the generalisation of the 'peasant path' in the discourses and programmes of anti-colonial and national democratic movements: the overthrow of landlordism as a condition of democracy as well as of economic progress.[34]

In the contemporary (postcolonial) periphery, characterised by generalised commodity production (however 'backward' some of its social forms and productive forces), capitalist development – with or without agrarian transition, marked by landlordism or not, or by the often vicious class struggle in the countryside generated by peasant capitalism [*Banaji*, 1990] – cannot provide an adequate or secure material existence, nor substantive political freedoms, to the great majority, urban and rural, proletarian and semi-proletarian.[35] The urgency of bread (or rice, or maize) *and* democracy will continue to distinguish the agrarian questions of the working masses, and to drive their struggles.

NOTES

1. Page references to Byres [1996] are to the final manuscript of the book and not to its published version. The systematic organisation of the book facilitates the checking and assessment of my discussion and quotations against the published text.
2. Earlier versions of this paper were first presented and published in 1986 [*Byres, 1986*]. The

trajectory of the intellectual project is described in the Foreword to Byres [1996]; see also Byres [1994; 1995].

3. At this point in the book, concepts of the productive forces focus exclusively on the *productivity of land* (yields) rather than the productivity of labour, which only assumes centre stage in the analysis of agrarian transition in the northern and especially western USA (see below).

4. Of course, there are tensions intrinsic to the ensemble of these mechanisms whereby agriculture can contribute to primary accumulation for industrialisation. The nature, form and extent of transfers from agriculture to industry must set limits to both (re)investment in farming (necessary to the development of the productive forces) and to rural demand for the products of industry. In terms of their abstract logic, these limits are eased by rapid growth of the productive forces in agriculture, but this is likely to be subverted (or 'delayed') by the extractive logic of Preobrazhensky-like primary accumulation (see also note 11). In concrete terms, how·these tensions are resolved (or otherwise) is determined by the course of class struggle in the countryside, by the relations between landed property (and agrarian capital where it exists) and nascent industrial capital, and by the actions of states. For an excellent elaboration of the economics of intersectoral resource flows, see Karshenas in this volume.

5. Byres [1996: 171 n92] quotes Deane [1979: 52] as follows:

> ... the agricultural revolution in England can be said to have contributed to the effectiveness of the first industrial revolution in four main ways: (1) be feeding the growing population and particularly the populations of the industrial centres, (2) by inflating purchasing power for the products of British industry, (3) by providing a substantial part of the capital required to finance industrialisation and to keep it going through a major war (with Napoleonic France, HB), (4) by releasing the surplus labour for employment in industry.

6. The Japanese landlord class of the agrarian transition was 'most unusual, if not unique' in its commitment to productive investment in, and management of, farming [*Byres*, 1991: 48)]

7. The two paths are indicated in the Preface to the second edition of *The Development of Capitalism in Russia* in 1907 [*Lenin*, 1964a] and developed in *The Agrarian Programme of Social Democracy in the First Russian Revolution, 1905–1907* [*Lenin*, 1962].

8. Presumably, supervision of the quality of labour on small sharecropped holdings [1996: 341] did not present the same obstacles or costs as supervising gang labour on plantations, whether under slavery (274–6) or after abolition when it proved impossible to reproduce the gang system with wage labour [1996: 318, 321].

9. In 1907 Lenin [1962] commented that in *The Development of Capitalism in Russia* he had identified the trend correctly but not the moment, while the opposite is the case here [*Byres*, 1996: 436]. That the trend apparent in the 1910 US census data used by Lenin was reversed soon thereafter, is also remarked by Djurfeldt [1981: 184].

10. For present purposes, I restrict myself to following Byres' framework and its substantive findings/interpretations, rather than assessing them against other contributions. Valuable examples of the latter include the work of Saith [1985; 1990] and Mundle [1985]. Saith [1985] similarly traces parallels and contrasts between capitalist and socialist agrarian transitions, with attention to the central reference point of Preobrazhensky's model, and his 1990 article elaborates an illuminating analysis of intersectoral linkages on a comparative and historical basis. Mundle [1985] compares the historic English and Japanese paths with colonial and independent India, including calculations of transfers from agriculture and an assessment of the differential weight of agriculture's various contributions to industrialisation.

11. This was one key point of divergence between Preobrazhensky and Kritsman and the Agrarian Marxists [*Cox and Littlejohn*, 1984]. Preobrazhensky's view of the necessary prior development of industry is echoed in later growth models such as WA Lewis' 'industrial trickle-down' process as Saith [1990: 197] terms it, and the Mahalanobis planning model in India in the 1950s. Whether initial Soviet industrialisation actually fulfilled Preobrazhensky's prescription is questioned by Ellman [1975]; see also the findings on China of Karshenas in this volume.

12. Byres [1996] does not provide data on the intersectoral terms of trade (ii), except to cite the observation of Mann and Dickinson (1980: 321 n51) that 'the increased volume of wheat production coupled with the general economic crisis of the 1880s and 1890s sent wheat prices plummeting'. This, however, is located in Byres' discussion of the 'persistence' of agricultural petty commodity production vs. capitalist farming in the USA (see note 31). On the significance of the global depression of the 1870s to 1890s, see note 24.

13. Byres [1991: 60] observes that 'agrarian transition is the outcome of a very long and complex process', which perhaps conflates the duration of transitions with what I have termed their 'prehistory' and privileges the timing, in world historical terms, of completed transitions. The latter may reflect the underlying influence of Marxist debate on the 'classic' *European* transitions from feudalism to capitalism [*Hilton*, 1976; *Brenner*; 1985], with its characteristic method of comparison of 'parallel histories'. This notion, and how it might obscure determination of the differential timing and duration of agrarian transitions by the uneven and combined development of capitalism on a world scale, is discussed next. Having said that, starting an account of the Japanese path at the Meiji restoration is problematic. In his interpretation of the Japanese transition, Mundle [1985: 67–71] suggests that its foundations were established in the long evolution of Tokugawa feudalism before 1868 – an assessment Byres would concur with; see also Barrington Moore [1966: 230–45], and Smith [1959].

14. There is also the vexed question of the intersectoral terms of trade in India, stressed by Mitra [1977] and Byres [1979] as inhibiting industrial accumulation. That was at a time when the terms of trade had been favourable to agriculture, but were soon to shift against it.

15. Although they did not limit themselves to the agrarian sources of the development of capitalism. While Byres' formulation of AQ3 is motivated by the purpose of identifying the specifically agrarian contributions to capitalist industrialisation, a further stage of analysis would need to integrate the account of agrarian change with issues of the role of merchant capital and of proto-industrialisation, which both Marx and Lenin considered at some length. A striking parallel with (or precedent of) the logic of Lenin's Prussian and American paths of agrarian transformation and of Byres' capitalism from above and below, is given in Marx's analysis of two paths of the formation of industrial capital, called upon by Post [1982: 45]. They are via the (self) transformation of merchant capital that takes control of and organises the process of production, or via the class differentiation of artisanal production which Marx designated 'the really revolutionary path' (echoed exactly in Lenin's characterisation of the American agrarian path). Post suggests that both these paths occurred in different branches of early industrialisation in the USA. The absence of any consideration of the social origins of industrial capital is somewhat like Hamlet without the Prince, when agrarian transition is defined by its outcome of industrialisation.

16. On specialised commodity production in feudalism, see Banaji [1976].

17. Byres [1996: 356] estimates Post's earlier article [1982] 'of considerable interest' while that of 1995 provokes a rapture that can only be conveyed in French: a *tour de force*, the *chef d'oeuvre*. Both are outstanding contributions, in my view, but for some purposes I find the earlier article more useful. The reasons should be apparent from my discussion. The earlier article examines how 'the realization of the necessary conditions for capitalist production in the United States took place through the articulation, expanded reproduction and transformation of three forms of production, and through a process of political class struggle that culminated in the American Civil War' [*Post*, 1982: 30]. The three forms in question are slavery, (agricultural) petty commodity production, and capitalist manufacture.

18. Of course, Byres knows this: 'colonial surplus appropriation has proved decisive' in some historical cases of capitalist industrialisation, although, he continues '*not* in the Prussian or American cases' [1996: 467, my emphasis]. However, territorial expansion was decisive to both, and the inward territorial expansion of the USA has led to its characterisation as 'an internal settler colonial state' [*Mann and Dickinson*, 1980: 290]. This refers primarily to warfare against, and dispossession of, Native Americans from early English colonisation of the Atlantic seaboard through to the late nineteenth century, which Byres narrates in detail and with passion [1996: 216–36]. If that process of primary accumulation expressed colonial expropriation rather than appropriation, the same does not hold for plantation slavery established by 'the colonial policy of the world-trading powers' (Preobrazhensky – see note

20). Nor does the independence from colonial rule of the USA after 1776 obviate the colonial character of slave plantation production, which *expanded* geographically in the American Southwest (as in Brazil and Cuba) in the first half of the nineteenth century, when slavery was being abolished in the New World territories of Britain and France [*Blackburn*, 1988: 548]; also Post [1982], as above.

19. The external circumstances, as so often in the history of capitalism, were those of war and its aftermath, in the case of South Korea of *two* wars: the Second World War which ended Japanese colonialism, and the Korean War which enabled the US military government after 1953 to force through the implementation of land reform (legislated in 1949) in the face of resistance by landlords. The internal circumstances reflected the Japanese colonial 'model' that combined intense exploitation of the peasantry with productive investment in agriculture, as in Japan itself [*ibid.*: 52–4] and by contrast with the legacy of European colonialism [*Saith*, 1990: 206–7].

20. With the exception again of Taiwan and South Korea, which again marks their close approximation to Preobrazhensky's model, and its intraversion of primary accumulation in the absence of the external sources of plunder of 'the colonial policy of the world-trading countries ... plundering in the form of taxes on the natives, seizure of their property, their cattle and land, their stores of precious metals, the conversion of conquered people into slaves, the infinitely varied system of crude cheating, and so on' [*Preobrazhensky*, 1965: 85].

21. While Taiwan and South Korea had their agrarian transitions, the other two Asian 'tigers' – the city states of Hong Kong and Singapore – lacked any agrarian base of industrial accumulation.

22. Mediated or *eliminated*, according to some analyses, for example, those stressing the 'disarticulation' of peripheral economies [*Amin*, 1974; *de Janvry*, 1981], or the globalisation of capital and the 'decline of national agricultures' [*Friedmann and McMichael*, 1989]. See further below.

23. And the half of the world's population with the greatest concentration of poverty [*World Bank*, 1990].

24. 1870 has a manifold significance. The Great Depression of 1873 to 1896 was the first sustained slump of global proportions in the series of long waves of industrial capitalism. It was a conjuncture of inestimable importance in the path of development of the capitalist world economy in the twentieth century, as many have shown, not least Lenin [1964c] in his analysis of imperialism.

25. On some of the recent twists in this trajectory:

> Promotion of agricultural exports, especially those called 'non-traditional' (geared to new niche markets for exotic foods, flowers, and other crops) is an explicit aim of structural adjustment conditions imposed by creditors ... the completely new markets in 'exotic' fruits and vegetables are global from the outset. Any state can enter, and in the push and shove of new markets, there is room for fly-by-night entrepreneurs and instant transnational corporations, as well as the giants of the postwar agro-food regime. Rapacious entrepreneurial practices are encouraged by slavish state policies to attract investments and promote exports. The paradise of eternal strawberries and ornamental plants for rich consumers depends on an underworld of social disruption and ecological irresponsibility [*Friedmann*, 1993: 50, 53–4].

26. On the theoretical basis for this hypothesis, see Gibbon and Neocosmos [1985], and on its applications Bernstein [1994].

27. See also, and most importantly, Neocosmos [1986]. Previously [*Bernstein*, 1996: 45 n37], I observed that the statement by Levin and Neocosmos cited loses none of its force by replacing 'primarily' with 'exclusively'.

28. Anderson [1974: 236–7n1, 277–8] suggests that Engels' concrete analysis of Prussia was superior to that of Marx in this respect.

29. Rosenberg [1996: 11], following Horowitz [1969], suggests that Barrington Moore's justly celebrated study of the *Social Origins of Dictatorship and Democracy* [1966], in which Prussia/Germany and Japan exemplify the passage of 'revolution from above' to fascism, follows the comparative method of 'parallel histories' which need to be complemented by

the location of Moore's case studies in uneven and combined development on a world scale.
30. Post continues: 'Sharecropping also eliminated plantation "self-sufficiency", making the direct producers more dependent on commodity circulation for their reproduction and deepening the social division of labour in the South'.
31. It is interesting that Byres' [1996] account of the USA extends beyond the completion of agrarian transition (while that of Prussia ends abruptly with 1871). There may be several reasons for this. One is to demonstrate how the succession of plantation slavery by sharecropping generated similarly negative consequences for industrialisation in the South. The other possible reason is both more complex and wide ranging, deriving from Byres' engagement with Lenin's American path *and* its generalising logic. As already noted, Lenin considered the agrarian question in the USA (AQ2) when its agrarian transition (AQ3) was already completed. While Byres grasps the nettle of Lenin's inaccuracy concerning American agriculture, Lenin's argument of the (inevitable) class differentiation of peasant or agricultural petty commodity production into classes of agrarian capital and wage labour may still haunt Byres' interpretation of the USA, which is formulated as 'the puzzle of why (petty commodity production) rather than full-blooded capitalism prevailed' in its agrarian transition [1996: 412], and again: 'Why, when the wage relation emerged relatively early elsewhere, did it fail to do so pervasively in American agriculture?' [*ibid.*: 427]. On his own account of seven cases of successful agrarian transition [*Byres*, 1991], the *only* instance of a 'relatively early' emergence of agricultural wage labour was in England (with the other instances of its emergence restricted to Prussia, and northern France from the 1840s, both exemplifying 'lateness'). It may be that the English path, noted above for its exceptionalism, here casts a long shadow from its historical time and space on that of American agrarian transition.
    Beyond the completion of transition, the 'puzzle' requiring explanation is that of the 'persistence' or 'survival' of petty commodity production in American farming, which is attributed to 'state intervention' [*ibid.*: 427, 433]. Does this carry an implication that, without such intervention, agricultural petty commodity producers will necessarily succumb to the superior 'efficiency' of capitalist farming? As Byres frequently and rightly observes, the role of the state is 'crucial' in all transitions to capitalism, and thereafter, of course. Why, then, the specific forms of state intervention in the USA since the 1920s? This is located in the next part of my discussion, but two further points can be recorded first. One is Byres' reticence in naming the *class* of agricultural petty commodity producers, unlike Post [1982: 39–40] who acknowledges the 'process of competition, innovation and accumulation' that leads to 'social differentiation into an *agrarian petty bourgeoisie* on the one hand, and a growing mass of property-less wage labourers on the other' [my emphasis; also *Post*, 1982: 43; 1995: 431–32]. This connects with a second issue (the tip of another iceberg among many which my present discussion can only hop between), namely the status of petty commodity production within capitalism. Djurfeldt [1981], among others, argues that petty rather than capitalist commodity production is the *characteristic* form of agricultural production in capitalism. See also note 32.
32. Djurfeldt [1981] provides a useful reminder of the importance of vertical integration in Chayanov. In the last part of *Peasant Farm Organization* (Chs.5 and 6), Chayanov turned from his analysis of the internal logic of peasant production (for which that work is most famous, or infamous) to consider its location in national and international capitalist economy: 'Where are the social threads that bind Sider Karpov's farm, lost in the Perm' forests, to the London banks and oblige him to feel the effects of changes in the pulse rate of the London stock exchange?' [1966: 257]. There follows a passage [257–64], all the more remarkable for having been written in 1925.

> The latest studies on the development of capitalism in agriculture, *particularly Lenin's work on American farming*, and partly Hilferding on finance capital, Lyaschenko on trading capitalism in Russia, and others, indicate that bringing agriculture into the general capitalist system by no means involves the creation of very large, capitalistically organized production units based on hired labour ... the new ways in which capitalism penetrates agriculture ... convert agriculture, despite the evident scattered and

independent nature of the small commodity producers, into an economic system concentrated in a series of the largest undertakings, and through them, entering the sphere controlled by the most advanced forms of finance capitalism. [*ibid.*: 257, 262, my emphasis].

In the second sentence quoted, 'evident' is better understood in the sense of 'apparent' rather than 'obvious'.

33 . An illuminating instance in terms of this discussion is provided by Friedmann and McMichael (1989: 93), concerning the assumption that advanced and peripheral capitalist economies are distinguished by the internal articulation (intersectoral exchanges) of the former as the basis of growth, and the 'disarticulation' of the latter:

> (T)his unexamined assumption applies possibly to one nation-state only, and then only for a brief historical period ... This case is the United States, in which agriculture was a source of demand for domestic industry during the period of protectionism accompanying late nineteenth century British hegemony ... Yet even then US agriculture was principally export-orientated. The ideal of national inter-sectoral balance nevertheless stems from this historical conjuncture, and gained currency with the rise of American hegemony and the proliferation of modernization and dependency theories that generalized the American model.

34. Byres [1996: 5–6] observes that Lenin's American path 'enters discourse on contemporary poor countries less frequently than does either the English or the Prussian path'. This suggests another insight into different appropriations and juxtapositions of the three agrarian questions. While the American path may not have featured much in discussions of AQ3, this is not so in relation to AQ1 and AQ2. First, it pervades AQ1 through the politics of the peasant path, as noted, of which Byres gives some telling examples elsewhere in his book: during the American revolution [1775–6] when landlord estates were seized and redistributed to their tenants [*ibid.*: 386, citing Post, 1995: 416], and after 1807 in Prussia and 1866 in the American South when the formal abolition of serfdom and slavery respectively was *not* accompanied by land reform, the expropriation and redistribution of landed property (unlike after 1789 in France and 1945 in Japan) [*ibid.*: 314]. Concerning AQ2, Lenin's model of class differentiation, of course, remains the virtually definitive reference point of materialist analysis of peasantries in the era of capitalism, not least in Byres' own work on India. Finally, could it be that the relevance of the peasant path to AQ3 is obscured by its widespread appropriation (and distortion) in *populist* discourses that celebrate peasant virtue and deny peasant class differentiation?

That this is not necessarily so is shown in an interesting instance reported in Levenson-Estrada's exceptional history of trade unionism in Guatemala City. The PGT in Guatemala in the 1940s and early 1950s 'like communist parties elsewhere in Latin America, identified feudalism and not capitalism as the principal cause of poverty and stagnation, and it supported an alliance with the native bourgeoisie to construct nationally owned capitalism; land reform would destroy the "feudal" landed oligarchy, create an internal market, and thus "open the path to industrialization of the country, prosperity and national economic independence"' [*Levenson-Estrada*, 1994: 19, quoting a PGT newspaper]. Again, from an interview with the communist leader of the (artisanal) shoemakers' union of that time: 'what the moment demanded in terms of industrial progress was the Agrarian Reform ... While the peasant masses had no capacity to consume, we said in our manifesto, industry had no possibility to develop because it depended on too small a market. What could you hope for from a market where only six per cent of the population wore shoes?' [*ibid.*: 21].

35. This resonates a theme which I have neglected, but was signalled by the analytical moment (iv) above: the 'freeing' of agricultural labour to join the urban proletariat. Hobsbawm's observation that massive exodus from the land in the contemporary periphery 'is only partly due to agricultural progress' can be sharpened: urban migration is often the result of rural distress, and its class (and gender) coordinates. This stands as one of the most compelling indicators of differences in agrarian transition (and capitalist development generally) 'then' and now in the trajectory of uneven and combined development on a world scale. Saith

[1985, 1990] puts issues of employment, livelihoods and poverty at the centre of his work on agrarian transition.

REFERENCES

Amin, S., 1974 *Accumulation on a World Scale*, New York: Monthly Review Press.

Anderson, P., 1974, *Lineages of the Absolutist State*, London: New Left Books.

Angelo, L., 1995, 'Wage Labour Deferred: The Recreation of Unfree Labour in the US South', *Journal of Peasant Studies*, Vol.22, No.4.

Banaji, J., 1976, 'The Peasantry in the Feudal Mode of Production: Towards an Economic Model', *Journal of Peasant Studies*, Vol.3, No.3.

Banaji, J., 1990, 'Illusions About the Peasantry: Karl Kautsky and the Agrarian Question', *Journal of Peasant Studies*, Vol.17, No.2.

Bernstein, H., 1994, 'Agrarian Classes in Capitalist Development', in L. Sklair (ed.), *Capitalism and Development*, London: Routledge.

Bernstein, H., 1996, 'The Agrarian Question in South Africa: Extreme and Exceptional?', *Journal of Peasant Studies*, Vol.23, Nos. 2-3.

Bhaduri, A., 1973, 'Agricultural Backwardness Under Semi-Feudalism', *Economic Journal*, Vol.83.

Bharadwaj, K., 1985, 'A View of Commercialisation in Indian Agriculture and the Development of Capitalism', *Journal of Peasant Studies*, Vol.12, No.4.

Blackburn, R., 1988, *The Overthrow of Colonial Slavery, 1776-1848*, London: Verso.

Brenner, R., 1985, 'Agrarian Class Structure and Economic Development in Pre-Industrial Europe', in T.H. Aston and C.H.E. Philpin (eds.), *The Brenner Debate. Agrarian Class Structure and Economic Development in Pre-Industrial Europe*, Cambridge: Cambridge University Press.

Byres, T.J., 1979, 'Of Neo-Populist Pipe Dreams: Daedalus in the Third World and the Myth of Urban Bias', *Journal of Peasant Studies*, Vol.6, No.2.

Byres, T.J., 1986, 'The Agrarian Question, Forms of Capitalist Agrarian Transition and the State: An Essay with reference to Asia', *Social Scientist*, No.162/3.

Byres, T.J., 1991, 'The Agrarian Question and Differing Forms of Capitalist Agrarian Transition: An Essay with Reference to Asia', in J. Breman and S. Mundle (eds.), *Rural Transformation in Asia*, Delhi: Oxford University Press.

Byres, T.J., 1994, 'The Journal of Peasant Studies: Its Origins and Some Reflections on the First Twenty Years', in H. Bernstein, T. Brass, T.J. Byres, *The Journal of Peasant Studies: A Twenty Volume Index 1973-1993*, London: Frank Cass.

Byres, T.J., 1995, 'Political Economy, the Agrarian Question and the Comparative Method', *Journal of Peasant Studies*, Vol.22, No.4.

Byres, T.J., 1996, *Capitalism from Above and Capitalism from Below. An Essay in Comparative Political Economy*, London: Macmillian.

Chayanov, A.V., 1966, 'Peasant Farm Organization', in D. Thorner, B. Kerblay, R.E.F. Smith (eds.), *The Theory of Peasant Economy*, Homewood, IL: Richard D. Irwin for the American Economic Association.

Cox, T. and G. Littlejohn (eds.), 1984, *Kritsman and the Agrarian Marxists*, special issue of *Journal of Peasant Studies*, Vol.11, No.2.

Deane, P., 1979, *The First Industrial Revolution*, Cambridge: Cambridge University Press.

de Janvry, A., 1981, *The Agrarian Question and Reformism in Latin America*, Baltimore, MD: Johns Hopkins University Press.

Djurfeldt, G., 1981, 'What Happened to the Agrarian Bourgeoisie and Rural Proletariat Under Monopoly Capitalism? Some Hypotheses Derived from the Classics of Marxism on the Agrarian Question', *Acta Sociologica*, Vol.24, No.3.

Ellman, M., 1975, 'Did the Agricultural Surplus Provide the Resources for Increase in Investment in the USSR During the First Five Year Plan?', *Economic Journal*, Vol.85.

Engels, F., 1970, 'The Peasant Question in France and Germany', in K. Marx and F. Engels, *Selected Works*, Moscow: Progress Publishers.

Friedmann, H., 1978, 'World Market, State and Family Farm: Social Bases of Household Production in the Era of Wage Labour', *Comparative Studies in Society and History*, Vol.20, No.4.

Friedmann, H., 1982a, 'The Political Economy of Food: The Rise and Fall of the Post-War International Food Order', *American Journal of Sociology*, Vol.88 (annual supplement).

Friedmann, H. 1982b, 'State Policy and World Commerce: The Case of Wheat, 1815 to the Present', in P. McGowan and C.W. Kegley (eds.), *Foreign Policy and the Modern World System*, Beverly Hills, CA: Sage.

Friedmann, H., 1993, 'The Political Economy of Food: A Global Crisis', *New Left Review*, 197.

Friedmann, H. and P. McMichael, 1989, 'Agriculture and the State System. The Rise and Decline of National Agricultures, 1870 to the Present', *Sociologica Ruralis*, Vol.29, No.2.

Gerschenkron, A., 1966, *Bread and Democracy in Germany*, Berkeley, CA: University of California Press (second edition).

Hilton, R. (ed.), 1976, *The Transition from Feudalism to Capitalism*, London: New Left Books.

Hobsbawm, E.J. 1994, *Age of Extremes: The Short Twentieth Century, 1914–1991*, London: Michael Joseph.

Horowitz, D., 1969, *Empire and Revolution*, Harmondsworth: Penguin.

Kautsky, K., 1988, *The Agrarian Question*, 2 vols., London: Zwan

Lenin, V.I., 1962, *The Agrarian Programme of Social Democracy in the First Russian Revolution, 1905-1907, Collected Works*, Vol.13, Moscow: Progress Publishers.

Lenin, V.I., 1964a, *The Development of Capitalism in Russia, Collected Works*, Vol.3, Moscow: Progress Publishers.

Lenin, V.I., 1964b, *New Data on the Laws Governing the Development of Capitalism in Agriculture, Collected Works*, Vol.22, Moscow: Progress Publishers.

Lenin, V.I., 1964c, *Imperialism: The Highest Stage of Capitalism, Collected Works*, Vol.22, Moscow: Progress Publishers.

Levenson-Estrada, D., 1994, *Trade Unionists Against Terror: Guatemala City, 1954-1985*, Chapel Hill, NC: University of North Carolina Press.

Levin, R. and M. Neocosmos, 1989, 'The Agrarian Question and Class Contradictions in South Africa: Some Theoretical Considerations', *Journal of Peasant Studies*, Vol.16, No.2.

Mann, S.A. and J.A. Dickinson, 1980, 'State and Agriculture in Two Eras of American Capitalism', in F.H. Buttel and H. Newby (eds.), *The Rural Sociology of the Advanced Societies. Critical Perspectives*, London: Croom Helm.

Marx, K, 1970, 'The Eighteenth Brumaire of Louis Bonaparte', K. Marx and F. Engels, *Selected Works*, Moscow: Progress Publishers.

Mitra, A., 1977, *Terms of Trade and Class Relations*, London: Frank Cass.

Moore, B., 1966, *Social Origins of Dictatorship and Democracy: Lord and Peasant in the Making of the Modern World*, Boston, MA: Beacon Press.

Mundle, S., 1985, 'The Agrarian Barrier to Industrial Growth', in Saith (ed.) [1985].

Neocosmos, M., 1986, 'Marx's Third Class: Capitalist Landed Property and Capitalist Development', *Journal of Peasant Studies*, Vol.13, No.3.

Post, C., 1982, 'The American Road to Capitalism', *New Left Review*, 133.

Post, C., 1995, 'The Agrarian Origins of US Capitalism: The Transformation of the Northern Countryside Before the Civil War', *Journal of Peasant Studies*, Vol.22, No.3.

Post, K., 1996, *Regaining Marxism*, London: Macmillan.

Preobrazhensky, E.A., 1965, *The New Economics*, Oxford: Clarendon Press.

Rosenberg, J., 1996, 'Isaac Deutscher and the Lost History of International Relations', *New Left Review*, 215.

Saith, A., 1985, '"Primitive Accumulation", Agrarian Reform and Socialist Transitions: An Argument', in Saith (ed.) [1985].

Saith, A. (ed.), 1985, *The Agrarian Question in Socialist Transitions*, special issue of *Journal of Development Studies*, Vol.22, No.1.

Saith, A., 1990, 'Development Strategies and the Rural Poor', *Journal of Peasant Studies*, Vol.17, No.2.

Smith, T.C., 1959, *Agrarian Origins of Modern Japan*, Stanford, CA: Stanford University Press.

World Bank, 1990, *World Development Report 1990: Poverty*, Washington, DC: World Bank.

Dynamic Economies and the Critique of Urban Bias

MASSOUD KARSHENAS

I. INTRODUCTION

T.J. Byres's critique of the urban bias thesis, which he developed more than two decades ago, can be usefully discussed under three interrelated themes. First and foremost was his challenge to the political economy foundations of the thesis. This involved a class-analytic attack on what he referred to as the 'neo-populist pipe-dreams' of the supporters of the urban bias thesis [*Byres*, 1977; 1979]. Rather than an undifferentiated mass of rural paupers, according to Byres, the rural population in different developing countries form differentiated entities structured along class lines as defined by the prevailing agrarian production relations in each country. The existing class relations defined in this way, not only influence the nature of state intervention and the thrust of government policy, but also limit the effectiveness of 'relatively autonomous' interventions by the state and shape the outcome of such interventions. This class-analytic perspective, which was also important in shaping the other dimensions of Byres's critique of the urban bias thesis, draws on the varied historical experiences of agrarian transition paths in both industrialised and developing countries and the implications of each path for broader socio-economic development, in particular the formation and functioning of states in the countries in question. 'Pipe-dreams' in this context contrast with actual historical processes of agrarian transition and possible policy interventions within the confines of each transition path.

The second dimension of Byres's critique of the urban bias thesis related to the definitions and factual evidence on the different mechanisms of intersectoral resource transfer as put forward by the proponents of the thesis, most notably by Lipton [1977] [*Byres*, 1974; 1979]. According to Byres, the admittedly insufficient and sporadic evidence that existed at the time in no way supported the urban bias thesis. The third aspect of Byres's critique related to the economic theories which constituted the analytical foundations

Massoud Karshenas, Department of Economics, School of Oriental and African Studies, University of London, Thornhaugh Street, Russell Square, London WC1H OXG.

of the urban bias literature. The marginalist analysis of neo-classical economics forms the conceptual basis for both the empirical studies in the urban bias literature as well as their prescriptive policy discussions. Within this framework the focus of analysis is on allocative efficiency, and policies are devised to correct the divergences from the marginal conditions needed to attain Pareto optimality at the point of equilibrium. The alternative view which forms the basis of Byres's critique of urban bias, has its lineage in the works of the classical political economists, particularly Smith and Marx, and views development as essentially a process of technological and organisational change, with patterns of resource flow between activities and sectors which could be considerably at variance with those prescribed by the marginalist analysis of general equilibrium models. Dynamic economies, externalities, learning, technological complementarities, increasing returns, and so on, which are anathema to the conventional general equilibrium models take centre stage in this alternative approach to economic development. While in conventional general equilibrium models the substitution aspects of sectoral allocations of output and factors of production are central, the alternative perspective focuses on the dynamic complementarity of different sectors in processes of development. As we shall argue below, both the measurement of intersectoral resource flows and the interpretation of the results in the literature have been crucially affected by the adoption of one or the other of these two points of view as the analytical framework of the study concerned.

In this study I mainly focus on the latter two themes of Byres's critique; namely the techno-economic conditions of possibility for different patterns of intersectoral resource flow, and new empirical evidence on these patterns in the process of development. The class-analytic investigation of the determinants of the flow and utilisation of resources in specific social formations involves a much more complex and detailed historical investigation beyond the confines of the present study. The next section discusses alternative theoretical approaches to the question of intersectoral resource flows, and investigates the likely determinants of resource transfer in a country undergoing growth and structural change. Section III discusses some of the more recent literature on urban bias, and examines empirical work in this field based on methodologies derived from conventional neoclassical theory. Section IV examines patterns of intersectoral resource flow in the development experience of five countries in Asia, and section V reviews the various implications of our findings.

II. THEORETICAL ISSUES AND CONCEPTS

Though the political economy aspects of the urban bias thesis are normally discussed in terms of the rural/urban distinction, much of the empirical measurement and economic policy discussion has focused on the sectoral distinction between agriculture and non-agriculture in what may be more appropriately termed as 'industrial bias' or 'agricultural squeeze' hypothesis. This lack of correspondence between socio-economic categories and their supposed political underpinnings in the urban bias literature, which is an indication of the *ad hoc* and ahistorical nature of the political economy framework of urban bias, has persisted even in the most recent literature on the subject.[1] This study follows the sectoral distinction between agriculture and non-agriculture, which is more appropriate from the political economy point of view. The urban bias hypothesis in this context translates into the agricultural squeeze hypothesis. This has been central in the growing criticism of the industrialisation policies pursued in developing countries over the past four decades. It has been argued that 'industrialisation bias', mainly characterised by the pursuit of import substitution industrialisation policies, has led to a squeeze of investible funds out of the agricultural sector with a negative effect on the growth of output and income in the sector and the economy as a whole. Agricultural surplus transfer has thus become a subject of some theoretical and empirical interest as witnessed by a growing number of studies, the most notable and influential of which has been the five volume study directed by Anne Krueger for the World Bank, covering case studies of 18 countries.[2]

Two broad approaches can be distinguished in the literature on intersectoral resource flows. The first, which one may refer to as the surplus approach, has its roots in the works of the classical political economists and has been further refined and developed in the conventional development economics literature in the post-war period.[3] Two basic observations underpin this approach to intersectoral resource flows in economic development. The first concerns the existence of dynamic economies or externalities associated with industrialisation, that is, dynamic and static economies of scale in modern manufacturing as well as the special role of manufacturing in inducing technological progress in other sectors. The second assumption, rather than referring to some intrinsic characteristic of certain economic activities, is more related to the observed characteristics of underdeveloped economies, which often exhibit persistent disequilibria particularly visible in rural labour markets with substantial surplus labour. The assumptions of surplus labour in agriculture and dynamic economies in the non-agricultural sector, give rise to a dynamic complementarity in the discussion of intersectoral relations in conventional development economics, which is absent in the general equilibrium models of neo-classical economics, the second broad approach to analysis of intersectoral resource flows (see the next section). Here, we shall first elaborate the concept of agricultural surplus and the mechanisms of surplus transfer and their likely determinants within the conventional development economics framework.

Net surplus outflow from agriculture, or what Kuznets [1964] has referred to as the 'net finance contribution' of agriculture to other sectors, is here defined as the sales of the agricultural sector to the rest of the economy (inclusive of exports) minus its purchases from the other sectors (inclusive of imports). This is sometimes also referred to as the 'net product contribution' of agriculture [e.g., *Millar*, 1970]. The net finance contribution of agriculture (R) can be defined from the real side according to the following formula:

$$R = X_a - M_a = F_a - (C_{af} + C_{nf}) - (I_{af} + I_{nf}) \qquad (1)$$

where agricultural sales to other sectors are denoted by X_a and its purchases from outside the sector are denoted by M_a. According to this equation, net agricultural resource outflow is equal to the net value added in the agricultural sector (F_a), minus the total consumption of agricultural households (partly produced within the sector, C_{af}, and partly purchased from outside, C_{nf}), minus total investment in the agricultural sector (partly produced by the sector itself, I_{af}, and partly purchased from the other sectors, I_{nf}). All the variables are measured in real terms according to some appropriate base point price system.

To begin with some static aspects of the resource flow process, as can be seen from equation (1), a basic precondition for a net surplus outflow from agriculture is that value added in the sector should be greater than the consumption of direct agricultural producers and the investment needs of agriculture for maintaining current levels of production. This means that in agrarian economies with high population pressure on land and low levels of labour productivity, where agricultural output is hardly sufficient to cater for the basic consumption needs of farm households, the possibilities for surplus outflow from the sector will be extremely limited. In a static context, therefore, for a surplus outflow from agriculture to be at all possible, the agricultural sector should have attained at least a minimum threshold of labour productivity. By implication, in a near subsistence economy where population growth and lack of absorption of the extra population by other sectors of the economy creates increasing population pressure on land, agriculture is likely to impose a growing financial burden on the rest of the economy. This, of course, is a direct outcome of the classical assumption of diminishing returns to labour under conditions of land scarcity, and assumes that technological progress in agriculture is independent of population pressure. With the further assumption of agricultural output being dependent on the level of consumption of agricultural labourers, as in efficiency-wage theories, this condition becomes even more stringent.

In a growing economy what happens to the real net surplus flow from agriculture depends, according to equation (1), on differential rates of change of agricultural value added on one hand, and real consumption and investment in the sector on the other. To take the consumption side first, the greater the increments in agricultural value added relative to the consumption of farm households, the greater agricultural resource outflow will be for any given amount of investment in the sector. The single most important determinant of agricultural or farm sector consumption is the disposable income of the farm household, which is largely determined by agricultural value added. There are, of course, other sources of farm income such as factor income from non-agricultural activities, net current transfers, and income gains from the terms of trade effect, to which we shall return shortly. Focusing on the agricultural value added component of farm income, and considering that the average propensity to save is expected to increase with the increase of per capita income, it could be maintained that the higher the value added per head or the productivity of the agricultural sector, the higher the net finance contribution of agriculture to other sectors will be. In a growing economy, therefore, the higher the growth of productivity of labour in agriculture, the higher the increase in surplus outflow from agriculture is likely to be over time, for any given rate of investment in the sector. In economies with fast rates of growth of labour productivity in the agricultural sector, whether due to rapid growth of the industrial labour force absorbing agricultural surplus labour or fast technological change in agriculture, the net finance contribution of agriculture is likely to increase over time. Of course, labour productivity growth in agriculture also depends on the rate and nature of agricultural investment, which introduces the investment side of the agricultural surplus flow as depicted in equation (1).

As can be seen from equation (1), the higher the incremental capital output ratio the lower will be the net finance contribution of agriculture to the rest of the economy. To the extent that capital intensity of production techniques could be varied in the agricultural sector, there exists the possibility of government intervention to influence the magnitude or direction of net resource flow through the choice of production techniques. In surplus labour economies, therefore, the adoption of more labour-intensive technologies for investment, which utilise the abundant supply of surplus labour within the agricultural sector, is obviously the optimum choice from the point of view of intersectoral resource flows as well.[4] In the long run in a growing economy, however, the marginal product of capital in agriculture is bound to decline in the absence of technological progress and under conditions of land scarcity. This is the familiar law of diminishing returns to investment in agriculture argued by Ricardo and other classical economists. As in the case of consumption-income flow balances discussed above, therefore, an important factor on the investment side in the long-run behaviour of agricultural surplus flow seems to be the pace of technological progress and increased efficiency of production inputs in agriculture.

There are, of course, various other intervening mechanisms which affect the magnitude and direction of resource flows, such as income distribution amongst farm households, stratification of agricultural producers, and various channels of income and capital flows. To consider the nature of these mechanisms, as well as their impact on the real side determinants of agricultural surplus flow, namely, value added, investment and consumption of the farm sector, it is helpful to consider the following decomposition of net agricultural surplus from the financial side:

$$R= X_a\text{-}M_a = (F_a\text{-}Y_f)\text{-}(K_{fg}\text{-}K_{gf})\text{-}(K_{fo}\text{-}K_{of})\text{-}(T_{fg}\text{-}T_{gf})\text{-}(T_{fo}\text{-}T_{of}) - TT \qquad (2)$$

where the right-hand side variables characterise the different financial mechanisms of agricultural resource outflow. The first term, $(F_a\text{-}Y_f)$, refers to value added in the agricultural or farm sector minus net factor income of farm households. It thus represents the outflow of net factor income from the sector, mainly comprising rent payments to absentee landlords, interest on loans and net factor income of the farm sector from non-farming activities (with a negative sign). The second term $(K_{fg}\text{-}K_{gf})$ represents net official capital transfers to the farm sector, and the third term $(K_{fo}\text{-}K_{of})$ denotes net private capital transfers into the farm sector from other sectors of the economy. $(T_{fg}\text{-}T_{gf})$ and $(T_{fo}\text{-}T_{of})$ denote the net inflow of respectively the government and private sector current transfers into the farm sector. The former primarily consists of net direct taxes/subsidies, and the latter largely of remittances of migrant members of farm households. All variables are in real terms, that is, deflated by the agricultural sales price index with some appropriate base point price system, and TT is the income gains in the agricultural sector arising from terms of trade improvements.[5]

The decomposition of the different financial mechanisms of surplus flow according to equation (2), (in addition to providing an aid to measurement of agricultural surplus when, due to data problems, it cannot be measured from the real side directly), also helps bring to light added considerations in the determination of agricultural surplus ignored in the above discussion. For example, in considering the consumption side of the resource flow process on the basis of equation (1), we assumed that the entire agricultural value added accrues to farm households and that it forms the only source of their income. As can be seen from the various financial mechanisms of surplus flow in equation (2), however, farm household disposable income is affected by various other mechanisms of income transfer, which introduce added dimensions to the analysis of consumption effects in the surplus flow process. To start with, not all of the value added in agriculture accrues to farm households. The extent to which it is siphoned off in the form of factor income outflows, such as rent and interest payments, depends on prevailing agrarian relations and the development of rural financial markets. For example, in economies dominated by large-scale absentee landlordism, a considerable share of the agricultural value added may flow out in the form of rents and interest on loans from informal credit markets at usurious interest rates. This outflow is reflected on the real side in the fact that, for any given level and rate of growth of labour productivity in agriculture, the level and rate of growth of consumption of farm households would be proportionately less. It would, however, be a mistake to infer from this that agrarian relations of this type necessarily imply a higher rate of surplus outflow from agriculture and a larger net finance contribution of agriculture in the long run. For these same relations may at the same time hinder the growth of labour productivity in agriculture by discouraging investment and technological innovations in the sector. In the long run the retardation effect on value added in equation (1) would outweigh the effect in reducing consumption.

The second source of factor income flow, which may lead to a higher rate of growth of consumption in agriculture over and above that warranted by the growth of labour productivity, is factor income inflow in the form of wage labour income by members of farm households partly engaged in non-agricultural activities. The same applies to income transfers by migrant workers and income gains through the terms of trade effect. In a predominantly agrarian economy with sluggish growth of labour productivity in agriculture and booming non-agricultural activities, these sources of income can lead to a much higher rate of growth of consumption per head in agriculture relative to labour productivity, and hence a growing financial burden by agriculture on the rest of the economy. This type of boom, however, cannot last long, as the food supply constraint and inflationary pressures in the economy would eventually end the boom in the non-agricultural sectors. It is sometimes argued that this sort of income transfer would itself contribute to the growth of labour productivity in agriculture by furnishing necessary funds for investment and, in the case of terms of trade effects, by additionally improving work incentives and providing the inducement to invest in the sector. For this proposition to be true, however, the existence of a host of other conditions related to agrarian relations, basic infrastructural investment, the availability of appropriate and profitable technological innovations, and the existence of institutions for the diffusion and efficient use of the new innovations, has to be ensured.

Of course, the increase in income transfers to agriculture need not necessarily be absorbed by consumption or investment in the sector itself. At high levels of agricultural productivity and income, and depending on the degree of development of financial markets in the countryside, increases in farm household incomes may create an equivalent outflow through private capital transfers in the form of voluntary private savings. As we will observe in section IV, this mechanism was at work in the later stages of development in countries such as Taiwan and Japan, where relatively high levels of agricultural productivity were already achieved and the network of financial institutions in the countryside was widespread. At the early stages of development when these conditions are not satisfied, however, a major part of such income transfers are likely to be spent in the agricultural sector itself, most probably on consumer expenditure. In these circumstances it may be necessary for the state to siphon off at least part of the new income transfers in the form of land taxes and other forms of direct taxation, in order to prevent agriculture from turning into a growing financial burden on the rest of the economy.[6] In doing so, however, due care must be taken so that high taxes do not diminish work and investment incentives in agricultural production.[7] The best way for ensuring this is for the state simultaneously to make adequate investment in basic infrastructure for agricultural production, and help introduce a stream of innovations so that profitability and productivity growth in the sector will be maintained. As we shall observe in section IV, the combination of these factors seems to have played an important part in the earlier stages of development in Japan and Taiwan, ensuring a net positive financial contribution by agriculture to other sectors of the economy.

So far we have neglected differentiation between farm households and its implications for intersectoral resource flows. The agricultural sector in developing countries does not normally consist of a homogeneous peasantry, and this introduces a further consideration in the analysis of surplus flow on the consumption side, namely the impact of the distribution of the agricultural incomes on surplus flow. Given the higher savings propensity amongst high income farm households, it may be postulated that the more skewed the distribution of income in the agricultural sector, the lower total consumption and the higher the net surplus outflow will be, at a given level of agricultural output [*Ishikawa*, 1967]. In a dynamic context this proposition can be restated in terms of growing differentiation amongst the peasantry and growing surplus outflow from the sector. However, for this to be a continuing process over time, that is, for differentiation to lead to an ongoing process of growing surplus outflow, it must be combined with technological advances which can give rise to increasing productivity of labour in agricultural production. Otherwise, the increase in the surplus outflow through such an income redistribution mechanism would have a once and for all effect as it is not the result of an increase in the productive potential of agriculture.

The various financial mechanisms of agricultural surplus flow, and their interactions with the real side variables bring to light the complex interaction of forces which determine the direction and magnitude of agricultural surplus. The discussion so far has, however, concentrated on the agricultural side of intersectoral resource flow accounts, assuming that other sectors respond accordingly to maintain equilibrium in the financial and commodity markets. This can give rise to a one-sided view of the determinants of intersectoral resource flows. The dynamic interactions between agriculture and industry could play an important role in the resource flow processes. For example, as argued above, the absorption of surplus agricultural labour by industry is an important determinant of the finance contribution of agriculture to economic growth. Similarly, industrial growth is necessary for the provision of the increasing amount of producer goods required by a technologically progressive agriculture. On the demand side also, the growth of non-agricultural sectors is essential for the absorption of the agricultural marketed surplus when a technologically dynamic agricultural sector makes a growing net finance contribution to the rest of the economy. This condition becomes particularly stringent because of the low income elasticity of demand for agricultural products, which gives an added significance to the absorption of surplus agricultural labour in non-agricultural sectors [*Mundlak et al.*, 1974]. In the absence of an adequate rate of increase in demand, excess supply of agricultural products leads to a decline in agricultural prices which can inhibit investment and technological innovation in the sector. It is sometimes argued that in an open economy the growth of the agricultural sector need not be constrained by the sluggishness of non-agricultural sectors. This argument, however, does not take into account the important complementarities on the supply side between agriculture and other sectors, for example, technological spillovers and surplus labour absorption. Historically, sustained growth in output and productivity in agriculture has generally been accompanied by substantial structural changes in output and employment in the economy as a whole, and by significant reductions in the share of agricultural employment.

From a long-term perspective, therefore, an important determinant of agricultural surplus flow on the real side appears to be the rate of technological innovation and productivity improvement in agricultural production. In technologically stagnant agrarian economies the agricultural sector would in the long run develop a growing financial burden on the rest of the economy. This may result from the natural growth of population and increasing population pressure on land with diminishing returns, eating into the marketed surplus of agricultural products on the consumption side; or it may result from the growth of demand for food in non-agricultural sectors leading to increasing inflow of investment goods into agriculture with diminishing returns.

III. RECONSTRUCTING HISTORY ACCORDING TO THEORY

The classical development economics approach to intersectoral resource transfer, sketched above, emphasises the crucial significance of dynamic factors such as the technological and institutional changes underlying the efficiency of resource use in agriculture, and the dynamic interactions between industry and agriculture in net agricultural surplus flow processes in the long run. The second approach, based on neo-classical general equilibrium theory, is more concerned with the efficiency of sectoral resource allocations within a framework where factors of production and sectoral outputs are viewed as substitutes, rather than being complementary in the development process. Within such a framework any attempt to accelerate the rate of growth of output of one sector has to be at the expense of other sectors. For example, attempts to accelerate the rate of growth of non-agricultural sectors through protective industrial policies would necessarily lead to a contraction of agricultural output, as under conditions of full employment and non-increasing returns such policies would involve a shift of resources from the unprotected to the protected sector. The main focus of this type of approach is the measurement of welfare losses due to the divergence of relative prices from market equilibrium prices under free trade, within a framework similar to the comparative static analysis of standard 'gains from free trade' literature. The terms of trade or relative price effect therefore plays a central role in the intersectoral resource flow mechanism within this approach. Unlike the classical surplus approach, where the terms of trade is viewed predominantly as a mechanism of income transfer, it is the allocative function of the terms of trade effect which is highlighted. Counterfactual historical simulations are used to measure the direction and magnitude of intersectoral surplus transfers, by contrasting the actual historical path with the counterfactual simulations of the free trade trajectory. The major shortcoming of this approach is that the comparative static analysis of standard general equilibrium theory does not lend itself to adequate study of complex dynamic interactions in the process of agricultural surplus transfer. A prominent example of this approach is the five-volume study directed by Anne Krueger for the World Bank, referred to in the previous section. In this section we take a closer look at the methodology and the findings of the World Bank studies.

Their mothodology is discussed by Krueger, Schiff and Valdes in appendices at the end of each case study volume, and along with a synthesis of the results it is further elaborated in more detail in Volume 4 of the World Bank studies by Schiff and Valdes [1992a]. The starting point and central focus of the methodology is on the terms of trade or relative price effect in intersectoral resource flows. It is maintained that direct and indirect interventions by the government can cause relative prices of traded goods to diverge from international prices, and can also lead to an increase in the relative price of non-traded goods over traded goods which constitutes an overvaluation of the exchange rate. Since most developing countries have followed development strategies favouring the industrial sector, both direct and indirect price interventions, it is argued, are likely to constitute a substantial tax on the agricultural sector through the terms of trade effect.[8]

The measurement of the relative price effect, and its impact on other aspects of intersectoral resource flows in the World Bank studies, is based on a two step estimation process. The first step is the measurement of taxes imposed on agriculture through the relative price effect by both direct and indirect government interventions. The second step is to estimate the impact of such intervention on output and income generation and distribution in agriculture and in the rest of the economy. This two step procedure is followed in individual country studies as well as in the synthesis volume where, starting from a discussion of the pattern of price intervention, Schiff and Valdes [1992a] continue with output, consumption, foreign exchange and income distribution effects of price intervention in succeeding sections of the book. Counterfactual historical simulations are compared to actual patterns of growth and resource flow to highlight losses resulting from price distortions introduced by government interventions. Before considering the problems associated with this type of methodology, a brief overview of the results presented in Schiff and Valdes [1992a] is useful.

The case studies cover eighteen countries in Asia, Africa and Latin America over a period from the early 1960s to the mid-1980s. The total tax imposed on agriculture through the terms of trade effect is measured as the percentage deterioration in the terms of trade compared to the hypothetical situation of free trade under an appropriate 'equilibrium' exchange rate. This is decomposed into two elements, that is, direct and indirect effects. The direct price intervention effect captures the terms of trade effect due to sector specific policies creating a wedge between producer prices and boarder prices of agricultural products at the prevailing exchange rate. The indirect effect measures the terms of trade effect resulting from the overvaluation of the exchange rate and industrial protection policies. The estimates indicate a substantial rate of taxation of agriculture averaging about 30 per cent for the sample countries, of which the major part (close to 75 per cent) is accounted for by indirect effects, namely the overvaluation of the exchange rate and industrial protection. While direct agricultural protection policies are subject to wide variations across countries and constitute less than eight per cent tax on agriculture for the sample countries on average, the indirect effects are more uniform across the countries and indicate a tax on agriculture of more than 22 per cent for sample countries on average (see Table 1). It should be noted, however, that while the measures of direct protection for individual agricultural commodities could convey useful information on relative protection given to different products and hence allocation of land and other resources within the sector, when applied to the agricultural sector as a whole, the separation of agricultural taxation into direct and indirect components is indeed no more than an artificial accounting construct with little information content. Under the prevailing exchange rate, trade and fiscal policies, free trade in agricultural products is unlikely to leave other prices in the economy intact. From the point of view of the agricultural sector as a whole, therefore, the total effect, namely the divergence of relative prices from those prevailing under the hypothetical free trade general equilibrium situation, is the meaningful concept.

After measuring the degree of price distortion in agriculture, the individual country case studies proceed to the second stage, namely the measurement of the impact of relative prices on agricultural output, balance of payments, government budget, and income transfers between and within sectors. Individual country studies measure the output response for disaggregated agricultural products, using both short-run and long-run price elasticities derived from times-series econometric studies. Estimates of loss of total agricultural value added are provided in the synthesis volume by Schiff and Valdes [1992a: Ch.4] using simulation results based on a pooled regression of value added on the estimated price distortions and some other variables for the sample countries over their respective reference periods. The latter estimates of output loss are reproduced in Table 1. According to these estimates, the terms of trade effect has led to substantial output loss over a 20-year period in all countries, with the exception of Korea, with an average of more than 26 per cent of total output for the sample average. Based on these estimates and those of adjustments in consumption and imports resulting from relative price changes under free trade, the studies proceed to estimate the foreign exchange loss resulting from the distorted relative prices. The cumulative foreign exchange loss as a share of total export earnings ranges between four to 140 per cent with an average of close to 30 per cent for the overall sample (Table 1). Various measures of net agricultural resource flow, made up of different relative price effects (measured under different assumptions) plus net direct producers subsidies and government investment in agriculture, are also presented. One of these measures, based on moderately conservative estimates of the scale of the

		Indirect Protection	Direct Protection	Total Protection	Cumulative 20 Year Effect(1)	Foreign Exchange Effect(2)	Real Income transfer Through:(3)			
							Relative Price Effect(4)	Input(5) Subsidies	Government Investment	Total
Cote dIvoire	1960–82	-23.3	-25.7	-49.0	50.0	-19.7	-21.0	2.0	13.0	-6.0
Ghana	1958–76	-32.6	-26.9	-59.5	86.9	-80.3	-26.0	2.0	3.0	-21.0
Zambia	1966–84	-29.9	-16.4	-46.3	32.8	-7.6	-37.0	19.0	5.0	-13.0
Argentina	1960–84	-21.3	-17.8	-39.1	17.3	-83.8	-16.0	-12.0	0.0	-28.0
Colombia	1960–83	-25.2	-4.8	-30.0	30.2	-19.3	-17.0	3.0	4.0	-10.0
Dominican Rep	1966–85	-21.3	-18.6	-39.9	24.2	-12.5	-32.0	0.0	12.0	-20.0
Egypt	1964–84	-19.6	-24.8	-44.4	65.2	-22.8	-12.0	-2.0	7.0	-7.0
Morocco	1963–84	-17.4	-15.0	-32.4	21.1	-17.7	-5.0	1.0	8.0	4.0
Pakistan	1960–86	-33.1	-6.4	-39.5	44.2	-148.2	-43.0	7.0	14.0	-22.0
Philippines	1960–86	-23.3	-4.1	-27.4	30.9	-5.3	-17.0	0.0	4.0	-13.0
Sri Lanka	1960–85	-31.1	-9.0	-40.1	24.2	-16.3	-52.0	3.0	19.0	-30.0
Thailand	1962–84	-15.0	-25.1	-40.1	40.7	-25.4	-26.0	1.0	8.0	-17.0
Turkey	1961–83	-37.1	5.3	-31.8	19.9	-41.1	-10.0	3.0	4.0	-3.0
Brazil	1969–83	-18.4	10.1	-8.3	23.1	-6.4	-4.0	21.0	12.0	29.0
Chile	1960–83	-20.4	-1.2	-21.6	8.7	-5.1	-21.0	8.0	4.0	-9.0
Malaysia	1960–83	-8.2	-9.4	-17.6	19.2	-6.1	-14.0	1.0	9.0	-4.0
Korea	1960–84	-25.8	39.0	13.2	-42.8	-21.9	-7.0	2.0	7.0	2.0
Portugal	1960–84	-1.3	9.0	7.7	-1.0	-3.8	7.0	-1.0	1.0	7.0
Average		-22.5	-7.9	-30.4	26.5	-28.9	-21.0	3.0	7.0	-11.0

Source: Schiff and Valdes [*1992a*].

Notes: (1) - as per cent of the beginning period output; (2) - as per cent of total value of exports; (3) - per cent of agricultural GDP; (4) - changes in the gross value of output of selected agricultural products as a result of price intervention; (5) - includes credit subsidies.

relative price distortion is shown in Table 1, which indicates relatively large outflows from agriculture for most countries with the average for the overall sample being more than ten per cent of the agricultural GDP.

The relative price effect, particularly the indirect component arising from economy wide policies leading to overvaluation of the exchange rate, appears to be the main source of net surplus extraction from agriculture in most country case studies. The significance of the terms of trade effect in these studies, however, goes beyond its relatively large magnitude. It is also central to agricultural growth, input use, government budget, balance of payments and other aspects of intersectoral resource flow processes. The terms of trade effect, or taxes on agriculture through relative price distortions, as noted above, is supposed to measure the distance between prevailing relative prices and those which would be obtained under free trade equilibrium. To estimate this distance, therefore, it is essential to estimate a set of general equilibrium models for the economies concerned over the study period, in which relative prices facing the agricultural sector will be endogenously determined. Though under certain small country assumptions it may be possible to assume that relative prices of traded goods under a free trade regime are given exogenously, the quintessential relative price of traded and non-traded goods, namely the equilibrium exchange rate, still needs to be endogenously estimated within a general equilibrium framework.

The sequential analysis of the World Bank case studies, starting from the estimates of relative price distortions and following with the impact of such price distortions on various other economic variables, will not do. This is a particularly important defect, as more than three-quarters of the estimated resource outflow from the agricultural sector in the sample countries, according to the World Bank case studies, is due to indirect interventions, most notably those associated with the overvaluation of the exchange rate. The equilibrium exchange rates in these studies are estimated on the basis of a simple elasticity model, using historical estimates of import and export elasticities, which essentially takes everything else in the economy over a 25-year period as given! This is a far cry from the equilibrium exchange rate under a free trade regime, which is supposed to bring about the fantastic changes in economic structure as highlighted in the concluding volumes by Krueger and others. To see the problems associated with this type of approach more clearly it would be necessary to examine the eighteen country studies individually. Since all the country studies use the same methodology, here we shall only consider the example of Korea, one of the better case studies in terms of availability of data and adherence to the methodology set up by Krueger and her associates. Korea also seems to be the only developing country in the sample found to have had a relatively favourable agricultural pricing policy for part of the study period. The case study of Korea is discussed in detail in Moon and Kang [1989] and the results are further discussed in the chapter on Korea in the edited volume by Krueger *et al.* [1992]. Korea had a persistent balance of payments deficit throughout the study period [960–84], which was particularly notable during the 1960s. The current account of the balance of payments had a deficit equivalent to about 60 per cent of exports in the first half of the 1960s and above 40 per cent in the latter half of the decade. This deficit, which was mainly financed by US aid grants, was substantially reduced in the subsequent period (Table 2). In addition, various trade restrictions and industrial protection policies during the 1960s implied that the balance of payments deficit under a free trade regime, everything else being the same, is likely to have been larger.[9] Based on these two sources of 'disequilibrium', and using fixed import and export price elasticities estimated from times-series historical data, the authors proceed to estimate the equilibrium exchange rate which would bring about a sustainable balance of payments deficit.[10] A sustainable deficit, as in almost all other 17 country case studies, is assumed to be zero throughout the period. The resulting estimates of the equilibrium exchange rate are shown in Table 2 alongside the official exchange rate. As can be seen, the estimated equilibrium exchange rate has close to 100 per cent premium over the official exchange rate during the 1960s, but the gap closes rapidly over the subsequent period in tandem with the reduction in the relative size of the foreign exchange gap. The estimated equilibrium exchange rate has an important bearing on the results regarding price distortions against the agricultural sector.

TABLE 2

FOREIGN EXCHANGE GAP, OVERVALUATION AND RELATIVE PRICE EFFECT ON AGRICULTURE IN KOREA, 1960–86

	Foreign Exchange Gap[1]	Exchange Rate		Relative Price Effect of Total Interventions[2]				
		Official	Equilibrium	Rice	Barley	Soybeans	Beef	Pork
1962–64	61.6	157.7	349.3	-21.0	1.7	-12.1	-39.7	-27.1
1965–69	41.2	274.6	461.4	-32.8	-29.9	2.9	-19.2	-3.5
1970–74	26.6	370.0	541.4	3.5	-3.2	15.1	-3.1	14.1
1975–79	12.4	484.0	594.0	73.1	55.3	57.9	75.8	10.2
1980–84	11.7	720.2	829.8	73.9	91.4	178.2	110.5	-5.3

Source: Moon and Kang [1992].

Notes: (1) - current account deficit as a percentage of export of goods and services; (2) short-term effect.

As shown by Moon and Kang's study, throughout the study period the Korean government provided substantial subsidies to agriculture through direct price support and trade protection. But when combined with the indirect effects arising from the overvaluation of the exchange rate, the resulting total impact adds up to a considerable relative price effect against agriculture during the 1960s. During the subsequent period, however, direct subsidies overshadow the indirect effects of the overvaluation of the currency, leading to a positive total price intervention effect in favour of agriculture (Table 2). The impact of the price distortions on the output of individual agricultural products are next estimated, using output response elasticities estimated from times series econometric models. It is estimated, for example, that over the 1960–69 period the short-run impact of adverse relative prices led to rice output being about 11 per cent lower than under free trade, barley being negatively affected by about 12 per cent, beef by over 10 per cent, and pork by about 13 per cent [*Moon and Kang*, 1989: 103]. During the 1970s and the 1980s, however, these trends were reversed as positive price discrimination in favour of agriculture is estimated to have led to substantial output gains compared with the free trade equilibrium situation (Table 3). These estimates of output effect, combined with the consumption effect of direct and indirect agricultural pricing policies, are then used to estimate the foreign exchange impact of government policy. It is estimated that the short-run impact effect of price discrimination against agriculture led to foreign exchange loss equivalent to more that 120 per cent of exports during the 1962–64 period and more than 40 per cent during

TABLE 3

EFFECT OF PRICE INTERVENTION ON OUTPUT, FOREIGN EXCHANGE EARNINGS
AND AGRICULTURAL INCOME TRANSFERS IN KOREA, 1962–84

	Changes in Output due to Price Intervention[1]					Effect on Foreign	Real Income Transfers[3]		
	Rice	Barley	Soybeans	Beef	Pork	Exchange Earnings[2]	Non-price	Price related	Total
1962–64	-11.0	-7.7	-8.0	-8.0	-20.3	-120.7	0.3	-16.9	-16.5
1965–69	-11.6	-13.8	-2.2	-9.4	-9.4	-40.8	2.4	-29.9	-27.5
1970–74	-0.8	-1.4	4.8	-2.6	10.0	-1.6	5.0	-1.4	3.6
1975–79	14.2	12.8	12.2	14.0	9.6	4.7	5.2	21.0	26.2
1980–84	22.8	43.0	48.8	25.4	-4.8	4.4	8.0	26.1	34.1

Source: Moon and Kang [1992].

Notes: (1) - short-run effect; (2) - short-run effect as a percentage of total exports; (3) - as a percentage of agricultural GDP measured in 1980 prices.

1965–69 (see Table 3). These trends are again reversed over the 1970s and the 1980s as the total price protection turns in favour of the agricultural sector. The study also provides estimates of real income transfers to and out of agriculture, combining non-price transfers such as government investment and low interest credit subsidies with the income transfers resulting from the terms of trade effect. Again, the estimated income transfers show a negative result for agriculture in the 1960s turning into a positive transfer during the ensuing period (Table 3). The culprit once more in this changing pattern of income transfers is the indirect price effects resulting from the suggested overvaluation of the exchange rate during the 1960s.

In fact, in all the 18 World Bank case studies the terms of trade effect resulting from the overvaluation of the exchange rate is negative, and is particularly significant in the case of poor countries with relatively large external borrowing and/or foreign aid flows, or those countries which resorted to large-scale foreign borrowing in the wake of the 1970s oil price shocks. In almost all the case studies the long-term sustainable balance of payments deficit used in the estimation of the equilibrium exchange rate is assumed to be zero throughout the study period. A judgement on what is deemed to be a sustainable balance of payments deficit needs to be made by any researcher interested in estimating an equilibrium exchange rate, no matter what estimation approach is adopted.[11] To assume that the sustainable deficit should be zero irrespective of the stage of development is to ignore important intertemporal aspects of economic development. It may be desirable for a poor surplus labour economy at the early stages of development to resort to foreign borrowing in order to supplement its domestic savings. Viewed in an intertemporal context, current account deficits in the initial stages of development cannot necessarily be interpreted as a sign of overvaluation of the exchange rate, nor can any surpluses which may appear in later stages of development to repay the debt be considered as a sign of undervaluation of the exchange rate.

The case of Korea is in fact a good example of this. During the 1960s the country heavily relied on foreign aid to increase its rate of investment and to encourage investment in the manufacturing sector, initially with large subsidies and government protection. The rate of investment increased from about 11 per cent of GDP in 1960 to over 24 per cent by 1970, with domestic savings increasing in tandem from about two per cent of GDP in 1960 to close to 15 per cent in 1970. Throughout this period foreign resources helped to finance domestic investment by a magnitude equivalent to ten per cent of the GDP. What is significant, however, is that despite the rapid rate of growth of investment and income the foreign exchange gap did not increase over this period. The direction of resources towards the setting up of a competitive manufacturing sector ensured a fast rate of growth of exports. The share of exports in GDP increased from 1.6 per cent in 1960 to over 10 per cent in 1970 and to over 35 per cent by the mid-1980s. By the early 1970s the share of manufacturing in total exports had already reached over 75 per cent, and it was indeed the existence of such a competitive manufacturing base that enabled Korea to sail through the two oil price shocks of the 1970s without falling into the type of debt problems which plagued other developing countries. Though from the early 1970s there was a declining trend in the share of foreign resources in financing domestic investment, during the two oil price shocks Korea once more resorted to high rates of external borrowing in order to maintain the momentum of growth.[12] From the mid-1980s, however, the current account of the balance of payments began to show sizeable surpluses. With historical hindsight it could be plausibly argued that the current account deficits, both during the 1960s and during the oil price shocks of the 1970s, were indeed sustainable. To argue that resort to foreign borrowing during these phases of Korean economic development was excessive and a source of foreign exchange overvaluation is absurd – particularly so with the presence of such phenomenal increases in the export / GDP ratios over the study period.

This lack of attention to the intertemporal aspects of intersectoral resource processes is the source of further serious problems in the methodology of the World Bank studies, which go beyond the determination of what constitutes a sustainable current account deficit. As we noted above, a serious shortcoming of the elasticities methodology in calculating equilibrium exchange rates is that it does not take into account the general equilibrium impact of devaluations. Devaluations, through their income effects, can influence the rate of absorption which influences the variables originally used to derive the equilibrium exchange rate – for example, the current account balance – as well as disturbing the equilibrium in the home market and the prices of non-tradables. Some of the World Bank case studies, including the Korean study, are totally oblivious to such possibilities. Others have mentioned the problems, but have simply assumed them away. For example, in the case study of Argentina [*Sturzenegger*, 1989: 56–7] the following are amongst many assumptions mentioned: the price of the home good is supposed to be fixed, permanent monetary equilibrium prevails, dynamic factors are excluded from the analysis, and 'income effects are not very large, or that the marginal propensity to spend on home goods is unity … '.[13] Some cynics may suggest that any assumption is justifiable as long as the desired results are derived. Unfortunately, however, even these assumptions are not enough to carry the World Bank case study results. The problem is that the structural parameters used to derive the results (for example, price elasticities) are estimated from the existing historical time series data which are unlikely to remain stable after switching to a free trade regime. Under these circumstances, and if all the above assumptions hold, the results can at best be interpreted as individual annual effects of free trade, given that the existing circumstances will be maintained in all the other years preceding and following the year in question. If so, all the cumulative effects discussed in individual country case studies, and forming the basis of discussion in the synthesis volume by Schiff and Valdes [1992a], will be undermined.

These problems of internal consistency in the methodology adopted by Krueger and associates essentially arise from the fact that they try to apply the comparative static analysis of pure theory to questions which are predominantly dynamic. While orthodox theory is concerned with propounding the allocative efficiency role of free trade under well known strict assumptions, the question at hand is essentially one of what Kaldor [1978] refers to as the creative functions of the price mechanism – namely its functions in transmitting impulses to economic change. As we observed above, the World Bank case studies have tried to get round this problem through the sequential analysis: first estimating the degree of relative price diversion from the free trade situation, and then estimating the impact of such price distortions on agricultural output and other economic variables. In doing so, they lose sight of important economy wide implications of relative price changes by focusing solely on the implications for the agricultural sector, in isolation from the interactions between sectors in the process of growth. The example of Korea would be again instructive in highlighting some of these omissions.

In the early 1960s Korea was still a low income, predominantly agrarian economy where more than 60 per cent of the labour force was engaged in agriculture. Furthermore, the country had one of the lowest agricultural land/labour ratios in the world, with an average of less than one hectare of land per household. More than two-thirds of farm households had one hectare or less of cropland, with about 99 per cent of cultivated land being in farms of three hectares and less. With a rapid rate of population growth of above 2.3 per cent during the 1960s, had it not been for fast rates of growth of labour absorption in non-agricultural sectors and high rates of rural outmigration, population pressure on land would have inevitably increased and declining productivity of labour set in sooner or later. The increase in labour absorption in the non-agricultural sector of close to six per cent a year during the 1960s, however, substantially reduced the rate of growth of the agricultural labour force and from the early 1970s the agricultural labour force indeed followed a declining trend (Table 4). Nevertheless, population pressure on land and the resulting fragmentation of the farm holding structure still appears to form a major stumbling block for the growth of Korean agriculture [*Moon and Kang*, 1989: 29–31].

Given the prevailing agrarian structure in the early 1960s and the relative size of the rural population (over 70 per cent), the sizeable predicted income gains through the terms of trade effect under free trade would have had an important impact on total consumption in the economy. How would that have affected the overall rates of savings and investment in the economy? In particular, how would investment in the non-agricultural sector and its rate of labour absorption have been affected? What would be the implications for population pressure on land, land fragmentation and agricultural productivity trends? What would be the implications of a free trade regime for the growth of manufacturing output and exports and for learning and competitiveness in that sector, and how would that impinge on the agricultural sector through possible technological externalities and the surplus labour transfer mechanism? How would the government budget be affected and the government's ability to provide the infrastructure and other agricultural support services necessary for the growth of the sector? And so on. Many of these questions are not raised in the World Bank studies, and those which are (for example, impact on government budget or exports) are only addressed from the narrow focus of changes envisaged in the agricultural sector alone – the rest of the economy is simply ignored. The task that the World Bank studies set themselves, namely a counterfactual historical simulation of the economy under free trade, could only be properly approached within an economy-wide dynamic model.

TABLE 4

INDICATORS OF GROWTH AND STRUCTURAL CHANGE IN KOREA, 1960–84

	Share of Employment in Agriculture	Percentage Share of GDP		Export/GDP Ratio	Share of Merchandise Exports		Savings and Investment Ratios		
		Agriculture	Manufacturing		Agriclture	Manufacturing	Saving	Investment	Foreign Savings
1960	60.2	38.7	14.6	1.6	15.2	na	1.9	11.2	9.3
1970	49.5	27.9	22.9	10.5	3.6	76.0	14.7	24.2	9.5
1980	32.3	16.5	32.5	28.6	2.6	90.0	25.6	33.1	8.5
1986	22.7	14.5	35.0	36.1	1.7	91.0	31.0	30.9	-0.1

Annual Growth Rates

	Employment Growth			Growth of GDP and its Components			Population Growth Rates:		
	Total	Agriculture	Other Sectors	Total	Agriculture	Manufacturing	Total	Agricultural	Non-agricultrual
1960–70	3.2	0.9	5.9	10.8	4.3	16.2	2.3	4.7	-0.1
1970–84	2.5	-0.7	4.7	8.1	2.2	14.6	1.5	3.5	-2

Sources: World Tables, World Bank; AGROSTAT, FAO, Rome; Moon and Kang [1989].

The main dynamic aspect of the World Bank studies seems to be the simulation of agricultural output growth under free trade, based on output response elasticities estimated from historical data. Assuming that the relative price and price elasticity estimates are plausible, this method can give reasonable estimates of output response in the case of individual crops. However, the individual output responses cannot be added up to arrive at the overall agricultural output response. One obvious reason is the substitution possibility between individual crops and the land constraint at the aggregate level. Secondly, at the aggregate level all the economy wide interactions discussed above come to the fore, making the elasticity estimates based on the actual historical data invalid. Factors such as government investment in infrastructure, irrigation, research, etc., as well as factors such as surplus labour transfer and technological capabilities which play an important role in price responsiveness, are all affected by switching to the free trade regime. In the synthesis volume of the World Bank studies, Schiff and Valdes [1992a: Ch.4] present estimates of agricultural growth effects arising from price distortions in all the sample countries over a 20-year period. These estimates which are presented in Table 1, compound the confusion in the rest of the World Bank studies beyond all proportions.

As noted above, the estimates are simulations based on a pooled cross-section time-series regression of value added on the estimated price distortions and other variables over the whole of the sample countries during their respective study periods. One problem with this regression model is that it imposes a common deterministic trend on all the countries in the sample, and thus variations in the growth rates are almost exclusively picked up by the total protection variable in the regression equation. What is more surprising is that the authors assert that the trend variable 'reflects the exogenously determined agricultural growth rate, say because of growth in agricultural labour force or increased public investment', thus implicitly assuming that the sample countries have followed similar trends in these variables. It would have been appropriate, at least, to test for the assumed common trends by including individual country dummy variables in the regression. A more serious problem is that the regression model imposes the same price response coefficient on all the countries in the sample! Thus, the output response to price changes in a country like Korea with family farms of average size of one hectare is assumed to be the same as that of Argentinean agriculture dominated by highly mechanised and commercialised *latifundios* of 200–5,000 hectares. What is even more surprising is that such an assumption is made in a synthesis volume of case studies where a wide range of price response coefficients are used in different individual country studies. Indeed, if the assumptions of the regression model used by Schiff and Valdes hold, then it should be possible

FIGURE 1
SCATTER PLOT OF AGRICULTURAL GROWTH vs TOTAL PROTECTION
1960–72

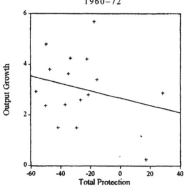

FIGURE 2
SCATTER PLOT OF AGRICULTURAL GROWTH vs TOTAL PROTECTION
1976–84

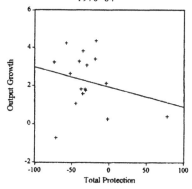

FIGURE 3
SCATTER PLOT OF AGRICULTURAL GROWTH vs CHANGE IN TOTAL PROTECTION
1960–72 AND 1976–84

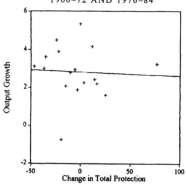

to observe some degree of correlation between the trend growth rates in agriculture across different countries and the level or change in the estimated price distortions in these countries. However, as can be seen from Figures 1–3, there does not seem to be any positive correlation between agricultural growth and the level, or increase in the level, of the total protection estimates in different countries over the 1960–72 and 1976–84 subperiods.[14]

So far we have mainly focused on the internal consistency of the methodology of the World Bank research project. This project, rather than being an objective investigation into intersectoral resource flow processes, seems to be more concerned with establishing the gains from free trade, and hence has concentrated mainly on one aspect of intersectoral resource flows, namely the terms of trade effect. The various financial mechanisms of intersectoral resource flows discussed in the previous section (with the exception of official transfers), and their interaction with real side variables, are by and large neglected. Factors such as technological and institutional change, central to the resource flow processes from a long term perspective, if not totally neglected, are taken as given within this methodology. The organisation of production in agriculture, which conditions both the generation of the agricultural surplus and the various forms that it takes, is treated in a cursory manner and agricultural response is modelled as a simple function of relative prices. As we have argued, even within such a limited perspective, in the absence of an economy wide dynamic model the World Bank methodology lacks the internal consistency necessary for meaningful interpretation of its findings. However, once we leave behind the world of well-behaved production functions and given and identical technologies across countries, and introduce factors such as increasing returns, economies of learning, and cumulative processes of innovation and diffusion of knowledge, even the setting up of an economy-wide model cannot help in the kind of *ex-ante* simulations that the World Bank project aimes at. Under these circumstances, gains from 'free' trade (in contrast to trade as such) cannot be established even at the abstract theoretical level, and *ex-ante* simulations of the type attempted by the World Bank project would involve a large area of indeterminacy left to the whims of the researcher. In a world of increasing returns and cumulative learning, the very notion of an equilibrium exchange rate loses its determinacy.[15] With the prevalence of such dynamic effects, any attempt to develop a general theory of surplus flow determination based on standard economic theory would be premature and can lead to misleading inferences.

Under these circumstances, and given the gaps in the present state of our knowledge about intersectoral resource flow processes, before embarking upon counterfactual historical simulations of the type attempted by the

World Bank case studies it is important to investigate actual historical patterns of resource flow and their likely determinants in the processes of development. Without such a prior understanding of the 'stylised facts', one could easily end up reconstructing history within the straitjacket imposed by the limitations of one's formal models. In the next section we shall try to highlight such stylised facts based on the experience of five countries in Asia and using the disaggregated accounting framework discussed in the previous section. It is, of course, recognised that with respect to the terms of trade effect one still needs to make a judgement as to the appropriate base point prices. Following Ishikawa [1967] we adopt base point prices prevailing in periods which are regarded as 'normal' years, and test the sensitivity of the results to changes in the choice of the base year (see further Karshenas [1995]).

III. LESSONS FROM HISTORY

The experience of the five countries, namely, China, India, Iran, Japan and Taiwan discussed in this section is based on the case studies in Karshenas [1995]. Here we summarise the findings of this earlier work, and try to highlight some of the broader implications of the intersectoral resource flow patterns observed in these country case studies for the kinds of questions raised in the previous section. We begin by providing a comparative overview of the pattern of net intersectoral resource flows in the sample countries.

The five countries studied can be broadly divided into two groups on the basis of their experience of agricultural surplus transfer. The first group, namely, *the surplus group*, includes Taiwan and Japan, where the finance contribution of agriculture to the rest of the economy was on the whole positive and agricultural surplus was growing over time. China, India, and Iran fall in the second category, *the deficit group*, where the net finance or net product contribution of agriculture to other sectors was negative, and over time the agricultural sector became a growing financial burden on the rest of the economy. This result may seem paradoxical, given that all the countries in the latter group pursued strong industrialisation policies of a highly protective type, and that such policies are normally associated with a resource squeeze from agriculture in the development literature. To explain this apparently paradoxical result we must first compare the working of the various mechanisms of intersectoral resource flow in the countries under review.

In order to facilitate our comparative study, a schematic picture of the financial composition of intersectoral balances for the countries studied is provided in Table 5. The positive and negative signs in the table are only indicative of the dominant tendencies in the direction of surplus flow during the reference periods for each country; for more elaborate analyses of the different mechanisms of surplus flow on an annual basis one has to refer to the individual country case studies. A positive sign is indicative of a net surplus outflow from agriculture and a negative sign indicates a net inflow of resources into the agricultural sector. The countries in the table are grouped into the surplus and deficit categories, with Taiwan and Japan showing a positive net finance contribution of agriculture, followed by the other three countries with negative contributions.

TABLE 5

MECHANISMS OF NET RESOURCE OUTFLOW FROM AGRICULTURE

Country	Current Terms of Trade (TT)	Factor Income $(F_a - Y_f)$	Government Transfers $(T_{fg} - T_{gf})$	Capital Transfers Government $(K_{fg} - K_{gf})$	Other[2] $(K_{fo} - K_{of})$	Total $(R = X - M)$
Surplus Countries						
Taiwan[1]	+	−	+	−	+	+
Japan	−	−	+	−	+	+
Deficit Countries						
China	−	−	+	−	−	−
India	−	−	+	−	−	−
Iran	−	−	−	−	−	−

Notes: 1 − in the case of Taiwan factor income flows and terms of trade in this table refer mainly to the post-colonial period;
2 − other capital in this table refers to private capital transfers including credits granted by government banks to agriculture.

The Case of Taiwan

Taiwan, at the top of the table, exemplifies the agricultural surplus case where the agricultural sector made a positive and growing net finance contribution to other sectors throughout the 1911–60 period. This was not because of a low or declining level of the gross inflow of resources into the agricultural sector; on the contrary, Taiwanese agriculture witnessed a significant and growing inflow of resources into the sector. What gave rise to the sizeable and increasing value of net agricultural surplus outflow was the larger and faster growing marketed surplus or sales of the agricultural sector relative to its purchases. This was made possible on one hand, by relatively efficient resource use and fast productivity growth rates in agriculture, and on the other hand, by the existence of effective mechanisms of surplus flow on the financial side. Effective government action, in both transforming the technological basis of agricultural production and siphoning off a large part of the fruits of its productivity growth through various financial mechanisms, was instrumental in the surplus transfer.

The need of the Japanese colonial administration to procure a sizeable exportable agricultural surplus from Taiwan played an important part in technological transformation of Taiwanese agriculture prior to the Second World War. Up to the 1920s, agricultural policy was mainly directed towards institutional reform, education, and infrastructure building. The growing population pressure on land, and rising demand for rice and sugar in the Japanese market, necessitated large increases in land productivity and transformation of the technological basis of Taiwanese agriculture. Heavy investment by the government in irrigation and land improvement during the 1920s, facilitated the move toward intensive farming based on increasing use of fertiliser and new varieties of seeds. This investment, together with other infrastructural investments during the early decades of this century, formed the foundation for the rapid spread of new crop technologies and productivity growth in agriculture, which carried on into the post-colonial period as well. A distinct feature of Taiwanese agriculture, shared only by Japan amongst the countries in our sample, was that the major part of output growth during the period under study was accounted for by the growth of productivity of resources deployed in the sector. This created the potential for agricultural surplus outflow on a substantial and increasing scale.

The financial channels through which this transfer took place are depicted schematically in Table 5. Official capital transfers, which mainly consisted of government investment in agriculture, were the only channels of resource flow which consistently registered a net surplus inflow throughout the study period.[16] This was, however, dwarfed by the sizeable outflows through other channels. During the colonial period the main mechanisms of surplus outflow were rents and government taxation. In the post-war period, rents lost their significance as a major mechanism of resource transfer, particularly in the aftermath of the land reform of the early 1950s, as government taxation and adverse terms of trade movements took over as the predominant sources of resource transfer. In fact, in the post-colonial period one can observe a net inflow of resources through factor income flows, as a result of a substantial wage income inflow and with rents losing their significance. However, this was easily overshadowed by other sources of surplus outflow. The terms of trade, which up to the mid-1930s moved in favour of agriculture, showed a substantial deterioration against agriculture in the post-war period. The income squeeze on the farm sector through the terms of trade movement in the post-war period was as large as

60 per cent of the increase in incomes resulting from real value added growth in agriculture during the same period. This rapid deterioration in agricultural terms of trade resulted from the government's pricing policies in its compulsory rice collection and fertiliser sales.

The terms of trade effect was supplemented to a major extent by government direct taxation which was another important source of surplus outflow. Taxation was in fact so high that, despite the significance of government investment in agriculture, the net consolidated government accounts showed a sizeable and growing net outflow of resources from agriculture. In other words, the outflow of resources through taxation was far greater than the inflow through capital investment and subsidies, and the difference grew over time. What stands out in the case of Taiwan in this respect, is that the tax burden on agriculture seems to have been much higher than on the other sectors of the economy.

Another source of surplus outflow from agriculture, particularly significant in the post-war period, was through private capital transfers which primarily took the form of outflow of voluntary savings by the farm sector through the credit system. This signifies the fact that agricultural surplus transfer need not necessarily take the form of compulsory government or landlord extraction; under conditions of rising productivity and incomes in the agricultural sector, surplus transfer can take place through voluntary savings, if appropriate financial institutions are in place.

A notable feature of the experience of Taiwan was that the substantial squeeze on agriculture through taxation, rents, and other mechanisms did not seem to have retarded the rates of technological advance and output and productivity growth in the sector. In the post-colonial period in particular, large increases in government taxation and substantial adverse terms of trade movements were combined with high rates of growth in output and productivity growth in agriculture. This signifies the fact that, in a technologically dynamic agriculture, productivity growth can help to maintain relative profitability, and hence the inducement to invest in agriculture, despite the adverse terms of trade movement.

The Case of Japan

The financial contribution of agriculture to the government budget during the Meiji period in Japan has become a classic example in the development literature of the financing role of agriculture in the early stages of development. Our empirical investigation of the case of Japan supports the conventional wisdom, and indeed goes further; in addition to its net contributions to the government's budget, the overall net finance contribution of agriculture to other sectors during the study period also seems to have been positive and considerable. We can distinguish between two phases in the behaviour of net agricultural surplus during the study period. The first phase (1888–1917) exhibited a large and expanding net agricultural surplus outflow, while in the second phase (1917–37) there was a deceleration in the rate of surplus outflow, even, according to some estimates, turning to an inflow. This behaviour in the rate of change of agricultural surplus flow reflects two distinct phases in the development of Japanese agriculture with different productivity and output performances.

The first phase, from the Meiji restoration (1868) to the end of the First World War was a period of relatively high productivity and output growth in the agricultural sector. Growth of agricultural output outstripped population growth, and in addition to providing food and raw materials for rapidly growing non-agricultural sectors, agriculture also produced an export surplus which made a significant contribution to industrial development. More than three quarters of output growth in this period was accounted for by productivity growth rather than an increase in inputs, which indicated the fast rates of technological innovation and the high and improving degree of efficiency of resource use in Japanese agriculture. Productivity growth in the agricultural sector during this phase was based on a continuous incremental improvement in technological practices within the traditional agrarian institutions inherited from the Tokugawa period. Technological innovations in the form of land improvement and extension of irrigation, as well as the introduction of new seeds, fertilisers, and better methods of cultivation, took place within small family holding units with, on average, one hectare of land. The government and rural-based landlord class played an important role in these technological improvements by both providing the finance for bulky investments and by promoting technological innovations and their diffusion. The rapid rates of productivity growth during this early phase created an increasing potential for agricultural surplus outflow.

The interwar period, the second phase of development of Japanese agriculture in the period under study, was one of agricultural stagnation and low productivity and output growth. During this period, productivity growth played a minor role in the growth of agricultural output, and the limited growth which did take place was mainly accounted for by the increase in inputs. The sources of technological improvement within the traditional institutions of Japanese agriculture seem to have been exhausted by the end of the first decade of the twentieth century, hence returns to investment in the sector within traditional agrarian institutions were diminishing. Thus the rate of increase of resources directed towards agriculture compared to the earlier period also slowed down, and agricultural output stagnated. The slow-down in the growth of agricultural output and productivity meant that the role of agriculture as a potential source of surplus became increasingly limited. This was indeed the underlying cause of the reversal of trends of net agricultural surplus flow during the interwar period.

The composition of surplus flow on the financial side, as depicted schematically in Table 5, shows the different mechanisms through which this took place. The difference in rates of productivity and output growth between the two subperiods itself had important implications for movements in the terms of trade and other mechanisms of financial flow. During the earlier dynamic phase of agricultural growth, the terms of trade improved only slowly in favour of agriculture and agricultural protection remained moderate. Indeed, during the first fifteen years of the twentieth century, the agricultural terms of trade in Japan relative to world prices declined substantially. This was, however, rapidly reversed during the interwar period, as the terms of trade in Japan improved considerably in favour of agriculture relative to the agricultural terms of trade at the international level. With the slow-down in the rate of productivity growth in the interwar period, the government had to intervene to protect agricultural incomes, and the degree of protection of the agricultural sector increased substantially.

Current official transfers formed an important source of net surplus outflow during the dynamic phase of agricultural growth prior to the First World War. Land taxes during the Meiji era formed the major share of government revenue, and by far exceeded the current and capital official transfers to agriculture. However, during the slow growth phase in the interwar period, the deceleration in the rate of increase in agricultural taxes, combined with increasing capital and current transfers by the government, led to a declining trend in the rate of surplus outflow from agriculture, which turned into an inflow towards the end of the period. As in the case of Taiwan, what stands out in Japan with regard to the pattern of official transfers, is the much higher burden of direct taxation on agriculture compared to non-agriculture. Despite the narrowing of the gap between relative tax burdens over the period under study, by the end of the 1930s the burden on agriculture was still twice as high as that on the non-agricultural sector.

An important source of income transfer into the agricultural sector throughout the study period in Japan was net factor income flows. These were due to the combination of low factor income outflow through rents, and large inflows in the form of labour income from the non-agricultural activities of farm household members. The former was due to the peculiarity of agrarian relations in Japan, with its rural based landlord class whose rental income did not constitute a factor income outflow from agriculture. The second factor, the wage income of agricultural households from non-agricultural activities, constituted a major source of income transfer into Japanese agriculture throughout the years under study. This signified the importance of the rate and nature of growth of the non-agricultural sector for intersectoral resource flows. The high rates of growth of the non-agricultural sector in Japan during the study period, and especially the high degree of labour absorption within this sector, created the conditions for farm households to supplement their agricultural incomes with substantial wage income generated in other sectors of the economy.

A final important feature of the Japanese experience of intersectoral resource flows was that, as in the case of post-colonial Taiwan, voluntary savings channelled through the credit system constituted an important source of financial outflow from the agricultural sector. While such net private capital outflow in the context of an economy at stationary state implies disinvestment and stagnation in the agricultural sector, in the context of a technologically dynamic economy undergoing rapid structural change it signifies the complementarity of sectors in processes of development and is normally accompanied by high rates of investment and productivity growth in agriculture.

The Case of China

Chinese agriculture underwent immense organisational changes during the period under study (1952–83). During the 1952–79 period, collectivisation and central planning of production and distribution were among the key features of agricultural organisation with important bearing on the processes of intersectoral resource flow. During the post-1979 reform era, the dismantling of collective organisations of agricultural production and gradual introduction of the household responsibility system and market incentives, meant that the pattern of intersectoral resource flows underwent considerable change. Despite this changing pattern of channels of resource flow, the net finance contribution of agriculture remained negative throughout the study period, with the gap widening over time. With the possible exception of the early 1950s, this result held both at current value and in real terms, at different base year or reference point prices, including world prices. It appears, therefore, that contrary to the common belief about central planning being a means of mobilisation of agricultural surplus for industrial accumulation, the finance contribution of agriculture to accumulation in non-agricultural sectors in China was negative.

Throughout the Maoist period, particularly during the 1960s and the first half of the 1970s, massive amount of resources in the form of intermediate and capital goods were diverted to Chinese agriculture. A significant share of industrial investment in this period was allocated to heavy industries producing capital and intermediate inputs for the agricultural sector, with their products sold to agriculture at highly subsidised prices. During this period China demonstrated some of the fastest rates of diffusion amongst developing countries of new agricultural inputs such as new seeds, fertilisers, pesticides and mechanical implements. By the end of the 1970s, China had achieved rates of use of modern inputs per hectare of cultivated land well above the average in the rest of the developing countries. However, output response to the growing amount of resources allocated to the agricultural sector during the 1960s and the 1970s, was relatively low. Yields did not increase commensurately with the growth in use of new inputs, and indeed labour productivity exhibited negative growth over these two decades. Given these trends in agricultural productivity, the government was severely constrained, and became increasingly so over time, in extracting a surplus from agriculture. With the declining productivity of labour in agriculture, the government had to provide substantial consumer subsidies, such as food subsidies in inter-regional grain sales, in order to ensure a basic living standard in the countryside. Furthermore, given the inefficiency of resource use in Chinese agriculture, to ensure an adequate growth of output and marketed surplus, the government diverted an increasing amount of new inputs into agriculture at subsidised prices. Consequently, agriculture became a drain on other sectors in terms of net resource flows.

The inefficiency of resource use in Chinese agriculture was partly due to overcentralised and inflexible agrarian institutions and their associated incentive and information problems. The rapid growth of output in the post-1979 reform period, which was largely based on the more efficient use of existing resources rather than increased flow of inputs, created the potential for a reversal in the growing trend of negative agricultural surplus flow. This, however, did not materialise as higher income and productivity growth in agriculture was more than neutralised by the surge in consumer expenditure by farm households. The share of consumer goods in the growth of total agricultural purchases during the 1978–93 period jumped to 83 per cent, from a value of slightly under 45 per cent during the 1952–78 period. The factors underlying this changing composition of intersectoral resource flow may be clarified further by investigating the financial mechanisms of resource flow as depicted in Table 5.

An important source of real income gain in the agricultural sector throughout the study period was the terms of trade effect. The income gains through the terms of trade effect during the 1952–83 period amounted to more that one and a half times the increase in the value of agricultural marketed surplus over the same period. Such substantial income gains were the result of indirect subsidies provided by the government, through its policy of keeping the prices of manufactured inputs supplied to agriculture constant while agricultural purchase prices increased over time. Such substantial income gains allowed a much larger inflow of producer and consumer goods purchased by agriculture from other sectors than could be financed by the internal resources of the agricultural sector itself. A major part of the gains in income terms of trade was concentrated in the post 1979 reform era, which played an important role in the rapid acceleration of consumer goods inflow into the agricultural sector.

There were, of course, other factors responsible for the growth of demand for non-agricultural consumer goods in the farm sector, over and above that warranted by growth of real agricultural output. The most important of these was relatively large net factor income inflows into the farm sector, predominantly in the form of wage income from the non-agricultural activities of the farm households. During the Maoist period, the relatively high rates of labour income inflow were due to the growing importance of commune-managed enterprises in rural areas as a source of non-agricultural income. In the post-1979 reform era, following decollectivisation and the introduction of commercial norms, the inflow of wage labour income to the farm sector accelerated. While the continuation of government subsidies to rural enterprises kept the old sources of factor income flow to farm households intact, new sources of income were added due to the rapid rates of growth of agricultural incomes and the resulting consumer boom in the first half of the 1980s, which encouraged a proliferation of non-agricultural commercial activities in the rural areas. Factor income flows, when added to income gains through the terms of trade effect, constituted a considerable inflow of external income to the farm sector, particularly in the post-1979 period.

In the context of a centrally planned economy, various items which in a market economy take the form of factor incomes – for example, rents and profits – can appear as public sector current transfers. There is indeed an established view which maintains that the state budget played an important role in siphoning off a large part of the agricultural surplus during the period under study. However, net current official transfers, though registering a positive outflow, remained relatively small compared to factor income flows, and, declined continuously during the period, even turning into an inflow by 1980. It is significant that during the post-1979 period, when agricultural incomes were rising rapidly due to the processes mentioned above, government direct taxation of agriculture indeed registered a negative growth in real terms. This was in sharp contrast to Japan and Taiwan, where government taxation of agriculture in the early stages of their development played an important role in generating a net positive finance contribution of agriculture. The lack of development of financial markets and the uncertainties regarding property rights and future developments in the economy, helped to translate income rises in the farm sector in the post-reform era into a surge in consumer spending. In this way, the widening financial resource gap of the agricultural sector continued even in the post-reform period, as already noted. While in the earlier period the growing financial burden of agriculture was due to the inefficiency of resource use and declining agricultural productivity, in the post-reform period the continuation of this trend was more due to lack of appropriate institutions and mechanisms of resource transfer.

The Case of India

India is another agricultural deficit country in our sample where the net finance contribution of agriculture to other sectors during its reference period (1950–71) was negative. The agricultural resource balance in the 1950s showed a relatively large deficit which followed a declining trend up to the mid-1960s. During this period there was an increasing trend in the value of marketed surplus as a proportion of agricultural value added, while purchases of the agricultural sector as a proportion of agricultural value added remained stable, thus creating a narrowing gap in the agricultural resource balance. From the mid-1960s, however, there was a sharp reversal in these trends, leading to a rapidly growing net inflow of resources into the farm sector. The growing financial burden of agriculture during the 1960s was closely connected to the 'new agricultural strategy' adopted by the Indian government.

The new strategy was introduced at a time when traditional agriculture seemed to be faltering because of the virtual exhaustion of new cultivable land frontiers and growing population pressure on land. Central to the new agricultural strategy was the seed-fertiliser technology of the green revolution which involved the introduction of a combination of new farming inputs, with obvious direct implications for the flow of resources. This, however, was not in itself a cause of increasingly negative net finance contribution of agriculture. In Japan and Taiwan, periods of a growing positive net finance contribution of agriculture coincided with intensified gross inflow of resources into the agricultural sector. What led, in the case of India, to different behaviour between the net and the gross flow of resources was that agricultural supply response was not commensurate with the increased flow of new inputs into the sector, as evidenced by the rapid rise in the ratio of producer goods purchases to agricultural value added during the 1960s

The inflow of new producer goods into the farm sector, however, was only one element of the purchases of agriculture from outside the sector. An even more important element was the increased flow of consumer goods into the farm sector, connected to the income gains in the sector through the terms of trade effect. An important aspect of the new agricultural strategy was the considerable improvement in the agricultural terms of trade over the 1964–70 period. This was intended as an incentive device, and also as a means of income transfer to make the adoption of the new technology affordable to farm households. The income gains through the improvement of agricultural terms of trade during 1964–70 were more than twice those resulting from the normal growth of agricultural output over the same period. Such income gains through relative price changes, exerted a double squeeze on the agricultural surplus; on one hand they increased the demand for consumer goods from outside the farm sector, and on the other they reduced the net sales of farm products to other sectors. This, of course, presupposes that such income gains were not siphoned off from the farm sector through various mechanisms, such as factor income, and official and private current and capital transfers.

As far as net factor income flows are concerned, the most plausible estimates seem to suggest a net inflow into the farm sector, although of a relatively much smaller magnitude than the other countries in our sample. Estimates of capital transfers, both official and private, also suggest a net inflow into agriculture – the former being mainly government investment in agriculture and the latter taking the form of subsidised loans by the banking system to the farm sector. While in Japan and Taiwan, at least in later stages of their development, such bank credits to the farm sector were substantially overshadowed by the savings deposits of farm households, this does not seem to have occurred in the case of India. Given the relatively lower per capita income of Indian farm households, as well as the backwardness of the rural financial institutions during the study period, such an outcome is not unexpected. What stands out in the case of India compared to Japan and Taiwan is the lack of net current official transfers as a significant source of surplus outflow from agriculture. This was due to the extremely low tax burden on agricultural incomes relative to incomes generated in other sectors of the economy, and particularly the decline in the tax burden in the latter half of the 1960s when agricultural incomes in real terms were rising due to the terms of trade effect. In this respect, the experience of India is similar to the post-1979 reform era in China, and to that of Iran.

The Case of Iran

An important feature of the Iranian economy, which distinguished it from the other countries in our sample, was the substantial inflow of external finance to the economy in the form of government oil export revenues. This provided ample resources which supplemented the investible funds mobilised from the domestic non-oil economy. The availability of external resources also facilitated a process of rapid structural change, and particularly fast income growth in the non-agricultural sector, which contributed to the formation of the popular belief that there was a resource squeeze from the agricultural sector. Contrary to such beliefs, however, empirical findings show that there seems to have been a considerable net resource flow into Iranian agriculture, which intensified with the 1970s oil boom. In fact, all the financial mechanisms of surplus transfer, both visible and invisible, recorded a net inflow into the farm sector.[17]

An important source of surplus inflow into Iranian agriculture on the invisible side was the terms of trade effect. There was a sustained terms of trade improvement in favour of agriculture which particularly accelerated during the oil boom years of the 1970s. The income gains through the terms of trade effect by the end of the study period were more than the real income gains arising from the normal growth of value added in the sector, measured at prices prevailing in the early 1960s. Even measured at base point prices prevailing at the world level, the agricultural terms of trade in Iran seemed to indicate an income gain to the agricultural sector for most of the study period. This formed one mechanism of transferring part of productivity gains in other sectors, including the increasing oil export revenues, to the agricultural sector.

The income gains through the terms of trade effect were supplemented by other visible inflows on the financial side of the resource flow accounts. An important source of net resource inflow into the farm sector was through the net factor income flow, which mainly consisted of wage labour income of members of farm households working in the non-agricultural sector. The rapid rate of growth of the non-agricultural sector meant that this source of income was large enough to overshadow factor income outflows such as interest on loans and rent payments to absentee landlords. With the implementation of land reform, the latter lost its significance as a source of surplus outflow from agriculture.

As with the other countries discussed above, on the capital account the net official flows showed an inflow into Iranian agriculture, which largely reflected the importance of government investment in the sector. This was a particularly large net inflow compared to other sources of resource transfer in the 1970s, as the government, benefiting from large oil price increases, undertook extensive investment projects in the agricultural sector. In addition, the government provided ample subsidised credit through the banking system to the farm sector. In the absence of a matching outflow of finance in the form of private financial investment by farm households, this meant that private capital flows also registered a net financial inflow into the agricultural sector. This aspect of intersectoral resource flows in Iran is in sharp contrast to agricultural surplus countries (Japan and post-colonial Taiwan) where private capital outflows in the form of financial investment of farm households formed an important mechanism of surplus outflow from agriculture. Another important feature of resource flows in Iran, which again contrasted sharply with these latter two countries, was the virtual absence of any government taxation of agriculture. As noted above, in Japan and Taiwan in the early stages of their development when rural financial markets were still undeveloped, government taxation formed an important source of surplus outflow from agriculture.

The growing net financial burden of Iranian agriculture during the study period was, of course, connected to developments in the economy on the real side. Substantial government subsidies on new inputs and credit, as well as government's direct investment in the agricultural sector, implied a sizeable and fast growing inflow of new intermediate and capital goods inputs into the sector. The use of new inputs such as chemical fertilisers and pesticides, as well as agricultural machinery and implements, increased at a phenomenal rate, particularly accelerating during the 1970s. The rapid growth of the gross inflow of new inputs into the agricultural sector in the case of Iran was not unlike the experience of Japan and Taiwan, where agriculture made a positive net finance contribution to the other sectors of the economy. What was distinct in the case of Iran, however, was the lack of commensurate response of agricultural value added to the inflow of new producer goods resulting from production and allocative inefficiencies within the agricultural sector. This was an important factor in turning agriculture into a net financial burden on the rest of the economy, as under these circumstances the marketed surplus grew at a slower rate than the purchases of the agricultural sector from other sectors. This effect was, of course, exacerbated on the consumption side, as due to sizeable income gains in agriculture through the terms of trade effect and factor income flows, the rate of growth of purchases of consumer goods by farm households surpassed those of output and marketed surplus of the sector.

IV. AGRICULTURAL SURPLUS AND INDUSTRIAL ACCUMULATION

The variety of experiences in terms of the direction, relative magnitude, and patterns and mechanisms of intersectoral resource flows in the five country case studies, reveals interesting results on different aspects of the role of agriculture in industrialisation. An important aspect of the debate in the development literature on the role of agriculture in economic development has centred on the financing role of agriculture in the process of early industrial accumulation. Our empirical results suggest that, at least in relation to the surplus labour economies studied here, there does not seem to be any significant relation between agricultural surplus and the overall savings and investment rates in the economy. In fact, in China, India and Iran, where agriculture imposed a large and growing financial burden on the rest of the economy, higher rates of national savings and investment were achieved in a shorter time as compared with countries such as Japan and Taiwan where agriculture provided a positive net finance contribution.[18] Furthermore, in the latter two countries, even during periods when the net finance contribution of agriculture was growing rapidly, the significance of agricultural surplus in the overall national savings declined over time. On the basis of the experience of the countries under study here, therefore, it appears that the role of agriculture in financing industrial accumulation has been historically less significant than suggested in the development literature. In fact, in China, India, and Iran, the non-agricultural sector not only managed to finance high rates of industrial investment, but also generated sufficient savings to finance a growing net financial burden by the agricultural sector.

The empirical findings also indicate that there seems to be no direct relation between net agricultural surplus flow and the growth of agricultural output. The growth of agricultural output in each country was certainly predicated upon a *gross* inflow of new producer and consumer goods from outside the sector on an increasing scale. Whether the final outcome turned out to be a positive or negative *net* flow of resources into the sector depended primarily on agricultural output response to the use of new inputs. In Taiwan, and Japan prior to the 1920s, with relatively high levels of production efficiency and fast rates of productivity growth in the agricultural sector, there was a net positive resource outflow from agriculture, despite the rapid growth of agricultural purchases from outside the sector. On the other hand, in China, India, and Iran, agriculture became a growing financial drain on the rest of the economy as a result of the relatively low levels of production efficiency and stagnant agricultural productivity.

Of course, other factors such as the existence of appropriate financial mechanisms of resource flow should be in place for productivity growth in agriculture to be translated into a net finance contribution by the agricultural sector. A notable example of the failure of the financial mechanisms of resource flow was in the post-1979 reform period in China, where agriculture continued to be a net financial burden on the rest of the economy on an increasing scale despite rapid rates of productivity growth in the sector. In the long run, however, productivity growth seems to be a *sine qua non* for preventing agriculture from turning into a growing financial drain on the rest of the economy. The experience of China during the Maoist period is a forceful reminder of this point. Despite the existence of institutions of central planning which were ideal mechanisms for the mobilisation and transfer of resources out of agriculture during that period, low productivity growth within the sector entailed a growing financial burden by agriculture on the rest of the economy. On one hand, low productivity of resource use within the sector meant that the government had to divert a massive amount of new producer goods at highly subsidised prices to agriculture in an attempt to maintain the growth of agricultural output. On the other hand, with growing population pressure on land and declining productivity of labour in the agricultural sector, other sectors had to increasingly subsidise the consumption of agricultural households. As a consequence, the institutions of central planning in the agricultural sector, which are widely believed to have been constructed as a means of mobilising agricultural surplus for industrial accumulation, had instead to be used to secure a net transfer of resources into the agricultural sector.

The experience of Japan provides a further example of the crucial link between the growth of agricultural productivity and net agricultural surplus flow. With the slow-down in productivity growth in Japanese agriculture during the 1920s and 1930s, agricultural surplus began a declining trend until by the end of the study period the balance of net intersectoral resource flows even registered a negative outflow from agriculture. The financial channels of surplus flow, which during the fast productivity growth period prior to the 1920s contributed to the outflow of relatively substantial surplus from agriculture, during the slow productivity phase turned into mechanisms of income transfer to agriculture.

The productivity of resource use within different sectors also provides the key to the understanding of the apparently paradoxical result that in countries such as China, India, and Iran, where strong import substituting industrialisation policies have been followed, the finance contribution of agriculture to other sectors has been negative, in contrast to Taiwan where agriculture has provided a sizeable net finance contribution to other sectors. This is contrary to the popular belief that import substitution industrialisation is tantamount to a resource squeeze from agriculture. The theoretical underpinning of such a belief, as we mentioned earlier, is provided by the full employment general equilibrium models of neo-classical theory – for which our empirical findings are indeed paradoxical. Within that framework, sectoral outputs become substitutes, as different sectors with given technologies of production compete for fully employed resources, and policies introduced to accelerate the rate of investment in industry would be necessarily at the expense of agricultural investment. As Kaldor [1978: 203] observed, 'this [general equilibrium] approach ignores the essential complementarity between different factors of production (such as capital and labour) and different types of activities (such as that between primary, secondary and tertiary sectors of the economy) which is far more important for the understanding of the laws of change and development of the economy than the substitution aspect'.

Post-war development economics, by making the assumptions of increasing returns in industry and surplus agricultural labour, reintroduced the complementary aspect of sectoral activities at the centre of the development process. Investment in industry makes fuller utilisation of surplus labour and thus increases the efficiency of resource use in the economy as a whole. At the same time such investment increases the supply of new land-augmenting producer goods to the agricultural sector — essential for the growth of agricultural output.[19] Agricultural growth would in turn enhance the possibilities for further profitable investment in industry as well as improving industrial productivity by expanding the market for industrial products. As discussed above, the massive inflow of producer goods into Chinese agriculture during the 1960s and 1970s was made possible only by a prior investment in industrial activities supplying agricultural producer goods. This was true also for the other countries in our sample, though the degree to which agricultural producer goods were supplied by domestic industry varied, depending on the openness of their economies and the orientation of their industrial investment. In none of the countries under study, were resources squeezed out of agriculture because of industrial policies and priorities, and in cases where such an interpretation could be possibly supported (for example, early Meiji Japan and Taiwan) this phenomenon was associated with agricultural growth and dynamism rather than stagnation.

By focusing on the dynamic and complementary aspects of sectoral interactions in development, post-war development economics highlighted the significance of sectoral analysis in the study of economic development. However, as in the rest of mainstream economics, little attention was paid by development economists to factors which govern production efficiency within sectors and activities. This was unfortunate because in later years the problems of poor agricultural performance in countries following industrialisation policies advocated by post-war development economics came to be automatically associated with the squeezing of resources from the agricultural sector without questioning the productivity of resources deployed in the sector. If the root of the problem is seen as the industrialisation policies followed by governments, then the abandonment of such policies and reliance on the free trade is said to restore agricultural growth. The mechanism through which this process is supposed to take place is the re-allocation of resources away from industry and towards a resource hungry agriculture, allegedly hitherto squeezed by the industrialisation bias of government policy.[20] The result of this simplistic approach has been the neglect of some of the most fundamental forces in the development process, namely production efficiency and the level and rate of change in productivity of resource use in different sectors.

As noted above, the problems of agricultural development in China,

India, and Iran, did not arise because of lack of investment and the diversion of resources away from agriculture; on the contrary, agriculture in these countries benefited from a relatively much higher rate of inflow of resources, both on a gross and net basis, than in Japan and Taiwan. What distinguished the latter two countries was rather the relatively much higher production efficiency and faster rates of productivity growth in agricultural production. With fast rates of productivity growth, relatively sizeable net resource outflows from agriculture could take place in these two countries through government taxation and adverse terms of trade movements, without apparently adversely affecting the relative rate of return on investment and production incentives in their agricultural sectors. On the other hand, in countries with slow agricultural productivity growth, despite generous tax exemptions and large income transfers into agriculture through favourable terms of trade movements and other mechanisms, agriculture continued to be a major constraint on economic growth.

It would of course be a mistake to make too many generalisations on the basis of the experience of the five countries studies here. There have been, no doubt, countries where agricultural output has suffered due to lack of investment and a general neglect by the government, which may have even led to a resource squeeze out of the sector. The case studies discussed here, however, establish that such a resource squeeze need not be a necessary by-product of development strategies favouring industrial growth. If anything, industrialisation seems to be a necessary condition for the rapid growth of inflow of new producer goods into agriculture, at least for the surplus labour economies of the type studied here. An even more important point highlighted by the present case studies is that from a long-term perspective, the efficiency of resource use *within* sectors, as determined by the organisational and technological capabilities of different economies, seems to play a more crucial role than sectoral allocation of resources, in explaining the different growth performances in the countries studied. Too much emphasis on the question of allocation of resources between sectors, with a focus on the substitution aspects of sectoral interactions, has led to a neglect of more dynamic considerations related to the efficiency of resource use, notably connected to the process of technological progress. It turns out that the critical question in the study of the long-term comparative performance of agricultural economies in Japan and Taiwan on the one hand, and India, China, and Iran on the other, is related more to the organisational and institutional relations which determine the efficiency of resource use within these respective economies rather than the relative magnitude of resources invested in each.

NOTES

1. See, for example, Sachs [1985] and Krueger [1992] for some recent examples, where the 'urban' bias thesis is provoked to furnish political explanations for the 'agricultural' squeeze hypothesis.

2. The results of the World Bank studies are summarised in Schiff and Valdes [1992a] and Krueger [1992].

3. By conventional development economics we refer here to the body of literature which developed in the post war period, initiated and highly influenced by the early ideas of economists such as Rosenstein-Rodan, Nurkse, Lewis, Hirschman, Prebisch, and Singer amongst others. Other influential contributors, arriving at a similar perspective following in the tradition of the classical political economists were Joan Robinson, Kaldor and Kalecki.

4. This depends on the reaction of farm household consumption to the wage labour income inflow from such investments. For the cut in gross inflow of resources made by the adoption of more labour-intensive technologies not to be neutralised by increased consumption in the farm sector, it is important to ensure that new investment leads to high rates of increase in yields and labour productivity in agricultural production. This is an added reason for emphasising the significance of technological innovations in agricultural surplus transfer.

5. For a more detailed discussion of intersectoral resource flow accounting and the choice of an appropriate base point price system see Karshenas [1995: 26–47].

6. This is particularly relevant to income gains through terms of trade effect, as such income gains are likely to accrue predominantly to the rich farmers and landlords who control the major share of the marketed surplus. The curtailment of non-essential and luxury consumption by this group is likely to have much wider beneficial effects in terms of financing accumulation in the economy as a whole [Kalecki, 1970].

7. It should be noted that land taxes could in themselves prove to be an important boost to work and investment incentives in agriculture, as they encourage an intensification in land use and discourage absentee landlords from keeping land idle.

8. It should be noted that our reference to the 'relative price' or the 'terms of trade effect', in the context of the World Bank sudies, is somewhat different from that of the classical approach discussed in the previous section. In the classical approach, where the main emphasis is on the income transfer effect of relative prices, the terms of trade effect refers to income gains resulting from the terms of trade between agricultural *sales* and *purchases*. In the context of the World Bank studies, however, assuming factor mobility and a tendency towards full employment of factors of production, the terms of trade effect refers to the relative prices between the agricultrural and non-agricultural sectors. As a result, in the World Bank studies the income transfers resulting from government subsidies on agricultural inputs are measured at later stages of the study as a separate source of income transfer, and are not included in the terms of trade effect, or what they refer to as the direct and indirect protection of agricultre, although in estimating agricultural price response they do seem to take into account the relative price effect of input subsidies. With these qualifications, we shall continue to use the terms 'relative price effec' and 'terms of trade effect' in this section.

9. As noted above, the assumption of 'everything else remaining the same', is central to the 'elasticity approach' adopted in the case studies for the estimation of the equilibrium exchange rate.

10. The price elasticity of imports is assumed to be -0.225 and that of exports 1.03. These elasticities which are mentioned in a footnote are based on the findings of other researchers [Moon and Kang, 1989: p.234]. There is no discussion of the method of estimation, their stability over time, and how the income effect of devaluations are dealt with in arriving at such estimates.

11. In the case of the purchasing power parity approach for example, this is translated into the choice of an appropriate base year.

12. During 1972–73 the current account deficit had fallen to about four per cent of the GDP, but in 1974–75 it once again increased to about ten per cent of the GDP. During 1976–78 the deficit declined to an average of about two per cent, with 1977 actually showing a surplus, but with the second oil price shock the resource gap increased to about six to seven per cent

of the GDP during 1979–81. From 1982 the deficit declined drastically and from 1984 it turned into a surplus. The current account surplus increased to seven per cent of the GDP on average during 1986–88.

13. For a theoretical discussion of the assumptions under which the absorption approach is compatible with general equilibrium analysis see Dornbusch [1975]. Dornbusch, however, hastens to add that 'The assumption of a zero marginal propensity to spend on traded goods is obviously quite extraordinary and the reader is reminded that I am not constructing the preferred model of the trade balance, but rather seek to explain the BRM [elasticity approach] model' [1975: 861].

14. This is also supported by a recent study by Teranishi [1996], where it is shown that rather than the estimated price distortions by the World Bank studies, the agricultural growth performances in different countries are more closely connected with factors such as government investment in irrigation and infrastructure, education and so on.

15. A good example of this is our earlier discussion on what can be deemed a sustainable balance of payments deficit. Any level can be justified assuming economies of learning of a sufficient strength.

16. It should be noted that the net inflow of factor income depicted in Table 5 only refers to the post-war period. For more details see Karshenas [1995: Ch.6].

17. Private bank capital flow, during the 1968–72 period, which showed a relatively small net positive outflow was of course an exception. The negative sign for 'Other' capital in Table 5 refers to the period under study excepting the 1968–72 period. For more details see Karshenas [1995: Ch.7].

18. For a detailed discussion of this point see, Karshenas [1995: Ch.10].

19. The agricultural producer goods need not necessarily be produced by domestic industry. The surplus labour could be employed in the export-oriented industries providing the foreign exchange for the purchase of agricultural producer goods in the international market.

20. This line of argument is particularly favoured by the World Bank as evidenced by the title of a recent World Bank publication, *The Plundering of Agriculture in Developing Countries* [*Schiff and Valdes*, 1992b]. This publication solely relies on the World Bank case studies which we have already discussed above. This argument is summed up in the preface to Schiff and Valdez [1992a] by Paul Schultz in the following words, 'the modernization of agriculture was being sacrificed at the altar of industrialization'.

REFERENCES

Byres, T.J., 1974, 'Land Reform, Industialization and the Marketed Surplus in India', in D. Lehmann (ed.), *Agrarian Reform and Agrarian Reformism*, London: Faber & Faber.

Byres, T. J., 1977, 'Agrarian Transition and the Agrarian Question', *Journal of Peasant Studies*, Vol.4, No.3.

Byres, T. J., 1979, 'Of Neo-Populist Pipe-Dreams: Daedalus in the Third World and the Myth of Urban Bias', *The Journal of Peasant Studies*, Vol.6, No.2.

Dornbusch, R., 1975, 'Exchanges Rates and Fiscal Policy in a Popular Model of International Trade', *The American Economic Review*, Vol.LXV, No.5, pp.859–71.

Ishikawa, S., 1967, *Economic Development in Asian Perspective*, Tokyo: Kinokuniya Bookstore.

Kaldor, N., 1978, 'The Irrelevance of Equilibrium Economics', in N. Kaldor, *Further Essays on Economic Theory*, London: Duckworth.

Kalecki, M., 1970, 'Problems of Financing Development in a Mixed Economy', in W. Eltis *et al.* (eds.), *Industrialisation, Growth and Trade*, Oxford: Oxford University Press.

Karshenas, M., 1995, *Industrialization and Agricultural Surplus: A Comparative Study of Economic Development in Asia*, Cambridge: Cambridge University Press.

Krueger, A.O., 1992, *The Political Economy of Agricultural Pricing Policy, Volume 5, A Synthesis of the Political Economy in Developing Countries*, Baltimore, MD: Johns Hopkins University Press.

Krueger, A.O., Schiff, M. and A. Valdes, 1992, *The Political Economy of Agricultural Pricing Policy, Volume 2, Asia*, Baltimore, MD: Johns Hopkins University Press.

Kuznets, S., 1964, 'Economic Growth and the Contribution of Agriculture: Notes on Measurement', in C. Eicher and L.Witt (eds.), *Agriculture in Economic Development*, New York: McGraw-Hill.

Lipton, M., 1977, *Why Poor People Stay Poor: Urban Bias in World Development*, Cambridge MA: Harvard University Press.

Millar, J.R., 1970, 'Soviet Rapid Development and the Agricultural Surplus Hypothesis', *Soviet Studies*, Vol.22, pp.77–91.

Moon, Pal-Yong and B. Kang, 1989, *Trade, Exchange Rate, and Agricultural Pricing Policies in the Republic of Korea*, World Bank Comparative Studies, Washington, DC: World Bank.

Moon, Pal-Yong and B. Kang, 1992, 'The Republic of Korea', in Anne O. Krueger, *et. al.* [1992].

Mundlak, Y., Danin, Y. and Z. Tropp, 1974, 'Agriculture and Economic Growth: Some Comments', N. Islam (ed.), *Agricultural Policy in Developing Countries*, New York: Stockton Press.

Sachs, J., 1985, 'External Debt and Macroeconomic Performance in Latin America and East Asia', *Brookings Papers on Economic Activity*, 2, pp.523–64.

Schiff, M. and A. Valdes, 1992a, *The Political Economy of Agricultural Pricing Policy: A Synthesis of the Economics in the Developing Countries*, Baltimore, MD: Johns Hopkins University Press.

Schiff, M. and A. Valdes, 1992b, *The Plundering of Agriculture in Developing Countries*, Washington, DC: World Bank.

Sturzenegger, A., 1989, *Trade, Exchange Rate, and Agricultural Pricing Policies in Argentina*, Washington, DC: World Bank.

Teranishi, J., 1996, 'Sectoral Resource Transfer, Conflict, and Macro-stability in Economic Development: A Comparative Analysis', in M. Aoki *et. al.*(eds.), *Role of Government in East Asia: A Comparative Institutional Analysis*, Oxford: Oxford University Press.

Output Per Acre and Size of Holding: The Logic of Peasant Agriculture Under Semi-Feudalism

GRAHAM DYER

The inverse relationship between farm size and productivity is widely accepted as a 'stylised fact' of agriculture in developing countries, a generalised phenomenon observed in widely differing agro-climatic conditions and agrarian structures. The significance of the inverse relationship as a crucial developmental issue cannot be overemphasised. The inverse relationship constitutes a major component of the economic rationale for redistributive land reform, and has obvious importance for policy issues concerning land reorganisation.

The debate over the inverse relationship has been extensive, constituted predominantly by two distinct agendas: first, a discussion of the factors which give rise to and explain the inverse relationship in the static context; second, and later, following the main thrust of the green revolution, a discussion of the breakdown of the inverse relationship in the dynamic context of changing technology. The former strand has focused on two main areas: first, qualitative factor differentials across farm size (soil quality, farm management, etc.) and the mechanisms that generate such differentials; second (quantitative) factor intensity explanations, for the most part within an explicitly choice theoretic framework.

The social context within which a differentiated peasantry operates, and which can generate an inverse relationship, is rarely discussed. Only Bharadwaj [1974a; 1974b; 1985] and Patnaik [1972; 1979; 1987] come close to this approach. However, while Bharadwaj lays the foundations for a political economy framework, she leaves the analysis at the level of technical and market relations and the constraints on participation imposed by resource positions. Patnaik, who operates very firmly within a class analysis framework, uses it to explain away the inverse relationship as a statistical illusion. This strand in the literature alludes only very briefly to the possibility of the inverse relationship breaking down under changing

Graham Dyer, Department of Economics, School of Oriental and African Studies, University of London, Thornhaugh Street, Russell Square, London WC1H 0XG.

production conditions. This latter strand in the literature often relies on the weaker (qualitative) explanatory foundations to discuss the disappearance of the inverse relationship in the dynamic context of the impact of the new technology and its differential adoption rate across farm size.

Byres [1972; 1974; 1977a; 1977b; 1981; 1986a; 1986b; 1990; 1991] and Byres and Dyer [forthcoming] made the first serious attempt to integrate both the static and dynamic analyses into a rigorous and unified class theoretic framework in the context of agrarian transitions. This approach explains both the generation of the inverse relationship and its breakdown. Class relations of exploitation in a relatively backward agriculture exert forces of economic compulsion on the poor peasantry to intensify cultivation, thus generating an inverse relationship. However, with the increasing penetration of capitalist relations of production and exchange, and with capital deepening on (proto-) capitalist farms, the inverse relationship breaks down as large farms capture the economies of scale associated with the new technology.

The empirical evidence for the existence of an inverse relationship between farm size and farm productivity is both historically and geographically widespread, ranging from pre-revolutionary Russia and China to contemporary poor countries in Asia, Africa and Latin America. Indeed, the inverse relationship is widely regarded as a 'stylised fact' of traditional agriculture [*Bardhan*, 1973: 1370], a generalised phenomenon observed in many developing countries characterised by widely different agro-climatic conditions, agrarian structures and cropping patterns [*Cornia*, 1985: 514–15; *Ghose*, 1979: 27].

Griffin [1974: 228] notes:

> A striking feature of the agricultural systems of virtually all poor countries is that yields per acre rise as average farm size declines. That is, the smaller the farm, the greater the average productivity of land. Conversely, the larger the farm, the greater the average productivity of labour. Since land is usually the factor in most acute shortage, the farms with the highest yields per acre are normally the most efficient. Even in countries where the average farm is very small, such as in India, it has been demonstrated that those farms which are smaller than average are economically the most efficient.

The modern debate comprises a large theoretical and empirical literature which came into being in the Indian context. Central to the modern Indian debate on farm size and productivity is the 17-volume Farm Management Studies (FMS) data collected by the Directorate of Economics and Statistics and the Research Programmes Committee over three years: 1954–55, 1955–56 and 1956–57.

The Indian debate proper begins with Sen's seminal 1962 article in the *Economic Weekly* [*Sen,* 1962]. There he notes the following observation: 'By and large, productivity per acre decreases with the size of holding.' Sen further notes that this trend holds in most areas for value-added too. Khusro [1964] and Bharadwaj [1974a] carry out more detailed studies using OLS regression techniques on the grouped FMS data. The constant generation and analysis of data since then continues to confirm the finding of an inverse relationship.

SOME APPARENT POLICY IMPLICATIONS

The significance of the inverse relationship as a crucial developmental issue cannot be overemphasised. Such a relationship has obvious importance for policy issues such as land ceilings and redistribution, as well as co-operative and other forms of land reorganisation, involving discussion of factors such as market imperfections and the institutional framework of traditional agriculture [*Bardhan,* 1973: 1371]. The apparent implications of such a relationship constitute a major component of the economic rationale for redistributive land reform and a small farm bias in agricultural development strategy.

Cornia [1985: 532] writes:

Because of the demonstrated superiority of small *vis-à-vis* large farming, land redistribution would have, if thoroughly implemented, immediate beneficial effects in terms of output growth, enhanced income distribution and, as a result, of alleviation of rural poverty. It would also bring about a resource use more in line with the factor endowment of developing countries by increasing labour absorption ... while forestalling premature labour-displacing mechanisation.

Berry and Cline, regarded by many as the definitive statement on the inverse relationship, argue that the finding of systematically higher land productivity and comparable levels of total factor productivity on small farms as opposed to large farms require redistribution of land to small farmers who apply labour more intensively, and the improvement of small farm access to credit and new technology. Both strategies will improve equity and increase output levels. With such land redistribution, the authors claim that: 'The optimal post-reform farm size, in the absence of technical returns to scale, will be merely the total agricultural area divided by the total number of families in the agricultural labour force' [1979: 128].

Estimates of output gains after land redistribution follow a two-step procedure: first, the average farm size is computed by dividing the available land by the number of families in the rural labour force; secondly, a statistical estimate of output per acre for that farm size is applied to the former result. Berry and Cline present [1979: 132–3, Table 5–1] estimates of the potential gains from such equalising land redistribution, ranging from ten per cent for Pakistan to 79.5 per cent for north-eastern Brazil.

The only caveats to the above procedure for calculating output gains given any prominence in Berry and Cline are those arising from price changes following shifts in output mix, and changes in labour input intensities [1979: 18–9]. However, the set of assumptions required for this astonishingly simplistic calculation to hold are both numerous and highly unlikely to occur in reality.

The first and most obvious problem with this procedure is that the estimates are not constrained by product mix or land quality. They assume that the total land available, defined as all land currently being used for agricultural purposes including pasture and woodland, can be converted to arable cultivation. Indeed, even marginal and waste land or land unsuitable for arable purposes can be so converted. Clearly, this assumption is inadmissible.

Furthermore, none of their calculations take into account the possibility of there being a minimum efficient scale or of there being a floor determined by subsistence income. In terms of the inverse relationship evidence, the optimal size of farm would be around one acre [Sen, 1962]. But when other criteria are considered, relating to viability, we find that the level of the floor rises considerably. One criterion might be that of minimum income. That is, the farm should be able to provide an adequate level of income for a peasant family – a subsistence income. This may turn out to be significantly larger than the optimal size based on the inverse relationship phenomenon (output maximisation). Other criteria might involve employment absorption: that is, the farm should be able to gainfully employ the working members of the average rural family; or technology absorption: that is, the minimum farm size should be such as to make efficient use of draught animals or machines. Consideration of these criteria may significantly raise the minimum feasible size of holding. Here there is a clear conflict between various criteria, in particular that based on the yield postulate of the inverse relationship on one hand, and those based on subsistence requirements or resource use on the other. Thus, the concept of viability sets a limit to redistributive land reform.

To draw on the inverse relationship to justify redistributive land reform, the general equilibrium effects also need to be considered: landless labourers have normally been excluded from access to redistributed land, and if land reform is implemented at the expense of large farms, then the landless may be worse off due to a fall in employment opportunities.

Even if the inverse relationship is empirically valid because small farms use more inputs per acre, land redistribution without ensuring the availability of extra inputs may not produce the expected results [*Bardhan*, 1973: 1371]. Estimates of output gains after redistribution of land assume that the required inputs exist and that no losses occur due to the process of redistribution. Such estimates do not take into account the extra investment costs of providing irrigation to unirrigated land, or of providing extra inputs (seeds, fertilisers, pesticides, etc.). The process of land redistribution itself may involve extra costs in terms of cadastral survey, boundary marking and the provision of access to plots, as well as the potential for the disruptive effects of land reform to reduce output.

The estimates further assume that the current input-output characteristics on existing farms of the 'optimal' size would also characterise farms of that size after land reform. This requires considering not only the availability and distribution of production inputs, but also the whole area of motivation governing labour effort. If incomes were to rise on small farms, this may relax the subsistence income or debt obligations constraint and allow small farmers either to relax labour effort with a lower application of labour per acre, and hence lower output per acre, or to reduce the proportion of output marketed. In such circumstances, while on-farm family consumption might increase, the supply of marketed surplus may well fall with serious consequences for economic activity outside agriculture.

SOME CONCEPTUAL AND STATISTICAL PROBLEMS

Neither the existence of the inverse relationship, nor its implications, have gone unchallenged. Indeed, Sen was one of the first to admit that the inverse relationship was by no means a well established fact and had not been proven 'beyond the legitimate doubts of exacting statisticians due to the fact that average data can be misleading' [1964a: 323].

A notable conceptual problem with respect to the inverse relationship was introduced into the debate by Utsa Patnaik [1972: 1613–24; also 1979 and 1987]. She argues forcefully that, if instead of taking acreage as the measure of farm size (size grouping) we take either annual value of gross output per farm or the value of tangible capital stock (scale grouping), we then may get, in certain circumstances, 'diametrically opposite results'. On the second measure of size (the scale grouping) output per acre may rise sharply with increasing scale of production. It may be the case that 'an intensive application of capital on the smaller holding results in its being larger [than a holding of higher acreage] on every economic index except acreage' [1972: 1614]. The reason for this is that holdings of 'varying levels of intensity, i.e. with varying production techniques and even varying organisation' [1972: 1617] are lumped together within the same size category, which may blur certain distinctions: between intensively and extensively cultivated holdings; and between different categories within the peasantry, so obscuring the extent of differentiation [1972: 1615]. It is possible to identify, say, a rich peasant with 80 acres and a rich peasant with just eight acres [1972: 1614].

If all of this is so, then the outcome is as follows, with the inverse relationship emerging on the size grouping, and certain crucial aspects concealed, which are clear on the scale grouping:

> When grouped by size, a small number of high-productivity holdings of small size, lumped with similar sized but low productivity extensively run holdings (which constitute the majority), raises the average yield for the small size group as a whole; while the large extensive farms, lumped with similar sized but much more intensive high-productivity capitalist farms, lower the average yield for the large-size group as a whole ... Not only with respect to yield, but also as regards all inputs, capital intensity and labour productivity, we find the same striking differences in the results of grouping by size and by scale respectively [1972: 1620].

Patnaik is making a very important point. It is, indeed, the case that 'when we are studying a process of agricultural change ... it becomes especially important to analyse the available data according to scale of production' [1972: 1621]. Two holdings of the same size may well differ in their class status. A holding may be smaller in size but larger as an economic unit [1972: 1614]. But note how she formulates the argument:

> What we are saying is that in the past, the set of rich peasants and the set of farms above 20 acres in UP probably had a very large number of common elements: while at present owing to the changes taking place in use of techniques and intensification of production the intersection of the two sets is getting smaller. Therefore the identification of the properties of one set with those of the other is now less justifiable and may be downright misleading [1972: 1624].

Observe the difference stressed between the past (a static situation) and the present (a dynamic one): in the Indian case, between the pre-'new technology' situation and the period when that 'new technology' had begun to spread and have an impact. The validity of her argument surely relates to circumstances of change. One might argue, on her own logic, that in the relatively static situation of the 1950s, when the inverse relationship was first established in the FMS studies, size was a useful measure, encompassing 'sets with a very large number of common elements'; while later, following the introduction of the green revolution technology, her argument begins to apply. She stresses: 'If techniques were absolutely uniform for all holdings then of course no problem of distinguishing between size and scale would arise. However techniques are far from uniform ... The possibility of adopting new, usually much more capital intensive techniques exists [by the 1970s] for the farms with an investible surplus' [1972: 1615].

This is the crucial point. We would argue that techniques tended to uniformity in the 1950s (certainly, to a far greater extent then than in the 1970s); and so size was then a useful stratifying variable: an acceptable index of economic status (class position). Where techniques of production have been only partially transformed, farm size may still be the relevant stratifying variable, but great care must be taken to avoid grouping farms with different systems of production. The exclusion or separate treatment of the latter of course requires theoretical and empirical investigation.

One further issue of crucial significance that needs to be flagged at this point, as it relates closely to the question of agrarian change, is the breakdown and disappearance of the inverse relationship in the context of the new technology. This widely documented phenomenon [*Chadha*, 1978; *Roy*, 1979; 1981; *Khan*, 1979; *Dyer*, 1991] is discussed later. Suffice it to state here that abundant evidence from India and Pakistan shows that following the introduction of green revolution technology, the inverse relationship seems to have disappeared, especially in those areas where the new technology has penetrated most deeply.

This, of course, is a very different phenomenon from that described by Patnaik, whose approach involves a statistical breakdown of the inverse relationship by switching from an area definition of farm size to a scale measure. The former approach, however, suggests that it is larger farms, due to their greater surpluses and access to and control over capital, which capture the productivity gains from the new technology, thereby structurally reversing the direction of the size–productivity relationship, despite the continued intensive application of family labour on small farms.

Another crucial distinction to be made is that between aggregated and disaggregated levels of analysis. At highly aggregated levels of analysis, whether at the cross-country [*Cornia*, 1985], national or regional level, a relatively high degree of land heterogeneity is to be expected. Those areas with better than average soil quality, in particular water availability, and hence higher than average natural land productivity, are historically likely to have attracted greater population settlement. Higher population density will, given limited land resources, lead to small average farm size over long time periods. Contrariwise for areas of relatively poor agricultural land where population settlement is likely to be less dense and average farm size larger. Hence, at this 'macro' level, an inverse correlation between land productivity (as measured by output per acre) and farm size is to be expected.

Note that this type of inverse relationship at the 'macro' level is fundamentally different from the inverse relationship which is the focus of our study. At the aggregate level, the direction of causality runs from land productivity (itself caused by better soil quality) to small average farm size. However, at the micro level (village level, for example) the causality is postulated to run in the opposite direction: specific factors associated with smaller than average farm size generate higher than average farm productivity. Moving from the macro to micro scale, the direction of causation is reversed: while exogenous factors are assumed to cause the inverse relation at the macro level, endogenous factors are assumed to cause the same inverse relation at the micro level – the inverse relationship at the 'macro' level is caused by diversity in natural conditions.

There are two further dimensions to the problem of aggregation. There is the related problem of aggregation over villages leading to a spurious inverse relationship. Even if no inverse relationship existed within villages, but there were different soil fertilities between villages, and high fertility villages had smaller average farm size, then an inverse relation would be shown by data aggregated over the group of villages. Alternatively, if fertility (average land productivity) was the same over villages, and the inverse relationship holds in each village, but villages have different size-ranges, then such a relationship could be eliminated [*Chattopadhyay and Rudra*, 1976: A–110]. Rudra [1968b] implies that the inverse relationship does not exist within any particular village, but arises as a spurious relationship when data for different villages are aggregated.

There is also the problem of grouped averages. Most of the analysis of the FMS data was carried out using size class averages for the principal variables, farm size and output per acre. Grouped data may generate an aggregation bias when the in-group variance is in fact greater than the between-group variance. Thus, farm level data which show no overall relationship between farm size and output per acre may, when grouped into size classes, show a spurious inverse relation.

Rudra [1968a: 1041] suspects the process of aggregation is responsible for what he calls the 'spurious correlation' of the FMS data. In a later study, Rudra presents data on rank correlation coefficients between farm size and yield per hectare *for individual crops* [1968b: A–35, Table 1]: producing only four statistically significant negative coefficients. Note, however, that there is a clear distinction to be drawn between physical yields of individual crops and total crop production in value terms (this reflects the importance of cropping intensity and crop pattern). Unlike the inverse relationship in value terms, little or no evidence has been produced for an inverse relationship in terms of the physical yields of individual crops.

THE INVERSE RELATIONSHIP VINDICATED AND SOME CONJOINT RELATIONSHIPS: CLUSTERED FACTORS

While Rudra is correct to assert the need to disaggregate the data, the divergence between his results and those of the FMS would persist even with disaggregation. Rudra's concept of yield per acre is biased toward eliminating the inverse relationship. Yields have been calculated as gross value of output per gross cultivated area [*Rudra*, 1968a: 1041]. Gross cultivated area or gross cropped area includes farm size plus those parts of the operated area multi-cropped.

However, factors such as double (or multiple) cropping and the percentage of land cultivated reflect the economics of farming. They are not exogenous factors. A farmer who cultivates land more intensively via double cropping and raising the percentage of land cultivated may be argued to be using land more efficiently [*Rao*, 1968: 1413]. Rudra's procedure corrects for the efficiency of land use by using gross cropped area. Moreover, it is important to establish why land is cultivated more intensively. Rudra's procedure, however, obscures cropping intensity differentials between farm size groups which may be of critical significance. If an inverse relationship exists between cropping intensity (the ratio of gross cropped area to net cropped area or farm size) and farm size, then Rudra's results are not surprising. Nevertheless, much of Rudra's criticism of the earlier FMS studies has a great deal of validity. While Chattopadhyay and Rudra challenge the universal validity of the inverse relationship, they do not reject that validity in all circumstances: in some places, at certain times, and for certain size ranges the inverse relationship may hold [1976: A–104].

Other writers have sought to answer some of the criticisms by using disaggregated data for individual farm households at the village level. Saini [1971] and Bhattacharya and Saini [1972: A–63] analyse disaggregated FMS data for 25 data sets in nine States, concluding: 'Thus, by and large, the inverse relationship between farm size and productivity is a confirmed phenomenon in Indian agriculture and its statistical validity is adequately established by an analysis of the disaggregated data' [1971: A–81–2].

The general conclusion after the spilling of much ink is that the inverse relationship between farm size and productivity has been confirmed as a valid empirical phenomenon in India, but not in the way conceived of in the earlier studies. Rudra and Sen in a joint paper [1980: 393] conclude: 'While … the inverse relation is more frequently confirmed than rejected, it would be a mistake to take it to be an empirical generalisation for Indian agriculture as a whole.' The inverse relationship findings in the Indian FMS, then, are not entirely conclusive. Moreover, some exceptions and complications are introduced by considering other factors besides land [*Sen*, 1964b: 441]. But the findings do suggest a persistent phenomenon that needs to be explained.

A wide range of relationships between farm size and other important factors are revealed by the various studies mentioned above that may throw some light on the theoretical understanding of this phenomenon. The major findings of the FMS studies and the wider debate which followed can be summarised as follows:

(1) An inverse relationship between output per net cropped acre for the total value of crop production and farm size exists for *most* regions of India, and for a wide range of other countries.

(2) That inverse relationship appears to be weakened when gross cropped area is used as the land measure in the productivity calculation.

(3) No inverse relationship is evident between the physical yield per acre of individual crops and farm size. Indeed, in most cases, physical yields of individual crops appear to be constant or even increasing across farm size.

(4) There is a strong inverse relationship between cropping intensity and farm size, where the cropping intensity index represents the ratio of gross cropped area to net cropped area.

(5) A further inverse relationship is evident between units of labour input per acre and farm size. As farm size increases, less human labour input is applied per acre.

(6) A related phenomenon is the declining ratio of family labour to total labour as farm size increases. The ratio of hired labour input to total labour increases with farm size.

(7) Along with increasing labour input intensity on the smaller farms, is a higher intensity of application of capital inputs (including animal labour power, seeds, fertilisers, and farm buildings).

(8) This latter association does not apply to purchased intermediate inputs which tend to increase proportionately or more than proportionately with farm size.

(9) An inverse relationship has also been noticed between the percentage of cultivated area irrigated and farm size.

It is already fairly obvious that these findings are closely interdependent. All the studies mentioned previously find these relationships clustered, suggesting a priori explanations for the inverse relationship based on factor input intensity, which will be discussed shortly.

THEORETICAL APPROACHES TO THE INVERSE RELATIONSHIP

We have seen then that empirical evidence points to a number of clustered relationships involving factors of production. That evidence has spawned a vast theoretical literature attempting to explain why an inverse relationship arises. It is convenient and logical to examine the principal theoretical approaches to the inverse relationship under three headings: (1) those that attempt to explain the inverse relationship in terms of qualitative factor differences between farm-size categories with respect to management, labour effort, technique, and soil quality; (2) a second and more substantial approach that attempts to explain the inverse relationship in terms of differential factor use intensities between farm-size categories; (3) the third is a class-based political economy explanation of the inverse relationship.

Management and Labour Quality Hypotheses

Given the essentially untestable nature of the concepts of management and labour quality, the researcher is forced to utilize various proxies, and hence this approach tends to be residual in nature. Some form of 'diseconomies of large scale' peculiar to agricultural production are normally invoked as giving rise to an inverse relationship.

This argument appears to have two distinct components: the first is a proposition concerning the increase in complexity of organisation that comes with size, and which appears to have inefficiencies inherent in it, compared with the small farm situation; the second is a proposition relating to supervision problems and incentives which seem to become problematic as size increases.

Clearly, complexity of organisation does increase with size, but why this should necessarily generate insuperable inefficiencies is not so clear. On the contrary, one might argue that the scope provided for division of labour and specialization leads to the possibility of increased efficiency.

Assuming that this argument has some validity, its force may hinge, to some extent, upon whether or not technical economies of scale exist. If there are indeed demonstrable potential economies of scale then these may compensate for possible managerial diseconomies. This implies a possible trade-off between technical economies of scale and managerial diseconomies of scale.

Thus, the argument simply in organisational terms is not wholly convincing, but the second part of the argument concerning incentives does seem, at first sight, to have considerable force. This argument suggests that any economies of scale arising from indivisibilities will be offset by the agency costs of managing wage labour and enforcing effort on the part of the hired workforce. Supervision costs and incentive contracts, it is posited, will have profound implications for the optimal size of farm [*Mellor and Johnston*, 1984: 558; *Mellor*, 1966: 368; *Nolan*, 1988: 41–2].

Related to this argument is the proposition that small farms have a productivity advantage with respect to the quality of labour, in turn related to incentive structures. This is a classic populist proposition in the literature, more often implied than stated explicitly. Unfortunately, no evidence is presented in support of the proposition, or against which one might test the hypothesis.

Lipton [1993: 1524] argues:

> people will produce more as small family groups, working for themselves and receiving the whole product of their labour, than as employees in larger units ... This points to the frequent superiority of the smaller, self-managed family unit, as expressed in the 'inverse relationship': namely, the generally higher productivity of land, and to a lesser extent all factors taken together, farmed in smaller holdings.

Because family members are residual claimants to profits, they therefore have higher incentives to provide effort than hired labour. They share the burden of risk and have no search or recruitment costs in the labour market: thus, the claimed superiority of family over large wage labour-based operations [*Binswanger and Deininger*, 1993: 1452]. Due to the advantages of peer monitoring, agents such as family farmers benefit more from supervising each other in small groups than from external supervision by costly foremen. Small farms reduce unit labour-related transaction costs (search, screening, supervision, shirking) by providing nearby, informed, rapid and flexible family overview of labour, and by building on intrafamily altruism and on the extended fungibility of family members between the household and the family farm [*Lipton and Lipton*, 1993: 648]. It is further argued that individual peasant farmers have better knowledge of local natural conditions than managers of large farms, and that potential losses from imperfect information are minimised by the ability of the small farmer to adjust to micro variations in the natural environment [*Binswanger and Deininger*, 1993: 1452]. This is accentuated by weather variability which requires rapid and flexible response by the farmer.

Many of the foregoing arguments, if they have any validity at all, would appear to have more relevance for vast landed estates or extensive ranch-type farming involving thousands of acres. They will have much less relevance for the types of large farms we are considering, in the range from 10 to 50 or even 100 acres.

Supervision costs, under such conditions, would seem to be greatly exaggerated. The use of attached labour in a supervisory role, or even better, the use of family labour, in setting work tasks and ensuring execution is sufficient to ensure that the requisite labour effort has been expended on the part of the workforce. The threat of losing access to wage labour opportunities will provide the incentive for the worker to supply the quantity and quality of labour effort demanded. The often highly personalised relationship between employer and labourer, sometimes involving access to credit and land, help to provide 'nearby, informed, rapid and flexible' supervision of labour [*Bhaduri*, 1973].

On the small farm side of the equation, idealised notions of 'family altruism' and 'fungibility of family members' ignores the unequal distribution of income within the farm household and intra-household exploitation. Further, the idea that small farmers have better information on the local environment is a dubious proposition, and is probably outweighed by the superior knowledge of large farmers concerning the use of modern technology.

The really critical problem, however, for these approaches is that if small farms are indeed characterised by superior management or labour quality, these should be reflected in a productivity advantage with regard to individual crops. However, as Bharadwaj [1974a] showed in her study of the FMS data, no systematic or significant relation between farm-size and the physical yields of individual crops exists (in fact, irrigated wheat-gram and cotton in Punjab showed a positive relation). This would seem to refute the hypothesis that the inverse relation arises from any superior entrepreneurship of the small farmer.

This approach is also undermined by the fact that the inverse relationship phenomenon is not limited to a simple comparison between small family labour farms and large hired labour farms. All the evidence shows that the inverse relationship runs across small family farms themselves. The adherents of the above approaches appear not to have recognised this problem.

Land Fertility Hypothesis

A second qualitative approach centres on the proposition that small farms are located on land of superior productive potential, leading to the fertility-based explanation of the inverse relation. A problem with this approach is that it is difficult to distinguish between inherent qualitative land differences and those arising from the application of fertility-augmenting inputs. Furthermore, superior soil quality may not be picked up by individual crop regressions because to some extent crop choice is dictated by soil type, and quality differences will be reflected predominantly in crop patterns [*Bharadwaj, 1974b: A14–15*].

Sen [1966] tends towards this fertility based approach. Over time, a correlation between land fertility and size of holdings will be established via population expansion on more fertile land. Faster population growth on more fertile land (due to higher growth of income opportunities) leads to greater subdivision of the land. This is easy to see in interregional variation where population expands faster due to natural increase and immigration, but also within regions, claims Sen, where the ability of a farm household to withstand famine or crop disease is greater with more fertile land. This approach ignores the crucial distinction noted earlier between the inverse relation at the macro level and at the micro level.

Sen's argument regarding fertility differentials relies upon a rather dubious Malthusian link between income and family size and between level of income and fragmentation, and ignores alternative employment opportunities off-farm. An alternative hypothesis proposed by Bhagwati and Chakravarty [1969] suggests that large farms build up holdings by land purchase and foreclosure on loans leading to a high degree of fragmentation, and consequently low productivity.

Of course, neither version of the fertility hypothesis (Sen or Bhagwati and Chakravarty) holds the promise of economic betterment for small farmers nor suggests that they have any inherently progressive characteristics. While the fertility hypothesis based on partible inheritance or small farm distress sales may appear plausible, it is weakened by the fact that small farmers may sell land to other small farmers. Likewise, land reform laws may simply lead to large farmers divesting their worst quality land. Bharadwaj [1974a] also points out that according to the FMS database, whereas large holdings do tend to be composed of a greater number of fragments, the intensity of fragmentation (number of fragments per acre) is higher on the small farms.

Any discussion of the land fertility-based explanation of the inverse relation would be incomplete without commenting on the perhaps curious empirical finding that small farms appear to have a greater percentage of acreage under irrigation. Many studies have focused on this fact as an explanation for the inverse relationship [Rao, 1963: 2043; Rao, 1966: 7; A.P. Rao, 1967: 1990].

Bharadwaj [1974b: A–19] offers two possible explanations for this: (1) better irrigation leads to greater soil fertility which over time produces greater land fragmentation; and (2) abundant family labour is deployed to create and maintain irrigation facilities. However, the first explanation along the lines of the macro inverse relation, would not explain why within a given district, small farms have a higher percentage of irrigated area. Secondly, if such irrigation facilities require capital investment, then the purported advantage of the small farmer will be counterbalanced. Thirdly, the irrigation ratio tells us nothing about the quality of irrigation facilities on various farm sizes: it does not indicate the effectiveness, source, quality, controllability or quantum of water supply. Indeed, a large proportion of the area officially classified as irrigated is often no better than unirrigated land, depending on rainfall as the source of water, which means that quantitative comparisons of irrigation ratios can be misleading.

Labour Intensity and Labour Market Dualism: The Sen Model

The extensive list of complementary relationships revealed by the FMS data tends to suggest that the inverse relationship is associated with variations in cropping intensity, with the quantum of labour and other production inputs per acre as the major explanatory factor: what we may call factor intensity explanations. One influential example is the argument that labour input intensity explains higher cropping intensity, with much attention, therefore, directed towards factors which explain labour input intensity.

Sen, in his seminal 1962 article, states that the FMS observations regarding the inverse relationship are to be expected given what he calls the 'mode of production' of Indian agriculture and its variation over farm size. The Sen model divides the rural economy into two parts: a modern, capitalist large farm sector based on hired labour, with the goal of profit maximisation; and a traditional peasant small farm sector based on family labour aiming to maximise gross output. While this approach, then, does hint at the question of determinacy alluded to above, Sen leaves the reasons for the primary motivation of output maximisation on the peasant farms unexplained, and concentrates on the causal factors behind higher labour input intensity.

On large wage labour-based farms labour is hired in up to the point where the marginal product of labour is equal to the market wage, thus maximising profits. On small family labour-based farms, 'provided labour has no outside opportunity of employment and provided there is no significant disutility of work in the relevant range of effort', labour will be applied beyond the profit-maximising point until its marginal product is zero [*Sen*, 1962: 245].

In a more sophisticated version of the model [*Sen*, 1966: 440], small farms maximise utility in a trade-off between increased income from extra output and leisure. Thus on the family labour-based farm, the marginal product of labour is not equalised to the market wage, but is determined by the subjective evaluation of the marginal disutility of effort. This family labour allocation rule is similar to that advanced by Chayanov [1966] in his theory of the peasant economy. Unlike Sen, however, Chayanov assumes the existence of family labour farms to the exclusion of wage labour-based farms. Nevertheless, they arrive at similar claims as to the relative superiority of the family labour farm. The subjective evaluation of labour is lower on the peasant farm than on the capitalist farm and this provides the former with greater resilience (via the ability of the peasant family to compress income). Thus, the inverse relation, according to Sen, is the natural result of an economy characterised by the existence of widespread surplus labour and family-based non-wage cultivation. The crucial factor is not size as such, but the system of farming [1962: 246].

A number of writers have criticised the Sen approach as being analytically deficient given that even small farms do not rely on family labour exclusively, and a large number of small farms are engaged in off-farm income generating activities. It is pointed out by these authors that the Sen model requires the non-existence of off-farm employment opportunities and the absence of labour-hiring on the small farms [*Khusro*, 1964; *Bhagwati and Chakravarty*, 1969; *Rudra*, 1973; *Taslim*, 1989; *Mazumdar*, 1963: 1259].

Of course, the fact that small farms hire in labour does not imply that they should follow marginalist rules. Time constraints may necessitate the hire of labour for urgent tasks to avoid harvest failure, which is quite consistent with under-employment throughout the rest of the year. Further, certain operations needing specialised skills may require hired labour which cannot therefore be seen as a substitutive category, for example the hire and operation of certain equipment. Furthermore, there may be sociological factors behind labour market imperfections: barriers to employment of women and children on account of status, or reluctance to work outside the farm [*Bardhan*, 1973: 1380]. Family labour and off-farm labour are not always coterminous. Social convention may determine the allocation of tasks, dependent on class, caste and gender status.

Neither hypothesis (that family and hired labour are exclusively separate categories so that family labour becomes a datum to the cultivating household, or that they are perfect substitutes so that the wage rate measures opportunity cost) is then justified. The wage rate is only one determinant of labour use and possibly not the most important factor [*Bharadwaj*, 1974b: A–18].

A second major criticism directed at the Sen model is an extension of the above argument. Clearly, farms are neither exclusively family labour-based nor wage labour-based, but this can be taken further: examination of the FMS data shows that the proportion of exclusively family labour farms is negligible among large farms (and not even very high among small farms) so that the labour allocation pattern posited by Sen on such farms cannot be used as a firm basis for an explanation of the inverse relation over the entire range of farm size. Hired labour is necessary beyond ten acres. Once 15 acres is reached, the fixed quantity of family labour wears thin (per acre use of family labour is negligible both on 15 acre and 50 acre farms, with both depending on hired labour). So the use of family labour cannot be used as an explanation of higher productivity on 15 acre as against 50 acre farms.

More explicitly neoclassical models exist which posit different sets of factor prices facing small and large farms as an explanation for the inverse relationship [*Srinivasan, 1973; Bardhan,* 1973; *Griffin,* 1974; *Bhalla,* 1979; *Berry and Cline,* 1979]. Here, the explanation involves optimal use of factor inputs in the context of relative scarcity: factor prices differ between large and small farms, such that the effective prices of land and capital are low for the former and the effective price of labour is low for the latter. The presence of relatively abundant family labour on small farms and the relatively low implicit price of land for large farmers dictate choices of technique with different factor intensities. Thus small farms have high labour/land ratios, whereas large farms use labour and land less intensively. Small farms with a lower opportunity cost of labour can exploit more marginal land, cultivate a larger proportion of their land, and achieve higher yields.

The thesis of differential factor prices between large and small farms is highly problematic. If indeed factor price differentials were the main explanatory mechanism at work, then we would expect to find higher capital intensities on large farms manifested in technological innovation, both biochemical and mechanical. However, as we will see later, in this context the inverse relationship breaks down. Indeed, this hypothesis would appear to be more appropriate as an explanation for the non-existence of an inverse relationship rather than its cause. Further, the supposed ability of small farmers to exploit more marginal land (because of a lower opportunity cost of labour) is hardly conducive to higher crop yields.

BEYOND THE MARGINALIST APPROACH: THE DEVELOPMENT OF A CLASS-THEORETIC FRAMEWORK

One common element between the Sen model and these more explicitly pricist variants is that they share the same marginalist conceptions and categories. The critical problems arise from the production function methodology employed. The only difference between Sen's model and the factor market imperfection theories mentioned above is that the latter consider all relative factor prices whereas Sen considers only one price: the cost of labour, which varies according to the system of production.

An important point of criticism of both the Sen model and the neoclassical variants concerns the simplifying assumption of a single crop and a single production cycle, which misses entirely the crucial significance of cropping intensity and cropping pattern. Thus, we see that both models are geared to explaining a non-existent relationship: while the inverse relationship can be observed in value terms, no such relationship exists with respect to the physical yields of individual crops. Of course, the models can be respecified to look at total value of crop output and labour input intensity, with a strong relationship between cropping intensity and labour application.

Production function studies, however, suffer from the problem that they are estimated with flow measures, which obscures the role of indivisibilities in agricultural production [*Sen,* 1981: 204]. The whole exercise of comparing marginal product and wage rates is meaningless for agricultural production, which is very different from industrial production. Agricultural production is sequential in nature, subdivided both temporally and operationally. The production cycle in agriculture is prolonged and varies greatly between crops. No straightforward marginal productivity rules can be applied here as the productivity of family labour inputs prior to harvest time will depend on the timely application of the necessary amount of labour during the harvesting period. Labour demand at the harvesting stage is largely determined by elements of previous stages. Labour at earlier stages thus has to be seen in the nature of fixed costs. Labour demand at harvest is a derived demand dependent on conditions earlier in the production cycle. Under such conditions, the meaning of the marginal product of labour in agriculture becomes extremely hazy almost to the point of becoming operationally useless [*Roy,* 1979: 20–23].

A second common element is that both approaches assume the same production function for all farm sizes and systems of production. Both peasant and capitalist farms are assumed to be operating on the same production function. Sen focuses on two different systems of production (small peasant farms and large capitalist farms), which have fundamental differences in their organisation of production and qualitative differences in their division of labour. It is not obvious therefore why these two systems are located on the same production function (the same marginal product of labour curve).

Indeed, Sen himself was later to admit: 'it is illegitimate to eulogize peasant farming on the basis of an analysis in which every type of farm has access to the same production function and to the same factors of production' [1966: 444]. A peasant farmer may be constricted to a less efficient set of production conditions including lack of access to economies of scale, lack of technical knowledge or access to particular factors, or risk aversion to using new inputs.

The use of a single production function to compare two very different systems of farming, points to the identification problem at the heart of the Sen model and its disciples. This concerns the assumption that large farms are capitalist farms, and small farms are peasant family labour-based farms.

This conceptual sleight of hand obscures the real relations at work which produce the inverse relation. This crucial point is further discussed below when we turn to a class-based approach to analysing the inverse relation. We must go deeper than the size of holding categories to the underlying social relations of production, in the dynamic context of agrarian transition.

Three possible explanations in terms of factor intensity have been posited: (1) labour input, (2) cropping intensity, and (3) choice of crop mix. A key point in the debate over the causal factors behind the inverse relationship, but one that is more often ignored or obscured, is which of these explanations is determinant? These findings are clearly inter-related, but what is the direction of causality? No simple econometric analysis can tell us the answer.

There are two possible interpretations however. The first, labour-based approach, we have already surveyed critically. The second is that it is higher cropping intensity and a cropping pattern associated with either higher labour absorption or remuneration (and hence the higher income derived from production) which implies greater factor use intensity, in particular labour intensity. Bharadwaj [1974b: A–16], indeed, suggests that value productivity differentials between farms boil down to the differential cropping intensity components of crop patterns. Here, the primary motivation is output maximisation, with cropping intensity appearing as the proximate cause of the inverse relation. Higher cropping intensities imply a higher intensity in the application of other factors of production, particularly labour.

Bharadwaj [1974b: A–16] notes from the FMS evidence that while there is a strong inverse relationship between labour input and size, this is not manifested in terms of individual crops. An explanation in terms of efficient factor substitution is undermined by the fact that there is no such relationship between labour productivity and size to be found in the FMS data.

Chattopadhyay and Rudra [1976: A–114], although taking a rather eclectic view of the inverse relationship, make the following powerful and incisive statement which takes us beyond the confines of the marginalist approach:

> Among the forces that drive a small farmer to more intensive effort the most important one, of course, is his need for survival. There is a certain basic minimum of consumption that a poor peasant family has to have without which it will be simply wiped out. It is only understandable that such a poor peasant family, depending on a small piece of land, submerged in a vast population of surplus labour in the countryside, and thus not having any alternative sources of employment and income, would try to produce the maximum output on his piece of land. He would not only ignore any marginal productivity calculations insofar as

family labour is concerned, he would employ hired labour whenever necessary to supplement family labour, and in doing that would pay no heed to marginal productivities. He would also try to apply non-labour and non-monetised inputs with maximum intensity, once again by using labour without any calculations. He would try to improve the quality of land by small-scale irrigation and other such means as can be procured with the help of labour. He will tend to leave fallow as little land as possible, and try to cultivate as many crops as possible and choose such crops which after meeting his minimum consumption needs would meet his minimum cash needs ... the tendency to intensify his effort would be all the more so [under sharecropping] because of the fact that he has now to meet his minimum needs with only a share of the results of his effort.

Despite the criticisms of the methodology and assumptions employed in Sen's labour utilisation model and the neoclassical 'pricist' variants, the former does have the great merit of attempting to locate an explanation of the inverse relationship in terms of the different conditions of production facing farm households. These Sen explores within the logic of what he calls the 'mode of production of Indian agriculture' and its correlation with farm size [1962: 245]. However, his notion of mode of production is conceptually nebulous and constrained by its choice theoretic framework based on relative resource endowments. There is clearly a need to go beyond farm size as the relevant stratifying variable to examine the underlying relations and forces of production.

The class-based approach proceeds from the proposition that the peasant farm is embedded in the socio-economic context of an emerging capitalist agriculture in which however, non-capitalist forms of surplus appropriation are still prevalent. Such a transitional state has been described by Bhaduri [1973] and Bharadwaj [1974b] as one of semi-feudalism, a situation in which the relations of production have more in common with feudalism than capitalism.

Agriculture remains backward inasmuch as 'the process of commercialisation has not culminated necessarily or rapidly in the pervasive dominance of capitalist relations' [*Bharadwaj*, 1985: 9]. The process of commercialisation has intensified peasant differentiation but has not generated a qualitatively changed peasantry: it has not resulted in a fully-formed capitalist agriculture in which rich peasants are transformed into capitalist farmers and poor peasants into wage labourers. Neither commercialisation nor the development of wage labour, however, are sufficient conditions for the development of capitalist agriculture.

This directly addresses Sen's and other writers' erroneous identification, on the basis of the labour-hiring criterion alone, of the large farms in their samples with capitalist farms. That identification needs an altogether more complex specification. The transition from rich peasant to capitalist farmer cannot simply be assumed (as it is generally in many studies of the inverse relationship) – it requires demonstration. While the use of wage labour and market participation may be important indications of processes of agrarian transition, the evidence contained in Bhaduri, Bharadwaj, Patnaik and others, of the lack of capital intensification on large farms, and of the continued existence of unfree relations between labour hirers and workers would suggest that Sen's (and others') elision of rich peasant/capitalist farmer is invalid.

It is within the context of a backward agriculture that we must seek the factors that give rise to and sustain the inverse relationship. Within a semi-feudal agriculture, the dominant classes are able to intensify and maximise surplus extraction from subordinate classes via interlocking modes of exploitation. By interlinking transactions in more than one market, the dominant class can maximise the rate of exploitation over time.

Here then is a very powerful mechanism, rooted in the social relations of production of an essentially pre-capitalist mode of production, that drives poor peasants to maximise output because their survival depends upon it. It would appear therefore that the factors *driving* poor peasants to intensify labour effort are more important than the factors *permitting* them to do so. The inverse relationship cannot be understood in terms of scale advantages among isolated farms, or simply in terms of the poverty and unemployment facing poor peasants. The inverse relationship arises because of factors which are related to farm size, but not because of some independent size effect *per se*. It is thus misguided to treat the inverse relationship as a sign of relative efficiency rather than of distress. Chattopadhyay and Rudra [1976: A–115] conclude: 'if the inverse relationship be made the basis of a policy for preserving small farmers as they are, the result would be the destitution and expropriation of poor peasants ... '. At the other end of the class spectrum, rich peasants, who have not yet been transformed into capitalist farmers, use the *same* technology, but with much lower labour intensity, and thus achieve lower yields.

THE BREAKDOWN OF THE INVERSE RELATIONSHIP IN THE DYNAMIC CONTEXT

We turn now to a further set of considerations that need to be taken into account: the essentially static nature of the Sen approach. The extension of a static result from a given set of unchanging circumstances to a dynamic context is invalid. The most significant change is likely to be with respect to technology.

In those areas where we find an inverse relationship, it is the case that all farm sizes have access to a more or less similar technology. Large and small farms use the same set of production inputs, and small farms achieve higher output per acre via far higher cropping intensities which in turn imply higher application of labour effort per acre. With the introduction of a new technology which favours large farms due to its associated economies of scale, then the so-called advantage which the small farms have with respect to labour input intensity, may be matched or more than matched by the new advantages which large farms have with respect to technology. In this situation, we might expect the inverse relationship to break down and eventually disappear, and with it part of the case for redistributive land reform.

In terms of the class-based approach, which is essentially a dynamic theory, with the development of the forces of production in the form of green revolution technology rich peasants are better placed to reap the benefits. When the new technology is transferred from laboratory test beds and research stations to agrarian production, large farmers benefit disproportionately. Institutions and services (extension, credit, input/output prices, information, marketing) and political power exhibit a strong bias in favour of large farmers who are the early adopters and therefore early gainers in terms of high output prices and low (subsidised) input prices [*Byres, 1972*].

Rich peasants have the resources, which poor peasants lack, to gain access to the package of new inputs (HYV seeds, chemical fertilisers, plant protection materials), and are able to monopolise the available credit necessary to purchase the green revolution package. Rich peasants dominate the institutions which supply and distribute the new inputs. While these biochemical inputs may be scale neutral, their adoption steps up pressures for mechanisation which has associated scale economies. This leads to the breakdown of the inverse relation with large capitalist farmers achieving higher yields.

The empirical evidence supports the proposition that following the introduction of the green revolution technology, the inverse relationship breaks down, markedly so in those areas where the new technology has penetrated most deeply: Chadha [1978] and Roy [1979] examine evidence from the Punjab to show a significant transition to modern capitalist agriculture. They divide Punjab into three heterogenous zones: the relatively backward eastern Punjab, the more recently advanced central districts, and the advanced western Punjab. The district regressions of yield on farm size show an inverse relationship still significant in the eastern zone, insignificant for the central zone, with the western Punjab exhibiting a statistically significant positive relation between output per acre and net cropped area. The fact that the inverse relationship is no longer in evidence in the latter region *despite* the still significant inverse relationship between cropping intensity and farm size suggests that large farmers have attained important scale advantages.

The hypothesis supported by Roy [1979; 1981] is that during the early period of transition, the institutional bias in favour of large farmers ensures that they are the first adopters of the new green revolution technology. Scale advantages become more important in the post adoption period, with large farmers maintaining high investment and growth rates. Thus, rather than small farmers being able to catch up, the initial advantages captured by large farmers are further strengthened over time due to intrinsic scale advantages.

THE INVERSE RELATIONSHIP IN THE EGYPTIAN CONTEXT

In an earlier contribution [*Dyer,* 1991], I presented a preliminary analysis of my fieldwork on the inverse relationship in the context of Egyptian agriculture. This work and the subsequent Ph.D. thesis [*Dyer,* 1995] were directly inspired by the class analytical framework suggested by T.J. Byres. Space here prevents me presenting the results in any great detail, but the broad outlines of my findings are as follows.

First, I showed that the evolution of cross-class land productivity in Egyptian agriculture was regionally heterogeneous [*Dyer,* 1989; 1991]. In a disaggregated study of ILO data for 18 villages in 1976 [*Radwan and Lee,* 1986], I was able to show that while some villages continued to exhibit an inverse relationship, others seemed to have experienced a breakdown and disappearance of that relationship. There was a high degree of correlation between the latter villages and areas of the Egyptian countryside which had experienced the development of capitalist relations and forces of production.

Later, I was able to identify in much greater detail the mechanisms adduced by political economy that lay behind the evolution of cross-class productivity indicated [*Dyer,* 1995; 1996]. At the heart of the analysis were processes of peasant differentiation and the important role played by the Egyptian state in the institutional development of the agrarian sector, in particular the relationship between rich peasants and the co-operative system.

After 1952, all land reform recipients had to join the co-operative system, at first confined to land reform areas. By the 1980s, there were over 5,000 agricultural co-operatives covering approximately three million farm families [*Rochin and Grossman,* 1985]. Rich peasants were able to dominate the co-operatives, especially those set up in non-land reform areas after 1963. The Egyptian state simply did not have the cadre to carry out such a massive extension without relying extensively on the local dominant classes [*Richards,* 1982]. Even where poor peasants were represented on co-operative boards, they were highly vulnerable to rich peasant pressure and bribery. Poor peasants are dependent on rich peasants for land, labour, input purchases, crop sales, cash loans, and intercession with state authorities [*Adams,* 1986]. These ties of dependence mean that the bulk of poor peasants have been 'captured' – not by the state – but by the rich peasants.

Rich peasants were able to use their direct or indirect control of co-operative boards to help themselves to co-operative supplies and monopolise tractors and other mechanised inputs, excluding the poor as systematically as a price system in an environment of unequal resource endowments would have done. Similar efforts characterised the subsidised credit programmes as well: most peasants could not gain access to medium and long term loans under the borrowing criteria set. The critical investment loans for livestock and machinery remained predicated on property, producing a large farm bias in the provision of credit.

By advancing loans to all farmers on the basis of the size of their cultivated crop, the Egyptian state clearly engaged in the unequal subsidisation of large farms. Those with less than five feddans, the vast majority of farms, received only half the credit advanced by the co-operative system, while the small minority of farms with over five feddans collected some 44 per cent of the total [*Sadowski,* 1991].

This rich peasant bias in access to co-operative and village bank credit resources also has important implications for the pattern of diffusion of modern technology in Egyptian agriculture. On the basis of their institutional control, large farms were able to obtain inputs before other farm households, the timely supply of such inputs constituting a major bottleneck and a condition of high productivity. Ownership of tractors, and other modern farm equipment such as irrigation technology, is strongly correlated with farm size, as Abdel-Fadil [1995] shows, with tractors being too large and indivisible an investment for poor and middle peasants. Tractor loans require collateral of at least five feddans and a 25 per cent down payment, and water pumps a collateral of three feddans. However, use of tractors via the private rental market was more widespread: in the 1981 agricultural census for Qena governorate in Upper Egypt, while only 2,500 farms owned or shared tractors, some 2,500 farms rented tractors from the public sector, and over 98,000 farms (66 per cent) rented tractor time from the private sector [*Ministry of Agriculture,* 1985].

As Abdel-Fadil [1995] notes, machine rental has become increasingly important as a mode of surplus extraction: those who own machinery rent to others on a piecemeal basis in return for cash or crop share. The profitability of such operations is enhanced by subsidised fuel, oil and machine purchase. Further, rental prices are set fairly high through tacit collusion between machine owners. Over the last 15 years or so, the emphasis has been on machine accumulation rather than land accumulation, reinforcing and accentuating the distinction between large and small farms. Such mechanisation reinforces the power and position of the rich peasants and the choice of technology reflects their perceived interests. In the past, reciprocal labour exchange between small peasant farms solved labour availability problems at peak periods, but mechanisation and monetisation have produced a pattern of hired labour with a high correlation between degree of mechanisation and hired labour use [*Hopkins et al., 1982*]. The benefits of tractorisation can be seen in terms of increased cropping intensity and yields, providing more flexibility in the cropping pattern, timeliness, and cost savings. In particular, mechanisation has increased the cropping intensity of rich peasants. The pattern of improved yields corresponds to the pattern of highly mechanised villages. Of course, what is important are the factors which generate differences in mechanisation levels in the first place [*El Sahrigi and Shepley,* 1984; 1985].

None the less, the diffusion of mechanisation throughout Egypt is very uneven. Levels of mechanisation vary considerably within and between villages according to the degree of social differentiation, and the unevenly distributed power of the rich peasantry in the Egyptian countryside, itself unevenly distributed. This heterogeneity has had profound implications for agrarian transition in Egypt. Dyer [1995; 1996] delineates two paths of agrarian transition from semi-feudalism in Egypt: a capitalist path (using hired wage labour and machinery) and a path dominated by petty commodity production with small farms producing for the market. In these studies, I provide a typology of villages reflecting these different paths of agrarian transition in Egypt: (1) land reform or resettlement villages which have moved in the direction of intensification of petty commodity production; and (2) villages in which capitalist agriculture and the emergence of capitalist relations of production around wage labour have appeared (see also Hopkins [1987] who identifies four possible paths for the Egyptian case).

Land reform villages are dominated by family farms of three to five feddans dependent on the use of intensive family labour. The effect of land reform here is to maintain the 'traditional' family farm as the unit of production and link it to the market through co-operatives. Larger farmers are not qualitatively different from smaller farmers, just quantitatively differentiated. These villages, characterised by small scattered land possessions, prohibit the application of modern technology and lead to the fragile formation of capitalism. Land fragmentation weakens their ability to adopt new agricultural methods, and intensify capital utilisation. Thus, land reform had the effect of slowing down capital accumulation, dampening the rate at which farm units are able to save and invest.

Direct state influence was certainly much stronger in land reform areas than elsewhere, where co-operatives were more easily dominated by rich peasants. Villages in which rich peasants have been able to accumulate land and other means of production such as machinery have exhibited a different outcome: increased social differentiation and the potential disappearance of small farmers rather than their survival. The capitalist villages have relatively greater concentration of land, larger area and population, and higher levels of mechanisation. Such villages also benefit from development efforts in the form of loans for machinery and other modern inputs. The mode of production changes because capital has penetrated the village and changes the system of production instead of being merely externally imposed via market relations. The family farm gives way to larger enterprises based on wage labour and the intensive use of machine inputs.

Within the uneven development of the Egyptian countryside, rich peasants are in many cases not 'technically more efficient' based on their use of modern technology. On the contrary, in those areas of relatively backward agriculture, rich peasants use essentially the same traditional technology as the poor and middle peasants, thus generating the circumstances under which an inverse relationship arises: with all farm sizes using more or less the same techniques of production, the higher cropping intensities of poor peasants (less than three feddans) which imply higher labour use intensities and higher value yields, have generated an inverse relationship between holding size and land productivity.

Only in areas where rich peasants have transformed themselves into a class of capitalist farmers are they more efficient, producing the conditions for a breakdown in the inverse relationship. In the capitalist regions, the significantly advanced level of the productive forces has allowed rich peasants to reap important scale advantages which more than outweigh the still higher labour and cropping intensities of poor peasant farms. The development of the forces of production here includes significantly different cropping patterns as well as use of modern inputs.

Thus, in the dynamic context of the development of both the relations and forces of production, in the shape of new technology, the inverse relationship breaks down and disappears. Rich peasants are able to capture the gains from the new technology, and with increased accumulation develop into capitalist farmers [Dyer, 1991]. These findings would seem to lay to rest the possibility of employing the inverse relationship evidence in favour of redistributive land reform.

REFERENCES

Abdel-Fadil, M., 1995, 'Class Differentiation and the Evolution of Agrarian Relations in Rural Egypt in the Liberal Era (1975-90)', Paper presented at the International Conference on Agricultural Productivity and Economic Development, Trondheim University, June 1995.

Adams, R.H., 1986, *Development and Social Change in Rural Egypt*, New York: Syracuse University Press.

Bardhan, P.K., 1973, 'Size, Productivity, and Returns to Scale: An Analysis of Farm-Level Data in Indian Agriculture', *Journal of Political Economy*, Vol.18, Dec.

Berry, R.A. and W.R. Cline, 1979, *Agrarian Structure and Productivity in Developing Countries*, Baltimore, MD: Johns Hopkins University Press.

Bhaduri, A., 1973, 'A Study in Agricultural Backwardness Under Semi-Feudalism', *Economic Journal*, Vol.83, March.

Bhagwati, J.N. and S.J. Chakravarty, 1969, 'Contributions to Indian Economic Analysis: A Survey', *American Economic Review*, Vol.59 No.4, Part 2, Supplement.

Bhalla, S.S., 1979, 'Farm Size, Productivity and Technical Change in Indian Agriculture', in Berry and Cline [1979].

Bharadwaj, K., 1974a, *Production Conditions in Indian Agriculture*, Cambridge: Cambridge University Press.

Bharadwaj, K., 1974b, 'Notes on Farm Size and Productivity', *Economic and Political Weekly*, Review of Agriculture, Vol.9, No.13.

Bharadwaj, K., 1985, 'A View of Commercialisation in Indian Agriculture and the Development of Capitalism', *Journal of Peasant Studies*, Vol.12, No.4.

Bhattacharya, N. and G.R. Saini, 1972, 'Farm Size and Productivity – A Fresh Look', *Economic and Political Weekly*, Review of Agriculture, Vol.7, No.26.

Binswanger, H.P. and K. Deininger, 1993, 'South African Land Policy: The Legacy of History and Current Options', *World Development*, Vol.21, No.9.

Byres, T.J., 1972, 'The Dialectic of India's Green Revolution', *South Asian Review*, Vol.5, No.2.

Byres, T.J., 1974, 'Land Reform, Industrialisation and the Marketed Surplus in India: An Essay on the Power of Rural Bias', in David Lehmann (ed.), *Agrarian Reform and Agrarian Reformism*, London: Faber & Faber.

Byres, T.J., 1977a, 'Output Per Acre and Size of Holding: The Logic of Peasant Agriculture Under Semi-Feudalism'. Paper presented at the IDS Rupag Seminar Programme, and in modified form at ISS, The Hague, April 1979.

Byres, T.J., 1977b, 'Agrarian Transition and the Agrarian Question', *Journal of Peasant Studies*, Vol.4 No.3.

Byres, T.J., 1981, 'The New Technology, Class Formation and Class Action in the Indian Countryside', *Journal of Peasant Studies*, Vol.8, No.4.

Byres, T.J., 1986a, 'The Agrarian Question and Differentiation of the Peasantry', Foreword to Atiur Rahman, *Peasants and Classes. A Study in Differentiation in Bangladesh*, London and New Jersey: Zed Books.

Byres, T.J., 1986b, 'The Agrarian Question, Forms of Capitalist Agrarian Transition and the State: An Essay with Reference to Asia', *Social Scientist*, Vol.14, Nos.11–12.

Byres, T.J., 1990, 'The Agrarian Question and Differing Forms of Capitalist Agrarian Transition: An Essay with Reference to Asia', in Jan Breman and Sudipto Mundle (eds.), *Rural Transformation in Asia*, New Delhi and Oxford: Oxford University Press.

Byres, T.J., 1991, "Agrarian Question, The" and "Peasantry", in Tom Bottomore *et al.* (eds.), *A Dictionary of Marxist Thought* (2nd edition), Oxford: Blackwell.

Byres, T.J. and G. Dyer, (forthcoming), *The Logic of Peasant Agriculture Under Semi-Feudalism.*

Chadha, G.K., 1978, 'Farm Size and Productivity Revisited – Some Notes from Recent Experience of Punjab', *Economic and Political Weekly*, Review of Agriculture, Vol.13, No.9.

Chattopadhyay, M. and A. Rudra, 1976, 'Size-Productivity Revisited', *Economic and Political Weekly*, Review of Agriculture, Vol.11, No.39.

Chayanov, A.V., 1966, *The Theory of Peasant Economy*, Homewood, IL: The American Economic Association.

Cornia, G.A., 1985, 'Farm Size, Land Yields and the Agricultural Production Function: An

Analysis for Fifteen Developing Countries', *World Development*, Vol.13, No.4.

Dyer, G.D., 1989, 'Agrarian Transition in Egypt: Technological Change in Egyptian Agriculture and Its Impact on the Relation between Farm Size and Productivity', unpublished M.Phil. thesis, University of Cambridge.

Dyer, G.D., 1991, 'Farm Size – Farm Productivity Re-examined: Evidence from Rural Egypt', *Journal of Peasant Studies*, Vol.19, No.1.

Dyer, G.D., 1995, 'Farm Size and Productivity in Egyptian Agriculture: An Analysis of Agrarian Structure and Technical Change', unpublished Ph.D. thesis, London University.

Dyer, G.D., 1996, *Class, State and Agricultural Productivity in Egypt*, London: Frank Cass & Co.

El Sahrigi, A.F. and S.C. Shepley, 1984, 'Farm Equipment Manufacture in Egypt', *Egypt Agricultural Mechanization Project*, Cairo: ARE Ministry of Agriculture.

El Sahrigi, A.F. and S.C. Shepley, 1985, 'Socio-Economic Evaluation of Farm Machinery Introduced in Project Villages from 1980 to December 1984', *Egypt Agricultural Mechanization Project, Working Paper No.19*, Cairo: ARE/USAID.

Ghose, A.K., 1979, 'Farm Size and Land Productivity in Indian Agriculture: A Reappraisal', *Journal of Development Studies*, Vol.16, No.1.

Griffin, K., 1974, *The Political Economy of Agrarian Change*, London: Macmillan.

Hopkins, N.S., 1987, *Agrarian Transformation in Egypt*, Cairo: AUC Press.

Hopkins, N.S., Mehanna, S.R. and B.M. Abdel Maksoud, 1982, 'The State of Agricultural Mechanization in Egypt: Results of a Survey 1982', *Agricultural Mechanization Project*, Cairo: ARE Ministry of Agriculture/USAID.

Khan, M.H., 1979, 'Farm Size and Land Productivity Relationships in Pakistan', *Pakistan Development Review*, Vol.18, No.1.

Khusro, A.M., 1964, 'Returns to Scale in Indian Agriculture', *Indian Journal of Agricultural Economics*, Vol.19, Nos.3–4.

Lipton, M., 1993, 'Land Reform as Commenced Business: The Evidence Against Stopping', *World Development*, Vol.21, No.4.

Lipton, M. and M. Lipton, 1993, 'Creating Rural Livelihoods: Some Lessons for South Africa from Experience Elsewhere', *World Development*, Vol.21, No.9.

Mazumdar, D., 1963, 'On the Economics of Relative Efficiency of Small Farmers', *Economic Weekly*, Vol.15, Nos.28–30.

Mellor, J.W., 1966, *The Economics of Agricultural Development*, Ithaca, NY: Cornell University Press.

Mellor, J.W. and B.F. Johnston, 1984, 'The World Food Equation: Interrelations among Development, Employment and Food Consumption', *Journal of Economic Literature*, Vol.22, No.2.

Ministry of Agriculture, 1985, *Nita'ig al-Ta'adad al-Zira'ai 'an al-Sinah al-Zira'aiah 1981–82, Muhafidhah Qena* (Agricultural Census 1981-2, Qena Governorate), Cairo.

Nolan, P., 1988, *The Political Economy of Collective Farms*, Cambridge: Basil Blackwell.

Patnaik, U., 1972, 'Economics of Farm Size and Farm Scale: Some Assumptions Re-Examined', *Economic and Political Weekly*, Vol.7, Nos.31–33.

Patnaik, U., 1979, 'Neo-Populism and Marxism: The Chayanovian View of the Agrarian Question and Its Fundamental Fallacy', *Journal of Peasant Studies*, Vol.6, No.4.

Patnaik, U., 1987, *Peasant Class Differentiation. A Study in Method with Reference to Haryana*, Delhi: Oxford University Press.

Radwan, S. and E. Lee, 1986, *Agrarian Change in Egypt: An Anatomy of Rural Poverty*, London: Croom Helm.

Rao, A.P., 1967, 'Size of Holding and Productivity', *Economic and Political Weekly*, Vol.2, No.44.

Rao, C.H.H., 1963, 'Farm Size and the Economics of Scale', *Economic Weekly*, Vol.15, No.51.

Rao, C.H.H., 1966, 'Alternative Explanations of the Inverse Relationship between Farm Size and Output Per Acre in India', *Indian Economic Review*, Vol.1, No.2.

Rao, C.H.H., 1968, 'Farm Size and Yield Per Acre – A Comment', *Economic and Political Weekly*, Vol.3, No.37.

Richards, A.R., 1982, *Egypt's Agricultural Development, 1800–1980*, Boulder, CO: Westview Press.

Rochin, R.I. and J.C. Grossman, 1985, 'Agricultural Cooperatives and Government Control in Egypt: A Historical and Statistical Assessment', Department of Agricultural Economics, University of California.

Roy, P.L., 1979, 'The Relation between Farm Size and Productivity in the Context of Alternative Modes of Production in Indian Agriculture', Ph.D. thesis, Delhi School of Economics, University of Delhi.

Roy, P.L., 1981, 'Transition in Agriculture: Empirical Indicators and Results (Evidence from Punjab, India)', *Journal of Peasant Studies*, Vol.8, No.2.

Rudra, A., 1968a, 'Farm Size and Yield Per Acre', *Economic and Political Weekly*, Vol.3, Nos.26–8.

Rudra, A., 1968b, 'More on Returns to Scale in Indian Agriculture', *Economic and Political Weekly*, Review of Agriculture, Vol.3, No.43.

Rudra, A., 1973, 'Allocative Efficiency of Indian Farmers: Some Methodological Problems', *Economic and Political Weekly*, Vol.8, No.3.

Rudra, A. and A.K. Sen, 1980, 'Farm Size and Labour Use: Analysis and Policy', *Economic and Political Weekly*, Vol.15, Nos.4–6.

Sadowski, Y.M., 1991, *Political Vegetables? Businessman and Bureaucrat in the Development of Egyptian Agriculture*, Washington DC: The Brookings Institution.

Saini, G.R., 1971, 'Holding Size, Productivity, and Some Related Aspects of Indian Agriculture', *Economic and Political Weekly*, Review of Agriculture, Vol.6, No.26.

Sen, A., 1981, 'Market Failure and Control of Labour Power: Towards An Explanation of "Structure" and Change in Indian Agriculture', *Cambridge Journal of Economics*, Vol.5, Nos.3–4.

Sen, A.K., 1962, 'An Aspect of Indian Agriculture', *Economic Weekly*, Vol.14, Nos.4–6.

Sen, A.K., 1964a, 'Size of Holdings and Productivity', *Economic Weekly*, Vol.16, No.18.

Sen, A.K., 1964b, 'Size of Holdings and Productivity – A Reply', *Economic Weekly*, Vol.16, No.18.

Sen, A.K., 1966, 'Peasants and Dualism with or without Surplus Labour', *Journal of Political Economy*, Vol.74, No.5.

Srinivasan, T.N., 1973, 'Farm Size and Productivity: Implications of Choice under Uncertainty', *Sankhya*, Series B, Vol.34, No.4.

Taslim, M.A., 1989, 'Supervision Problems and the Size-Productivity Relation in Bangladesh Agriculture', *Oxford Bulletin of Economics and Statistics*, Vol.51, No.1.

Communist Revolution and Peasant Mobilisation in the Hinterland of North China: The Early Years

R.G. TIEDEMANN

'If they [the peasants] become class conscious and arise in class struggle, our social revolution, Communism, will be assured. Therefore since they have this tendency, waiting for their natural, slow progress is not as good as using some man-made methods to accelerate them, thereby enabling them to become class-conscious a day earlier and avoid a day of suffering' – Anon. in *Gongchangdang* (7 April 1921).[1]

It is, of course, generally accepted that peasants were an essential factor in the successful staging of the Chinese Communist Revolution. It is assumed – especially in Chinese mainland historiography – that it was primarily Mao Zedong's ideas and actions in South and Central China in the late 1920s and early 1930s which laid the foundations for the shift of the revolution from the cities to the countryside. Moreover, after the Communist were forced to abandon their red bases in Central China in 1934, the revolution was successfully revived under Mao's leadership in Northwest China during the Anti-Japanese War (1937–45), culminating in Communist victory during the subsequent Civil War (1946–49). Thus, until a decade or two ago scholarly writings focused on Central China during the Jiangxi phase and on Northwest China during the Yan'an phase of the Chinese revolution, giving the impression that wherever Mao went, the revolution went also. It is only in recent times that some attention has been paid to Communist mobilisations in other parts of China, both prior to 1927 and during the war against Japan. As far as North China[2] is concerned, we now have studies for Huaibei [*Perry*, 1980]; Jin-Cha-Ji (that is, Shanxi, Chahar, Hebei) [*Hartford*, 1980]; Shandong [*Paulson*, 1982];[3] the Taihang mountains [*Thaxton*, 1983]; and Henan [*Wou*, 1994]. Indeed, some scholars are beginning to promote the idea that it was in the North China base areas

R.G. Tiedemann, Lecturer in the History of Modern China, School of Oriental and African Studies, University of London, Thornhaugh Street, Russell Square, London WC1H 0XG.

where the revolution was ultimately won, rather than in the much vaunted Shaan-Gan-Ning border region of the Northwest [*Goodman*, 1994: 1007–10, with respect to Jin-Ji-Lu-Yu (that is, Shanxi, Hebei, Shandong, Henan)]. However, while a more comprehensive record of the history of the Communist revolution in wartime North China is now in the making, far less is known about the earlier attempts at radical peasant mobilisation there in the 1920s. This contribution will, therefore, explore the origins of rural activism in North China, and more specifically the circumstances which brought together, albeit only briefly, revolutionaries and peasants in settings that had long been noted for their endemic rebelliousness. Consequently, a brief outline of the contextual factors that both facilitated and inhibited radical mobilisation is essential.

CONTEXTUAL VARIATIONS AND CHANGING SOCIAL ECOLOGIES

Certain parts of North China had a long tradition of collective violence, and it would be some of these violent collectivities that were to draw the attention of radical activists in the 1920s. In keeping with Skinner's concept of macro-regional cores and peripheries, spatial variations in the patterns of socio-economic differentiation were certainly prevalent within the North China macro-region. Topography and climate made the harsh environment that affected cropping patterns, tenurial relations and a host of other social institutions. Moreover, since at least the eighteenth century certain secular developments contributed to accelerating socio-economic change. These include rapid population growth and the attendant decline of the person–land ratio since the eighteenth century. Given the cultural requirement for a family to produce many sons, partible inheritance (that is, the absence of primogeniture) consequently was not uncommon. This meant that holdings became ever more fragmented over time. Demographic pressure in turn led to migration and the opening up of marginal lands, as well as the increasing need for wood fuel, led to deforestation, erosion and more frequent ecological disasters, aggravated by official corruption and administrative inefficiency that accompany dynastic decline. The massive mid nineteenth-century rebellions represent the first major shock during the Qing dynasty to the state and social structure.

Although reliable economic data is virtually nonexistent,[4] impressionistic accounts indicate that most peasants in northern China were poor, barely able to rise above subsistence level even in good years. There were, of course, variations in the extent of poverty and in the strategies which peasants employed to improve their chances of survival. While the majority of North China's peasants employed a variety of non-violent survival strategies (including sideline activities, begging, seasonal or permanent migration), in certain areas rural dwellers were more likely to turn to violent strategies. It is the latter which are of particular relevance to this contribution.

In her important study of rebellion and revolution in the Huaibei area, Elizabeth Perry [1980] has analysed certain chronic forms of *competitive* violence, consisting of either *predatory modes* (feud strife, traditional banditry, illegal production and distribution of salt) or *protective modes* (crop-watching societies, village fortification, armed self-defence organisations). Although feud strife was more common in south-eastern China [*Lamley*, 1977], this form of collective action was not unknown in North China. The parties to a feud usually fought over access to scarce resources. Property disputes tended to be associated with lineage feuds, whereas conflict arising from water management (irrigation, flood control) were more likely to involve entire communities (villages, districts, or the inhabitants of two different counties). Such strife could simmer for generations, intermittently exploding into open conflict over apparently trivial matters. It was intimately connected with litigation which was often merely the continuation of a feud by other means and 'an effective way of gaining revenge' [*Cohen*, 1966: 1214].

Banditry was the most prevalent and enduring form of rural violence in certain parts of the North China Plain. These predatory activities were not so much a response to particularly severe hardship, but part of a generally violent milieu. Here the inhabitants were more inclined than those in other parts of northern China to turn to violent survival strategies. Brigandage had long been an integral part of the local society, with bandits maintaining a symbiotic relationship with local communities. This clearly increased the problem of bandit suppression. The local civil and military authorities, lacking both the means and the inclination for bandit suppression, were notoriously ineffective [*Tiedemann*, 1982].

In response to the escalating predatory activities, rural dwellers devised certain protective strategies. Since the middle of the nineteenth century, crop-watching societies had been set up and a good many villages been surrounded by protective earth walls. Towards the end of the nineteenth century, a variety of local armed self-defence organisations emerged. However, as Perry [1980: 3–5, 94–5] has pointed out, in an unstable environment where the use of private violence was accepted, predatory and protective strategies could be employed simultaneously. While protecting *their* resources, it was not uncommon for such local groups to seek to acquire the resources of other, similar collectivities.

As noted above, in the late nineteenth century competitive violence tended to be concentrated only in certain areas of North China, namely at the provincial border districts on the North China Plain. Economic conditions and opportunities were not necessarily worse here than in other parts of North China's macro-regional periphery. The crucial factor which permitted violence to break out and persist in these districts was of a geopolitical nature, namely their strategic location at the administrative peripheries, as the North China Plain is dissected by the boundaries of five provinces, resulting in notorious lacunae of state power in late imperial times. In this economic and political hinterland the inhabitants had long ago acquired a reputation for violence [*Tiedemann*, 1991: 51–2].

In many ways, the environment in the North China border districts was similar to that of Sicily, where 'the use of violence and intimidation was part of the regional culture; the capacity to coerce with physical violence was valued in itself' [*Blok*, 1974: 172]. The crucial factor in this situation was the State's failure to monopolise the use of physical violence. The lack of effective government control in the North China border areas was attributable to several factors. First of all, there was an underlying secular trend of general administrative deterioration during the late Qing and early republic. Magistrates, expecting rapid turnover, preferred to keep a low profile rather than intervene in conflicts and risk demotion and dismissal [*Kuhn*, 1975: 262]. Furthermore, the local official's position was weak in the border districts, because he lacked adequate forces of repression. The notoriously corrupt and oppressive underlings in the county *yamen*, for their part, were more likely to provoke unrest than reduce it. Moreover, in view of the paucity of degree holders in these areas, the State could not rely on local elites to act as informal representatives of the State [*Wakeman*, 1975: 2, 4; *Kuhn*, 1975: 260–62].

In imperial times local notables in the peripheral areas lacked, moreover, the ties with provincial and national elites that would have enabled them to settle local disputes by calling in the forces of repression. To the contrary, in spite of widespread internal factional conflict, the inhabitants of these districts – the local elite included – tended to unite to resist all encroachments from the outside. This paradox of internal conflict and parochial solidarity to preserve local autonomy was and remained the most important characteristic of the North China border regions. However, in the early twentieth century the traditional forms of violence began to spread from the peripheries into hitherto peaceful core areas. Furthermore, the escalation of competitive conflict now was intimately linked with the rise of more spontaneous forms of collective violence, namely fiscal conflicts and food riots. Such *reactive* violence occurred wherever local rights were violated or vested interests threatened, and was symptomatic of the late Qing state-building New Policies reforms.

This process of 'state' penetration of rural society accelerated dramatically after the 1911 Revolution, and more destructively with the advent of the warlord era. The warlord period is a most confusing chapter in the history of modern China. Military rule and consequent political fragmentation began in 1916 with the disintegration of the Beiyang Army in the North, and was aggravated by the independent actions taken by non-Beiyang militarists in the South. Since it was necessary to maintain a large and effective fighting force to contain or destroy rival factions, militarists and their civilian subordinates extracted enormous revenues from the local inhabitants. The collection of a multitude of exorbitant taxes was inevitably accompanied by extortion and confiscation.

In addition to the economic disruptions caused by excessive taxation, the inhabitants of warlord China were also exposed to the more direct destructive aspects of warlord conflict. During the interminable clashes and confrontations between warlord factions, the civilian population suffered loss of life, crops and property. Retreating armies looted the area before leaving it, followed by a new regime of terror by the victorious troops. Peasants were forced to supply food, quarters, draft animals, and carts. Young men had to accompany military expeditions as coolies, and were left destitute in distant places with little prospect of returning to their homes. Refusal to accede to military demands invited looting, burning, raping and killing by undisciplined troops. Perhaps not surprisingly, this process of increasing intrusion of a weak centralising state as an extractive institution occurred simultaneously with the significant escalation of lawlessness in local society. The dramatic decline of law and order and the rapaciousness of what passed for 'the state' had a significant effect on the rural population, affecting local elites and masses alike. Prasenjit Duara [1987] has called this paradoxical pattern 'state involution'.

As long as the major warlord factions were preoccupied with defending or acquiring strategic and lucrative bases, a large number of what might be termed 'marginal' militarists were able to lead a relatively autonomous existence in the less desirable interstices of power, thereby adding greatly to the instability of rural China. These 'mini-warlords' were generally even less interested in maintaining a degree of stability in their base areas and ruthlessly extracted as much as they could before moving into another area.

These smaller military formations were difficult to distinguish from bandit gangs, especially since they drifted back and forth between warlordism and pure banditry. Given the widespread disorder during the years of military separatism (that is, warlordism), it is not surprising that banditry reached unprecedented proportions. Furthermore, a dramatic change in the nature of brigandage can be observed. Whereas in the nineteenth century traditional bandits had to some extent adhered to the principle of 'social banditry', the brigands of the 1920s employed far more brutal and indiscriminate strategies. This new type of predatory activity has been aptly called 'soldier banditry' [*Billingsley*, 1988; *Tiedemann*, 1982]. Soldier bandits were for the most part the casualties of the ever shifting constellations of warlord cliques and factions. Deserting, disbanded and defeated troops were the main contributors to this phenomenon.

As a result of the breakdown of the state's repressive capacity during the warlord era, the rural inhabitants reacted to pandemic banditry and oppressive military exactions by establishing or reviving local self-defence groups. Although in reality the distinctions were not so clear-cut, we can distinguish three basic types of protective organisations for analytical purposes: (1) regular county-level militia units (*mintuan*); (2) so-called 'village federations' (*lianzhuanghui*); and (3) the so-called 'semi-religious' self-defence organisations [*Tai*, 1985: 82–4; *Perry*, 1980: 178–80]. It is the last-named group which is of particular significance to this contribution. These semi-religious defensive associations appeared under a bewildering variety of names such as Red Spears, Red Flags, White Flags, Yellow Sands, Big and Small Knives, Heavenly Gates.[5]

Such protective collectivities, commonly referred to as Red Spear associations, were generally not organised by members of the upper rural elite, but by local power holders of lesser prominence. These Red Spear-type groups were neither 'religious sects' nor 'secret societies' or the 'sworn-brotherhood' type, but essentially local community self-defence organisations that employed certain 'heterodox' elements in their preparatory rituals (certain formulae of which were said to be 'secret'). They would seek the assistance of travelling religious and/or martial arts specialists who would teach them spells and incantations designed to make the rustic fighters invulnerable to sword cuts and rifle bullets. Membership in these village organisations was usually compulsory. Describing a Red Spear Society near Tai'an (Shandong), Sidney Gamble [1963: 302] observed that 'The Society became practically one of the village activities, with the village head leading it, with most of the villagers enrolled as members and with the organized groups giving protection against soldiers and bandits.' These Red Spear-type organisations were most prominent in Henan, but were also quite common in Shandong and southern Zhili.

The areas where rural self-defence associations were most prominent were also areas with a long history of internal competitive conflict. Hence it is not surprising that the semi-religious self-defence organisations, too, were plagued by internal and external rivalries. This helps explain why there was such a great diversity of names for defensive collectivities. Some such protective groups might even make temporary alliances with a warlord faction to fight against another local self-defence league. Such short-lived alliances were dictated by local inter-group rivalries and tended to be opportunistic in nature. Although self-defence organisations were established primarily in response to escalating traditional group violence, they often became the instrument of elite resistance to demands by the state. As early as 1922 there were indications that the local self-defence associations could be mobilised also against oppressive taxation, corrupt officials, avaricious troops and military conscription. In the mid-1920s large-scale Red Spear uprisings against all authority were widespread in northern China [*Bianco*, 1972; *Perry*, 1980; *Slawinski*, 1972; *Tai*, 1985; *Wou*, 1994]. Their primary concern was the defence of local interests against all outsiders. Consequently, self-defence groups were willing to enter into temporary alliances with any force that was also engaged in fighting their entrenched oppressors.

Attacks by Red Spears and similar organisations were, however, not solely directed against outside oppressors, but also against the militarists' local representatives: the local police force, and those members of the upper elite who were collaborating with the warlords as tax collectors, hence the frequent clashes between Red Spears and the upper gentry-dominated local militia. Thus patterns of local violence were becoming ever more complex in the 1920s, containing both competitive and reactive forms [*Perry*, 1980]. Rural conflict in the 1920s was in many ways a continuation of the familiar pattern of traditional collective violence. People, especially in certain parts of northern China, were accustomed to employing violent survival strategies while at the same time exercising reactive solidarity against outsiders. In view of the multiple contradictions, the boundaries between the various types of collective action were often rather blurred. Local collectivities developed elaborate systems of alliances.

At this point a brief reference to the prevailing economic debate would seem to be in order. Reliable socio-economic data is scarce for inland North China, and especially for those areas of particular interest to this study. While it is generally agreed that economic factors played a significant role in the revolutionary mobilisations in the 1940s, there is considerable disagreement as to when conditions became intolerable in the Chinese countryside. Two major opposing views prevail. While some scholars have argued that rural conditions did not get worse until the 1930s, others have made a case for the long-term immiseration of the peasantry [*Huang*, 1985: 3–32]. Given the widespread dislocations caused by warlordism, and aggravated by a spate of severe natural disasters, it is difficult to accept the view that the 1920s were years of relative prosperity. Rather, it seems reasonable to argue that the decade saw the culmination of a gradual and long-term process of immiseration in inland North China. There is, however, general agreement that landlordism was not a major institution in North China [*Shepherd*, 1988], an issue of more immediate relevance to Communist mobilisation efforts.

Several things should be noted about traditional collective rural violence: (1) it was organised on a community basis or along kinship lines – not along class lines; (2) it was organised hierarchically by local power holders for the protection of parochial interests; (3) such groups were hostile towards or at least suspicious of outsiders. During the early republican period, the country was left in a political vacuum, and collective violence became pandemic. In the 1920s much of northern China was disrupted by frequent warlord struggles, civil war, soldier-banditry, and fierce resistance by local self-defence organisations against all outside predators. The various forms of social conflict were, however, still very much part of the traditional order, and its is impossible to distinguish within the above categories any form of collective violence that was amenable to a modern revolutionary movement. It is against this background of escalating predatory and protective violence that the embryonic Chinese Communist revolutionary movement made its first attempts at peasant mobilisation in North China.

COMMUNIST RURAL MOBILISATION

Although the role of the peasantry in revolutionary movements had been discussed at the Second Congress of the Communist International in 1920, as set out in the 'Theses on the Agrarian Question' [*Riddell*, 1991: 635–70, 949–59], the emerging Chinese Communist Party (CCP) promoted a strictly urban strategy of revolution in the early 1920s, advocating the establishment of party cells and mass organisations amongst the modern working class in the larger cities. Nevertheless, in South and Central China a few activists independently turned to the countryside at this time. The earliest peasant mobilisation was Shen Xuanlu's Yaqian Peasant Association in Xiaoshan District, Zhejiang province, in the summer of 1921 [*van de Ven*, 1991: 119–20], followed by Peng Pai's well known efforts in Haifeng, eastern Guangdong, in August 1922 [*Hofheinz*, 1977; *Marks*, 1984; *Galbiati*, 1985]. A year later local revolutionaries started a peasant movement in Hunan province [*Yokoyama*, 1975; *McDonald*, 1978], followed by Fang Zhimin's Xinjiang peasant movement in northeastern Jiangxi in 1924 [*Sheel*, 1989].

In North China, too, Communist cells were established in the larger cities in the early 1920s, with the northern bureau of the fledgling revolutionary movement situated in Beijing. The small band of Communist organisers operated secretly amongst railway workers along the Beijing–Hankou and Longhai railways, in a few mining centres and certain other relatively small-scale industrial establishments. Schoolteachers and middle and normal school students played an important role in these endeavours. Moreover, when some of these radical intellectuals returned to their native villages during vacations or upon completion of their studies, some of them began to spread the urban-centred revolutionary movement to the countryside,[6] relying on kinship or other local connections in these attempts. 'Because the peasants' primordial loyalty was directed toward kinship and community groups such tactics allowed the Communists to win the trust of the peasants, who otherwise would have been apprehensive about joining a Communist movement. To the peasants, these radical students were respected kin leaders' [Wou, 1994: 118]. However, these early activities could rarely be sustained in any meaningful way, as the pull of lineage and locale proved stronger than revolutionary commitment.

The CCP's commitment to peasant work increased in the mid-1920s, when Communist activists began to implement rural policies under the united front with the Guomindang (Nationalist Party) that had been arranged by the Soviet Union. Indeed, as early as 1923, the Comintern representative Mikhail Borodin had advised Sun Yat-sen to start a peasant movement in Guangdong and to promise the peasants land as well a lower rents [van de Ven, 1991: 163]. Accordingly, the revolutionary united front government at Guangzhou (Canton) established a Peasant Department and a Peasant Movement Training Institute, where Communist activists, including some from North China, received training in anticipation of the Northern Expedition to unify the country.[7]

As it became clear that the urban proletariat was too small to provide the basis for a revolutionary takeover, the CCP began to pay more attention to rural mobilisation in North China. The May Thirtieth Movement of 1925, although initially a nation-wide movement of urban industrial workers and students, did spill over into the countryside and accelerated the growth or rural mobilisation. In the 'Resolution on the Peasant Movement' of the Fourth Congress of the CCP (January 1925), peasants were recognised as the most important ally of the proletariat in the national revolution. As part of the emerging agrarian united front policy, the formation of peasant associations and peasant self-defence bodies was promoted, but class struggle was not encouraged at this time [Wilbur and How, 1989: 122–23]. Although these policies were primarily designed to develop the peasant movement in Guangdong province, the establishment of peasant associations in the northern provinces now became an urgent task also. Leaders such as Li Dazhao and Chen Duxiu began to promote the idea of transforming existing rural collectivities into Communist-controlled mass organisations.

In an article published in 1926, Chen Duxiu insisted that the Red Spears were not bandits, but organised groups of peasants and small landowners engaged in anti-bandit activities and tax and rent resistance [Wou, 1994: 80]. Li Dazhao asserted in August 1926 that the Red Spears were public-minded civic groups who turned to superstitious beliefs to make up for military weakness and primitive weaponry. Equating the Red Spears' parochial attachment with class consciousness, he assumed that they could be transformed into Communist-controlled mass organisations [*Wou*, 1994: 80–81]. Indeed, the Second Enlarged Plenum of the CCP's Central Committee, held at Shanghai from 12–18 July 1926, passed specific resolutions on the co-opting of existing protective or predatory bodies in Henan, Shandong and Zhili [*Wilbur and How*, 1989: 746–8].

The Red Spears, since they were opposing the militarist political regimes in North China, were now hailed as the real armed force in the National Revolution. Although they were addicted to superstition, full of destructive tendencies and lacking constructive tendencies, they should nevertheless be made the armed peasants' organisation of the general peasant organisation. Furthermore, their superstitious dogma should not be actively opposed [*Wilbur and How*, 1989: 750–51]. At this time, the Central Committee also worked out a similarly lenient policy toward bandits, insisting that those bandits who did not oppress the peasantry should be kept in a neutral position so they could not be utilised by 'bad gentry and local bullies' [*Wilbur and How*, 1989: 748].

Early attempts to tap the potential of existing militarised rural organisations were made in Henan on the eve of the impending Northern Expedition by the CCP and Comintern agents among the Red Spears and Heavenly Gates [*Perry*, 1980: 213–24; *Thaxton*, 1983: 70–92; *Tai*, 1985: 103–14]. More recently, Odoric Wou [1994: 51–97] has produced a rather more detailed account of Communist attempts to transform the Henan Red Spears into armed peasant associations. In Henan Red Spear-type self-defence activities were particularly widespread, and given the fact that the new revolutionary government had been established in nearby Wuhan after the successful completion of the first stage of the Northern Expedition, Communists were particularly active in Henan in anticipation of the resumption of the Northern Expedition.

However, the events in the summer of 1927 were to bring about the introduction of rather a rather more radical Communist peasant mobilisation programme. As a consequence the virtual destruction of the CCP's urban bases following the Shanghai Massacre in April 1927 and the break with the left-wing Guomindang in the summer of 1927, many of the remnants sought refuge in the countryside. This was the case also in Shandong, where Communist work among the Red Spears and similar collectivities had started somewhat later than in Henan. However, in Shandong it was warlord suppression which forced radical activists out of the cities. Thus, the British consul-general at Ji'nan reported in the spring of 1927 that no revolutionary activities had been noted in the province.[8] In June 1927 he reported that the extermination of Communists and Nationalists was continuing in the cities of Shandong, following the disclosures from the raid on the Soviet Embassy in Beijing.[9]

It would appear that many revolutionary activists were forced to leave for the countryside, for Tours noted that many students had disappeared from Ji'nan.[10] Against a background of urban suppression campaigns, Communist activists began to pursue a more radical policy of peasant mobilisation, reflecting the 'August 7 Directive' of 1927 which proclaimed that the Chinese revolution was in transition from the bourgeois-democratic revolution to the socialist revolution [*Pak*, 1971: 48]. Now the process of taking over existing armed rural collectivities was to involve both economic and political struggles, including resisting grain requisitions, splitting leaders from the rank and file of local organisations by killing 'bullies and bad gentry', as well as the distribution of confiscated land.[11]

In late 1927, the CCP tried to absorb existing local defence groups into Communist-controlled peasant associations (the latter were virtually non-existent at that time) in a few rural districts of Shandong. On 23 November 1927 the Shandong Provincial Committee of the CCP instructed the Tai'an-Laiwu county committee in connection with Red Spear activities in the Tai'an-Laiwu area of the Central Shandong Massif that 'we need not (and should not) expand and extend the strength and life of the Red Spear Association but take advantage of them' and 'subvert their organizational system and incorporate it into the peasant association' [*Pak*, 1971: 302, 303].

The CCP took a similar approach at the time of the spontaneous anti-warlord Red Sparks and Big Swords uprisings in the Wangtai area south of Jiaozhou in eastern Shandong in the summer and late autumn of 1927. Although the Shandong provincial committee had urged radical measures, such as confiscation of land of bad gentry and local bullies, corrupt officials and landlords, as well as the distribution of this land among the peasants [*Pak*, 1971: 291], the local party branches seem to have had little control over the insurrection. As the provincial committee admitted afterwards in a somewhat ambiguous statement:

> During the uprising in Chiaotung [Jiaodong, i.e. the Shandong promontory] what had been especially neglected was probably the peasant association. The Chiaotung uprising was [undertaken] with the bandits and the Big Swords as the core. We should bring out the peasant association. We should first insist in principle that the Big Swords, the bandits, and the peasant association are the same [in goal] (never mean to follow the Big Swords and bandits), and then gradually break up their organizational system getting hold of their

masses from below to make them join the peasant association. [*Pak*, 1971: 292]

However, as a Japanese observer noted, the local Communists joined the spontaneous struggle when it was already under way and were not able to influence its course [*Tanaka*, 1930: 309; also *Pak*, 1971: 305]. Further mobilisational attempts were made in Shandong in 1928–29, when radical Guomindang party branches (*dangbu*) carried out a programme of land confiscation and set up peasant associations in parts of northern Jiangsu and southern Shandong. In Shandong, these associations were, however, broken up and their leaders arrested by Yang Hucheng's warlord troops because they were said to be as 'bolshevistic' as the party branches. In the Haizhou (Jiangsu) area the *dangbu* confiscated the estates of *dongshi* (rural managers), as well as temple land (*North-China Herald*, 8 Sept. 1928, p.402). The extent to which Communist activists were involved in these actions is not clear, although local authorities and foreign observers were convinced of their partcipation.[12]

Another example of early radical peasant mobilisation in Shandong involved the attempted takeover by revolutionary activists of a large bandit gang in Yanggu county in the western part of the province. The local Communist party branch had organised some rudimentary peasant associations in Yanggu county before 1927 and contact had been established with the Red Spear associations in the area, but without concrete results [*Pak*, 1971: 306]. In December 1927 the local people were already agitated, fearing an outbreak of war in anticipation of the resumption of the Northern Expedition and the overthrow of local warlords Chu Yupu and Zhang Zongchang. On 14 January 1928 a group of bandits calling themselves the *Wandaohui* suddenly occupied the mission station of the Society of the Divine Word in the village of Poli, holding some German Catholic priests and sisters hostage. It transpired afterwards that these bandits, whose six leaders were said to be fairly well off, had staged this 'uprising' as a result of a broken promise to incorporate them into a warlord army.

According to local Communist Party accounts, two or three cadres had been sent from the local party bureau in Dongchang to work with the Poli bandit leaders, and others to engage in propaganda work among the ordinary bandits. It was hoped that by friendly persuasion they could gradually be brought under CCP control. The leaders did, in fact, agree to distribute grain on five occasions, the last of which is said to have attracted some 2,000 peasants. Since the distributions were perceived to be acts of bandit generosity rather than the result of Communist intervention, the local CCP leadership instructed the cadres to openly use Communist slogans, and set up peasant associations. Since this would have resulted in a split with the bandits, the party workers ignored the instructions. Discouraged with their lack of progress in converting the bandits, most of them returned to their homes. When local militia and warlord armies began to lay siege to the fortified mission station, the bandits eventually broke through the encirclement on 7 February and escaped into the neighbouring province of Zhili.

As David Paulson [1982: 31] has pointed out, this incident is glorified in later Communist accounts as the earliest revolutionary insurrection in the province. However, he goes on to say that

> the contemporary report concluded that it was nothing more than 'marsh bandits doing mischief' (*shui-fei de hu-nao*). It observed that the bandits continued to use the slogan 'kill the landlords and redistribute the grain' even when their aim was to find ways to rise to be officials. The poor peasants appreciated the bandits 'charity' toward them, and hoped that they would return.

Indeed, few peasants were, in fact, aware that Communist activists had been involved in the affair. Nor is there the slightest hint of any Communist presence in the detailed German missionary accounts.[13]

LIMITATIONS OF REVOLUTIONARY PEASANT MOBILISATION

While Communist activists had considerable success in South and Central China in the late 1920s and early 1930s, peasant mobilisation proved rather disappointing in the North. Since a successful peasant movement did emerge in the notorious hinterland of North China in the 1940s, how can we account for the marked absence of revolutionary fervour here during the 1920s? Given the ephemeral nature of the Communists' North China work in the 1920s, a detailed discussion of the broader issues concerning the Chinese revolution (summarised in Skocpol [1982]; Wou [1994: 1–19; Esherick [1995: 45–76]) will not be entertained here. However, it may be useful to look briefly at the main lines of discussion concerning the factors that were responsible for the success of the revolution during the Anti-Japanese War, for they may help us understand the failures of the 1920s. Of course, even for the later period scholarly opinion is divided [*Hartford and Goldstein*, 1989]. Chalmers Johnson [1962], for instance, has stressed the importance of 'peasant nationalism'. Mark Selden [1971; 1995], focusing on the Shan-Gan-Ning border region of Northwest China during the Anti-Japanese War, put the emphasis on social revolution. Most writers in the 1960s and 1970s had no doubt that it was the Chinese Communist Party's 'organisational weapon' that provided the vital leadership which turned tradition-bound peasants into active revolutionaries [*Kataoka*, 1974; *Hofheinz*, 1977].

In other words, it is argued that peasants are generally thought to be incapable of autonomous, organised, co-ordinated and sustained large-scale action. The most notable exception to this interpretation has been Ralph Thaxton's more recent study [1983]. Relying heavily on a strong version of 'moral economy' theory, he concludes that it was the peasants of North China who imposed their own more local revolutionary objectives upon the CCP's agenda. However, the proponents of the moral economy theory [*Scott*, 1976], especially when applied to North China [*Thaxton*, 1983], have been severely and justly criticised [*Chen and Benton*, 1986; *Little*, 1989: Ch.2; *Averill*, 1991]. Indeed, as has been shown above, North China's peasants were often an integral part of elite-dominated hierarchical structures, with village social institutions cutting across class lines and conforming to established patterns of competition and collaboration. In other words, an autonomous and homogeneous peasantry required by moral economy theory did not exist in the North China hinterland. Nor does the problematical moral economy explanation take into account the persistence of intra-elite conflict as part of endemic collective rural violence. Still, although it is difficult to find evidence for genuinely autonomous organised peasant action, this is not to deny that peasant motivations, values and practices had to be taken into account by both rural elites and local Communist activists when bringing forward their programmes. That is certainly a factor which shaped the revolutionary activities in the hinterland of North China during the 1920s. Thus, as Stephen Averill [1991: 92] has suggested, a moral economy perspective may form a useful element in a pluralistic analysis of the Communist-led revolution. As far as the multi-faceted approach is concerned, Chen Yung-fa's [1986] multi-causal arguments offer a more convincing interpretation of the protracted and at times contradictory nature of the revolution in East-Central during the Anti-Japanese War.

Similarly, the Communist failure in North China in the 1920s can be attributed to a combination of factors. Certainly some of the significant circumstances of the 1940s – most notably the military occupation of North China by a foreign power – were absent in the 1920s. Moreover, the lack of independent coercive power was a crucial weakness in the North. The Communist organisers thus were easily suppressed, first by warlords and upon the completion of the Northern Expedition in the spring of 1928 by the Nationalists. Unlike the Yan'an period when they were in a rather better position to survive adversity, in the 1920s the party organisation was too minuscule and spread too thinly[14] to create secure base areas and sufficient party-controlled peasant associations, engage in multi-class mobilisation against external threats or transform rural society into a revolutionary movement. Nor is it very likely that the early rural cadres had a reasonable grasp of Marxist ideology or had studied Lenin's *What Is to Be Done?* They were thus ill equipped and too inexperienced to grasp and deal with the objective internal situation in the hinterland of North China. In these zones with a long history of collective violence, they failed to gain appreciable support, because the dominant mode of conflict was between similar factions. Such conflict was segmental rather than along class lines and reinforced the internal solidarity of hierarchical collectivities. As Hamza Alavi [1973: 44] has remarked more generally, in such conflicts

> rival factions, or faction leaders, fight for control over resources, power, and status as available within the existing framework of society rather than for change in the social structure ... An important aspect of factional conflict is that rival factions are, in general, structurally similar, namely that they represent similar configurations of social groups.

Thus, in spite of widespread rural distress in the warlord period in the 1920s, the response to Communist appeals to the peasants' socio-economic interests was negligible in northern China. Moreover, issues such as tenancy, commercialisation of agriculture,[15] and incorporation into the world market were, on the whole relatively unimportant in the notorious zones of endemic violence. Here modern economic penetration had been far too marginal to have brought about the kind of socio-economic disruptions which had facilitated the transition from segmental conflict to conflict along class dimensions, noted by some writers in areas of early Communist mobilisation in South China [*Marks*, 1984]. In the harsh environment of much of rural northern China, where the old socio-economic and socio-political order was largely intact, community solidarity remained a powerful inhibitor of class antagonism, and 'endemic rebelliousness' – that is, opposition to any and all impositions of and encroachments by outside authority – remained a formidable obstacle to revolutionary change in the 1920s. The inability to subdue or co-opt local militarised collectivities such as Red Spear-type associations and local bandit gangs were a significant factor in the CCP's failure to create revolutionary bases.

In this context, the abandonment of an united front programme following the 'August 7 Emergency Conference' and the subsequent 'Li Lisan adventurist line', and the insistence of implementation of policies formulated by Party Central, Comintern and Moscow, proved particularly harmful. While such demands as 'establishing soviets' and 'land revolution' may have been effective mobilisational tools in Central and South China, they were found to be inappropriate in the North. Poor communication between the Centre and local party cells, as well as different interpretations of Party Central instructions by CCP branches and cells as to what was appropriate policy in the local context further complicated matters. In any case, it is difficult to see how the contradictory policies of taking over local militarised collectivities, when the leaders of these organisations were to be the victims of mobilisation campaigns that ranged from anti-rent and debt movements, 'land to the tiller' struggles, confiscation of arms and grain, to driving out and killing landlords, 'evil gentry' and other 'reactionary forces'. Neither CCP leadership, nor the Comintern, nor local party activists were willing to adapt their programme for the future to the 'traditional rural vision of an ideal world in which the state left the village alone' [Hartford, 1995: 166].[16] Instead, the Central Committee and Comintern continued to advocate suicidal insurrections well into the 1930s. 'Class struggle, uprising, soviet, so the litany ran. And so, in the attempt to set the spark to light a prairie fire, the movement repeatedly sent up columns of smoke that brought in the cavalry' [Hartford, 1995: 166]. Thus, when local cadres did manage to establish the only peasant-based soviet government in all of North China – in Gaoyang and Li counties of Hebei – in the summer of 1932, it was quickly destroyed by government forces [Grove, 1975].

CONCLUSION

As Kathleen Hartford [1995: 145] has pointed out with respect to Hebei, the CCP had a history in the villages of North China:

> It was a history both of radical initiatives on land issues and of uprisings based on community opposition to state encroachments. It was also a history of betrayal, stupidity, ineptness, dashed hopes, suppression, and failure. Such a history of negatives may be every bit as formative for a revolutionary movement as the more positive record of the CCP in the south.

Linda Grove [1975: 244] has argued that the Gaoyang experience 'left behind a legacy of peasant involvement with the revolutionary movement which was the base for rapid organization of the CCP-led movement during the anti-Japanese war'

A new opportunity to integrate the militarised – but essentially reactionary – defensive and offensive rural collectivities into an effective revolutionary movement presented itself during the Japanese occupation of North China after 1937. But this was a different situation. Since the Japanese could hold only the important cities and the lines of communication, the Communists took the opportunity to construct relatively secure base areas behind enemy lines. Under a new multi-class united front approach, CCP activists coped more successfully with existing rural social structures by implementing reformist agrarian policies to achieve revolutionary ends. At the same time, they were able to organise 'anti-Japanese' guerrilla units and improve their military capabilities with peasant support. At that time the CCP would employ an effective policy that allowed it to engage in class struggle while operating within a multi-class resistance movement against an external enemy. In the final analysis the North was more receptive to the CCP than the high-tenancy regions of Central and South China. It was the instability and insecurity of rural life, rather than tenurial conditions, that made North China more receptive to revolutionary mobilisation [*Huang*, 1990: 161]. As Joseph Esherick [1995: 60] has argued, the enduring commitment of the few thousand cadres who had survived in North China before 1937 was instrumental in this process: 'The rapid growth of the North China base areas during the early years of the war relied on the critical role of these local cadres. Their survival to play this role is testimony to a remarkable revolutionary dedication.' The experience they had gained from the bitter lessons of these years of failed risings in the 1920s helped them to mobilise the peasantry of the socially complex and notoriously violent North China hinterland.

NOTES

1. This passage is quoted in Brantly Womack [1982: 51] who calls the article from which he translated it 'the first and one of the most interesting CCP articles on the peasantry". The article is entitled 'Gao Zhongguo de nongmin' [To the Chinese peasants] and was published in *Gongchangdang* [The Communist], Vol.1 (7 April 1921), pp.3–7.
2. In this essay 'North China' refers to the North China macroregion as delineated by G. William Skinner [1977]. However, examples will be drawn primarily from Shandong province and adjacent districts in neighbouring provinces on the North China Plain, i.e. southern Zhili (from 28 June 1928 called Hebei), parts of northern Jiangsu, northern Anhui and much of northern and eastern Henan.
3. Elise A. DeVido has quite recently completed a doctoral dissertation on the Shandong base area at Harvard University.
4. Although a number of other works have appeared over the years [*Myers*, 1970; *Jing and Luo*, 1978; *Huang*, 1985; *Duara*, 1988], they do not provide sufficient detail of conditions in the areas of particular interest to this essay. The recent publication by Kenneth Pomeranz [1993] stands out as a major study focusing specifically on an underdeveloped part of North China. In any case, China's overall rural economic development in the late imperial and republican periods remains a matter of considerable scholarly controversy. Informed critiques of the most recent works on China's agrarian economy are offered by Michael F. Martin [1991] and Jürgen Osterhammel [1993].
5. For a long list of North China protective societies contemporary with the Red Spears, see Perry [1980: 269–73].
6. The precedent of elite involvement in radical activities had been established before 1911, when the Revolutionary Alliance mobilised middle school teachers and students in North China to propagate revolutionary ideas in the countryside. Likewise, such ideas were spread along secret society and bandit networks [*Zhang*, 1994].
7. The Nationalist government launched its Northern Expedition from Guangzhou in July 1926, and by 10 October 1926 the city of Wuhan in Central China had been occupied and the Nationalist government formally transferred there.

8. B.G. Tours to Sir Miles Lampson, No.13, Ji'nan, 25 April 1927 (Intelligence Report), Public Record Office (London), FO 228/3638.
9. Tours to Lampson, No.22, Ji'nan, 26 June 1927 (Political Summary), Public Record Office (London), FO 228/3638. The raid on the Soviet Embassy in Beijing was undertaken on 6 April 1927 by the security forces of the northern warlord Zhang Zuolin. Many Communist documents were seized and a number of Chinese activists arrested, among them the co-founder and head of the northern branch of the CCP, Li Dazhao, who was executed on 28 April 1927.
10. Tours to Lampson, No.38, Ji'nan, 4 Oct. 1927 (Intelligence Report), Public Record Office (London), FO 228/3638.
11. Letter from the Shandong Provincial Committee to the Gaomi *xian* committee, 9 Nov. 1927, Document 45 in Pak [1971: 291-293]. On the Wangtai uprising, see Affleck to Lampson, No.10, Ji'nan, 4 April 1928 (Intelligence Report), Public Record Office (London), FO 228/3824; see also Tanaka [1930: 308-09].
12. Nikolaus Tabellion, 30 May 1929, in *Tsingtauer Missions-Korrespondenz*, Vol.1, No.3 (1 July 1929), p.29. On the radical nature of the *dangbu*, see also Edgar Snow's early observation on the Chinese revolutionary scene [1931: 524], to the effect that 'in many districts remote from Nanking Communists secured control of the [dangbu] and manipulated them as they pleased'. He reported that they had been responsible for 'many of the oppressive acts … Their object was to undermine public confidence in the Kuomintang by causing it to appear despotic and deceitful.' By the late 1930s Snow had, of course, become an admirer of Mao Zedong's revolutionary movement [*Snow*, 1941; 1957; 1961]. On the limitations of Left Guomindang mass mobilisation, see Dirlik [1975].
13. Later Communist accounts of the Poli uprising are Sheng Beiguang [1984]; County Party History Office, 'Dang lingdao de Shandong zui zao de yici nongmin baodong–Yanggu Poli baodong' [The earliest peasant uprising in Shandong under the leadership of the Party: the Poli uprising in Yanggu], in Yanggu Committee of the Chinese People's Political Consultative Conference, *Yanggu wenshi ziliao xuanbian* [Selected Yanggu historical materials], Liaocheng: Shandong sheng chuban zongshe, 1989, pp.22–32; Ji-Lu-Yu bianqu geming shi gongzuozu [Working group on the revolutionary history of the Hebei-Shandong-Henan border region], *Ji-Lu-Yu bianqu geming shi* [Revolutionary history of the Hebei-Shandong-Henan border region], Ji'nan: Shandong daxue chubanshe, 1991, pp.46–9. For some German missionary accounts, see Blandina [1928]; Weiß [1928]; Henninghaus [1927/28]. See also Adolf Boyé to Auswàrtiges Amt, No.175, Beijing, 24 Jan. 1928; No. 201, Beijing, 27 Jan. 1928; No.389, Beijing, 20 Feb. 1928, in Archives of the German Foreign Office (Bonn), Abt. Pol IV 652/2: Politik 16, China, Vol.2. In the German sources the attack on Poli occurred on 14 January; the Chinese sources give 22 January as the date.
14. According to Harrison [1972: 99], party membership in April 1927 consisted of 3,101 members in Zhili (Hebei)-Shanxi-Inner Mongolia; 1,300 in Henan, and 1,015 in Shandong.
15. As Philip Huang [1990: 102–04] has pointed out, a significant degree of agricultural commodity production had long existed in the North China hinterland, but it was either what he calls 'extraction-driven commercialisation' to make tax and interest payments, or 'survival-driven commercialisation' to provide for subsistence needs. However, production for profit, or 'enterprise-driven commercialisation', was not well developed here in the 1920s.
16. In this connection, the competing but rather moderate reformist ventures in rural North China by James Yen [*Hayford*, 1990] and Liang Shuming in Shandong [*Alitto*, 1986] should be noted.

REFERENCES

Alavi, Hamza, 1973, 'Peasant Classes and Primordial Loyalties', *Journal of Peasant Studies*, Vol.1, No.1.
Alitto, Guy S., 1986, *The Last Confucian: Liang Shu-ming and the Chinese Dilemma of*

Modernity, 2nd edn. Berkeley, CA: University of California Press.

Averill, Steven, 1991, 'Moral Economy and the Chinese Revolution', *Peasant Studies*, Vol.18, No.2.

Bianco, Lucien, 1972, 'Secret Societies and Peasant Self-Defense, 1921-1933', in Chesneaux [1972].

Billingsley, Phil, 1988, *Bandits in Republican China*, Stanford, CA: Stanford University Press.

Blandina, Sr. [Anna Mairon], 1928, *Unsere Gefangenschaft unter 1000 chinesischen Räubern*, Steyl: Missionsdruckerei.

Blok, Anton, 1974, *The Mafia of a Sicilian Village 1860-1960: A Study of Violent Peasant Entrepreneurs*, Oxford: Basil Blackwell.

Chen, Yung-fa, 1986, *Making Revolution: The Communist Movement in Eastern and Central China, 1937-1945*, Berkeley, CA: University of California Press.

Chen, Yung-fa and Gregor Benton, 1986, *Moral Economy and the Chinese Revolution*, Amsterdam: Anthropological-Sociological Centre, University of Amsterdam.

Chesneaux, Jean (ed.), 1972, *Popular Movements and Secret Societies in China, 1840-1950*, Stanford, CA: Stanford University Press.

Cohen, Jerome Alan, 1966, 'Chinese Mediation on the Eve of Modernization', *California Law Review*, Vol.54.

Dirlik, Arif, 1975, 'Mass Movements and the Left Kuomintang', *Modern China*, Vol.1, No.1.

Duara, Prasenjit, 1987, 'State Involution: A Study of Local Finances in North China, 1911-1935', *Comparative Studies in Society and History*, Vol.29, No.1, pp.132–61.

Duara, Prasenjit, 1988, *Culture, Power, and the State: Rural North China, 1900-1942*, Stanford, CA: Stanford University Press.

Esherick, Joseph W., 1995, 'Ten Theses on the Chinese Revolution', *Modern China*, Vol.21, No.1.

Galbiati, Fernando, 1985, *P'eng P'ai and the Hai-Lu-Feng Soviet*, Stanford: Stanford University Press.

Gamble, Sidney D., 1963, *North China Villages: Social, Political, and Economic Activities before 1933*, Berkeley, CA: University of California Press.

Goodman, David S.G., 1994, 'JinJiLuYu in the Sino-Japanese War: The Border Region and the Border Region Government', *China Quarterly*, No.140.

Grove, Linda, 1975, 'Creating a Northern Soviet', *Modern China*, Vol.1, No.3.

Harrison, James Pinckney, 1972, *The Long March to Power: A History of the Chinese Communist Party, 1921-72*, New York: Praeger.

Hartford, Kathleen J., 1980, 'Step by Step: Reform, Resistance, and Revolution in Chin-Ch'a-Chi Border Region 1937-1945', unpublished doctoral dissertation, Stanford University.

Hartford, Kathleen J., 1995, 'Fits and Starts: The Communist Party in Rural Hebei, 1921-1936', in Tony Saich and Hans van de Ven (eds.), *New Perspectives on the Chinese Communist Revolution*, Armonk, NY and London: M.E. Sharpe.

Hartford, Kathleen and Steven M. Goldstein, 1989, 'Introduction: Perspectives on the Chinese Communist Revolution', in Hartford and Goldstein (eds.), *Single Sparks: China's Rural Revolutions*, Armonk, NY and London: M.E. Sharpe.

Hayford, Charles W., 1990, *To the People: James Yen and Village China*, New York: Columbia University Press.

Henninghaus, Augustin, 1927/28, 'In den Händen der Räuber', *Steyler Missionsbote*, Vol.55, No.9.

Hofheinz, Roy, Jr., 1977, *The Broken Wave: The Chinese Communist Peasant Movement, 1922-1928*, Cambridge, MA: Harvard University Press.

Huang, Philip C.C., 1985, *The Peasant Economy and Social Change in North China*, Stanford, CA: Stanford University Press.

Huang, Philip C.C., 1990, *The Peasant Family and Rural Development in the Yangzi Delta, 1350-1988*, Stanford, CA: Stanford University Press.

Jing Su and Luo Lun, 1978, *Landlord and Labor in Late Imperial China: Case Studies from Shandong*, translated from the Chinese with an Introduction by Endymion Wilkinson, Cambridge, MA: Harvard University Press.

Johnson, Chalmers, 1962, *Peasant Nationalism and Communist Power: The Emergence of*

Revolutionary China, 1937–1945, Stanford, CA: Stanford University Press.
Kataoka, Tetsuya, 1974, *Resistance and Revolution in China: The Communists and the Second United Front*, Berkeley, CA: University of California Press.
Kuhn, Philip A., 1975, 'Local Self-Government under the Republic: Problems of Control, Autonomy, and Mobilization', in Wakeman and Grant [1975].
Lamley, Harry J., 1977, "*Hsieh-tou*": The Pathology of Violence in Southeastern China', *Ch'ing-shih wen-t'i*, Vol.3, No.7.
Little, Daniel, 1989, *Understanding Peasant China: Case Studies in the Philosophy of Social Science*, New Haven, CT and London: Yale University Press.
McDonald, Angus W., Jr., 1978, *The Urban Origins of Rural Revolution: Elites and the Masses in Hunan Province, China, 1911–1927*, Berkeley, CA: University of California Press.
Marks, Robert, 1984, *Rural Revolution in South China: Peasants and the Making of History in Haifeng County, 1570–1930*, Madison, WI: University of Wisconsin Press.
Martin, Michael F., 1991, 'Rural Living Conditions in Pre-Liberation China: A Survey of Three Recent Studies', *Journal of Peasant Studies*, Vol.19, No.1.
Myers, Ramon H., 1970, *The Chinese Peasant Economy: Agricultural Development in Hopei and Shantung, 1890–1949*, Cambridge, MA: Harvard University Press.
Osterhammel, Jürgen, 1993, 'Bauern und ländliche Gesellschaft im China des 20. Jahrhunderts. Zwischenbilanz einer Debatte', *Internationales Asienforum*, Vol.24, No.3–4.
Pak, Hyobom (trans. and ed.), 1971, *Documents of the Chinese Communist Party 1927–1930*, Hongkong: Union Research Institute.
Paulson, David, 1982, 'War and Revolution in North China: The Shandong Base Area, 1937–1945', unpublished doctoral dissertation, Stanford University.
Perry, Elizabeth J., 1980, *Rebels and Revolutionaries in North China 1845-1945*, Stanford, CA: Stanford University Press.
Perry, Elizabeth J., 1985, 'The Red Spears Reconsidered: An Introduction', in Tai [1985].
Pomeranz, Kenneth, 1993, *The Making of a Hinterland: State, Society, and Economy in Inland North China, 1853–1937*, Berkeley, CA: University of California Press.
Riddell, John (ed.), 1991, *The Communist International in Lenin's Time: Workers of the World and Oppressed People's, Unite! Proceedings and Documents of the Second Congress, 1920*, New York: Pathfinder, 2 vols.
Scott, James C., 1976, *The Moral Economy of the Peasant: Rebellion and Subsistence in Southeast Asia*, New Haven, CT: Yale University Press.
Selden, Mark, 1971, *The Yenan Way in Revolutionary China*, Cambridge, MA: Harvard University Press.
Selden, Mark, 1995, *China in Revolution: The Yenan Way Revisited*, Armonk and London: M.E. Sharpe.
Sheel, Kamal, 1989, *Peasant Society and Marxist Intellectuals in China: Fang Zhimin and the Origin of a Revolutionary Movement*, Princeton, NJ: Princeton University Press.
Sheng Beiguang, 1984, 'Yanggu nongmin yundong he Lu-xi dang zaoqi huodong' [The Yanggu peasant movement and early activities of the Party of western Shandong], *Shandong dang shi ziliao* [Materials on Shandong party history], No.1.
Shepherd, John R., 1988, 'Rethinking Tenancy: Explaining Spatial and Temporal Variation in Late Imperial and Republican China', *Comparative Studies in Society and History*, Vol.30, No.3.
Skinner, G. William, 1977, 'Cities and the Hierarchy of Local Systems', in G. William Skinner (ed.), *The City in Late Imperial China*, Stanford, CA: Stanford University Press.
Skocpol, Theda, 1982, 'What Makes Peasants Revolutionary?', in Robert P. Weller and Scott E. Guggenheim (eds.), *Power and Protest in the Countryside: Studies of Rural Unrest in Asia, Europe, and Latin America*, Durham, NC: Duke University Press.
Slawinski, Roman, 1972, 'The Red Spears in the Late 1920s', in Chesneaux [1972].
Snow, Edgar, 1931, 'The Bolshevist Influence', *Current History*, Vol.33, No.4.
Snow, Edgar, 1941, *The Battle for Asia*, New York: Random House.
Snow, Edgar, 1957, *Random Notes on Red China (1936–1945)*, Cambridge, MA: Harvard University, East Asia Research Center.
Snow, Edgar, 1961, *Red Star over China*, New York: Grove Press.

Tai Hsüan-chih, 1985, *The Red Spears, 1916–1949*, trans. Ronald Suleski. (Michigan Monographs in Chinese Studies No.54.) Ann Arbor, MI: University of Michigan.

Tanaka Tadao, 1930, *Kakumei Shina nōson no jisshoteki kenkyū* [A definitive study of revolutionary China's villages], Tokyo: Shūjinsha.

Thaxton, Ralph, 1983, *China Turned Rightside Up: Revolutionary Legitimacy in the Peasant World*, New Haven, CT: Yale University Press.

Tiedemann, R.G., 1982, 'The Persistence of Banditry: Incidents in Border Districts of the North China Plain', *Modern China*, Vol.8, No.4.

Tiedemann, R.G., 1991, 'Rural Unrest in North China 1868–1900: With Particular Reference to South Shandong', unpublished doctoral dissertation, University of London.

van de Ven, Hans J., 1991, *From Friend to Comrade: The Founding of the Chinese Communist Party, 1920–1927*, Berkeley, CA: University of California Press.

Wakeman, Frederic, Jr. 1975, 'Introduction: The Evolution of Local Control in Late Imperial China', in Wakeman and Grant [1975].

Wakeman, Frederic, Jr. and Carolyn Grant (eds.), 1975, *Conflict and Control in Late Imperial China*, Berkeley, CA: University of California Press.

Weiß, Josef, 1928, 'Tausend Räuber in Puoli', *Stadt Gottes*, June, Vol.51.

Wilbur, C. Martin and Julie Lien-ying How, 1989, *Missionaries of Revolution: Soviet Advisers and Nationalist China, 1920–1927*, Cambridge, MA: Harvard University Press.

Womack, Brantly, 1982, *The Foundations of Mao Zedong's Political Thought, 1917–1935*, Honolulu, HI: University Press of Hawaii.

Wou, Odoric Y.K., 1994, *Mobilizing the Masses: Building Revolution in Henan*, Stanford, CA: Stanford University Press.

Yokoyama Suguru, 1975, 'The Peasant Movement in Hunan', *Modern China*, April, Vol.1, No.2.

Zhang Xin, 1994, 'Reconsidering the 1911 Revolution: The Case of Henan', *Chinese Historians*, Vol.7.

Popular Culture, Populist Fiction(s): The Agrarian Utopiates of A.V. Chayanov, Ignatius Donnelly and Frank Capra

TOM BRASS

'The populist tradition offers no panacea for all the ills that afflict the modern world' – Christopher Lasch [1991: 532].

'We were created to live in Paradise, and Paradise was designed to serve us. Our purpose has been changed; that this has also happened with the purpose of Paradise is nowhere stated' – Aphorism 84 in Kafka [1973: 97].

'You don't win a hat like that playing mumbly pegs' – An aside by Bob Hope to Bing Crosby, about the size of the hat worn by the High Lama, in the film *Road to Hong Kong* (1962).[1]

In a world characterised on the one hand by dystopic images of widespread poverty, unemployment, famine, 'ethnic cleansing', refugee flight, depeasantisation, ecological disaster and war, all generated by a seemingly unstoppable neo-liberal capitalism, and on the other by a triumphalist and widely announced 'death' of Marxism together with its vision of progress rooted in the possibility/desirability of planning, technology, industry and urbanisation, one of the most urgent and frequently-asked questions has become: are there any alternative visions of the future, and if so of what do they consist? In short, if Marxism is no longer to be permitted a role in the design of Paradise/Utopia/('community'), what sort of place will the latter be, and who/what will decide this?

One alternative vision of the future is that advocated by populism, an 'a-political'/'third-way' ideology that has a long history, and which projects itself in terms of a discourse-against that is simultaneously anti-capitalist

Tom Brass is at the Faculty of Social and Political Sciences, University of Cambridge, Free School Lane, Cambridge CB2 3RQ, UK.

and anti-socialist. In a variety of guises and forms, populism has emerged and re-emerged periodically as a reaction by (mainly, but not only) peasants and farmers to industrialisation, urbanisation and capitalist crisis: first in the 1890s, subsequently during the 1930s, and now in the 1990s when non-socialist concepts of 'community' are once again on the political agenda. Then, as now, it could be argued that a vision of a rural arcadia composed of an independent peasantry is viable only in a non-existent context such as a populist utopia.

Accordingly, here it is intended to examine the depiction by populism in the domain of 'popular culture' of what purports to be its non-capitalist/non-socialist alternative: in short, the socio-economic and political structure of its 'imaginary' as this involves a symptomatic opposition between the utopic and dystopic (or the combination within populist ideology of a discourse-for and a discourse-against about utopia and its 'other'). This dystopic/utopic opposition structures each of the three populist texts considered below: the American novel *Caesar's Column* (1890) by Ignatius Donnelly [1960]; the Russian text *The Journey of My Brother Alexei to the Land of Peasant Utopia* (1920) by A.V. Chayanov [*Kremnev*, 1977]; and *Lost Horizon* in both its literary and cinematic forms, the English novel by James Hilton [1933] and the film produced in America during 1937 and directed by Frank Capra.

These three literary/filmic texts share a common negative/positive vision, in which a dystopic/('evil') urban is contrasted with an utopic/('good') rural. To the 'natural'/god-given social order of the populist utopic, therefore, is counterposed the dystopic chaos of a dark/dangerous/closed world inhabited by the variants of non-natural *untermensch* ('mob', 'lower classes', 'underclass'). Accordingly, it is argued here that what is significant about the fictional portrayals of utopia by Donnelly, Hilton and Capra – all of which had a powerful impact in the domain of 'popular culture' – is not just that each text was a reaction in the midst of a capitalist crisis to capitalism itself, nor that each was nationalist, orientalist and even racist in outlook, but also (and perhaps most importantly) that all were an expression of fear that such a situation would lead to socialism. This latter anxiety also informs the fictional utopia of Chayanov, except that in his case the danger is now in the past.

I

The Return of Populist 'Community'

The received wisdom that utopias have been and are basically the 'imaginaries' of the political left overlooks the long history of similar attempts by those on the centre/right of the political spectrum to construct an alternative 'imaginary'. It is not without significance, therefore, that following the demise of the Soviet Union much (non-Marxist) social theory is currently engaged in an attempt to recuperate a specifically non-socialist variety of community. This project extends from the currently fashionable 'communitarianism' of MacIntyre [1981], Etzioni [1990; 1993] and Lasch [1991; 1995], with its fear of the loss of and an advocacy of a return to traditional family and community values, to a community of autonomous individuals that structures the contractarianism of Rawls [1993] and the postmodernism of Rorty [1989].[2] Such a project could be said also to include the tribal/peasant/gender/ethnic/national 'communities' implied or disclosed in much recent social theory about the so-called Third World that is produced from within the 'cultural-not-racial-difference' discourse of the allegedly 'post-fascist' European 'new' right on the one hand and the postmodern framework of the new social movements and Subaltern Studies on the other.[3] Despite some obvious theoretical differences, all the latter share a common characteristic: the attempt either to identify or to construct an ethically based 'moral' community, without either having regard to class differences or having to transform substantially existing property relations.[4] In short, this search for a de-politicised form of 'community' is yet another variant of populism.[5]

Although it shares with Marxism a discourse-against that attacks big business, political injustice, and the effects of capitalism generally, populism does this not in the name of the common ownership of the means of production (as does Marxism) but rather in the name of individual, small-scale private property. Since it downgrades/denies the existence of class and accordingly essentialises the peasantry, populism also perceives smallholding proprietors as socio-economically undifferentiated and thus casts them all in the role of 'victims', uniformly oppressed by large-scale institutions/monopolies located in the urban sector (the state, big business and 'foreign' capital). An important consequence of the reproduction by populist ideology of this opposition between state and peasant is a quasi-mystical belief in the efficacy of any/all anti-state discourse/action-from-below. In contrast to Marxism, therefore, the problems and negative effects of capitalism are attributed by populism to the distortion (= 'greed') and not the structure of capitalism.[6] Most significantly, and as many Marxists have constantly pointed out, the political anxiety that structures the discourse-against of populism is an underlying fear of socialism rather than capitalism. For this reason, the populist discourse-against is directed not so much at capitalism *per se* as at its large-scale monopoly/('foreign') variant which gives rise to the very conditions that lead in turn to socialism.[7]

Like Marxism, populism also combines a pessimism about the present with an optimism about the future. Unlike Marxism, however, populism fails to distinguish between a progressive/modern anti-capitalism which seeks to transcend bourgeois society, and a romantic anti- (or post-) modern form the roots of which are located in agrarian nostalgia and reactionary visions of an innate 'nature'. Accordingly, the pessimism which structures the discourse-against of populism in general and agrarian populism in particular generates an optimism which is not forwards-looking but much rather backwards-looking, and thus corresponds to an attempt to reinvent tradition in a way that has been (and continues to be) supportive of conservative, nationalist and even fascist ideology.[8]

A potent form of ruralism with roots in romantic and conservative notions of an organic society, agrarian populism historically has proclaimed the necessity of an 'above politics' mobilisation on the basis of the agrarian myth ('peasants-as-the-backbone-of-the-nation'), an ideological position defended in most contexts with reference to a common and mutually-reinforcing set of arguments. The first of these was about economics, and entailed a discourse in which agriculture was presented as the historical and continuing basis of social organisation, peasant farming as the source of national food self-sufficiency, and the peasantry as the source of military personnel – and thus the defence of the nation.[9] The second argument concerned politics, and advanced claims about the peasantry as upholders of the existing hierarchy, and thus as a bulwark against the spread of socialist ideas and the guarantors of political stability. The last and perhaps the most powerful component of this discourse was about culture: this entailed a critique of industrialisation, urbanisation and modernity based on nostalgia for a vanishing way-of-life, linked in turn to perceptions of an idyllic/harmonious/folkloric village existence as an unchanging/unchangeable 'natural' community and thus the repository of a similarly immutable national identity. Linked to the latter was the view of the countryside generally as the locus of myths/legends, spiritual/sacred attributes, non-commercial values, and traditional virtue.

The way in which populism has been propagated historically demonstrates the problematic nature of claims that it corresponds to an authentically grassroots discourse-against. Hence in a significant number of historical cases from the 1890s to the 1940s the agrarian myth has not only been disseminated in the domain of 'popular culture' in a form that is either aristocratic (literature) or bourgeois (cinema) but its politico-ideological content has similarly been an historically and/or contextually specific response from above to an actual/potential threat from below, posed in the case of the bourgeoisie by the proletariat. However, this fear of the crowd (= the revolutionary proletarian 'mob-in-the-streets') subsides to the degree that the urban working class can be controlled and/or deflected politically, and this indeed has been one of the important tasks of populism generally; to the extent that it celebrates the variety of existing grassroots conservatism subsumed under the rubric of 'popular culture', therefore, postmodernism is currently the theory of this practice.[10]

II

The rise of agrarian populism in Russia, America and Japan during the second half of the nineteenth century and its resurgence during the 1920s and 1930s not just in the latter contexts but also in Central Europe, England, France, Italy, Germany, China and India, suggests that it was an almost universal national response to the capitalist crisis of those periods.[11] In most of these contexts, therefore, the resurgence in the face of a double threat (an 'alien'/international finance capitalism 'from above' and an equally 'alien'/international socialism 'from below') of populism and its agrarian variant (Nōhonshugi, 'Merrie England', volksgemeinschaft, narodnism, the pioneering frontier spirit, etc.) was in turn linked not just to nationalism (as in England, the United States and Russia) but also to fascism (as in Italy, France, Germany and Japan).[12] In most of these countries, therefore, it is unsurprising to encounter the fact that significant elements of the agrarian myth structured 'popular culture' in general and its most powerful component, the cinema, in particular.[13]

Much of the populist discourse which structures the agrarian myth is present in the films of Frank Capra, who directed not only Lost Horizon (see below) but also Mr Deeds Goes to Town (1936), Mr Smith Goes to Washington (1939) and It's a Wonderful Life (1946).[14] All these films celebrate the populist values associated with the rural conservatism of an idealised small-town America, as epitomised by an individual saviour in the form of 'the little man' from a small-scale rural background (= purity, innocence) who takes on and triumphs over city bankers, financial interests in the corrupt and large-scale urban setting. Thus Mr Deeds Goes to Town celebrates a seemingly irrational/insane use of inherited wealth to resettle farmers dispossessed by the capitalist crisis, and culminates in a courtroom reaffirmation of small community anti-intellectualism (= 'natural rural common-sense') against the false sophistication of the city. Similarly, in It's a Wonderful Life Capra contrasts the small/'good' capitalist from an unchanging/small-scale rural community background with the large/'bad' financial capitalist and a nighmarish largescale/mechanised urban future.[15]

Agrarian Utopiates, Populist Fiction(s)

Two of the three texts considered here were produced in the context of a capitalist crisis, and all three idealise the small-scale, rural life, the lone individual, and are against the large-scale, finance capital, against the city, against the state. Set in New York a century into the future, the first of the three agrarian populist utopias, *Caesar's Column* (1890) by Ignatius Donnelly, consists of a series of letters written to his brother by Gabriel Weltstein, a sheep farmer from the new African state of Uganda.[16] Like all the rest of modern capitalist civilisation, Donnelly's New York of 1988 is polarised between on the one hand a small aristocratic ruling class of wealthy finance capitalists (= the Plutocracy), and on the other a large urban industrial proletariat (= the 'great, dark, writhing masses' which inhabit the 'underworld'). Organised into the Brotherhood of Destruction and led by an ex-farmer called Caesar, the American working class overthrows the ruling aristocracy of financial capitalists, in the course of which modern urban industrial civilisation worldwide is itself extinguished. While Caesar celebrates the victory of the proletariat amidst the ruins of New York by building a column out of the bodies of the slain, Weltstein and a few others succeed in escaping to an idyllic rural 'garden in the mountains' located in Africa.[17]

Using the pseudonym of Ivan Kremnev, the Russian neo-populist theoretician A.V. Chayanov wrote the utopian fiction *The Journey of My Brother Alexei to the Land of Peasant Utopia* (1920).[18] The central character in this narrative is Alexei Kremnev, a socialist living in the drab Soviet Russia of 1921, who is suddenly transported forward in time by 60 years to Moscow in 1984, where he is mistaken for an American visitor.[19] Half a century on, he finds that socialism has collapsed, towns have been abolished, and Moscow is now a rural arcadia without either heavy industry or proletariat.[20] Established as a result of peasant opposition to socialism, the labour-intensive agrarian economy of what has now become the Russian Peasant Republic is in the fiction of Chayanov based on the restoration of private property in the form of the peasant family farm, and the corresponding absence of planning and state intervention. Discovering that half a century earlier he himself was responsible for the supression of the peasant movement in Soviet Russia, and by implication the idyllic pastoral (= agrarian utopia) that Russia would have become had this not been done, Kremnev repents and rejects his socialism in favour of populism.

For a number of reasons, perhaps the most interesting of the three examples of agrarian populist utopia considered here is that projected in the book *Lost Horizon* by James Hilton, and in the film of the same name, directed by Frank Capra.[21] Both film and book versions of *Lost Horizon* follow roughly the same plot.[22] Escaping from a revolutionary crowd in China, European passengers on the last plane out are kidnapped and transported to a mysterious, idyllic Tibetan 'garden in the mountains' (the Valley of the Blue Moon or Shangri-La) high in the Himalayas.[23] In the film version those kidnapped consist of the British Foreign Secretary elect, Robert Conway, and his brother George, together with a paleontologist (Alexander P. Lovett), an incurable invalid (Gloria Stone), and a speculator (Chalmers Bryant, whose alias is Henry Bernard) who swindled small investors during the Wall Street crash. 'Discovered' on the unexplored Tibetan plateau by a Capuchin priest at the beginning of the eighteenth century, Shangri-La remains mountain-locked and unaffected by the economic depression, the impending world war, or indeed time itself.[24] In short, it embodies the Garden of Eden of legend, in which no one grows old or lacks for anything. However, shortly after the death of the two-hundred years old High Lama, the original 'discoverer' of Shangri-La, the main protagonist Robert Conway and his brother attempt to return to external 'civilisation'. In the course of this journey, one of the accompanying inhabitants of Shangri-La ages rapidly and dies, while Conway's brother falls off the mountain to his death. Conway himself reaches the plains below, but then changes his mind about staying and decides to return once more to Shangri-La, which he succeeds in doing as the film ends.

The context – and the background to the successful appeal – of both novel and film versions of *Lost Horizon* is the capitalist crisis of the 1930s, which has in turn given rise to the criticism that the narrative corresponds simply to an unfocussed form of escapism, a discourse-against that lacks an 'other'.[25] This critique, which is reinforced textually by the flight from (and the juxtaposition of) a context governed by chaos/war to one structured by order/peace, is true only in a superficial sense.[26] *Lost Horizon* is not simply an expression of pessimism devoid of an accompanying optimism, but is rather the combination of a pessimism/optimism couple in which the optimism possesses (and thus projects) a particular socio-economic configuration. Although pessimism generated by economic crisis in metropolitan capitalism is not confronted internally, in that no solution is sought within (and arising from) the structure of modern industrial capitalism itself, it does contain an external 'other'. An alternative is present, therefore, in that the optimistic 'other' is to be found not in the form of a transformation of existing society but rather outside industrial capitalism altogether, in an idyllic arcadia located deep within the Himalayas. Accordingly, this is a case not of (an 'otherless') escapism *per se*, as many of the critics maintain, but rather its opposite: the *reaffirmation* of a traditional and – as is argued here – a conservative form of 'otherness' which, as well as being anti-industrial (anti-modern/anti-urban/anti-technological) in outlook, is not only (and therefore) specifically rural but also populist and orientalist.[27]

Utopic/Dystopic Discourse

These three agrarian populist texts combine and simultaneously juxtapose what might be termed the symptomatic discourse about the 'dystopic' and 'utopic', an opposition which delineates a form of political, economic and social existence that is either desirable (small-scale production, yeoman farmer, rural arcadia) or undesirable (technology, large-scale industry, urbanisation, socialism, finance capital and the proletariat).[28] In short, for agrarian populism utopia corresponds to its 'community' while dystopia constitutes the absence of the latter. More generally, the discourse about utopia/dystopia extends from (and epistemologically unites) the 'high culture' of the ancient world and traditional Christian beliefs on the one hand to the literary/filmic depiction of 'future worlds' in modern science fiction (time-travel and/or space-travel) on the other.[29] In so far as it addresses the desirability/undesirability of the structure/content of future worlds, therefore, it is a genre that not only transcends the 'high'/'low' cultural divide but also and thereby licenses the political construction/ reproduction of a 'popular culture' that is specifically populist.

An important distinction between the texts considered here is that whereas for Chayanov the dystopic is disclosed and warned against by a shift in time, for Hilton and Capra the same objective is achieved by a shift in space. The text by Donnelly combines a shift in both time and space. Accordingly, the utopic vision of Chayanov entails traversing time but not space; the protagonists in his narrative are projected forward into a future within the same demarcated space. By contrast, in the the utopic vision of Hilton and Capra it is space which is traversed and not time; both utopic and dystopic exist in the same moment but occupy a different terrain. Central to the discourse about 'the utopic' and/or 'the dystopic', therefore, is a sub-text concerning the sacredness (or profanation) of nature, space and time.

Utopic/Dystopic Nature

An important element of the discourse about utopia/dystopia is the concept of a violent/harmonious 'nature', whereby dystopia is equated with all that is 'unnatural' and utopia with 'natural' forms of social organisation and existence. Seemingly antithetical, violent/harmonious concepts of 'nature' are actually different sides of the same ideological coin, and constitute a Social Darwinist discourse in which humanity (instead of shaping) is shaped by 'nature'. Accordingly, the harmony which exists in the pastoral version is in fact underwritten by the violence of the 'red-in-tooth-and-claw' variant, in that a 'natural' order is not merely incribed in 'nature' but the latter periodically exercises its physical power in order to restore/maintain this. This discourse of Social Darwinism, or the view that change of all kinds is organic, and beyond the capacity of human agency to alter, licenses in turn a pessimistic view about humanity and historical progress, and thus about the possibility, the effectiveness and even the desirability of social change: where/when it takes place, the latter is regarded as a 'natural' process, as part of a project of innateness.

Fears about the destruction of 'nature' – and with it a 'natural' peasantry – invariably structure the utopic/dystopic portrayals that arise historically as a response to the depeasantisation that accompanies economic crisis. This kind of anxiety manifests itself in the implicit/explicit identification of a combined threat: (financial) capitalism and its even more nightmarish 'other', socialism. Thus the economic depression of the 1880s in England generated a whole literary genre projecting contrasting dystopic/utopic images of society, at the centre of which is a discourse about 'nature'.[30] In the utopias of William Morris and Richard Jefferies, for example, not only is 'nature' central to the narrative but in each instance it represents two different sides of the same coin; the former depicts a pastoral and the latter a Social Darwinist image of nature.[31] For the agrarian populist utopic, therefore, the objective is not, as with Marxism, one which entails that humanity be in control of nature, but much rather its opposite: that (an active) nature be in control of (a passive) humanity. Linked to this is the perception of a technology-that-is-out-of-control, the ultimate form of alien (= de-humanised = non-human = robotic) 'otherness' that structures many dystopic texts.[32]

Utopic/Dystopic Space

The ideological and metaphorical significance of symbolic spacing in the utopic/dystopic project derives in part from Christian tradition, in which a salvation that is non-material but spiritual is always to be found in heaven – located above (literally and metaphorically) the earth – where the innocence/purity/light of the Garden of Eden (= pastoral) is to be recuperated. Thus high physical space (= mountaintop) signals not only salvation but also the recovery of innocence and its accompanying primitive essence which is also rural (heaven = purity = redemption = peace = nature = utopia = 'the above'). By contrast, in the same religious tradition the earth (= purgatory, limbo) is the physically intermediate domain of 'the material' and the 'sinful-but-redeemable', a context that is both 'pure' (= rural) and 'impure' (= urban) where the (class) struggle (between capital and labour) for salvation which takes place results in either redemption or damnation.

Beneath them all, however, lies the underworld (= hell = violence = dystopia = 'the below'), the domain of 'the unredeemable-sinful' and thus metaphorically and literally the 'other' of Eden/heaven: the dark realm of death and the damned (= the urban proletariat, the 'underclass' or the 'mob-in-the-streets').[33] Unsurprisingly, the dystopic character of this symbolically potent physical 'otherness' is a pervasive theme in many of the literary/cinematic depictions in 'popular culture': examples from the science fiction genre include *The Underground Man* by Gabriel Tarde [1905], the film *Metropolis* (1926) directed by Fritz Lang, and – most notably – *The Time Machine* by H.G. Wells [1895], in which 'those below' were the violent/ (productive) Morlocks, the workers underground who provided for and then consumed the gentle/(parasitical) Eloi, 'those above' who led an idyllic rural existence in the 'Upper World'.

The importance of symbolic spacing in *Lost Horizon* is twofold. First, like the 'mountain' film genre in Germany during the same period, the physical location of Shangri-La within the highest/(undiscovered) peaks of the Himalayas similarly projects an aura of sacredness/spirituality linked to it being the abode of the gods, a perception reinforced by its mythical/legendary status.[34] And second, the physical occupation by the lamasery of the middle foreground raised mightily over the valley floor (a spatial distinction that is very evident in the film), accurately conveys the relative importance in the class structure of its respective inhabitants: its mainly European rulers are situated 'up above', while the indigenous peasantry (= 'natives') that is the object of this rule occupies the space 'down below'.

The same kind of symbolism is if anything even more pronounced in the physical ordering of space in *Caesar's Column*: in the underworld, below everyone, is the 'under-class' or proletariàt, while immmediately above them occupying the middle ground is the aristocracy of finance capital; above them all, 'amidst the high mountain valleys of Africa', is the colony of 'the saved'.[35] As significant is the fact that, as Donnelly [1960:38] observes, those below (= the urban proletariat) cannot by travelling 'that narrow, gloomy, highwalled pathway, out of which they could never climb' escape from their dystopic situation up the mountain to utopia: like the case of Shangri-la in *Lost Horizon*, therefore, the working class inhabitants of the 'Under-World' in *Caesar's Column* will not be permitted to reach Eden, there to find redemption.

Utopic/Dystopic Time

As important and symbolic as space in the 'utopic' project is the element of time. Accordingly, in the sacred context of utopia the passage of time is itself suspended, and with it history, the object being to halt – if not to reverse – the economic development which licenses the double threat of socialism and the feared 'mob-in-the-streets'. Unsurprisingly, such views (whereby a-historicism merges with and becomes anti-historicism/anti-science/anti-progress) combine to structure the contextually-specific perceptions of 'a decadent civilisation in decline' that are themselves part of a conservative response to (or reaction against) capitalist crisis. The suspension of time in 'utopic' discourse also contributes to the reproduction of a number of interrelated politico-ideological stereotypes: the myth of an ever-present, self-sufficient/subsistence-oriented a-historical peasant farmer, the eternal 'lazy native' whose alleged indolence stems from the 'unchanging timelessness' (= the essential sameness) of nature itself, a conceptualisation which in turn lies behind most of the orientalist notions about the 'primitive'/'otherness' of Africa and the East.

The questioning of progress as 'unnatural' is itself linked historically to the rejection by conservative intellectuals such as Nietzsche, Spengler, Pareto, Ortega y Gasset and Le Bon of a linear conception of time, and its replacement by cyclical notions of time based on the annual cycle of birth/death in nature.[36] Nature/time is accordingly suspended in an 'eternal present', which is divinely and/or 'naturally' ordained and ordered, and its hierarchy/'difference' (= heterogeneity, diversity) is therefore sacred and/or 'natural'. Perhaps the most potent ideological manifestation of the latter view is the redemptive myth of a 'golden age', which not only structures the many and recurring proclamations in the midst of capitalism by populists/populism announcing the 'end-of-history' and the 'end-of-ideology', but is also present in the symbols, rites, and religious customs/ceremonies of most non-capitalist social formations [Eliade 1954], where it involves the ideological attempt to replace the mortality of profane time (= history) with the immortality of sacred time.[37] Hence the timelessness of Shangri-La in *Lost Horizon* represents the attainment of sacred time, the eternal present of the Garden of Eden: no one who does not leave Shangri-La grows old.[38]

III

Before considering the positive elements of the populist utopic as presented in these texts by Donnelly, Chayanov, Hilton and Capra, it is important to establish the negative structure (together with its determinants) of their dystopic 'other': that is, the mirror image of the utopic.

Dystopic Capitalism, Dystopic Crisis, Dystopic Rulers

Unlike *Journey of My Brother*, in which the dystopic is socialist, both *Caesar's Column* and *Lost Horizon* are characterised by a capitalist dystopia. In both the latter texts, however, the anti-capitalist discourse is of a specific type: in each case the responsibility for – and hence the target of their political attack – is not capitalism *per se* but finance capital (= usury). Not only does Donnelly portray finance capital as all-powerful (a force that 'has the whole world in its grasp') and responsible for the plight of the indebted yeoman farmer and thus the undermining of the agrarian myth, but he also – and most significantly – inculpates financial capital with creating the urban proletariat which destroys the whole of existing civilisation.[39]

As depicted in *Caesar's Column*, therefore, the ruling class responsible for the dystopic condition of New York in 1988 is not only composed of aristocratic representatives of finance capital, but the latter is also closely associated in Donnelly's narrative with an ethnically 'foreign'/'alien' Jewish 'other'.[40] This opposition between an idealised and ethnically 'pure' American republicanism and its 'impure' aristocratic ruling class 'other' is underlined in the narrative by the fact that one of the two principal female characters, who is a lineal descendent of the first president, is sold as a concubine to Prince Cabano, the ruling financier.[41] Hence the purchase by 'Jewish finance capital' of that most sacred of American symbols permits a relay-in-statement of negative identities (urban = foreigner = Jewish = finance capital = non-American 'otherness'). By contrast, the two principal female characters (Christina, Estrella) not only come from (and thus symbolically represent) rural backgrounds, but also (and thereby) embody moral virtue and racial 'purity', licensing a series of symbolically interchangeable positive identities (woman = virtue = purity = rural = nature = Aryan = civilisation = authentically American).[42]

Much the same is true of *Lost Horizon*, in which the economic crisis of the 1930s is presented not as a systemic effect of capitalism itself but rather as the fault of financiers and intellectuals, thereby combining populist anti-capitalism and anti-intellectualism.[43] Significantly, the representative of (unproductive) finance capital, the speculator Bernard/Bryant, not only finds redemption in Shangri-La, where he reverts to a productive role, but is exonerated by Conway who, as the representative of the state, also inculpates himself for the existing capitalist crisis.[44] The sub-text in this particular case is that the capitalist system would function adequately if financiers, intellectuals and the state were all prevented from interfering with it.

Dystopic Workers, Dystopic Struggle, Dystopic Socialism

Perhaps no other component of agrarian populist discourse-against is allocated quite such a negative role in precipitating a dystopic armageddon, and thus depicted in quite the same pathological manner, as the urban working class. Symptomatically, therefore, for Donnelly the existence of the urban industrial proletariat in the New York of 1988 is the mirror image of his rural paradise: in contrast to the yeoman farmer of the agrarian myth, the 'haggard', 'hopeless' workers inhabit an urban anti-utopia which corresponds to a literal and metaphorical 'underworld' that is 'death in life', 'the resurrection of the dead' and 'hell'.[45] Like its 'other' and creator, finance capital, the American proletariat of *Caesar's Column* is similarly 'impure', being composed of ethnically diverse migrants (= 'invading Mongolian hordes').[46] Indeed, the less 'controllable' and the more revolutionary the working class becomes, the more the narrative of *Caesar's Column* focuses on its ethnic composition, a discourse in which the latter is equated with the 'alien'/'darkness' both of urban 'otherness' and of the destructive 'otherness' of 'barbarism'/'chaos'.[47]

Of greater concern to Donnelly than the oppression and exploitation of the industrial workforce, however, is the fact that a century hence it has become organised, and formed the Brotherhood of Destruction.[48] Not only does the latter have a global membership of one hundred million, but workers are now routinely familiar with Marxist theory and have acquired a consciousness of class, as a consequence of which it is no longer possible to control them.[49] Most significantly, for Donnelly this is a transformation that is not only unnecessary but one that must be reversed, a view which contrasts with that of Marxism which *celebrates* such a transition. His fear is that by de-naturing the peasantry of the agrarian myth, and turning the yeoman farmer into a landless labourer in the city, finance capital creates not just its 'other' but an 'other' in its own brutal image.[50]

Once a peasantry is transformed into a proletariat, Donnelly warns, it loses not only its land but also its passivity and thus its political inhibitions: accordingly, he implies, the yeoman farmer of the American agrarian myth should be retained not so much for economic reasons (= the viability of self-sufficient cultivation) as for political reasons.[51] In short, to prevent an historically 'eternal' category of petty commodity producers from being separated by (finance) capital from its traditional means of production, in the process becoming what all fractions of the bourgeoisie fear most: a class conscious urban proletariat no longer under their collective control, or the 'mob-in-the-streets' that pervades the dystopia of agrarian populism.[52]

Since much of the anti-modern and anti-technological discourse of agrarian populism is founded on the fear of the 'mob-in-the-streets', it is unsurprising to encounter in *Caesar's Column*, in *Journey of My Brother* and in *Lost Horizon* a pervasive anti-socialist politics. In the case of *Lost Horizon*, therefore, the film version by Capra commences with a literal and symbolic flight by Conway (and the others) to escape from a Chinese revolutionary 'mob-in-the-streets'. Hence the journey which ends in Shangri-La/utopia commences by leaving behind the 'twin evils' that structure the dystopia of agrarian populism: finance capital and its 'other', the revolutionary working class.[52a] For Donnelly the impossibility/ undesirability of socialism is similarly evident from his apocalyptic vision of New York once the proletarian revolution is realised: not only is the latter process depicted as nihilistic, a pointless act of destruction by the 'mob-in-the-streets', but for him the overturning of the existing division of labour appears 'unnatural'.[53] Furthermore, the revolutionaries are presented as in the end being no different from the financiers who ruled them, and thus incapable of constructing an alternative to the whole oppressive/exploitative system which they have overthrown.[54]

Chayanov regards a socialist alternative to capitalism in similarly negative terms, although in his case it is an alternative that has already been tried and found wanting. In the course of his time-travel to the Moscow of 1984, therefore, Kremnev learns that the socialist system of the 1920s was of short duration, and collapsed into its national components amidst a more general process of war and European fragmentation, since when 'the system had been slowly evolving towards an increasingly peasant regime'.[55] Significantly, it was the collapse of socialism that led to the re-emergence of its 'other': the system of peasant family farming. Dismissing the Bolsheviks as 'ideologists of the working class', Chayanov concludes by claiming that they were 'enlightened absolutists' who had been responsible for reducing Russia to 'a condition of anarchic reaction'.[56]

IV

Turning to the physiognomy of the agrarian populist utopia, not only are finance capitalism, technology, the urban proletariat and socialism – the dystopic effects of time and historical progress – absent, but in terms of class position and ethnic origin political power is exercised by a different subject.

Agrarian Populist Utopia as Non-Technological 'Other'

Since at the centre of most literary/filmic representations of anti-modern dystopias lies the nightmare vision of a planned (= rational) future, unsurprisingly an important aspect of existence in the utopic 'other' is its non-/anti-technological socio-economic structure.[57] The historical appeal of the latter to agrarian populism is unsurprising, since technology has been the visible manifestation of the large-scale economic power of capital, and the method whereby smallholders were not only separated from their means of production (= physically displaced-from/replaced-on the land) but also lost control over both their land and their own labour-power, each of which were ideologically deeply rooted in a discourse about 'nature'.[58]

In *Caesar's Column, Journey of My Brother* and *Lost Horizon*, therefore, a large-scale technology/industrialisation (and, by implication, modernity itself) is represented in negative terms.[59] Hence the government of the utopian 'garden in the mountains' located in the Uganda of 1988 discourages the invention of labour-displacing techniques, since in this context the desired objective is 'not cheap goods or cheap men, but happy families'.[60] Similarly, the Moscow of 1984 has reverted to a non-technified labour-intensive peasant agriculture, while in Shangri-La technology – like modernity generally – is presented as an unwelcome 'contamination' from the 'outside' below, the process of 'machine-power multiplying' being equated with the familiar dystopic theme of technology-beyond-the-control-of-humanity.[61]

Agrarian Populist Utopia as Oriental/Pastoral 'Other'

Given the negative/dystopic elements (capitalism, socialism, urbanisation, technology) which structure the discourse-against of agrarian populism, it is equally unsurprising that its positive/utopic reproduces and reaffirms the importance of two distinct forms of 'otherness': it is both orientalist and rural. A return to this rural/'primitive'/Eastern 'otherness', therefore, is celebrated in a specifically orientalist mode: imperial colonisation. Hence the utopia of *Caesar's Column* is not only located in the new state of Uganda in the African confederation, where English is the universal language, but has been colonised by the family of the main character for a period of 70 years.[62] Furthermore, Africa is depicted as the exotic/ mysterious/unknowable 'other' of imperial discourse, the mirror image of urban New York in 1988; it is accordingly described by Donnelly both as 'primitive' and as 'that strange, wild, ancient, lofty land'.[63]

Much the same is true of *Lost Horizon*. Just like the Southern Agrarians in the United States, whose response to the capitalist crisis of the 1930s was to advocate a return to the non-capitalist 'natural' values embodied in the cultural 'otherness' of the antebellum American south, so Frank Capra in the midst of the same capitalist crisis similarly attempted to recuperate a seemingly 'authentic' non-capitalist, agrarian and culturally-specific form of 'otherness' physically removed from the present, but this time located in the 'orient'. For Capra and Hilton, therefore, the utopia of Shangri-La in *Lost Horizon* is orientalist, located in the domain of the Eastern 'other' in Tibet.[64] Indeed, the utopias in *Caesar's Column* and *Lost Horizon* both share the same geography, and thus symbolic spacing: rural arcadias in exotic colonial settings, situated within – and protected from the outside by – high mountain ranges. Hence the description by Donnelly of the physical location of his utopia-in-Uganda in the inaccessible high mountain valleys of Africa could just as easily apply to Shangri-La in *Lost Horizon*.[65]

In literary practice the pastoral tradition is structured by the opposition between on the one hand a simple/ happy/('natural') life in the tranquillity of the countryside that is light and open, and on the other the corruption/ depravity/pollution of 'unnatural' existence in the city, which is dark, narrow and dangerous. The utopic of agrarian populism, therefore, is essentially the attempt to recuperate the traditional values associated with a 'natural' but vanishing rural social order threatened by the violent expansion of industrial/financial capitalism and its accompanying 'other', socialism. This is especially true of the utopia in *Caesar's Column*, which constitutes the epitome of the American agrarian myth based on nostalgia for a 'golden age': that is, a 'little world [that] is a garden of peace and beauty', or a combination of 'the primitive, simple shepherd-life' and homestead farming, a situation characterised by an 'equal distribution of wealth' in which no individual landholding would exceed one hundred acres.[66] Similarly, the Valley of the Blue Moon in *Lost Horizon* is described by Hilton as 'nothing less than an enclosed paradise of amazing fertility ... crops of unusual diversity grew in profusion and contiguity, with not an inch of ground untended.' The idyllic nature of this rural arcadia emerges most clearly in the pastoral imagery which structures the film version, the visual impact of which led Graham Greene to describe Shangri-La as a place of 'flirtatious pursuits through grape arbours, splashings and divings in blossomy pools under improbable waterfalls and rich and enormous meals'.[67]

The same is true of *Journey of My Brother*. The Russia of 1984, in which towns no longer existed, was now a land of abundance, an agrarian society dominated economically by the peasant family farm, which emerged and consolidated following the implosion of socialism during the 1920s and peasant revolution of the 1930s.[68] As in *Caesar's Column* and *Lost Horizon*, the resulting social order of utopia based on peasant farming is depicted by Chayanov as a return to an ancient and natural condition which neither capitalism nor socialism had been able to supress for long.[69] Accordingly, the Russia of the mid-1980s is characterised by an absence of 'large fortunes', an economic situation referred to by Chayanov as 'the democratisation of national income'.[70] In short, a context in which no socio-economic differentiation of the peasantry occurs, and consequently an economy in which all petty commodity producers remain the same.

Class Structure in the Agrarian Populist Utopia

Claims about peasant economy notwithstanding, it is important to note that the agrarian populist utopia does not exclude the possibility of small-scale capital accumulation, and hence the persistence and/or development of class relations. Thus it is only finance capital and not capitalism *per se* that is to be banished from the agrarian populist utopia of *Caesar's Column*. Criticising usury which 'kills off the enterprising members of a community by bankrupting them', therefore, Donnelly not only presents small-scale manufacturing in a positive light but also accepts in principle the process of accumulation and the unequal distribution and inheritance of wealth, maintaining that 'only in their excess [do] they become destructive'.[71] The same appears to be true of Russia in 1984 where, as Chayanov makes very clear, the continued existence of the peasant family farm is not itself incompatible with the survival of the market, a 'residual capitalism' described by him as 'tame' and non-exploitative.[72]

As with the dystopia of agrarian populism, the nature and ethnic origin of the ruling class in its utopia is equally specific. Accordingly, in *Caesar's Column* those who flee from the New York in 1988 to the safety of 'the garden in the mountains' in Uganda are in the main of 'Aryan' ancestry, while in the case of *Lost Horizon* the traditional political ruling hierarchy in Shangri-la is a theocracy at the apex of which are similarly to be found representatives of the 'Nordic' races, a ruling class that is periodically replenished mainly by Europeans who arrive from the outside.[73] Although neither the Ugandan colony in 1988 nor the Moscow of 1984 is a theocracy, Christian religion discharges an important role in the former while in the latter context political power is exercised by a monastic order (the Brotherhood of Saints).[74]

The structure of class rule in utopia is evident from the similarity in the nature of political power and role of the state in all three texts considered here. As Donnelly makes clear, although nominally democratic, state power in his agrarian populist utopia is actually exercised by a ruling class, albeit of a different kind from that which ruled its dystopic urban 'other'.[75] In Chayanov's Moscow of 1984, the state operates on a *laissez-faire* principle whereby the ruling peasant regime 'for the most part relied on social methods of solving problems, not measures of state coercion'. Based on peasant councils, the state has neither role nor substantial power, having been stripped of 'virtually all social and economic functions' and replaced by what appear indistinguishable from grassroots non-government organisations.[76] Symptomatically, the benign role of the state attributed by Chayanov to the peasant regime is contrasted with the coercive, surplus-extracting state apparatus under socialism: in the latter context, it is argued, the state exploited the workers in order to maintain a wasteful bureaucracy, thereby reproducing once again a central ideological premiss not just of agarian populism but also of the political right.[77] Exactly the same *laissez-faire* principle structures politics in Shangri-La, where the 'prevalent belief' of its ruling class is in 'moderation'.[78]

Notwithstanding the tranquillity implied in the idyllic character of ruling class existence in the utopias of *Caesar's Column*, *Journey of My Brother* and *Lost Horizon*, each is nevertheless structured by a sub-text that is aggressively nationalist and/or Social Darwinist.[79] Thus 'the saved' who manage to escape from a dystopic New York of 1988 not only take with them examples of ruling class culture but also as the inhabitants of 'the garden in the mountains' in Uganda then erect a wall to prevent those still on the outside from entering utopia.[80] In the case of Moscow during 1984, the Russian Peasant Republic conscripts 'nature' itself (a cyclone) in order to protect itself from and to vanquish Germany, characterised by Chayanov as 'the defeated hordes', a conflict which itself mimics the nationalist defence of a subsistence-oriented smallholding peasantry mounted by Slavophile populism against German (= 'foreign') capitalist penetration of Russia during the late nineteenth century.[81] Much the same kind of discourse is evident in *Lost Horizon*, where – as in the case of *Caesar's Column* – the fear is that the capitalist crisis 'outside' will result in the destruction not so much of society but of ruling class culture; accordingly, the object of the 'utopic' is in this case to protect/preserve the latter against a rapacious modernity and its machine.[82]

Most importantly, in none of the utopias depicted in these three agrarian populist texts is there a sizeable urban working class. Thus a potentially threatening proletariat is largely absent from Donnelly's Uganda in 1988, and wholly absent from the Shangri-La of Hilton and Capra in the 1930s: in both these contexts, the main producers are self-sufficient cultivators.[83] Neither is there an urban proletariat in the Moscow of 1984 as depicted by Chayanov. The reason for this is significant: towns had been abolished because of the threat posed by the proletariat which resided and worked in them. In short, for Chayanov the fear of industrialisation and urbanisation that would lead to socialism – via the kind of apocalypse predicted in the texts by Donnelly, Hilton and Capra – had resulted in the pre-emptive and counter-revolutionary destruction by the Russian peasantry of urban habitation and the decentralisation of production.[84]

For all these reasons, it is necessary to disagree with Marin [1993: 9–10], for whom utopia represents an equilibrium, a neutral space between rival powers in which neither prevails. Although corresponding to many other aspects of 'the utopic', therefore, Shangri-La during the 1930s, Moscow in 1984 and Uganda in 1988 are not so much 'neutral'/'in-between' (= liminal) spaces, in which power is negated, but much rather a locus of its *expression*.

V

Concluding Comments

The resurgence in the current crisis of capitalism of a 'communitarian' political agenda which seeks to construct a concept of 'community' (= utopia) that does not entail a radical transformation in property relations indicates yet again the historical pervasiveness amidst recurring capitalist crises of populist ideology. To a significant degree, the agrarian populist discourse-for and discourse-against in *Caesar's Column*, in *Journey of My Brother* and in *Lost Horizon* overlaps with and is thus supportive of the oppositions which in turn structure utopic/dystopic discourse (high/low space, time/timelessness, and most importantly the rejection/recuperation of 'nature'), albeit with some variations and additional elements.

Hence the dystopic 'other' of these agrarian populist texts is characterised by the absence of 'community', or a situation in which a modern financial capitalism generates an urban environment, a technology and a workforce none of which can be controlled: that is, an urban industrial proletariat which threatens armageddon/(damnation) by becoming both revolutionary and socialist. The latter possibility is the subject of warnings contained in all three texts; Chayanov, however, issues his from within the context of a socialist dystopia which already exists and which can thus be avoided if an alternative path based on peasant economy is not supressed, whereas Donnelly, Hilton and Capra do so in reverse, by charting the dystopic role of finance capitalism which occurs precisely because such an agrarian populist course was not followed.

Furthermore, both finance capital and the proletariat are united in their 'otherness' for agrarian populism by virtue of being not merely the harbingers of the dystopic but also because each is the 'inauthentic' ethnic/national 'other'. Accordingly, it is Jewish finance capital that is blamed for creating its 'other', an urban proletariat containing a large black component, a discourse which mimics that of the political right (for which Jewish finance capital creates its 'other', Jewish Bolshevism). All the dystopic elements (finance capital, the proletariat, urbanisation, industrialisation) in *Lost Horizon* and *Caesar's Column* not only have a specific ethnic identity but have their origins in and/or are associated with 'western civilisation'. By contrast, all the utopic elements (small-scale accumulation, the rural, the peasantry) tend to be located in the domain of the Eastern 'other', thereby implicitly conceding the fear by agrarian populism of large-scale industrialisation/urbanisation associated with both capitalist and socialist development as in nationalist terms a specifically 'alien' and Western 'other'.

The desired utopia (= 'community') in all three texts is therefore not only orientalist and rural, but is also characterised by the suspension of time, and with it history, the object being to halt economic development, if not to reverse it. An effect of this a-historical timelessness is that it permits in turn the celebration/(salvation) of the traditional small-scale producer (artisan, farmer, peasant) in the context of an Edenic pastoral. Although in each case the discourse is against capitalism, the latter – like socialism – encompasses only large-scale industrial manufacturing: specific forms of small-scale accumulation, such as handicraft/artisan/peasant production, are thus acceptable within the context of the agrarian populist utopia.

The refusal to admit large numbers of those on the 'outside' who might wish to enter both the Ugandan colony and Shangri-La as a result of the capitalist crisis suggests further that access to these particular utopias is Social Darwinist in two specific ways: not only is it restricted in terms of ethnic and class composition, but it is also limited to those who appreciate/ know/respect the upper-class cultural values that it desires to conserve/ preserve. These agrarian populist utopias constitute, in short, the 'utopic' as ordered by a (mainly) white European ruling class, in which hierarchy is ordained by God, is 'natural', is based on nature, and is presented either as acceptable to (and thus not challenged by) those below, or beyond the capacity of the latter to challenge.

NOTES

1. Although less serious than the utterances of Robert Conway about Shangri-La in the film *Lost Horizon*, this aside by Bob Hope a quarter of a century later nevertheless makes an oblique reference to the same kinds of 'otherness' (the 'East' in general, the Tibetan lamasery in particular, and the kind of the power exercised in the latter context).

2. For much the same reason – attempting to identify 'community' where none exists – the 'communitarianism' of Etzioni has come under attack from those on the neo-liberal political right as well as those on the political left. Accordingly, those on the left criticise 'communitarianism' from the viewpoint of a socialist alternative, based on the control by the state of market forces. Similarly accepting that markets destroy communities, neo-liberals on the political right (for an example of which see John Gray, 'Hollowing Out the Core', *The Guardian*, London, 8 March 1995) maintain by contrast that the impossibility of 'communitarianism' derives from the unviability/undesirability of state control over the market. For the heterogeneity of political and economic views subsumed under the concept 'community', see Kamenka [1982].

3. For the 'culturalist' discourse of those on the European 'new' right, and why in some instances it takes a pro-Third World position, see among others Miglio [1993], Durando [1993], de Benoist [1994], and Taguieff [1990; 1994a; 1994b]. Examples of development theory influenced by a postmodern new social movements and/or a Subaltern Studies framework include Laclau [1985; 1993], Guha [1982–89], Omvedt [1994], Shiva [1989; 1991], and Booth [1994]. For the common epistemological lineage of the latter, together with a critical discussion of their postmodern/populist/conservative politics, see Brass [1991; 1995a; 1995b]. Political disagreements notwithstanding, it is important to differentiate the theoretical work of those such as MacIntyre, Etzioni, Lasch, Rawls, Rorty, Guha, Shiva and Omvedt, all of whom are at the intellectually serious end of the populist spectrum, from the varieties of inconsequential dilettantism (for example, Hawthorn [1991]) to be found at its non-serious end.

4. Hence the current appeal of a 'communitarian' ideology to a wide spectrum of centre/right political opinion (for example, Democrats in America; Liberal Democrats, Labour and Conservatives in Britain) is precisely because it does not to any great degree question existing property relations. It is in short an attempt to construct a concept of 'community' that is compatible with the continued reproduction of capitalism. As Etzioni himself observes: 'But what about socio-economic rights? What is the communitarian economic agenda? The short answer is, there is none ... Our agenda, so far, has largely been "cultural" ... Cultural factors need attending to and are, indeed, at the core of the communitarian mission. ('Common Values', *New Statesman and Society*, 12 May 1995). Moreover, the work of MacIntyre [1981] suggests that communitarian ethics are traditional and thus backward-looking, to be retrieved from an idealised 'golden age' of Mediaeval Christianity and Ancient Greece. Unlike the concept of 'community' which structures the liberal social theory of Etzioni, Rawls and Rorty, the same concept as used by socialists can have an existence only

where all means of production are also subject to common ownership. Significantly, the attempt by current 'communitarian' ideology to establish 'community' without transforming property relations is itself prefigured in the views of agrarian populists in America. Thus for Lasch [1995] – as for Donnelly – the threat to democracy comes from 'new elites' which control not just information (= intellectuals) but also globally-mobile money (= international finance capital); again like Donnelly, the suspicion remains that what communitarians such as Lasch really fear is that 'the revolt of the elites' in the form of a refusal by the rich to recognise the existence of social obligations to and a shared humanity and common bonds with the poor and less-well-off will lead to 'the revolt of the masses'. Noting that communitarianism and populism both attach importance to small-scale property, family values and tradition, and each is anti-state and rejects the untrammelled freedom of the market (because this undermines small property), Lasch [1995: 92–114] accepts that both ideologies are essentially the same. In contrast to Marxism, which seeks to abolish both private property and class by means of revolutionary action, therefore, communitarians such as Lasch and agrarian populists like Donnelly [1960: 5, 66] want merely to reform the existing system and establish a 'brotherhood between classes' while leaving property relations largely intact. Evidence of this earlier communitarianism in *Caesar's Column* takes the form of, for example, appeals by Gabriel Weltstein to the ruling class to spare humanity, his defence of a clergyman preaching reconciliation between capital and labour, and the conversion of political conservatives to utopian ideals [*Donnelly*, 1960: 137–9, 167–71, 310]. There are also constant references in the film version of *Lost Horizon* to Shangri-La as a 'community'.

5. Unfortunately, this distinction is overlooked in much of what passes for 'analysis' of the discourse 'from below', with the result that there has been a shift from critical engagement with to an uncritical celebration of 'popular culture' (for a recent example of which, see Samuel [1995]). Although they have always been aware of the role of the media in the class struggle, socialists have nevertheless tended to underestimate both the importance and the extent of its negative impact in constructing/reproducing/reinforcing/deflecting particular forms of political consciousness. As Raymond Williams (Britton [1991: 106]) reminds us:

> What was often not noticed on the left, and is perhaps not fully noticed even today, is that there are others besides radicals and democrats who are interested in being popular. What was supposed to be a monopoly in one selected sense of the people fighting for their rights and freedoms, turned out to be very different ... Certainly radicals and democrats fought for the new [media] forms and the new freedoms, but so did commercial entrepreneurs [and] capitalists from that day to this. They saw their own versions of possibility in the new technologies, the new audiences which were being formed ... .

Hence the enthusiasm manifested among those on the left in Europe and the United States during the 1920s for cinema as a form of 'popular culture' that would contribute substantially to the political advancement/emancipation of the working class was in many ways similar to the current postmodern obsession with 'popular culture' as a medium for 'self-empowerment'. Only later did politically progressive film criticism recognise that in a capitalist context the agenda of what constituted the 'popular' was set largely from above and not below. In this connection, it is impossible to overlook the important political role of film music in the reproduction of ideological forms (the longing for, 'belonging' to, and celebration of nationalism/religion/'nature') that are themselves supportive of the agrarian myth. Nowhere perhaps is this crucial function more evident than the way in which the music produced for the Hollywood cinema during the 1930s and 1940s was a pastiche of (and thus reproduced the nostalgia inherent in) its nineteenth century Romantic variant [*Flinn*, 1992]. Since the interpretation by the audience of the cinematic image is to an important degree structured by an accompanying melody the imperceptability of which makes such ideological framing all the more effective, the resulting 'innocence'/'naturalness' of the music permits a powerful emotional conditioning of the visual experience in terms of its dramatic/spiritual/mythic/real/positive/negative meaning. It is not without significance, therefore, that the orchestral score by Dmitri Tiomkin was among the Academy Award nominations made in connection with the film version of *Lost Horizon*.

6. This characterisation by populism of capitalist crisis as the effect not of accumulation but

rather of 'human greed' emerges most clearly in two of the texts considered below, in which the dystopic is a specifically capitalist phenomenon. In *Lost Horizon*, therefore, Hilton [1933: 148–9] observes that the Great Depression of the 1930s which resulted from speculation on the financial markets was itself the consequence of people 'want[ing] something for nothing'. Similarly, in the case of *Caesar's Column*, the apocalyptic destruction of modern civilisation is blamed by Donnelly [1960: 71–2] on 'human greed, – blind, insatiable, human greed – ... selfish instincts, these have done this work!'. Such a theorisation, in which the solution to the crisis entails not systemic but individual transformation, is of course compatible with the continued existence of capitalism, albeit on a small scale.

7. This is evident not only from the discourse-against of Donnelly in America during the 1890s and Chayanov in Russia during the 1920s (see below) but also from an observation (cited in Mitrany [1951: 119, 241]) by G.K. Chesterton in England during the 1920s that: 'What has happened in Europe since the [1914–18] war has been a vast victory for the peasants, and therefore a vast defeat both for the Communists and the capitalists ... In a sort of awful silence the peasantries have fought one vast and voiceless pitched battle with Bolshevism and its twin brother, which is Big Business, and the peasantries have won.'

8. There are unfortunately many instances of the displacement of socialist ideas by populist ones because of a failure to distinguish between these two forms of anti-capitalism. One example is Genovese [1994], who now finds merit in the political opposition by Southern Agrarians to the expanding power of the free market and the stong state, and consequently makes common cause with the reactionary discourse-against of southern conservatism. Another example, also from North America, is the journal *Telos*, the rightwards political trajectory of which has – for much the same reason – moved from Western Marxism through Critical Theory, communitarianism and populism, to its present ultra-conservative position: a platform for the recuperation/dissemination of the reactionary views held by those (such as Carl Schmitt, Gianfranco Miglio, Alain de Benoist) whose ideas are associated with the old or 'new' (= allegedly 'post-fascist') right in Europe.

9. The theme of peasant-as-warrior, together with the negative consequences for the nation of this ceasing to be the case, is particularly marked in the agrarian populist discourse of *Caesar's Column*. Noting that in America towards the end of the nineteenth century the numerous uprisings by the working class were supressed by 'sons of farmers', one of the characters [*Donnelly*, 1960: 96] laments that as the number of farmers had declined this source of defence can no longer be relied upon. The resulting situation is clearly outlined by Donnelly [1960: 97]:

> Hence the materials for armies have disappeared. Human greed has eaten away the very foundations on which it stood ... when the Great Day [of the revolution] comes, and the nation sends forth its call for volunteers, as in the past, that cry will echo in desolate places ... [there will be no] desire or capacity [among those farmers which remain] to make soldiers and defend their oppressors.

Of especial significance, therefore, is the fact that by proletarianising yeoman farmers, and transforming them into their 'other' (= the 'mob-in-the-streets') finance capital has destroyed not only the peasantry (= warriors) which protected its own class power by defending the latter against the proletariat but also and thereby the nation itself.

10. However much its exponents attempt to deny it, the existence of a substantial epistemological and political overlap between on the one hand currently fashionable variants of postmodernism and populism, and on the other much conservative philosophy, cannot be dismissed as accidental, irrelevant and/or unimportant. Like populism and postmodernism, conservatism is distrustful of overarching/'foundational' materialist theories, which each dismisses as false optimism propounded by those (mainly marxists) who adhere to unacceptable/irrelevant meta-narratives and universals. By contrast, populism, postmodernism and conservatism are similarly respectful/protective of an a-historical/idealised concept of the past, notions both of locality and of 'community' that do not question property relations, and all celebrate difference/diversity generally and that of the autonomous/fragmented individual subject in particular.

11. For agrarian populism in these contexts over this period, see Hicks [1931], Saloutos and

Hicks [1951], Mitrany [1951], Hofstadter [1962; 1969], Walicki [1969], Furth [1976], Havens [1974], Cardoza [1982], Conkin [1988], Fritzsche [1990], and Soucy [1995]. For the centrality of the pastoral to English culture generally, and the contrast with a demonic image of its urban 'other', see Williams [1973: 8–12; 1985]. After the 1914-18 war, 'a rural England where clocks have stopped' was epitomised in the pastoral idiom of the Georgian poets (Timms [1985: 113]), for whom '[p]overty is quaint because it is rural ... [t]hese are poets who have closed their minds to merely to social change, but to the transformation of discourse which accompanied it'. Like the character Conway in *Lost Horizon*, '[t]hey are refugees, not merely from the city but from the twentieth century'. It is not necessary to endorse the conclusion presented in the text by Weiner [1981], that in England from the mid-nineteenth century onwards the pastoral myth blocked the development of industrial capitalism, therefore, to accept the validity of his argument regarding the pervasiveness of this ideology. In America the agrarian myth overlapped with and was itself structured by the frontier myth (on which see Hofstadter and Lipset [1968]), in that the latter enabled an infinite expansion of the smallholding economy idealised by the former. (Significantly, the liminality of the frontier is one of the properties identified by Marin [1993] as constitutive of 'the utopic') That the agrarian myth still structures the discourse of the far right in America is clear from Sargent [1995: 19, 156, 340].

12. As is clear from various sources (Rogger and Weber [1965], Havens [1974], Cardoza [1982], and Blinkhorn [1990]), many of the characteristics of agrarian populist ideology mobilised by the political right in Germany, Italy and Japan during the 1920s and 1930s were also important in the rise of fascism in other European countries. Thus one sympathetic observer of agrarian populism [*Mitrany*, 1951:149] concedes that:

> It was significant of the two reactionary mass movements which made their appearance in western Europe that both laid great store upon peasant life and work ... German National-Socialism especially set the fashion for an almost mystical glorification of the peasant ... The Spanish Falangists were telling the peasants that 'Spain was the countryside'. In Germany as in Spain, and later in Vichy France, the peasant family was set up as the hope for national revival ... France, said Marchal Pétain, 'will recover all her strength by contact with the soil'. And a Nazi spokesman demanded the 'de-urbanisation of our whole way of thinking'.

13. For cinematic themes of 'peasant-as-warrior-defending-the-nation' in the case of Japanese and German 'popular culture' during the 1930s and early 1940s, see Richie [1972: 43–44, 45, 51], Kracauer [1947: 261ff.], Hinz [1980: 111–17, 125], and Welch [1983: 105–8].

14. Belton [1994: 313] suggests that a similar nostalgia for the 'lost innocence' of smalltown family/community values – but now located in the 1950s – pervades many films of the late 1970s and 1980s, such as the time-travelling *Back to the Future*. For the connection between Capra's films and populist ideology, see Richards [1970], Rohdie [1970], Levy [1991], and McBride [1992: 253–4, 259]. Capra, who himself invested substantially in land and became a millionaire by the end of the 1930s, can aptly be described [*McBride*, 1992: 329, 382] as someone whose film *oeuvre* 'balances ... Republican economic principles with a democratic fantasy of nonconformity ... by and large, a safe nonconformity, without risk of adverse economic or social consequences and therefore a meaningless form of pseudo-revolt'.

15. Interestingly, in the version of *It's a Wonderful Life* scripted by Dalton Trumbo, one of the Hollywood Ten who was blacklisted by the McCarthyite House Committee on Un-American Activities (HUAC), no distinction is made between 'good' and 'bad' capitalist. As McBride [1992: 521–2] notes:

> Trumbo's George [Bailey] is a politician who rises from an idealistic state assemblyman to a cynical congressman contemptuous of the people he represents ... [in Trumbo's script] there is no [Henry S.] Potter to serve as George's nemesis, for George, in effect, serves as his own Potter – a ruthless modern businessman who carelessly spoils the town for his own profit. The harsh, explicit social criticisms of Trumbo's script cut too close to the bone for Capra [who] retreats from the Marxist implications of Trumbo's view of capitalism, carefully balancing its unfavourable (and unbelievable) portrait of an evil

businessman (Potter) with a favourable portrait of a good businessman (George) ... *It's a Wonderful Life* paints the Bailey–Potter conflict in the Manichaean rhetorical terms of the Populist Party in the 1890s, showing the extent to which Capra had become locked into an anachronistic, and by then reactionary, thought pattern.

16. Ignatius Donnelly, who was born in Pennsylvania in 1831 and died in 1901, was perhaps the most influential agrarian populist in the United States during the latter part of the nineteenth century. Like Chayanov, he was engaged in a wide range of activity; in addition to *Caesar's Column* Donnelly not only wrote books on a wide variety of subjects, but also founded a Populist newspaper, drafted the programme of the People's Party, played an important role in the Farmers' Alliance, led the Granger movement against railroads, and was a senator for Minnesota and a vice-presidential candidate [*Ridge*, 1962]. Together with his political activity and speeches, the fiction/non-fiction of Donnelly contributed to the construction/consolidation of anti-finance/anti-foreign capital, anti-state discourse that constituted the mobilising ideology of farmers' protest movements (the Grangers, the Greenbackers, the Farmers' Alliance) in the mid-western and southern states of America over the last three decades of the nineteenth century, a mobilisation that culminated in the formation of the People's Party in 1892. The mass appeal and hence political impact of *Caesar's Column* in the domain of 'popular culture' is beyond question; a decade after publication some 230,000 copies of the book had already been sold in the United States and 450,000 in Europe [*Ridge*, 1962: 267], and as Vann Woodward [1938: 139] has noted: 'Thumbed copies of Donnelly's *Caesar's Column* ... were circulated from hand to hand. Those [farmers] who did not read them heard them quoted by those who had'.

17. Contrary to the assertion by Kumar [1987: 128] that 'the insurrection [of the Brotherhood of Destruction] is brutally crushed', it in fact succeeds, which for Donnelly (and populism generally) is the crux of the problem. However, the victory of the proletariat in *Caesar's Column* is short lived, and – with the single exception of 'the saved' in the mountain valley of Uganda – the world quickly reverts to a state of Social Darwinian 'nature' (starvation, famine, plague), in which three quarters of all humanity perish [*Donnelly*, 1960: 310]. The dystopic symbolism of both the building of and the form taken by Caesar's column itself is unmistakable: a pyramid of dead bodies covered with cement, it carries an inscription – composed by Gabriel Weltstein – commemorating 'The Death and Burial of Modern Civilisation' [*Donnelly*, 1960: 274, 282]. What is being celebrated, therefore, is the destruction of a multiplicity of 'othernesses' which are the targets of agrarian populist discourse-against: the end of the proletariat and finance capital, the bodies of which constitute the column, of modern industrial society, and the death of the city itself. All are interred beneath a structure of concrete (= the building material of the urban) in the shape of a pyramid (= tomb of past civilisations, never to rise again).

18. Like that of Ignatius Donnelly, the written work of Alexander Vasilevich Chayanov is wide-ranging, and includes not just literature but extends also to cover rural sociology, economics, art and history (see the bibliography in Chayanov [1966: 279ff.]). Best known and most influential as an agronomist, Chayanov was a prominent neo-populist theoretician who took an important part in the debates about the nature and future development of the peasantry in the Soviet Union during the 1920s (see Kerblay [1971], Jasny [1972: 200–204], Harrison [1975; 1977], Cox [1979], Durrenberger [1984] and Ellis [1988: 102ff.]). Born in 1888, he was Director of the Moscow Institute of Agricultural Economy until the 1930s, and 'disappeared' in Stalin's purges at the end of that decade. The views expressed by him in the *Journey of My Brother* constitute an attempt to represent in fictional form the systemic effect of his economic theory: in short, it is an account of what a future society composed of and ruled by an economically viable peasantry might look like in practice. In the theoretical framework of Chayanov [1966; 1991], therefore, not only is peasant economy itself a specific mode of production, but the reproduction of the peasant labour farm is determined endogenously, by the consumption needs of the family that works the land. Accordingly, output on the peasant farm is in his view determined not by external factors (such as rent, taxation, or the extraction of surplus labour by those who own/control the means of production) but rather by the motivation of its individual members (= self-exploitation).

Designated the producer/consumer balance, this 'natural' equilibrium – which is linked by Chayanov to land area, the size of and working members in the family – constitutes a 'natural' limit to the output of peasant cultivation. From this analysis it follows that substantial capital accumulation and class differentiation cannot occur either in peasant agriculture or in a society organised around the latter. Critiques of Chayanov's theory of peasant economy point out that it conflates rich and poor peasants, it is an historically static entity abstracted from the national and international economy, it embodies a subjective concept of value, it overlooks the operation/effect of land/labour markets and capitalist competition, and ignores class divisions between/within peasant farms together with a differential capacity to utilise technology.

19. The date 1984 immediately invites a comparison with the dystopic novel by Orwell [1949], and raises the issue of a possible connection between the latter and Chayanov, via the dystopic novel by Zamyatin [1977], not least because (as Deutscher [1955: 35–50] has shown) the plot of Orwell's *1984* is based on Zamyatin's *We*. The possibility of a Chayanov–Zamyatin–Orwell link arises from the fact that – as Smith [1977: 9–10] suggests – Zamyatin, who knew Chayanov, himself spent time in England, in this way disseminating via literary circles the utopic significance of 1984 that was subsequently incorporated by Orwell into his own text.

20. In this fictional portrayal of Moscow as it would be in the mid-1980s, Chayanov [*Kremnev*, 1977: 90] reproduces one of the central arguments made by agrarian populists in Russia during the 1920s, namely that: 'Thanks to its fundamentally healthy nature, agriculture had avoided the bitter cup of capitalism and [the ruling peasant regime of 1984] had no need to direct [its] developmental process into that channel.' Such a view contrasts with that of the Bolsheviks in general and in particular Lenin [1960], who argued that the Russian village community was not a bulwark against capitalism (as populists maintained) but much rather had already been penetrated by this economic form, as a result of which the peasantry was disintegrating along class lines.

21. First published in September, 1933, the book had already gone through sixteen printings by August 1936 (the edition owned by this writer). The 1937 film of *Lost Horizon* was produced by Columbia Studios and cost US$2 million (= US$30–40 million at current prices) to make; similarly popular, the film was nominated for four Academy Awards and eventually became a box-office success. For the background to the making of the film, and the quarrels between director and producer over budget and editing, see McBride [1992: 351–66]. Interestingly, a 1973 remake of the film *Lost Horizon* – but this time as a musical – was a critical failure and incurred a financial loss; made just after the development decade, the message of the film seemed at that particular conjuncture to be irrelevant.

22. There are a number of differences between the book and film versions of *Lost Horizon*. For example, in the film Father Perrault is Belgian, whereas in the book he is of Luxembourgeois nationality; Hugh Conway, the main character in the book, becomes Robert Conway in the film; Captain Charles Mallinson, one of the two colonial officials in the book, is in the film transformed into George Conway, brother of Robert; and the character Roberta Brinklow, a missionary in the book, is in the film version changed into Gloria Stone, an incurable invalid. The film also contains an additional character: Alexander P. Lovett, a paleontologist (played by Edward Everett Horton). Significantly, perhaps, the only character who retains his identity and name in both book and film versions is the speculator, Chalmers Bryant alias Henry Bernard. In the book Robert Conway is merely a minor colonial administrative official (HM Consul) who flees a revolutionary uprising in Baskul (= Kabul?) on the north-west frontier of India; the kidnap flight to Tibet and Shangri-La is eastwards, across the Karakorum mountains. In the film version, however, both Baskul and the revolutionary uprising are located in China, Conway is now the British Foreign Secretary elect travelling to Shanghai, and the kidnap flight towards Tibet and Shangri-La goes westwards (but remains within the domain of 'the East'). There are also differences between book and film in terms of chronology: whereas the book is set in 1931, the film locates the same episode in 1935. The significance of the latter date is that it coincided with the Long March of 1934–35, a period that signalled the re-emergence of the Chinese Communists, and thus underlined the element of a socialist 'threat'. The year in which film itself was made is also crucial in reinforcing its

warnings: the Marco Polo Bridge incident, which took place in 1937, marked the start of Sino-Japanese conflict and – along with the Civil War in Spain – the beginnings of the Second World War.

23. Since a horizon is by definition a place which is never reached, and thus like Utopia itself is a non-existent place, plus the fact that the name of the valley makes an oblique reference to a time ('once in a blue moon') that is similarly rare, the 'lost' element has a twofold meaning. It refers both to a double unattainability (that-which-cannot-be-reached either in physical or temporal terms), reinforcing thereby its element of mystical 'otherness', and also to a literal and symbolic opacity in relation to the surrounding world (= chaos).

24. For references by Conway and others to the economic depression 'outside' Shangri-La, see Hilton [1933: 133–4, 148–52]. The metaphorical opposition between the 'outside' and Shangri-La itself is highlighted early on in the film when, following their rescue from the plane crash, Conway and the other passangers enter Shangri-La for the first time: outside the entrance a storm continues to rage, whereas inside it is calm and peaceful. This contrast is underlined visually by the astonished reaction of Conway himself, who first looks down into the valley and then once again glances behind him at the tempest on the other side of the entrance. The assumption about the pivotal role of Robert Conway, and hence the politico-ideological importance of his utterances, is based on the fact that Capra himself strongly identified with the character [McBride, 1992: 356].

25. McBride [1992: 355–6] misses the underlying element of continuity that structures Capra's populist discourse when he complains that, unlike the director's previous films in which positive solutions (a vindication of and a return to the 'common-sense' traditional values of the countryside) are counterposed to and overcome the negative elements (the corrosive effect of technology, corruption, and finance capital in the big city), Lost Horizon lacks a coherent alternative to the chaotic world Conway leaves behind, and is thus merely an exercise in escapism. Much the same point is made by Graham Greene, who claims similarly that Capra's discourse-against is merely unfocussed escapism. Hence the observation (Parkinson [1993: 270]) that: 'The director [Capra] emerges as a rather muddled and sentimental idealist who feels – vaguely – that something is wrong with the social system. … it is useless trying to analyse the idea behind the Capra films; there is no idea that you'd notice, only a sense of dissatisfaction, an urge to escape … .'

26. The box-office failure of the Korda film, Things to Come, based on H.G. Wells's Shape of Things to Come and the success of Lost Horizon is attributed by Brosnan [1978: 63–4] specifically to a negative audience reaction to the issue of technological progress; in other words, a popular rejection of of Wells' celebration of technology/modernity and a corresponding endorsement of the anti-technological/anti-modern themes projected by Hilton/Capra. Such a view is supported by the adverse audience reaction to the Orson Welles radio dramatisation in the United States of H.G. Wells' The War of the Worlds in October 1938 [Cantril, 1982], when panic was generated not only by insecurity linked to the capitalist crisis but also the impending European war and the technological/mechanical means by which this would be waged.

27. It is clear from research conducted by Mass Observation (Richards and Sheridan [1987: 96, 122, 127, 131, 132, 200ff.]) into audience reaction to films screened during a period extending from the late 1930s to the early 1940s not only that the film Lost Horizon had a strong appeal to cinema audiences generally but also that the latter perceived an optimistic programmatic element ('uplifting moral vision') in the message both of the film itself and in its ending. This perception by cinema audiences of a programmatic aspect is evident, for example, from responses such as: 'the discussion in town after that picture's [i.e. Lost Horizon] visit shows that spiritual uplift is beginning to attract in pictures' (original emphasis); and 'Lost Horizon [had] a certain amount of moral behind it'. Similar kinds of positive reaction were elicited by its ending (= the final cinematic 'fade out' in which Conway struggles back over the mountains to Shangri-La). In dismissing Lost Horizon as 'the typical middlebrow novel', therefore, Graham Greene (Parkinson [1993: 426]) unwittingly identifies one of the main reasons for its successful appeal to film audiences. On this point he asks rhetorically: 'What common ideas can be assumed between the middle-western farmer and the Cockney clerk, between the New York stockbroker and the

unemployed man in a Welsh village? Few, I'm afraid, less vague and sentimental than the ideas of *Lost Horizon*. (For a similarly dismissive view, see Morton [1952: 205–06]) Significantly, in his consideration of the way in which populist ideas were disseminated in America, Hofstadter [1962: 6] allocates an important role precisely to 'middlebrow writers'.

28. Despite conforming to a classical dystopian/utopian framework, neither *Journey of My Brother* nor *Lost Horizon* is mentioned in two recent texts on utopia/utopianism (Kumar [1987], Bann and Kumar [1993]), and *Caesar's Column* is referred to only in passing – and then incorrectly (see note 17 above).

29. For the political heterogeneity and the long historical lineage of discourse about the utopic/dystopic, see among others Manuel [1967; 1972: 69ff.], Passmore [1972], Finley [1975: 178–92], Manuel and Manuel [1979], and Kumar [1987].

30. The political trajectory covered by such arguments may be illustrated by reference to the ideological fusion of the ideas advanced by W.H.Hudson, H.J.Massingham and Rolf Gardiner (about which see Griffiths [1983: 142–6] and Abelson [1988]). The pro-agrarian/anti-industrialisation views propounded by Hudson were instrumental in persuading Massingham to question and then strongly reject the desirability/possibility of modernism, progress, industrialisation and urbanisation. The importance of Massingham, a widely-read writer about the English countryside, is twofold. First, by arguing for the centrality to notions of 'Englishness' and 'belonging' of 'nature', the aesthetics of landscape and the countryside generally, it was he more than any other writer who (re-) constructed the agrarian myth in English 'popular culture' during the inter-war period, thereby reproducing/reinforcing the view that national identity was essentially rural. And second, this combination of a lament for the cultural decline of England, the nostalgia for and romanticisation of a vanishing rural arcadia, and his anti-socialist/anti-industrial/anti-urban views, led Massingham in turn to endorse the attempt by Gardiner – a prominent Nazi sympathiser and enthusiast of 'Nordic solidarity' – to re-invent what was belived to be an authentic 'Merrie England' through the restoration of the 'traditional village community' composed of cultivators and artisans.

31. Examples include Morris [1885/1970], Jefferies [1885/1939], Hudson [1887], and Forster [1909/1947]. The view taken here is different from that advanced by Fortunati [1993: 84ff.], who maintains that the structuring principle of these texts is the Biblical myth of the Apocalypse. Here it is argued that as important as the millenarian element is the fear about the way in which capitalism was transforming rural society; indeed, given the sacred ideological status of 'nature' itself in this discourse, and further the ideological interchangeability of 'nature'/'nation'/'sacred', this difference is merely one of emphasis, since both are variants of the same discourse. (For the extent to which current Hollywood films are structured by religious themes of Armageddon (= the end of time), see Ostwalt [1995].)

32. This theme, which stems from a fear of the effects of tampering with the 'naturalness' of humanity, has a long history and is a pervasive element of popular culture. For example, it structures the discourse about the dystopic in the genre of science fiction, extending from the 1950s BBC television series *Quatermass and the Pit* [Kneale 1960] to the 1980s and 1990s films such as *Terminator, Robocop* and *Blade Runner* (on which see see Bukatman [1993] and Rushing and Frentz [1995]). Where humanity is itself perceived as part of nature, as part of the 'natural', and is displaced in the narrative of 'the utopic' by an alien/(robotic) technology, this constitutes a metaphor for the replacement by capital of living labour with its dead equivalent. In this discourse, therefore, humanity = 'nature'/'the natural', whereas technocop/robocop = the 'other'. In terms of positive/negative forms of the populist utopic, the impact of this alien technology on humankind also amounts to a process of de-naturing, which suggests in turn the existence of a continuity with earlier versions of the dystopic wherein 'the natural'/'nature' is confronted by a dangerous form of 'otherness'.

33. The same opposition between above/good and below/bad structures the dystopia of E.M. Forster [1947: 115–58], where an anomic, unnatural, undesirable existence – controlled by 'the Machine' – in the city underneath the surface of the Earth is contrasted with the long lost and now forbidden 'natural'/rural/desirable existence on the surface of the Earth. Although in the 1936 film *Things to Come* directed by Korda, the utopia of H.G. Wells is located underground – thereby transgressing this most fundamental symbolic spacing – this

contradiction is resolved ideologically by locating salvation above ground, in the form of an escape by means of a 'space gun' to the Moon.

34. For the ideological importance and influence in Germany during the 1930s and early 1940s of the 'mountain' film genre, as mediated in the work of directors such as Leni Riefenstahl and Luis Trenker, see Kracauer [1947: 110–12, 257–63]. It could be argued that the physical location of Shangri-La actually *within* the mountain peak itself (a visual image that is very clear in the film version) signifies protection by the gods.

35. Donnelly [1960: 7]. As with *Caesar's Column*, the above/good and below/bad metaphor in *Lost Horizon* also extends to include the opposition between dark (= bad) and light (= good). In contrast to the dark and ominous atmosphere of scene in which Conway and the others escape from the revolutionary 'mob-in-the-streets' at the beginning of the film, the arrival in Shangri-La is by contrast bathed in light.

36. All these elements are present in what Bailey [1958] terms the sociology of pessimism. The vehemently anti-Marxist/anti-socialist conservativism of those such as Le Bon [1924] and Pareto [1963] was structured by a discourse about the decay of existing civilisation (= the central emplacement of the sociology of pessimism), itself premissed on the fear of revolution by the crowd (= 'the mob in the streets') which in their view would destabilise what they perceived as a 'natural' social equilibrium. Because human behaviour is regarded by Pareto as innate and in the main irrational (= non-logical), it follows that there can be no point in trying to change it for the better, and social progress as a goal of human activity is therefore impossible (for a similar view held by de Maistre, see Berlin [1990: 122]; for an example of a more recent exponent of this position by a conservative, see Nisbet [1980]). However, because such irrational/non-logical behaviour may nevertheless be useful for society, Pareto maintains that traditional beliefs (such as religion, hierarchy) should not be displaced. Anticipating by a century many of the disillusioned views advanced by postmodern theory, therefore, the anti-statist economic liberalism of Pareto not only invokes diversity/difference in defence of traditional behaviour (= customs) but denies thereby the possibility of change/progress, because it is both useless/undesirable to attempt the latter and such beliefs are anyway useful (= functional).

37. Far from disappearing, it is argued by Bausinger [1990] that such traditional beliefs expand/extend to accompany the spread of capitalism, a process structured by the commodification/reinvention of folklore.

38. '[L]ike some baulked monster, waiting outside the valley to pounce', time is represented by Hilton [1933: 101, 185–6, 201] as an 'external contamination', a specifically Western and dystopic characteristic, whereas timelessness is presented as a characteristic of the utopic Eastern 'other'. A similar theme structures the Powell and Pressburger film *Black Narcissus* (1947), in which the spirituality of an innate and timeless Oriental 'otherness' overcomes Christian nuns who attempt to establish a convent in the Tibetan Himalayas.

39. For these points, see Donnelly [1960: 26, 43, 95]. Significantly, the 'unnatural'/Machine-controlled urban industrial civilisation of the dystopic underground city in 'The Machine Stops' by E.M. Forster [1947] is also destroyed.

40. Hence the many anti-semitic utterances: for example, 'the aristocracy of the world is now almost altogether of Hebrew origin', Jews 'are the great money-getters of the world', 'the real government is now a coterie of bankers, mostly Israelites ... ', 'Europe is a banking association conducted extensively for the benefit of bankers ... The world today is semitised' [*Donnelly*, 1960: 31–2, 97–8]. This anti-semitism – a pervasive element of agrarian populism (see Vann Woodward [1938: 431ff.]) – is not confined to observations about members of the Plutocracy: hence the vice-president of the Brotherhood, himself of Jewish ethnic origin, ultimately absconds with the funds belonging to the proletariat [*Donnelly*, 1960: 283]: 'He took several of his trusted folowers, of his own nation, with him. It is rumoured that he has gone to Judea; that he proposes to make himself King in Jerusalem, and, with his vast wealth, re-establish the glories of Solomon, and revive the ancient splendours of the Jewish race, in the midst of the ruins of the world.'

41. On this point, see Donnelly [1960: 48–9].

42. The importance of 'Aryan ancestry', which is in turn equated with 'civilisation', is made clear by Donnelly [1960: 242].

43. 'High finance ... is mostly a lot of bunk ... A feller does what he's being doing for years, and what lots of other fellers have being doing, and suddenly the market goes against him. He can't help it, but he braces up and waits for the turn. But somehow the turn doesn't come as it always used to, and when he's lost ten million dollars or so he reads in some paper that a Swede professor thinks it's the end of the world. Now I ask you, does that sort of thing help markets', Bernard/Bryant observes, and when challenged by Mallinson that the money he lost belonged to other people, replies: 'There isn't safety anywhere, and those who thought there was were like a lot of saps trying to hide under an umbrella in a typhoon ... the whole game's going to pieces ... there isn't a soul in the world who knows what the rules [of the game] are' [*Hilton*, 1933: 148–9, 150].

44. 'As for Bryant, whom [Conway] decided he would still think of and address as Bernard, the question of his exploits and identity faded instantly into the background, save for a single phrase of his – "the whole game's going to pieces." Conway found himself remembering and echoing it with a wider significance than the American had probably intended: he felt it to be true of more than American banking and trust company management. It fitted Baskul and Delhi and London, war making and empire building, consulates and trade concessions and dinner parties at Government House; there was a reek of dissolution over all that recollected world, and Barnards's cropper had only, perhaps, been better dramatised than his own. The whole game *was* doubtless going to pieces, but fortunately the players were not as a rule put on trial for the pieces they failed to save. In that respect financiers were unlucky' [*Hilton*, 1933: 151–2, original emphasis]. Ironically, a recent financial scandal reproduces much of the symbolic structure of *Lost Horizon*: in February 1995, therefore, a 'rogue trader' Nick Leeson (= speculator Bernard/Bryant), accused of being responsible for losses of £800+ million and the collapse of Barings Bank, fled eastwards from Singapore to Malaysia, where he travelled to Kota Kinabalu and took refuge in an hotel named the 'Shangri-La'. Unlike the Bernard/Bryant character in *Lost Horizon*, however, Leeson found no redemption in his particular Shangri-La.

45. Donnelly [1960: 36, 38].

46. Donnelly [1960: 37–8]. Much the same theme – blaming an ethnically specific (Jewish) finance capital for importing ethnically specific (black/hispanic) cheap labour with which to undermine an ethnically specific but indigenous (white or 'authentic American') workforce – is central to the discourse of American fascism [*Sargent*, 1995: 126].

47. Thus Donnelly [1960: 71, 123–4] compares the approaching 'universal conflict, savagery, barbarism, chaos' of working class revolution in New York of 1988 to the 1791 slave revolt in Santo Domingo, and notes that all the black workers in the American South are members of the Brotherhood of Destruction because: 'Their former masters have kept them in a state of savagery, instead of civilising and elevating them; and the result is that they are as barbarous and bloodthirsty as their ancestors were when brought from Africa, and fit subjects for such a terrible organisation [= the revolutionary proletariat].' Later the working class leader, Caesar, is described by Donnelly [1960: 149] in the following terms: 'his [Caesar's] skin was quite dark, almost negroid'. And when Caesar captures the palace belonging to – and in effect becomes – his 'other', Prince Cabano, Donnelly [1960: 272] comments: 'He [Caesar] was so black with dust and blood that he looked like a negro ... his eyes were wild and rolling'. For Donnelly, therefore, the proletariat = revolution = black = blood/bloodthirsty = dirt = savage/wild = uncontrollable. That agrarian populism in America has a long history of complicity with racism in general and southern racism in particular is clear from many sources (see, among others, Van Woodward [1938] and Conkin [1988]). Significantly, the way in which black Americans from the inner cities are currently perceived by the white middle class as a 'problem' of an 'uncontollable underclass' (as theorised by Murray [1990; 1994]) reproduces much of the discourse which structured this century-old agrarian populist fear of the 'mob-in-the-streets'.

48. It should be emphasised that Donnelly is not unaware of the dynamics of capitalist exploitation and oppression. For example, he observes [*Donnelly*, 1960: 39] that: 'It was the same story everywhere. Here we saw exemplified, in its full perfection, that "iron law of wages" which the old economists spoke of; that is to say, the reduction, by competition, of the wages of the worker to the least sum that will maintain life and muscular strength enough

to do the work required.'

49. On these points, see Donnelly [1960: 67, 161], who notes that workers 'are wonderfully intelligent ... there have arisen, from among the very labourers, splendid orators, capable organisers, profound students of politics and political economy ... '. The inability of employers to control a class conscious (= 'intelligent') proletariat is attributed by Donnelly to the benefits of state education, the implication being that the revolutionary overthrow of capitalism has in an important sense been made possible by public expenditure ('our taxes'). Interestingly, the latter point anticipates the argument currently advanced by many of those on the neo-liberal political right in metropolitan capitalist countries for cutting public expenditure.

50. As Donnelly [1960: 149, 280] makes clear, a proletarianised/brutalised peasantry is 'not natural' (depeasantised peasant ≠ warrior ≠ nation ≠ nature):

> Brutality above had produced brutality below; cunning there was answered by cunning here; cruelty in the aristocrat was mirrored by cruelty in the workman ... [...] Crowds of farmers from the surrounding country kept pouring into the city. They were no longer the honest yeomanry who had filled, in the old time, the armies of Washington, and Jackson, and Grant, and Sherman, with brave Patriotic soldiers; but their brutalised descendents ... They [de-natured peasants] were murderers not warriors.

51. See Donnelly [1960: 92, 96], whose view about the political necessity of reproducing what may in fact be an economically unviable peasant economy contrasts with that of Chayanov [1966; 1991], for whom the survival of the peasantry was determined by its economic viability.

52. An example of the dangers inherent in such a transformation effected by finance capital is the case of Caesar himself, the commander of the Brotherhood of Destruction. Originally a peasant farmer and a 'good' man, Caesar is transformed by cumulative, high-interest debt into his 'other', a 'bad' man at the head of the 'mob-in-the-streets': consequently, he 'who was once a peaceful farmer' becomes a 'brute' responsible for 'universal conflict, savagery, barbarism, chaos' [Donnelly, 1960: 71, 126–7, 190]. The moral of this particular fable is clear: the dangers inherent in tampering with 'nature' (= a 'natural' peasantry, which is 'naturally' passive) – which is precisely what finance capital stands accused of in agrarian populist discourse-against.

52a. This hostility to socialism on the part of the author of Lost Horizon emerges clearly both in another novel published in the same year [Hilton, 1933a] and also in the 1937 film based on this, Knight Without Armour, directed by Jacques Feyder, which incorporates the similar theme of a successful flight from the Bolshevik revolution by a Russian countess.

53. Not only does he dismiss the efficacy of revolutionary transformation, therefore, but Donnelly [1960: 60–61, 65–6, 70–71, 256, 257] also describes the revolutionary proletarian 'mob-in-the-streets' as: 'the molten mass of horror ... sweeping away all this splendour into never-ending blackness and ruin. [...] A foul and brutal and ravenous multitude ... dark with dust and sweat, armed with the weapons of civilisation, but possessing only the instincts of wild beasts ... Civilisation is gone, and all the devils are loose! ... That which it took the world ten thousand years to create has gone in an hour.' In his view [Donnelly, 1960: 227–8], moreover, the building of Caesar's column 'was Anarchy personified: – the men of intellect [merchants, lawyers, clergymen] were doing the [manual] work; the men of muscle were giving the orders'.

54. For Donnelly [1960: 190, 258], therefore, the proletarian revolutionaries who constitute the 'mob-in-the-streets': 'have decided to keep all these fine residences for themselves! They will be rich. They will do no more work. [...] The difference is, they [the financiers] are brutes who are in possession of the good things of this world; and Caesar is a brute who wants to get into possession of them.'

55. Kremnev [1977: 86–7]. The fact that the earlier dystopia of E.M. Forster [1947] is ruled by a Central Committee suggests that it, too, might be socialist.

56. For evidence of Chayanov's anti-Bolshevik/anti-communist discourse, see Kremnev [1977: 89, 90–91, 92]. In attributing the collapse of Bolshevism during the 1920s to a combination of socialist 'anarchy', the impossibility of planning, and an innate nationalism, and

maintaining that communism 'removed all incentive [to] work' and merely reproduced the inherent 'servitude' of the proletariat, Chayanov not only omits to mention external factors (for example, the invasion of Soviet Russia during 1918–19 by Polish, British, American, French, Czech and Turkish forces in an international anti-Bolshevik crusade) but also reproduces the arguments about the impossibility/collapse of socialism advanced by those on the political right.

57. Thus it is mathematical rationality to which Zamyatin [1977] objects in his dystopic novel *We*. Much the same is true of the underground, urban dystopia in 'The Machine Stops', about which Forster [1947: 148] observes: ' ... Humanity, in its desire for comfort, had over-reached itself. It had exploited the riches of nature too far. Quietly and complacently, it was sinking into decadence, and progress had come to mean the progress of the Machine.' On the historical pervasiveness of anti-science ideology, see Passmore [1978]. As always, it is important to distinguish between two distinct forms of anti-scientific/technological discourse. On the one hand, a Marxist critique of science/technology as value-free technique, which points out that under capitalism it constitutes the productive forces whereby capital extracts more surplus-value from labour-power, but which under socialism could be used for social rather than private ends (for the benefit of rather than against workers). And on the other, an idealist all-embracing rejection of science and technology *per se*, as presented for example in the work of Shiva [1989].

58. Symbolically, therefore, the (capitalist) machine becomes the method whereby capital consumes both land/('nature') and ('natural') time spent working on this. That anti-technological discourse necessarily categorises American populism as a form of conservatism is denied by Lasch [1991: 226], who observes that: 'Populists condemned innovation because it undermined proprietary independence and gave rise to "wage slavery", not because it tore apart the delicate fabric of custom. They had little use for custom as such, nor did they cultivate a reverence for the past.' Because it ignores the discursive imbrication between national identity, custom, tradition and 'proprietory independence' on the one hand, and on the other mistakenly regards non-specific opposition to wage slavery as politically progressive (rather than as motivated by fear of a potentially/actually revolutionary 'mob-in-the-streets'), this attempt by Lasch to de-link populism and conservatism fails to persuade.

59. Observing that the physical isolation of Shangri-La would prevent it from being 'contaminated' by the outside world, Conway points out that the word 'contaminated' encompasses most aspects of modernity ('dance bands, cinemas, electric signs, and so on'). 'Your plumbing', he explains [*Hilton*, 1933: 88], 'is quite rightly as modern as you can get it, the only certain boon, to my mind, that the East can take from the West. I often think that the Romans were fortunate; their civilisation reached as far as hot baths without touching the fatal knowledge of machinery'.

60. Donnelly [1960: 309].

61. Thus Kremnev [1977: 84] asks: 'Why the devil do you [Russians] expend so much human labour on the fields? Surely your technology, which easily controls the weather, is capable of mechanising agricultural labour to free work hands for more skilled occupations?' To which the reply is: 'Agriculture has never been as manual as now. And at our population densities, this is no fad, but sheer necessity.' Chayanov goes on to describe large-scale manufacturing industry as 'a pathological, monsterous condition' [*Kremnev*, 1977: 90]. For the anti-technological views (= 'machine-power multiplying') of those who rule Shangri-La, see Hilton [1933: 190–91].

62. For these points, see Donnelly [1960: 13, 26].

63. See Donnelly [1960: 7, 141]. A recent text by Pieterse [1992] that examines the way in which images of Africa structured Western 'popular culture' unfortunately fails to make any mention of the way these pictorial/visual stereotypes were themselves reinforced by the references to Africa contained in *Caesar's Column*.

64. Thus the central character in *Lost Horizon*, Conway, is not only described at the beginning of the film version as 'a man of the East' but is said in the book to 'get on with' the Chinese, and to be reminded of China by the Valley of the Blue Moon [*Hilton*, 1933: 130]; for rather less idyllic versions of the socio-economic conditions 'enjoyed' by the peasantry in China at this time, see Buck [1930] and Tawney [1932; 1938]. Notwithstanding its literary/filmic

impact on the domain of 'popular culture', and the resulting popularisation/reinforcement within pre-war metropolitan capitalism of the stereotypically timeless/mystic/Eastern 'other', *Lost Horizon* is not mentioned by Said [1978; 1993] in his consideration of the historical instances and dissemination of orientalist ideology.

65. For descriptions of utopia as 'the garden in the mountains' that is 'shut out from attacks by ice-topped mountains', see Donnelly [1960: 245, 299].

66. On these points, see Donnelly [1960: 7, 45, 105, 313]. Denying the grassroots efficacy of the agrarian myth, some revisionist texts are now engagaged in the attempt at the political rehabilitation of the American populist tradition (see, for example, Goodwyn [1976; 1978; 1986; 1991] and Lasch [1991]), maintaining among other things that it was not based on nostalgia but was 'broadly egalitarian and humanistic [on] issues of race and gender as well as economics' [*Goodwyn*, 1991: 42–3]. In a similarly sympathetic account of populism, Donnelly's utopia is wrongly described by Canovan [1981: 57] as involving 'a fairly socialistic program'.

67. For these descriptions of Shangri-la, see Hilton [1933: 129] and Greene [1972: 148]. Much the same is true of the description in 1920 by Chayanov [Kremnev 1977: 94–5] of Moscow as it would be fifty years in the future, where

> The passing centuries had changed nothing in rustic delights, and only a careful observer would have noticed the considerable quantities of preserved pineapple, the bunches of bananas and the extraordinary abundance of good chocolate. As in the good old days, little boys whistled on gilded clay cockerels, just as they had done in the days of Tsar Ivan Vasilevich and in Novgorod the Great. A double accordion played a fast polka. In a word, everything was fine.

The recuperation/rejection of the 'primitive'/'natural' element in the film version of *Lost Horizon* is mediated through the four main relationships: between Robert Conway and Sondra, Lovett and Bernard, and the latter and Gloria, all of whom either remain in or return to Shangri-La and whose relationships symbolise the realisation of an 'authentic' selfhood, and between George Conway and Maria, who deny this 'authentic' selfhood and each of whom dies whilst attempting to escape from Shangri-La. In the case of Lovett, for example, this self-realisation is depicted filmically by a rejection of his own facial image reflected in a mirror on the lid of a Chinese lacquer box, which he shuts (= denying selfhood): having accepted Shangi-La, and decided to stay, he then opens the same Chinese lacquer box in order now to enjoy his own reflection (= discovery of selfhood in Shangri-La/'Eastern' artefact). The key relationship in the film is that between Robert Conway and Sondra: she is the one who suggests that Conway be brought to Shangri-La, and thus represents its desirable 'otherness'. Their relationship blossoms amidst the idealised rural imagery depicting the Valley of the Blue Moon: indeed, his initial pursuit of her through its arcadian scenery (waterfalls, lake) mimics the hunt in the classic pastoral, and his subsequent meeting with her takes place among similar bucolic images, after Robert Conway encounters further evidence of harmonious unchanging/unchangeable 'nature' in the form of 'natives' herding livestock and 'native' artisans at work. On this occasion he takes over from her conducting singing 'native' children, a metaphor for his inheritance of power over the 'natives' in the rural Eden of Shangri-La itself. Lovett and Bryant/Bernard also experience conversion and redemption in a similarly arcadian context: the former abandons plans to mine gold in favour of an engineering project to improve the water supply in Shangri-La while the latter undertakes to teach 'native' schoolchildren (informing Chang of his discovery that the 'native' artisans seem very happy), again metaphors for transcendance of two forms of 'otherness' unacceptable to agrarian populism (finance capital, intellectuals). Much the same happens to the invalid Gloria Stone, who simultaneously recovers her health and discards her makeup, thereby signalling her rejection of the 'evil'/'outside' (= 'unnatural'/corrupting modernity) by regaining her 'natural' physical/(spiritual) purity. By contrast, Robert's brother George not only persists in his desire to leave Shangri-La, an attitude signalled by his retention of 'western' clothing long after the others have 'gone native', but he also takes with him an inhabitant of Russian origin, Maria, who symbolises the expulsion of the socialist 'other' from the Eden of agrarian populism.

68. For the civil war of the 1920s, the peasant revolution of the 1930s and the re-emergence of both abundance and the Russian peasantry, see Kremnev [1977: 75, 86–7, 88, 90]. Consequently, Kremnev [1977: 82] is informed, the situation is now one in which: 'the whole area for hundreds of miles around Moscow is a continuous agricultural settlement, intersected by rectangles of common forest, strips of co-operative pastures and huge climatic parks. In areas of farmstead settlement, where the family allotment is no more than 8–10 acres, you will find peasant houses almost side by side for dozens of miles.'

69. In reply to his question about the origins of the new organisational form based on peasant agriculture, Kremnev [1977: 88] is told:

> You want to know about those new principles ... which peasant power introduced into out social and economic life. In fact, we had no need of any *new* principles; our task was to consolidate the *old*, centuries-old, principles on which from time immemorial the peasant economy had been based ... Our economic system, like that of the ancient Rus', is founded on the individual peasant farm. We considered it, and still do so, the ideal model of economic activity. In it, man confronts nature ... This is man's natural condition, from which he was exiled by the demon of capitalism (original emphasis).

70. Kremnev [1977: 96].

71. Donnelly [1960: 26, 101–4].

72. For the existence of residual capitalist production in the fictional Russia of the mid-1980s, see Kremnev [1977: 91, 92]. The peasant regime which replaced socialism, argues Chayanov [*Kremnev*, 1977:92], 'took over the management of the economy [and] immediately put in motion all the mechanisms which stimulate private economic activity – piece rates, bonuses for managers and premium prices for those products of peasant farming which it was essential to develop ... .'

73. For the rural, ethnic and national origins of 'the saved' in the case of *Caesar's Column*, see Donnelly [1960: 225–6, 236, 242]. On the nature of theocratic rule in Shangri-La, together with the ethnic composition/recomposition of its ruling class, see Hilton [1933: 123, 174–5]. 'Our best subjects,' observes Perrault [*Hilton*, 1933: 181], 'undoubtedly, are the Nordic and Latin races of Europe; perhaps the Americans would be equally acceptable ... '. Given that in *Journey of My Brother* Kremnev is himself mistaken for a visitor from America, the ethnic composition in all three agrarian populist utopias is roughly the same: European and/or North American whites.

74. On this point, see Donnelly [1960: 3, 292–3, 297, 302, 309, 313] and Kremnev [1977: 83].

75. The governing body of the utopia in Uganda is known as 'The People', and is composed of three branches: producers (peasants, workers), employers (merchants, manufacturers), and intellectuals, who hold the balance of power: 'For good purposes and honest instincts we may trust the multitude,' observes Donnelly [1960: 301–2], 'but for long-sighted thoughts of philanthropy, of statesmanship and statescraft, we must look to a few superior intellects'.

76. On these points, see Kremnev [1977: 89, 98–9, 100]. Should any organisation defy or exceed the wishes of grassroots opinion, Chayanov suggests, it will be subject to the power of 'moral authority' exercised by these same grassroots. However, no mention is made of what happens in the event of a confrontation between competing but mutually irreconcilable interests.

77. For evidence of Chayanov's anti-state discourse, and in particular the equation by him of the state with the bureaucracy, see Kremnev [1977: 89, 91, 97–9]. On the question of exploitation of the worker by the bureaucracy, Chayanov [*Kremnev*, 1977: 91] claims that: '[the] labour laws protect the worker from exploitation even better than the laws of the dictatorship of the proletariat under which a colossal share of surplus value was absorbed by the herds of officials in the Chief Administrations and the Administrative Centres.' For the centrality of this kind of claim (state = wasteful, unnecessary bureaucracy) to the discourse of agrarian populism in general, and in particular the new farmers' movements that emerged in India during the 1980s, see Brass [1995a].

78. The *laissez-faire* principle structuring political power in Shangri-La is clear from the observations by Chang [Hilton, 1933: 90–91, 137, 139], that: ' ... I should say that our prevalent belief is in moderation ... [i]n the valley ... there are several thousand inhabitants living under the control of our order ... we rule with moderate strictness, we are satisfied

with moderate obedience ... we believe that to govern perfectly it is necessary to avoid governing too much.'

79. In response to an observation by Conway that 'there are many people in the world nowadays who would be glad enough to be here', Perrault replies [*Hilton*, 1933: 234]: '*Too many* ... [w]e are a single lifeboat riding the seas in a gale; we can take a few chance survivors, but if all the shipwrecked were to reach us and clamber on board we should go down ourselves (original emphasis).'

80. On these points, see Donnelly [1960: 245, 300], who notes that those fleeing to 'the garden in the mountains' in Uganda take with them 'a great library of books ... - literature, science, art, encyclopedias, histories, philosophies...', and then build a wall 'that would completely cut off communication with the external world', adding that it 'was a melancholy reflection that [the 'saved'] were thus compelled to exclude [their] fellow men'. This twofold course of action is also followed by the inhabitants of Shangri-La in *Lost Horizon*.

81. Kremnev [1977: 106].

82. Hence the reply given to Conway by Perrault [*Hilton*, 1933: 191], to the effect that: 'We may expect no mercy [from the chaos outside], but we may faintly hope for neglect. Here we shall stay with our books and our music and our meditations, *conserving the frail elegancies of a dying age* ...' (emphasis added). Asked by the High Lama whether or not he considered Shangri-La to be unique, Conway answered no, because [*Hilton*, 1933: 210]: ' ... it reminds me very slightly of Oxford [University], where I used to lecture. The scenery there is not so good, but the subjects of study are just as impractical ... .' Indeed, the parallel is exact, since in both contexts the object of existence is precisely to conserve 'the frail elegancies of a dying age'. This sense of the impending loss of traditional values which must themselves be preserved is reinforced by what Hilton writes elsewhere; describing the menaced tranquility of his public school in Cambridge (Brookfield = The Leys) during the First World War, he observes [1938: 44]: 'Behind the murmur of genitive plurals in dusty classrooms and the plick-plock of cricket balls in the summer sunshine, there was always the rumble of guns that were destroying the world that Brookfield had made and that had made Brookfield.' '[I]t seems to me', concludes Hilton [1938: 49], implicitly contrasting an internal and idyllic pastoral/(cultural) setting (public school/ancient university/Shangri-La) threatened by an external chaos, 'that Brookfield in wartime was ... less barbarian than the world outside it'. This protective attitude towards traditional culture is also encountered in *Journey of My Brother*: the futurist painting that symbolised revolutionary socialism in Russia during the 1920s has been replaced in the Russian Peasant Republic of 1984 by a return to the artistic styles of the pre-revolutionary ruling classes [*Kremnev*, 1977: 77].

83. For the abundance of food grown by inhabitants in their own smallholdings in 'the garden in the mountains' in Uganda, and the presence of self-sufficient cultivators in Shangri-La, see Donnelly [1960: 310] and Hilton [1933: 139].

84. Noting that the 'rising of 1937 was the last manifestation of the political role of the towns before they dissolved in the sea of the peasantry', Chayanov [*Kremnev*, 1977: 80, 87] observes that:

> In 1934, when power was firmly in the hands of the peasant parties, the ... government, persuaded by many years' experience of the danger to a democratic regime from huge conglomerations of urban population, decided on a revolutionary measure. At the Congress of Soviets they carried through a decree ... on the abolition of towns with more than 20,000 inhabitants ... The factories were gradually evacuated to new railway junctions throughout Russia.

REFERENCES

Abelson, E. (ed.), 1988, *A Mirror of England: An Anthology of the Writings of H.J. Massingham (1888-1952)*, Bideford: Green Books.

Bailey, R.B., 1958, *Sociology Faces Pessimism: A Study of European Sociological Thought Amidst a Fading Optimism*, The Hague: Martinus Nijhoff.

Bann, S. and K. Kumar (eds.), 1993, *Utopias and the Millennium*, London: Reaktion Books.
Bausinger, H., 1990, *Folk Culture in a World of Technology*, Bloomington, IN: Indiana University Press.
Belton, J., 1994, *American Cinema/American Culture*, New York: McGraw Hill, Inc.
de Benoist, A., 1994, 'Three Interviews with Alain de Benoist', *Telos*, Nos.98-99.
Berlin, I., 1990, *The Crooked Timber of Humanity*, London: John Murray.
Blinkhorn, M. (ed.), 1990, *Fascists and Conservatives: The Radical Right and the Establishment in Twentieth-Century Europe*, London: Unwin Hyman.
Booth, D. (ed.), 1994, *Rethinking Social Development*, Harlow: Longman Scientific & Technical.
Boyte, H.C. and F.Riessman (eds.), 1986, *The New Populism: The Politics of Empowerment*, Philadelphia, PA: Temple University Press.
Brass, T., 1991, 'Moral Economists, Subalterns, New Social Movements, and the (Re-) Emergence of a (Post-) Modernised (Middle) Peasant', *Journal of Peasant Studies*, Vol.18, No.2.
Brass, T. (ed.), 1995a, *New Farmers' Movements in India*, London: Frank Cass.
Brass, T., 1995b, 'Old Conservatism in "New" Clothes', *Journal of Peasant Studies*, Vol.22, No.3.
Britton, A. (ed.), 1991, *Talking Films*, London: Fourth Estate.
Brosnan, J., 1978, *Future Tense: The Cinema of Science Fiction*, London: McDonald & Jane's.
Buck, J.L., 1930, *Chinese Farm Economy*, Chicago, IL: University of Chicago Press.
Bukatman, S., 1993, *Terminal Identity: The Virtual Subject in Post-Modern Science Fiction*, Durham, NC: Duke University Press.
Canovan, M., 1981, *Populism*, London: Junction Books.
Cantril, H., 1982, *The Invasion from Mars: A Study in the Psychology of Panic*, Princeton, NJ: Princeton University Press.
Cardoza, A., 1982, *Agrarian Elites and Italian Fascism*, Princeton, NJ: Princeton University Press.
Chayanov, A.V., 1966, *The Theory of Peasant Economy* (edited by D. Thorner, B. Kerblay and R.E.F. Smith), Homewood, IL: The American Economic Association.
Chayanov, A.V., 1991, *The Theory of Peasant Co-operatives*, London: I.B. Tauris & Co., Ltd.
Conkin, P.K., 1988, *The Southern Agrarians*, Knoxville, TS: The University of Tennessee Press.
Cox, T.M., 1979, *Rural Sociology in the Soviet Union*, New York: Holmes & Meier Publishers, Inc.
Deutscher, I., 1955, *Heretics and Renegades*, London: Hamish Hamilton.
Donnelly, I., 1960/1890, *Ceasar's Column: A Story of the Twentieth Century*, Cambridge, MA: The Belknap Press of Harvard University Press.
Durando, D., 1993, 'The Rediscovery of Ethnic Identity', *Telos*, No.97.
Durrenberger, E.P. (ed.), 1984, *Chayanov, Peasants and Economic Anthropology*, New York: Academic Press.
Eliade, M., 1954, *The Myth of the Eternal Return*, New York: Pantheon Books Inc.
Ellis, F., 1988, *Peasant Economics*, Cambridge: Cambridge University Press.
Etzioni, A., 1990, *The Moral Dimension: Toward a New Economics*, New York: The Free Press.
Etzioni, A., 1993, *The Spirit of Community: Rights, Responsibilities and the Communitarian Agenda*, New York: Crown.
Finley, M.I., 1975, *The Use and Abuse of History*, London: Chatto & Windus.
Flinn, C., 1992, *Strains of Utopia: Gender, Nostalgia, and Hollywood Film Music*, Princeton, NJ: Princeton University Press.
Forster, E.M., 1947/1909, 'The Machine Stops', in *The Collected Stories of E.M.Forster*, London: Sidgwick & Jackson.
Fortunati, V., 1993, 'The Metamorphosis of the Apocalyptic Myth: From Utopia to Science Fiction', in Bann and Kumar (eds.) [1993].
Fritzsche, P., 1990, *Rehearsals for Fascism: Populism and Political Mobilisation in Weimar Germany*, New York: Oxford University Press.
Furth, C. (ed.), 1976, *The Limits of Change: Essays on Conservative Alternatives in Republican China*, Cambridge, MA: Harvard University Press.
Genovese, E.D., 1994, *The Southern Tradition: The Achievement and Limitations of an American*

Conservatism, Cambridge, MA: Harvard University Press.

Goodwyn, L., 1976, *Democratic Promise: The Populist Movement in America*, New York: Oxford University Press.

Goodwyn, L., 1978, *The Populist Movement: A Short History of the Agrarian Revolt*, New York: Oxford University Press.

Goodwyn, L., 1986, 'Populism and Powerlessness', in H.C.Boyte and F.Riessman (eds.).

Goodwyn, L., 1991, 'Rethinking "Populism": Paradoxes of Historiography and Democracy', *Telos*, No.88.

Greene, G., 1972, *Graham Greene on Film: Collected Film Criticism, 1935-39*, New York: Simon & Schuster.

Griffiths, R., 1983, *Fellow Travellers of the Right: British Enthusiasts for Nazi Germany 1933-39*, Oxford: Oxford University Press.

Guha, R. (ed.), 1982-89, *Subaltern Studies I-VI*, Delhi: Oxford University Press.

Harrison, M., 1975, 'Chayanov and the Economics of the Russian Peasantry', *Journal of Peasant Studies*, Vol.2, No.4.

Harrison, M., 1977, 'The Peasant Mode of Production in the Work of A.V. Chayanov', *Journal of Peasant Studies*, Vol.4, No.4.

Havens, T., 1974, *Farm and Nation in Modern Japan: Agrarian Nationalism, 1870-1940*, Princeton, NJ: Princeton University Press.

Hawthorn, G., 1991, *Plausible Worlds*, Cambridge: Cambridge University Press.

Hicks, J.D., 1931, *The Populist Revolt: A History of the Farmers' Alliance and the People's Party*, Minnesota, MN: The University of Minnesota Press.

Hilton, J., 1933, *Lost Horizon*, New York: Grosset & Dunlap.

Hilton, J., 1933a, *Knight Without Armour*, London: Ernest Benn Ltd.

Hilton, J., 1938, 'A Chapter of Autobiography', in *To You, Mr. Chips*, London: Hodder & Stoughton.

Hinz, B., 1980, *Art in the Third Reich*, Oxford: Basil Blackwell.

Hofstadter, R., 1962, *The Age of Reform: From Bryan to FDR*, London: Jonathan Cape.

Hofstadter, R., 1969, 'North America', in G. Ionescu and E. Gellner (eds.), *Populism: Its Meanings and National Characteristics*, London: Weidenfeld & Nicolson.

Hofstadter, R. and S.M. Lipset (eds.), 1968, *Turner and the Sociology of the Frontier*, New York: Basic Books.

Hudson, W.H., 1887, *A Crystal Age*, London: T. Fisher Unwin.

Jasny, N., 1972, *Soviet Economists of the Twenties*, London: Cambridge University Press.

Jefferies, R., 1939/1885, *After London*, London: J.M. Dent & Sons.

Kafka, F., 1973, *Shorter Works - Volume I*, London: Secker & Warburg.

Kamenka, E. (ed.), 1982, *Community as a Social Ideal*, London: Edward Arnold, Publishers.

Kerblay, B., 1971, 'Chayanov and the Theory of Peasant Economies', in T. Shanin (ed.), *Peasants and Peasant Societies*, London: Penguin Books.

Kneale, N., 1960, *Quatermass and the Pit*, London: Penguin Books.

Kracauer, S., 1947, *From Caligari to Hitler: A Psychological History of the German Film*, London: Dennis Dobson, Ltd.

Kremnev, I. [ps. A.V. Chayanov], 1977/1920, 'The Journey of My Brother Alexei to the Land of Peasant Utopia', in R.E.F. Smith (ed.), *The Russian Peasant in 1920 and 1984*, London: Frank Cass.

Kumar, K., 1987, *Utopia and Anti-Utopia in Modern Times*, Oxford: Basil Blackwell.

Laclau, E., 1985, 'New Social Movements and the Plurality of the Social', in D.Slater (ed.), *New Social Movements and the State in Latin America*, Amsterdam: CEDLA.

Laclau, E., 1993, 'Power and Representation', in M. Poster (ed.), *Politics, Theory, and Contemporary Culture*, New York: Colombia University Press.

Lasch, C., 1991, *The True and Only Heaven: Progress and Its Critics*, New York: W.W. Norton & Co.

Lasch, C., 1995, *The Revolt of the Elites and the Betrayal of Democracy*, New York: W.W. Norton & Co.

Le Bon, G., 1924, *The World Unbalanced*, London: T. Fisher Unwin.

Lenin, V.I., 1960, 'The Development of Capitalism in Russia', *Collected Works*, Vol.3, Moscow:

Foreign Languages Publishing House.

Levy, E., 1991, *Small-Town America in Film: The Decline and Fall of Community*, New York: Continuum.

MacIntyre, A., 1981, *After Virtue*, London: Duckworth.

McBride, J., 1992, *Frank Capra: The Catastrophe of Success*, London: Faber & Faber.

Manuel, F.E. (ed.), 1967, *Utopias and Utopian Thought*, Boston, MA: Beacon Press.

Manuel, F.E., 1972, *Freedom from History*, London: University of London Press.

Manuel, F.E. and F.P. Manuel, 1979, *Utopian Thought in the Western World*, Oxford: Basil Blackwell.

Marin, L., 1993, 'The Frontiers of Utopia', in Bann and Kumar (eds.) [1993].

Martin, J.W. and C.E. Ostwalt (eds.), 1995, *Screening the Sacred: Religion, Myth, and Ideology in Popular American Film*, Boulder, CO: Westview Press.

Miglio, G., 1993, 'The Cultural Roots of the Federalist Revolution', *Telos*, No.97.

Mitrany, D., 1951, *Marx Against the Peasant*, Chapel Hill, NC: University of North Carolina Press.

Morris, W., 1970/1885, *News from Nowhere*, London: Routledge.

Morton, A.L., 1952, *The English Utopia*, London: Lawrence & Wishart.

Murray, C., 1990, *The Emerging British Underclass*, London: Institute of Economic Affairs.

Murray, C., 1994, *Underclass: The Crisis Deepens*, London: Institute of Economic Affairs.

Nisbet, R., 1980, *History of the Idea of Progress*, London: Heinemann.

Omvedt, G., 1994, 'Peasants, Dalits and Women: Democracy and India's New Social Movements', *Journal of Contemporary Asia*, Vol.24, No.1.

Orwell, G., 1949, *Nineteen Eighty-Four*, London: Secker & Warburg.

Ostwalt, C.E., 1995, 'Hollywood and Armageddon: Apocalyptic Themes in Recent Cinematic Presentation', in Martin and Ostwalt (eds.) [1995].

Pareto, V., 1963, *A Treatise on General Sociology*, Vols.1–4, New York: Dover Publications.

Parkinson, D., 1993, *Mornings in the Dark: The Graham Greene Film Reader*, London: Carcanet.

Passmore, J., 1972, *The Perfectibility of Man*, London: Duckworth.

Passmore, J., 1978, *Science and Its Critics*, London: Duckworth.

Pieterse, J.N., 1992, *White on Black: Images of Africa and Blacks in Western Popular Culture*, New Haven, CT: Yale University Press.

Rawls, J., 1993, *Political Liberalism*, New York: Columbia University Press.

Ridge, M., 1962, *Ignatius Donnelly: The Portrait of a Politician*, Chicago, IL: University of Chicago Press.

Richards, J., 1970, 'Frank Capra and the Cinema of Populism', *Cinema*, No.5.

Richards, J. and D. Sheridan (eds.), 1987, *Mass-Observation at the Movies*, London: Routledge & Kegan Paul.

Richie, D., 1972, *Japanese Cinema*, London: Secker & Warburg.

Rogger, H. and E. Weber (eds.), 1965, *The European Right: An Historical Profile*, London: Weidenfeld & Nicolson.

Rohdie, S., 1970, 'A Structural Analysis of *Mr Deeds Goes to Town*', *Cinema*, No.5.

Rorty, R., 1989, *Contingency, Irony, Solidarity*, Cambridge: Cambridge University Press.

Rushing, J.H. and T.S. Frentz, 1995, *Projecting the Shadow: The Cyborg Hero in American Film*, Chicago, IL: University of Chicago Press.

Said, E.W., 1978, *Orientalism*, London: Routledge & Kegan Paul.

Said, E.W., 1993, *Culture and Imperialism*, London: Chatto & Windus.

Saloutos, T. and J.D. Hicks, 1951, *Agricultural Discontent in the Middle West 1900–1939*, Madison, WI: University of Wisconsin Press.

Samuel, R., 1995, *Theatres of Memory*, London: Verso.

Sargent, L.T. (ed.), 1995, *Extremism in America: A Reader*, New York: New York University Press.

Shiva, V., 1989, *Staying Alive: Women, Ecology and Development*, London: Zed Books.

Shiva, V., 1991, *The Violence of the Green Revolution: Third World Agriculture, Ecology and Politics*, London: Zed Press.

Soucy, R., 1995, *French Fascism: The Second Wave, 1933–1939*, New Haven, CT: Yale University Press.

Smith, R.E.F., 1977, 'Notes on the Sources of George Orwell's 1984', in R.E.F. Smith (ed.)., *The Russian Peasant in 1920 and 1984*, London: Frank Cass.

Taguieff, P.-A., 1990, 'The New Cultural Racism in France', *Telos*, No.83.

Taguieff, P.-A., 1994a, 'Discussion or Inquisition? The Case of Alain de Benoist', *Telos*, Nos.98–99.

Taguieff, P.-A., 1994b, 'Origins and Metamorphoses of the New Right', *Telos*, Nos.98–99.

Tarde, G., 1905, *Underground Man*, London: Duckworth.

Tawney, R.H., 1932, *Land and Labour in China*, London: George Allen & Unwin.

Tawney, R.H., 1938, *Agrarian China*, Shanghai: Kelly & Walsh.

Timms, E., 1985, 'Expressionists and Georgians: Demonic City and Enchanted Village', in Timms and Kelley (ed.) [1985].

Timms, E. and D. Kelley (eds.), 1985, *Unreal City: Urban Experience in Modern European Literature and Art*, Manchester: Manchester University Press.

Vann Woodward, C., 1938, *Tom Watson: Agrarian Rebel*, New York: Macmillan.

Walicki, A., 1969, *The Controversy over Capitalism*, Oxford: Clarendon Press.

Wiener, M.J., 1981, *English Culture and the Decline of the Industrial Spirit 1850–1980*, Cambridge: Cambridge University Press.

Welch, D., 1983, *Propaganda and the German Cinema 1933–1945*, Oxford: Clarendon Press.

Wells, H.G., 1895, *The Time Machine*, London: Heinemann.

Williams, R., 1973, *The Country and the City*, London: Chatto & Windus.

Williams, R., 1985, 'The Metropolis and the Emergence of Modernism', in Timms and Kelley (eds.) [1985].

Zamyatin, Y., 1977/1924, *We*, Harmondsworth: Penguin Books.

Globalisation and Restructuring in the Indian Food Industry

JAIRUS BANAJI

In April 1996 Unilever announced the merger of its two major group companies in India, Hindustan Lever Ltd. and Brooke Bond Lipton India Ltd.[1] Brooke Bond came into the Unilever fold in 1984 when it was acquired internationally for £376 million. Then in 1992 the Brooke Bond and Lipton businesses were merged to form a single company. The latest merger, however, is important in several ways. First, it makes Hindustan Lever the largest company in the Indian private sector in terms of market capitalisation, the first time any foreign company has occupied such a high rank. Secondly, for Hindustan Lever it means instant diversification into a sector whose rapid expansion has attracted a host of foreign companies and, till October 1995 at any rate, approved foreign investments worth some Rs 22 billion, between a third and a half of the totals approved for power and oil respectively![2] Thirdly, the merger with Brooke Bond Lipton India is simply the culmination of a series of mergers and acquisitions through which S.M. Datta, Lever's flamboyant and aggressive chairman, pushed Hindustan Lever into the forefront of a period of spectacular growth, *far above global averages*,[3] in the face of stiff opposition from the unions, with whom he refused to negotiate, and of the resurgent ground-swell of economic nationalism ('swadeshi'). In a sense, Hindustan Lever's growth in the nineties was the most spectacular or strident symbol of the deregulation of large-scale industry, but also of the dilemmas facing Indian capitalism in the period of globalisation. Having called for liberalisation for years, most Indian businesses now find themselves vulnerable to the expansion of foreign business, and faced with the clear choice of either internationalising their own operations or becoming marginal players. Finally, the merger can also be construed as a *response* to global competition, in particular to Procter & Gamble in the core business and Nestlé in the new areas of

Jairus Banaji is at Wolfson College, Oxford, UK. Part of the research for this study was conducted jointly with his colleagues Gautam Mody and V. Janardhan, and much of it was supported, financially, by the IUF/Asia Pacific. The author is grateful to all of them and to Bennet D'Costa, Franklyn D'Souza, and Rohini for their help.

growth, with the restructuring of Unilever's Indian businesses reflecting international priorities and the drive to sustain group profitability through product and geographical diversification. This aspect is in fact explicit: 'Talking about the need to take foreign competition head on, Mr Datta said: "We need to move more speedily because the new business environment in India has provided a vast opportunity for our global competitors to bring in their latest in technology and branding"'.[4]

'OUR GLOBAL COMPETITORS'

The current wave of globalisation is being driven by international firms attracted to large and expanding markets in the unsaturated regions of the world economy. Globalisation is restructuring global *investment* patterns, a fact consistently ignored in most of the recent literature on the subject.[5] Secondly, for Marxists it is worth noting that the restructuring of investment flows is not bringing about an 'export' of capital to areas of *lower* organic composition, as some classical versions of Marxist theory have supposed, but, *fundamentally*, a surge of investments in highly capital-intensive production facilities (in oil, chemicals, automobiles, food processing, and so on) geared to expanding domestic and regional markets. The *design* of manufacturing is dictated by the same considerations which prevail elsewhere (high-volume capital-intensive technology, economies of time, flexible manufacturing systems, automation) but its location, globally, is determined by where the most rapid expansion is foreseeable. Thus Nestlé's Management Report for 1994 notes, 'Of the eleven new factories opened worldwide over the last two years, nine are in emerging markets. Particular emphasis is being placed on the Far East/Pacific area'. For Nestlé the emerging markets were characterised by a sales volume growth in excess of 10 per cent. In PepsiCo's Annual Report for 1995, these are called 'Growth markets' and said to be 'markets where we are *investing heavily because we believe they have high growth potential*'. 'Growth markets primarily include Brazil, China, Eastern Europe and India.' In 1995 PepsiCo registered volume advances of $194 million, largely through the contribution of these markets. Procter & Gamble's Annual Report for 1995 states, 'Asia recorded 24 percent volume growth led by excellent progress in China and India'. Grand Metropolitan's Annual Report for 1995 tells us, 'India is one of IDV's fastest growing emerging markets, with both international and national brands ... experiencing significant growth'. In a similar vein, Seagram announces that it 'established affiliates in Colombia, India, the Philippines, and South Africa. *We believe the potential for India, in particular, is enormous*'. Unilever has likewise gone on record as saying, 'the areas of fastest growth which present the best business opportunities for businesses we are in are Southeast Asia, Latin America and countries like India and China'.[6] Finally, the same heady optimism is true of international majors in other industrial sectors, for example, the US aerospace giant AlliedSignal, which sees itself being 'led' into 'untapped regions of the world such as India, China and Mexico', and ICI which recently announced plans to invest £800 million in Asia over the next ten years (£200 million in India) and stated that it would increase the contribution of its Asian operations from the present level of 15 per cent of global turnover to 25 per cent.[7] Since 1993, headlines in the Indian corporate press have consistently emphasised the strong interest of international firms in the Indian market and in Asian markets more generally.

REFORMS

The reforms of July 1991 included the 'substantial deregulation of industry, promotion of increased competition by the opening up of many areas previously reserved for the public sector, and policies to attract increased foreign investment'. To attract a larger share of global investment flows, the government abandoned the key provision of the Foreign Exchange Regulation Act (FERA) and allowed direct foreign investment with 51 per cent or more equity in high priority industries. It also produced a significant change in the Monopolies & Restrictive Trade Practices legislation so as to 'completely eliminate the need of prior approval for establishment of new undertakings, expansion of existing undertakings, merger, amalgamation, etc.' which companies above the threshold limit of assets were required to obtain from the Central Government. Some spokespersons of large industry, such as T. Thomas, former chairman of Hindustan Lever, were strong advocates of the need for rapid concentration as a growth strategy; in May 1992 he wrote, 'Our industrial licensing policy and MRTP compelled industry to be fragmented and small; instead of creating a few large scale companies having the capability to invest and compete, we have ended up with a motley collection of medium to small size companies by international standards. It is inevitable that there has to be a shakedown through mergers and acquisitions.' Thus the progressive liberalisation which began in the summer of 1991 under the pressure of a severe foreign exchange crisis would immediately expand the range of corporate strategies available to companies. Companies were free to invest more in local operations and convert them into subsidiaries, to buy up other companies, to consolidate their business operations through mergers, and to aim for global stature in a world characterised by fierce competition for international markets. The throwing open of the core sectors to private investments, domestic and foreign, is clearly intended to encourage the expansion of private capital, especially of the big business groups.

'The liberalisation process currently on in India has evoked much interest with multinational companies around the world', said one multinational representative while inaugurating Brooke Bond's frozen desserts plant near Nasik. Actual flows of foreign direct investment have swelled from $620 million in 1993–94 to $1.31 billion in 1994–95 and around $2 billion in 1995–96.[8] It is clear that India is in the middle of her second foreign investment boom, and that this, together with the liberalisation, is the background against which we have to look at the effects of restructuring in food and related sectors.

The current foreign investment boom is distinguished from the previous one in the 1950s and early sixties[9] by at least three major features. Firstly, the renewed flow of investments is part of a new restructuring of *global* investment patterns, with companies which face a downturn in the well-established markets targeting Asia as 'the fastest growing region in the world for the rest of the decade'.[10] For example, it was reported in April 1994 that 'the major focus of German industry has shifted to Asian countries' and that 'India is ranked top among them'.[11] It is clear that the revival of the world economy depends to some extent on the further expansion of the Asian countries. Second, the current boom in direct foreign investment is marked by the entry of the world's *biggest* corporations. Among comparatively new investors, that is, multinationals with a previously low or zero exposure in India, 30 per cent of the world's 100 largest corporations are making new investments, followed by only 12 per cent of the next 100, 10 per cent of the third 100, and so on. In the top 50, the proportion of firms investing in India (for the first time) is as high as 40 per cent. These firms include General Motors, Shell, Exxon, Ford, General Electric, British Petroleum, Daimler Benz, Mobil, Philip Morris, Samsung, Du Pont, Chevron, Elf Aquitaine, Renault, Peugeot, Alcatel, Sony, Daewoo, and Total of France. Of course, the expansion of foreign capital is considerably more than this list suggests, since smaller multinationals are also rushing to India, and, besides, firms with established business interests, such as Nestlé, Unilever, Philips, ABB, Hoechst, Siemens, BASF, Bayer (from the top 50) are making or are certain to make new investments. For example, Hoechst AG is joining Reliance in a joint venture at Hazira,[12] Bayer AG is setting up a huge chemicals complex at Manali,[13] Barnevik of ABB regards India as the world's second largest market for power plants and rail transportation,[14] and so on. A third characteristic is that the new investments are more widely dispersed, with a strong attraction for the so-called 'backward areas' where union organisation is either weak or non-existent.

CORPORATE STRATEGIES

Companies' strategies can be characterised at different levels. At the most general level, the main players in the Indian food industry have been pursuing one of the following main strategies: (1) to become no.1 in specific industries; (2) to re-concentrate the operations of a local subsidiary and diversify independently; (3) to establish global capability and emerge as an Indian multinational. Thus Unilever's expansion in India has been based on the first of these 'main' strategies, Cadbury Schweppes is a good illustration of the second, and ITC is the best example of the third. At another level, 'corporate strategy' can also refer to the types of expansion and restructuring through which companies have implemented their main strategy. Acquisitions have played a key role here, both because they reduce the costs of investment and because they provide quicker access to markets and/or manufacturing capacities. In the food business, acquisitions have been made either to help companies to expand market shares in sectors where they face volume stagnation or to enable (mostly tobacco) companies to recentre their operations by diversifying into food. In India, Unilever companies can show both types of acquisitions. On the other hand, most mergers have been internal operations intended to consolidate businesses through the formation of bigger companies which can acquire market leadership more rapidly or which are better able to withstand the competition of new multinationals. Acquisitions especially have been used to effect rapid diversification into the foods business. But for the major companies, diversification has been counterbalanced by considerable emphasis on the core businesses. Thus ITC is today a strategically diversified conglomerate but it is still heavily involved in the tobacco industry. Hindustan Lever is still largely a soaps and detergents company, and Brooke Bond derives 86 per cent of its turnover from tea. In fact, all these companies have continued to invest heavily in their traditional product lines, despite rapid growth of new areas of business. Thus today diversification is no longer *at the cost of* core businesses but complementary to them, and the companies which are likely to emerge from the current phase of restructuring will have a structure akin to large conglomerates with parallel interests in related lines of business. Some impression of the sheer pace and scope of restructuring can be got by looking at Brooke Bond, which has been Unilever's bridgehead into the Indian food industry.

Brooke Bond's growth strategies can be divided into (1) *consolidation* in mainline businesses, (2) diversification into *processed foods*, and (3) entry into *contract farming*.[15] Of these the first strategy has been achieved by mergers and new investments, the second mainly through acquisitions. The mergers came in two stages, starting with the decision, announced in

1992, to merge Tea Estates and Doom Dooma with Brooke Bond. These were plantation companies in which Unilever held a 74 per cent stake, and one effect of the merger would be that the latter's stake in Brooke Bond would increase from 39.4 per cent to close to 50 per cent. Tea Estates owns 12 plantations in South India, of which four are in the Nilgiris, five in Coimbatore district and three in Madurai district. The estates comprise some 3,400 hectares, and during 1990 the average yield per acre was said to be one of the highest in the industry. Doom Dooma Tea has three tea estates in Dibrugarh district of Assam, with 2,964 hectares under cultivation and a reported workforce of 6,000 plus. One of the features of the food industry is the ability of large-scale producers to achieve substantial increases in productivity and/or yield, and this is illustrated by the Doom Dooma plantations. In 1991 it was reported, 'Although Doom Dooma is burdened with old tea bushes with low outturn, the post-Brooke Bond management has succeeded in raising the output through intensive replanting. It introduced the continuous manufacturing process in place of batch manufacture to trim wastage.' In the following year these amalgamations were followed up by the merger of Lipton and Brooke Bond which resulted in the 8th largest company in the Indian corporate sector and the formation of the *biggest foods company* in the country. Simultaneously, Brooke Bond made new investments in the tea business, announcing plans to set up a tea blending and packaging factory in Assam at a cost of Rs 5 crores, inaugurating a composite tea processing and packing unit at Dharwar in Karnataka in May 1993, and starting a 100 per cent export oriented unit at Etah in UP for the manufacture of instant tea powder, at a cost of Rs 20 crores, financed by Unilever's increased stake in Lipton. To this list of fresh investments in mainline businesses we should add the company's new instant coffee agglomeration plant at Hosur. When this was started around 1989, the only other major manufacturer of instant coffee in India was Nestlé's Food Specialities Ltd. Finally, the acquisition of 52 per cent equity in Kothari General Foods, most of this (33 per cent) from General Foods Inc of the US (currently Kraft General Food International) gave Brooke Bond a further stake in the coffee business. Brooke Bond paid only Rs 7 per share of KGF and proposed to pay off the KGF shareholders in cash to avoid diluting Unilever's holding in the company. In return it acquired an 'ultra-modern coffee plant at Mysore', paying a little over Rs 10 crores for a gross block of Rs 30 crores in fixed assets.

Not content with consolidation, Brooke Bond entered the processed foods business with one major acquisition and one substantial new investment. In 1993 the company bought Kissan Products for Rs 25 crores, after Nestlé offered Vijay Mallya Rs 23 crores in an attempt to outbid Brooke Bond, and in addition to the £300,000 which changed hands in an overseas deal involving the purchase by Unilever of Cadbury Schweppes' 33 per cent stake in Kissan. It was said that the Kissan takeover would give Brooke Bond roughly 79 per cent of the squash and fruit juice market in India, 68 per cent of the jam and preservatives market, and 42 per cent of the tomato ketchup market. In early 1994 it was also reported that Brooke Bond was keen to take over Ready Foods' processed foods plant on the outskirts of Bangalore. This is a Rs 63 crore state-of-the-art plant which began operations only recently and is said to have a capacity of 24,000 tonnes of frozen fruits and vegetables. But ITC is also interested in Ready Foods and till the end of June no deal had been announced. However, so far Brooke Bond's biggest investment in food has been the frozen desserts factory at Sinnar (near Nasik in Maharashtra), inaugurated in January 1994. Established in a record time of thirteen months with a capital investment of Rs 56 crores (financed entirely through internal accruals) and a capacity of 8 million litres, this is 'the single largest investment made in the processed foods industry by any business house'. According to the company's publicity during the inauguration, *'The key factory personnel have been trained overseas in Unilever research laboratories and manufacturing units for extended periods of up to 2 years'*. On the company's description, 'The bulk intake and processing of indigenous raw materials, computer controlled processing equipment, automatic cleaning systems and automated filling lines mean that human contact with the product during manufacture is eliminated'. Thus the Sinnar factory is probably typical of the *highly automated*, capital-intensive plants which the new wave of foreign investments is introducing into remote rural areas which lack both industrial experience and of course any sort of union tradition. Finally, BBLIL's entry into frozen vegetables will probably absorb even bigger investments, since this is Brooke Bond's major thrust area in the processed foods business in India. In 1993 the company stated, 'An exercise has begun to identify areas where vegetables and fruits are grown *so that a complete network of processing and distribution facilities can be created across the country'*. By November 1993 Brooke Bond had started marketing frozen peas, mushrooms, cauliflower and other vegetables in Kanpur and Lucknow, sourcing the vegetables from Tarai Foods Ltd., which is reported to have set up capacity for 7,200 tonnes per annum, at Rudrapur in UP. According to the memorandum of understanding signed with Tarai Foods, Brooke Bond was to have the first right on the company's entire production, would market the product under its own brand name and have complete control over the final pricing of the product. Since then, however, ConAgra has reportedly picked up a majority stake in Tarai Foods![16] There is a vast potential demand for frozen fruits and vegetables within India itself, but also a growing worldwide market, especially in Europe and the US, and Brooke Bond's eagerness to acquire Ready Foods is partly explained by the fact that 'Conditions in the Madanapalle belt, on the outskirts of Bangalore, where the Ready Foods plant is located, are proving to be ideal for growing high demand "European preferred" vegetables such as cauliflower, tomatoes and zucchinis round the year'.

This leads directly to the third of Brooke Bond's strategic moves, backward integration into agriculture based on contract farming. A company press release issued at the time of the merger with Lipton states:

> The agriculture based products proposed to be introduced will spur BBLIL to establish a *direct backward linkage with the farming community in and around the existing/future factories that will come up* as a part of the company's ambitious diversification programme. The company will organise superior extension services and distribute high quality inputs such as seeds to raise productivity ... It is estimated that annually farm produce worth over Rs 3000 crores currently goes waste. *The introduction of practices such as contract farming, required for the backward integration of BBLIL's proposed new businesses* such as frozen vegetables, will help prevent such waste and also generate employment in rural areas.

Like Brooke Bond, ITC too has earmarked the foods business as a major thrust area, but ITC started diversifying much earlier and moves into the food industry as a remarkably diversified concern with significant international interests and a strong base in agriculture.[17] In the late 1980s the fastest expanding division was agribusiness, but this had already been preceded by diversification into hotels and has been followed by even more rapid diversification in the early 1990s. Consequently, ITC now operates in seven main areas of business (tobacco and cigarettes, hybrid seeds and edible oils, hotels, paper and paperboard, packaging and printing, international business, and financial services) and is said to be working on a restructuring plan involving a series of mergers and demergers which will redefine the core businesses and make it 'the strongest agri-products company in the subcontinent, with focus on tobacco, oilseeds and edible oils'. Unlike Unilever group companies, ITC's expansion has been almost entirely through new investments and the flotation of new companies, and whereas the growth strategies of Hindustan Lever and Brooke Bond are strongly influenced by Unilever's priorities, ITC is bent on emerging as an *Indian* multinational. Chugh was quoted by the London *Financial Times* as saying: 'Our objective is to become a multinational company. *We are happy that BAT is supportive of our ambition.*'[18] In other words, ITC's plans are no longer governed by BAT's strategies.

Cigarettes

Although ITC is the undisputed cigarette-industry leader with about 63 per cent market share, global giants' expected entry will increase competition in the long term.[19] ITC's response is to *upgrade* cigarette manufacturing facilities to *global standards* with substantial investments. According to Chugh, 'We must be ready to compete in India with global players and compete globally with the multinationals'. Thus ITC 'is planning to set up an ultra-modern cigarette factory at a cost of Rs 100 crore on the Bellary Road' some 20 km from Bangalore.[20] The new site will occupy 100 acres of land. A report appearing in January 1994 claimed that ITC was 'planning to *gradually shift the existing plant to a location outside Bangalore'*.[21] On the shopfloor, the drive to take the global competition head on also means a massive thrust for productivity. According to a report which appeared in the *Business Standard* in May the same year,

> ... the ITC management has called for an immediate increase in production at its Kidderpore factory..The workers have been asked to increase the production level to 16 million cigarettes a day. The daily average production at the Kidderpore factory between April 1993 and March 1994 was 12.3 million cigarettes. The increase in output "has become essential" ... because of recent developments "which make it imperative for us to be competitive on all fronts". The issue was discussed threadbare with the CITU-affiliated India Tobacco Workers' Union and the INTUC-affiliated Tobacco Employees' Union in the last week of April. (According to the company) Global competition is fast becoming a reality with RJ Reynolds setting up a factory near Hyderabad. Philip Morris is also planning to enter the Indian market with its Marlboro brand. ITC signed a long-term agreement with the TUs on March 30 last year. Under the terms of the agreement "We were required to produce 16 million sticks a day for the first few months and then move up steadily to 18 million", said the company note ... The production in March and April this year was 204.9 and 330.8 million cigarettes respectively against 197 and 294.4 million in the corresponding months last year. *Since the introduction of the VRS* [Voluntary Retirement Scheme] *in September 1992, the number of workers at the Kidderpore factory has come down from 735 to 464.*[22]

Oilseeds

ITC is also setting up one of the country's largest oilseeds processing units. This will be based at Alwar in Rajasthan, and the areas identified for crop development are Alwar for rapeseed and mustard, Ganganagar, Bharatpur and Alwar for sunflower, and Kota Bundi and Tonk for soyabean. The cost of this project is around Rs 100 crores. ITC entered the edible oils business in 1987 with a 30,000 tonnes per annum refinery at Mantralayam in Kurnool district of Andhra Pradesh. Mantralayam is in the dry Rayalaseema tract, where land under sunflower cultivation is said to have increased eleven-fold to 440,000 hectares in only five years. Contract farming is not permitted under general oilseeds, and with overcapacity in crushing and refining there has been a 'virtual scramble for the seed'. Management claimed ITC was moving towards contract farming in sunflower and groundnut (the growers are mostly farmers with three to ten acres of land). The investments in Rajasthan should likewise mean a rapid growth of contract farming, since the company plans to produce substantial yield increases and will be buying back commercial seed from farmers for processing into edible oil. Finally, the edible oil businesses are going to be further strengthened with the launch of a subsidiary, ITC Palm-Tech, for the production and extraction of palm oil. In June 1993 it was reported that Kumpulan Emas Bhd, a Malaysian plantation group, would be teaming up with ITC to build India's first integrated palm oil complex. This could involve some 100,000 hectares, also in Andhra Pradesh. Since the oil palm has a longish gestation period of four to seven years, ITC plans to build farmers' commitment to the crop by involving them directly in the equity of the new company.

Food Processing

ITC's newest diversifications include financial services, software, menswear, footwear, probably power, and certainly food processing. ITC's interest in food processing was first announced in September 1993 when the group was reported to have 'identified the food processing industry as a *major focus area*'. A few months later, in March 1994, the ITC board approved a proposal to create a separate foods division within the company, and 'it is reliably learnt that *ITC is to set up a food processing plant [near Bangalore]* at a project cost of about Rs 40 crores'. It is likely that the Bangalore factory will produce fresh frozen tinned fruits and vegetables. ITC may be entering the beer market in a tie-up with Heineken. It is also planning a substantial investment in Aquafarming, using a combination of local sourcing ('marketing tie-ups') and own production. In November 1993 it was reported that ITC

> had finalised agreements with at least five parties that are engaged in setting up aquaculture complexes. While two of these units are at Nellore, others are coming up at Ongole, Kakinada, Belasore on the east coast, and Ratnagiri ... A 5000 tonnes per annum processing plant is also fast coming up at Vizag which will help boost the company's exports in the marine field from the rich hinterland of

prawn cultivation in the coastal districts of Andhra Pradesh. The Vizag unit is a joint project of ITC Ltd ... and the foreign collaborators Showa Trading Corporation of Japan

One of ITC's sourcing partners is Coromandal Aqua which is setting up a Rs 11.17 crore integrated prawn project at Kothakodur in Nellore district, inclusive of grow-out ponds, hatchery and a processing plant. According to the agreement, 'ITC will pick up 50 per cent of the output for export using its brand name. The balance will be marketed by ITC on Coromandal's behalf' for a royalty of one per cent. Thus even sourcing arrangements are being rationalised through marketing tie-ups with aqua firms, against the earlier pattern of sourcing shrimps directly from a large number of small farmers.

Globalisation and International Sourcing

ITC's drive to emerge as an independent multinational was clearly reflected in the resistance it posed to BAT's attempt to up its stake in the company to 51 per cent. *BAT was willing to pay something in the region of $1 billion to have majority control.* Press reports claimed that BAT wanted ITC to '*pull out* of the businesses in which BAT itself does not have a presence ... ' An alternative proposal was that ITC should transfer its tobacco operation to a new company in which BAT would have 51 per cent shareholding. The ITC top management reacted with vigorous opposition and BAT was forced to retreat, declaring publicly, 'We have no plans to take control of ITC' (BAT chief executive Martin Broughton). For BAT loss of control over ITC means a further source of competition in the global tobacco industry. For example, in March 1993 BAT's main competitor in the deal for a joint venture with Prilucky Tobacco Factory, one of the biggest and best factories in the Ukraine, was ITC. Undeterred by its defeat, ITC stated that it 'hoped to clinch a deal soon with a Russian partner'! Thus BAT and its erstwhile subsidiary are now clearly global competitors. However, this does not preclude a partnership between the two firms. BAT's decision to make India a manufacturing base by sourcing some of its production through ITC and VST – subcontracting brands like Hollywood, Belmont, Derby and Horizon for export to South American, Asian and African markets – is an example of this. Moreover, currently 90 per cent of ITC's leaf tobacco exports are to BAT plc and its subsidiaries/associates. However, ITC has consolidated its own international operations by establishing ITC Global Holdings, a Singapore-based subsidiary which is involved in international trading. In December 1993 ITC Global purchased S.A. Unibel NV's commodities dealing business from the Unilever group, 'to gain access to lucrative markets in Central America and West Africa'. In IT consultancy and software services, ITC has started a subsidiary in the UK, ITC Infotech, which is designed to 'spearhead the group's software business using the UK as the basis to penetrate markets on a global scale'. Welcomgroup, ITC's hotel division, now merged with ITC Hotels Ltd., has been looking for properties abroad to start off its international career. 'To start with, the company is concentrating on S.E. Asia ... It is also looking for properties in east Europe.' In Nepal the largest private sector organisation in that country is an ITC associate, Surya Tobacco Co. Pvt. Ltd. Again, both ITC and ITC Hotels have gone in for overseas capital issues. ITC's Euro-issue in October 1993 was oversubscribed ten times and pulled in $92 million. Finally, the fact that ITC is a BAT affiliate and not a BAT subsidiary means that ITC's expansion may involve an indefinite series of foreign tie-ups. For example, it has tied up with Filtrona International for the manufacture of filter rods, mostly for the company's own consumption. Other recent collaborations include Reebok (in the shoe business), Lotus (software), Heineken (beer), Threadneedle (financial services), ICI-controlled Zeneca Seeds (agribusiness), and the Technology Funding Venture Capital Group.

The example of ITC shows that unions in India are no longer confronting some inert 'national' capitalism but an increasingly sophisticated global capitalism which cannot be handled effectively if unions themselves do not establish a new level of coordination. *Global capital wants tighter control over investments, cost-effective production structures, and pliable workforces isolated from the influence of unionism.* All this is underpinned by the increasingly ruthless nature of competition in world industry. When existing businesses lose market share or fail to diversify successfully, parent firms may sidestep those operations and seek fresh entry points. Thus Cadbury Schweppes has floated a 100 per cent subsidiary to effect its entry into the soft drink market.[23] It has also, of course, raised its stake in Cadbury India to 51 per cent. It is clear, however, that the existing operation will be refocused on chocolates, partly because attempts to diversify have been unsuccessful but mainly due to the entry of Mars. Cadbury India is planning a new Rs 40 crore chocolate plant, probably at its existing premises at Malanpur. This factory was started in 1989 with a production capacity of 8,000 tonnes per annum, and it is clear from recent reports that the company will eventually *shift most of the production from Thana to Malanpur*, which is near Gwalior in Madhya Pradesh. According to employees, Cadbury has sold half the land at its existing premises (in Pokhran) to a local builder. Moreover, for most of 1993 the factory was on four-day working, in July the company introduced a Voluntary Retirement Scheme which was accepted by some 350 employees, mostly older workers, and finally, according to employees themselves, 'They are certainly not planning any investments in Thane.' All the signs are that Cadbury may close down the unit at Thana and concentrate the bulk of its activity at the new site. Thus Kelkar's report in

Business Standard that 'Cadbury has decided to *refocus its operations from its factory in Thane, which is a high wage island, to its plant in Malanpur* ... ' is in all likelihood correct.

These decisions are part of the attempt to break the bargaining power of organised workforces and restructure profitability in union-free territory. The new global capital wants to minimise the intervention and impact of new unionisation by staving off the entry of unions for as long as it can. The crudest example of this is Hindustan Lever's ferocious struggle to keep the employees' federation out of its new plants. At a more insidious level, Cadbury reflects production strategies which have the same effect of undermining union strength. Thus Cadbury's managing director C.Y. Pal was quoted as saying, 'Besides our own facilities *we have the Dr. Writer's facility at Phaltan for making our products.*' The reference here is to a private limited company called Dr.Writer's Food Product Pvt.Ltd. This unit, owned by Madhav Apte, ran up huge losses (Rs 5.89 crores against a paid up capital of just Rs 35¼ lakhs!) and was declared sick. In October 1989 Cadbury entered into a revival agreement under which it would inject fresh capital in the form of machinery. Apte is rumoured to be one of the chief funders of the Shiv Sena. The factory is said to employ only 55 workers. Another unit which works for Cadbury is the Warora Co-operative in Kolhapur where Bournvita is produced. Altogether the company relies on *extensive* subcontracting. For Dollops it used a loan-licence agreement with Indian Ice Creams Ltd., which has a modern facility on the outskirts of Bangalore. Bournvita is also made using third party capacity of 1,000 tonnes in Hyderabad.

DOWNSIZING, RELOCATION, AND FLEXIBILITY: UNION REPORTS

The picture is one of extensive rationalisation with cutbacks in employment and continuous pressure for increases in production. *The most important fact about Bombay plants is the lack of new investment.* According to the Hindustan Lever Employees' Union, there has been no new investment in the Sewree factory for the last five years. In fact, no investment is planned unless the Dove proposal goes through. The 'Dove proposal' is the idea of *sourcing the entire Asian demand for Dove soap from the Sewree establishment.* Currently the Asian markets are serviced by US exports, against which local managers feel that given the quality standards of the factory in Bombay, which are the best in India in toilet soaps, it would make more sense for the whole production to be concentrated in Bombay. Indeed, the union claims that Bombay quality is said to be equal to international quality. At Herbertson's Bhandup factory, now controlled by Unilever through Brooke Bond's acquisition of Kissan from the UB group, the mood is one of widespread and persistent uncertainty. The union's feeling was that the new management considers the Bhandup factory to be 'excess'. There has already been a drastic cut in employment from 300 employees in 1986 to a current strength of 140, including staff. Yet, further cuts are planned: Brooke Bond want to increase the Kissan turnover through volume increases, say they are willing to bring in Unilever technology: but want a reduction in employee strength. The bulk of new investment has been at the factories in Bareilly and Bangalore, which also account for the largest share of turnover, Rs 30–40 crores at Bangalore against Bhandup's miserable 3½ crores. The Bhandup factory is also the least advanced technologically: for example, packing is still entirely manual. In fact, there has been no new investment since 1974.

At Cadbury's Thana factory, from a peak employment of 1,250 employees some eight years ago, staff strength has come down to 750. Bombay managements have seen the example of Ciba-Geigy negotiating a closure entirely through a Voluntary Retirement Scheme involving some 900 employees. The next major mass retirement was at Procter & Gamble's Richardson factory on the Thane-Belapur Rd, where the vast majority of 373 employees accepted early retirement in 1995. In a neighbouring plant CPC International managed to retire the bulk of its workforce and shift production (temporarily?) to a shed in Dharwar. It is likely that the company intends to automate the Kalwa factory.[24] Cadbury itself is likely to see a second VRS, as part of a clear attempt to relocate production elsewhere. The Indori factory is said to have around 400 workers, Malanpur around 200. At Thana there is 'no pressure for production'. There has been no investment either. When the company raised Rs 40 crores through a rights issue, 'Not a single paisa of this was invested in the Thana factory.' The position is similar in Britannia in one respect; here too, on Wadia's own admission, 'very little has been ploughed back for modernisation'. Fresh recruitment stopped around 1977 and employee strength has come down to 1,157, excluding staff, whereas only five years ago it was upwards of 2,000. However, there is an important difference with Cadbury. In Britannia it is quite clear from the union's description that BSN plans to make Reay Road a renovated manufacturing base. BSN technicians have visited the plant in the last seven to eight months and have 'suggested a lot of changes to management'. Moreover, in Britannia there *is* pressure for production. The union gave a 10 per cent production increase in each of the last three agreements (1987, 1990, 1994), and in the last round of discussions around the Charter the company also wanted demanning on all machines. At Hindustan Lever the union felt that company was planning to run down the workforce to a target level of 1,200–1,400 from the current 1,900. In Britannia, likewise, the union stated that BSN was planning to have a workforce of 650 within the next five to six years, which means that over half the labour force will be retired. Sales employees have also seen strong pressures for retrenchment. According to the All-India Brooke Bond Employees' Federation, in the last round of bargaining (in 1994) management wanted *restructuring of the distribution system* with the complete shutdown of some 600–700 sales depots (325 were closed in 1990, 219 in 1992), and the centralisation of sales offices into four large regional blocs instead of 40 dispersed establishments. Indeed, Brooke Bond has restructured distribution on the basis of the private agency system, with the appointment of wholesalers in lieu of sales staff. In 1991, the Vice-President of Sales and Marketing was quoted as saying, 'The direct selling system is very cost-effective, but when remote rural areas are brought under it, it becomes very expensive', and that Brooke Bond's new thrust was mainly to achieve 'rural penetration'.

Beyond the precincts of the metropolitan labour market, in distant and barely accessible rural locations, managements have had considerable flexibility in the deployment of labour: for example, in the SmithKline Beecham Horlicks factory at Nabha (in Patiala district of Punjab) the company still retains a pool of several thousand temporaries, in addition to some 860 permanent employees, and in ITC's leaf processing factory at Chirala (in the coastal area of Andhra Pradesh) seasonal workers have always been a majority of the labour force. At Chirala, however, the feature of particular interest is that the company had retrenched some 5,000 women in the early eighties (in this factory alone) and had done so in response to directives from BAT for an improved quality of leaf and a corresponding shift from manual stripping of the leaves to mechanised threshing. The women, mostly Dalits, were forced back into agriculture, where earnings were considerably lower. According to one manager, 'There was a little bit of resistance, nothing significant'. Finally, the newer plants in these more remote locations are highly capital-intensive: for example, 60 permanent employees and five managers in PepsiCo's snack foods plant at Channo (in Punjab) for an investment of Rs 24 crores, 60 permanent workers and 14 managers at Kellogg's Taloja factory for a projected annual capacity of 5,700 tonnes of cereals. Moreover, unencumbered by the legacies of unionism, even established investors like Unilever can transform the new plants into exemplars of 'best proven practice', as in the Khamgaon soap factory where "teamwork" and high levels of productivity are still compatible with average wages of Rs 1,500/- per month.

NEW INVESTORS

The entry of the global food and drinks giants is both rapid and comprehensive:

Lowenbrau,[25] Holsten,[26] Foster's,[27] Carlsberg,[28] Anheuser-Busch,[29] and probably Heineken[30] in beer, International Distillers and Vintners (GrandMet),[31] United Distillers (Guinness),[32] Allied Domecq, Seagram,[33] Brown-Forman, American Brands, and Pernod Ricard[34] in distilled spirits, Coca-Cola and PepsiCo in soft drinks, United Biscuits in biscuit manufacturing,[35] Hershey Foods,[36] Mars,[37] and Nestlé in confectionery, Seagram, Cadbury Schweppes,[38] and Coastlog[39] in fruit juices, ConAgra,[40] McCain, and Unilever in frozen foods, Tyson Foods in poultry, H.J. Heinz in ketchups and baby foods, Danone in dairy products and mineral water, Japan Tobacco in rice, Kellogg and Quaker Oats in breakfast cereals, Burns Philp in yeast and bakery ingredients, Pillsbury (GrandMet) and Philip Morris in flour and vegetable-based products. Some of these are collaborations, others 100 per cent subsidiaries. Thus Carlsberg is tying up with United Breweries, R.J. Reynolds with the M.K. Modi group, Rothmans with GTC, Pillsbury with the Godrej group,[41] Anheuser-Busch with Shaw Wallace, Quaker Oats with the 'practically unknown' Cremico Agro Industries,[42] and (possibly) Heineken with ITC (which is also close to a tie-up with ConAgra):

> Heineken is said to have planned a $417 million investment in its Asian businesses over the next five years. The Dutch brewing company's interest in India is seen as an offshoot of the plan to increase its presence in the Asian region. The beer industry in India is growing at the rate of 15 per cent annually, with major global brands all set to hit the local market this year [1994]. The worsening downturn in the European beer markets has prompted continental brewers to target the fast-growing Asian region.[43]

International Distillers and Vintners has set up a joint venture with Polychem of the Kilachand group to produce Smirnoff vodka and other IDV brands. 'According to Mr Christopher Pearson, President of IDV's Asia Pacific operations, the Indian company will be the first in Asia to produce Smirnoff, and *will be a production base for exports to the Asia–Pacific region.'*[44] But the last few years have also seen a dramatic tightening of control over investments, with international firms rushing to form *subsidiaries* and increasing their stake in existing ventures through 'preferential allotments', open market purchases and the buying out of partners. Food firms with fully-owned subsidiaries include Unilever, Heinz,[45] Hershey Foods, Kellogg,[46] Philip Morris, Mars, Groupe Danone,[47] Cadbury Schweppes, the Pillsbury Co, Burns Philp, and McCain. For example, it was reported recently that Philip Morris 'is not interested in a joint venture. Instead, it plans to set up a 100 per cent subsidiary as the project [for pasta, vegetable purée, etc.] requires big money and the joint venture partner may not be willing to put in investment. Moreover, it is company policy not to part with state-of-the-art technology in the food processing field to its partners.'[48]

The rise of holding companies, in particular, reflects both long-term commitments to the Indian market and the flexibility of rapid diversification in terms of future investment strategies. But foreign majors have also repeatedly failed to gain majority control in existing or proposed ventures with dominant Indian businesses or even middle-size firms (Philip Morris in Godfrey Philips, where it currently holds a 36 per cent stake,[49] Heineken in discussions with the UB group,[50] Danone in discussions with Indiana Dairy Specialities[51]) and it is likely that this has increased the preference for 100 per cent subsidiaries. Finally, Heinz's entry into India has been through acquisitions. It bought Glaxo's family products division for a record $67 million (Rs 210 crores),[52] and in June 1994 was close to acquiring PepsiCo's tomato paste factory at Zahura in Punjab,[53] but this was rapidly acquired by Unilever. Cargill was said to be in the race for Glaxo's stake in KG Gluco Biols, 'as part of its overall bid to build up synergies in the core agricultural and commodities businesses in the region'.[54] Also in 1994, PepsiCo acquired Duke and Sons, the oldest drinks company in the Bombay area.[55] In 1995 ConAgra acquired a 51 per cent stake in Tarai Foods through its subsidiary Lamb-Weston. And of course Unilever has established a strong position in prepared tomatoes and vegetables through its acquisitions of Kissan and PepsiCo's tomato business.

CONCLUDING REMARKS

To sum up, the current wave of expansion in India's burgeoning food industry has seen rapid penetration of markets through joint ventures and acquisitions, tighter control over investments through the consolidation of equity and formation of subsidiaries, major and rapid restructuring of entire businesses, including relocation of investments and restructuring of older manufacturing establishments, and, finally, vertical integration into agriculture through contract farming. All of this is, as I have argued, part of the global production expansion of firms whose survival depends on continuing market expansion. For example, Carlsberg plans large-scale investments in China and joint ventures in Brazil, Burma, and Vietnam, Heineken is building breweries in Burma, Cambodia, Thailand, and China, Kellogg has opened high-technology cereal plants in China and Argentina, Heinz is expanding in southern Russia and South Africa. As between global sourcing capability and market-seeking investments, I have argued that the present wave of expansion is essentially driven by the latter. Global expansion is driven by rapidly expanding markets. But within these markets investments are being structured to emphasise the expendability of labour, to intensify the fragmentation of workforces, and to secure compliance through submission. The widespread hostility to unions is a logical consequence of these strategies. The idea that Indian business can found a viable long-term competitive advantage on labour costs is an illusion, however. For example, 'Most MNCs feel it is not smart to chase the low labour type of markets. *It's a dead end for the country to chase competitive advantages in labour costs'.*[56] This has important implications for trade union strategy in the big emerging markets where competition is most fierce. Secondly, with a whole cycle of foreign investments behind us and the *long-term* integration of established foreign producers (firms like Hindustan Lever, Siemens, Philips, Glaxo Wellcome, and so on), the dilemma for Indian business is knowing where to draw the line between 'Indian' and 'foreign'. Is Indian capitalism 'Indian' in the racial sense of companies confined to the ownership of indigenous entrepreneurs and public enterprises, 'Indian' in the territorial sense of all firms with an established position in Indian manufacturing, or do these levels of definition lose their practical significance in the context of the increasing international integration of firms from different national settings?[57] In the Indian political context, both Left and Right have tended to view the dynamics of capitalism in nationally limited or racial categories, advocating the primacy of local ownership in the face of the *explosive* globalisation of equity markets[58] and the renewed upsurge of foreign direct investment. Thirdly, firms like Heinz, Nestlé, Brooke Bond, ITC, ConAgra and McCain will surely be involved in contract farming. The evolution of these 'process markets' will be a major development for the agrarian sector, and signify a corresponding need for future work in 'peasant studies' to master a more complex dynamism and set of relationships than differentiation of the peasantry conceived as a purely autonomous process.

NOTES

Note on abbreviations and company names: ET = The Economic Times (Bombay), *BS = Business Standard* (Calcutta), *FT = The Financial Times* (London); BAT refers to BAT Industries plc, which regards ITC as an associate company; ABB is the power engineering giant Asea Brown Boveri; BSN was recently renamed Groupe Danone; GDR is 'Global Depository Receipt'. A lakh is 100,000, a crore is ten million. Rs 30 to the US$ might be a reasonable exchange-rate.

1. *ET,* 20 April 1996, 'Lever, Brooke Bond Merging to Form Megacorp'.
2. *FT, India Business Intelligence,* 51, 10 Jan. 1996, p.17.
3. *ET,* 6 March 1996.
4. *ET,* 26 April 1996.
5. For example, Ruigrok and van Tulder [1995], otherwise very stimulating.
6. *ET,* 31 Jan. 1994, interview with Michael Perry, chairman of Unilever.
7. *ET,* 10 March 1996.

8. *ET,* 14 Jan. 1996, 'FDI doubles to $1,314m'.
9. Kidron [1965].
10. Ernest Stern of the World Bank, cited *ET,* 4 June 1994.
11. *ET,* 30 April 1994, cf. Henkel, President of the Federation of German Industries, 'Now we realise that the EC is not growing as fast as the Americas or Asia. To avoid oblivion, we have turned our attention to these continents,' *ET,* 17 Feb. 1996.
12. *ET,* 7 April 1994.
13. *ET,* 13 March 1994.
14. *ET,* 11 March 1994.
15. The sources for this and the following paragraphs are press clippings and company circulars contained in the Brooke Bond and ITC files in the *Business India* library in Bombay. I am particularly grateful to Arun Subramaniam for the chance to consult those files. Lack of access to my notes has prevented detailed referencing. On Brooke Bond see the company press releases dated 30 July 1993, 15 Sept. 1993, 25 Jan. 1994 and 8 March 1984; and *Financial Express,* 24 Dec. 1989; *ET,* 25 Oct. 1990; *BS,* 16 April 1993 ('Brooke Bond to Acquire Kissan for Rs 25 Crore'); *ET,* 13 Dec. 1991; *BS,* 24 Feb. 1994 ('Brooke Bond to Take Over Ready Foods Operations'); *BS,* 19 April 1994 ('ITC Vies with Brooke Bond for Ready Foods Takeover'); *Business and Political Observer,* 22 Jan. 1994; *BS,* 2 Nov. 1993; *BS,* 31 March 1994.
16. *ET,* 7 Nov. 1995, 'US company to acquire majority in Tarai Foods'.
17. Smith New Court, 'ITC Ltd.', 10 Sept. 1993, is an excellent source on ITC, prepared on the occasion of the company's GDR issue in October 1993.
18. *FT,* 12 May 1994, 'BAT Drops Indian Subsidiary Plan'. K.L. Chugh was chairman of ITC from 1991 to 1995, when he was forced to resign following concerted pressure from BAT for his removal, cf. *FT,* 23 March 1995, 'BAT Urges Head of Indian Group To Go' (where Chugh is quoted as saying, 'BAT is stifling the interest of ITC, which is aspiring to become an Indian multinational'!).
19. See Smith New Court, 'ITC Ltd.' (note 17 above). Sources for ITC include: *Business and Political Observer,* 15 April 1993 ('ITC Setting Up 100-Crore Oilseed Complex'); *BS,* 24 June 1993; *Times of India,* 8 July 1993; *BS,* 7 Sept. 1993 ('ITC Plans to Diversify in Food Processing'); *ET,* 20 April 1994 ('ITC May Enter Beer Industry with Heineken); *Financial Express,* 6 Nov. 1993 ('ITC Signs MOUs for Aqua-culture Complexes'); *BS,* 18 April 1994 ('ITC Resists BAT Bid for Majority'); *ET,* 6 May 1994 ('BAT Industries Denies Plan to Take Over ITC'); *ET,* 18 June 1993; *BS,* 17 April 1993; *BS,* 19 June 1993; and a company press release dated 4 Dec. 1994.
20. *ET,* 26 Nov. 1993, 'ITC Plans Rs 100-cr Cigarette Factory'.
21. *ET,* 28 Jan. 1994.
22. *BS,* 17 May 1994, 'ITC Moves to Raise Cigarette Production', by T. Bandyopadhyay.
23. *ET,* 7 June 1994, 'Cadbury Schweppes to Float Own Company in India'. On Cadbury see *Financial Express,* 18 Sept. 1992; *ET,* 12 Feb. 1993; *BS,* 20 Dec. 1993 (report by Kelkar); *BS,* 24 Dec. 1990; and *Business and Political Observer,* 12 June 1991 ('BIFR May Approve Dr Writer's Tie-up with Cadbury India').
24. Banaji and Hensman [1995].
25. *BS,* 17 May 1995.
26. *ET,* 7 Sept. 1994.
27. *ET,* 14 Sept. 1994, *FT* 19 May 1995.
28. *ET,* 8 July 1994, 3 April 1996.
29. *ET,* 31 Dec. 1994, 10 May 1996.
30. *ET,* 20 April 1994, *FT,* 13 April 1995 (second thoughts).
31. *ET,* 13 July 1995.
32. *ET,* 28 Sept. 1994, 8 April 1996.
33. *BS,* 15 Sept. 1995.
34. *ET,* 4 Aug. 1995.
35. *BS,* 12 July 1995.
36. *ET,* 13 May 1995.
37. *BS,* 15 Jan. 1995.

38. *ET,* 7 June 1994.
39. *BS,* 23 Aug. 1995.
40. *ET,* 7 Nov. 1995.
41. *ET,* 17 June 1995.
42. *FT, India Business Intelligence,* 53, 7 Feb. 1996, p.14.
43. *ET,* 20 April 1994.
44. *ET,* 19 Nov. 1993.
45. *ET,* 12 Aug. 1994.
46. *ET,* 29 Oct. 1993.
47. *BS,* 11 July 1995.
48. *ET,* 13 June 1996, 'Philip Morris Recasts India Plans'.
49. *ET,* 2 May 1994, 'The US-based company was earlier reported to be in talks with its Indian affiliate, Godfrey Philips India ... These talks were initiated as early as three years ago, with the Philip Morris-GPI combine wanting to make a foray into the beer segment. Last year, however, the talk veered around Philip Morris' wanting to increase its stake to 51 per cent. The move, however, fizzled out, with reports suggesting that the Modis did not want to dilute their stake in GPI.'
50. *ET,* 8 July 1994, 'Interestingly, the UB group has tied up with Carlsberg after its talks with Dutch brewery giant Heineken failed. The Dutch group was insisting on a 51 per cent holding in McDowell. In contrast, Carlsberg has agreed to a minority holding in the joint venture company.'
51. *BS,* 17 Aug. 1995, 9 Nov. 1995, 'According to Indiana Dairy sources, the deal with Danone fell through because the French major was asking for a majority stake in the venture.'
52. *ET,* 1 Oct. 1994, cf. *ET,* 16 Sept. 1995, 'Heinz India Seeks More Acquisitions'.
53. *ET,* 27 June 1994, 'Heinz May Buy Pepsico's Tomato Paste Plant'.
54. *ET,* 6 Feb. 1994.
55. *ET,* 11 April 1994, 'Pepsi Foods Keen to Possess Entire Stake in Duke and Sons'.
56. Timothy M. Devinney, cited *ET,* 24 Jan. 1996 (emphasis mine).
57. For discussion of a related case, see Zeitlin and Ratcliff [1988].
58. Bryan and Farrell [1996: 35]: 'Gross cross-border equity transactions, including all foreign purchases and sales of corporate securities in the United States, increased from under $93 billion in 1980 to over $1.5 trillion in 1994.'

REFERENCES

Banaji, J. and R. Hensman, 1995, 'India: Multinationals and the Resistance to Unionised Labour', *International Union Rights,* Vol.2, No.2.
Bryan, Lowell and Farrell, Diana, 1996, *Market Unbound: Unleashing Global Capitalism,* London: John Wiley & Sons.
Kidron, Michael, 1965, *Foreign Investments in India,* London: Oxford University Press.
Ruigrok, Winfried and Robert van Tulder, 1995, *The Logic of International Restructuring,* London and New York: Routledge.
Zeitlin, Maurice and Richard Earl Ratcliff, 1988, *Landlords and Capitalists: the Dominant Class of Chile,* Princeton, NJ: Princeton University Press.

Trade as a Mechanism of Economic Retrogression

PRABHAT PATNAIK

The purpose of this study is to explore the circumstances under which an economy's being opened up for trade or engaging in larger trade can result in a contraction in its employment and output *even when its exports and imports balance one another*. Economic historians, especially those who have worked on the experience of colonial economies, attest to the fact that such circumstances, where trade is a mechanism for economic retrogression, have been historically observed [*Bagchi*, 1976; *U. Patnaik*, 1991]. Our concern in this study is with the question: what are these circumstances?

Standard Keynesian macroeconomics, let alone neo-classical macroeconomics, would not recognise any such circumstances. According to Keynesian macroeconomics, a country *can* witness a contraction in its employment and output through engaging in trade, but only if it has an import surplus which entails a net contraction in aggregate demand. The converse argument is that a country can witness an expansion in its output and employment through trade *only* if it runs up an export surplus, an argument which was used by Kalecki [1971], and Bukharin [1972] before him, in his critique of Rosa Luxemburg's theory (we are ignoring here the indirect effects of trade via stimulating investment and so on).

The reason why Keynesian macroeconomics does not recognise the possibility of economic retrogression through trade lies in a fundamental assumption which underlies its entire structure, namely that more of *every* commodity can be produced if only the demand for it is larger. It follows then that with balanced trade some sectors would expand and others would contract and, barring differences in employment coefficients across sectors which I ignore, there would be no net contractionary effects. Putting it differently, the unemployment generated in the contracting sectors can, as it were, be absorbed into the expanding sectors, since *ex hypothesi* no sector is *immediately* supply-constrained. Once this assumption breaks down however, as I believe it does in the usual context of an underdeveloped

Prabhat Patnaik, Centre for Economic Studies and Planning, Jawaharlal Nehru University, New Delhi-110067, India.

economy, we get a very different kind of macroeconomics where a very different kind of multiplier deetermines the level of overall employment and output and where trade can easily play the role of an agent acting towards economic retrogression.

The fact that this assumption does not hold in the case of underdeveloped countries was argued forcefully by none other than Kalecki himself. In a paper [*Kalecki, 1963*] dealing with what he called the crucial difference between the economic problems of developed and underdeveloped economies he argued that employment expansion in the former could be achieved through a budgetary trick, while in the latter there were institutional constraints, arising from extant agrarian relations, upon the expansion of wage goods output, and consequently upon employment expansion.

Without in the least detracting from the necessity of land reforms which Kalecki underscored, I feel nonetheless that Kalecki went too far in his emphasis on the rigidity of the wage goods output under extant agrarian relations. Experience has shown that larger investment in agriculture can call forth larger agicultural output (upon a socially narrow base of landlord capitalism), perhaps not indefinitely but certainly up to a point. What is essential is investment, and private investment here is complementary to public investment. More public irrigation for instance results not only in more private adoption of the seed-fertiliser technology, but also in more private irrigation. In short, the wage goods output may be given in the short run, but is augmentable within limits in the long run through appropriate investment. In what follows I shall make the extreme assumption, in order precisely to highlight the specific argument of the present paper, that wage goods output is capacity constrained in any single period, but that this capacity is *perfectly* augmentable, with a given capital-output ratio, through investment. And yet it turns out that even for such an economy trade can engender economic retrogression.

II. SINGLE PERIOD EQUILIBRIUM BEFORE TRADE

In this section and the one which follows I shall examine respectively the single-period equilibrium of a very simple economy before and after it has been opened up to trade. Section IV looks at the impact of trade upon the dynamics of this simple economy, while section V restates the argument for the more general case (as opposed to the simple case). Section VI comments on the contemporary relevance of the argument, while section VII contrasts it with some other arguments of this *genre* and discusses certain wider issues thrown up it.

Consider an economy with two sectors, a food sector, assumed for the present to be synonymous with the wage goods sector, which produces at full capacity and where the price consequently is demand-determined, and a manufacturing sector where output is always at less than full capacity and pricing consequently is prime-cost plus (both sectors being vertically integrated this means unit labour cost plus). The workers of both sectors earn the same wage rate and spend the entire wage bill on the consumption of food; capitalists in the two sectors consume fixed proportions of their profits (not necessarily identical between the sectors) and capitalists' consumption, government expenditure, and all investment takes the *material form* of the manufactured good. I assume in this simple case that government expenditure is entirely deficit-financed.

The basic equations for such an economy can be set out as follows:

$$O^f = w.l^f.O^f + w.l^m.O^m \qquad (1)$$

where O stands for output, l for the labour coefficient per unit of output, w for the real wage rate and the superscripts f and m for the food and the manufacturing sector respectively.

Taking food as the numeraire, the price of the manufactured good is given by

$$p = w.l^m (1 + \pi) \qquad (2)$$

The output of food is given by the capital stock in this sector multiplied by the (technological) output–capital ratio:

$$O^f = K^f. \beta^f \qquad (3)$$

Total output in the economy is simply:

$$Y = O^f + p.O^m \qquad (4)$$

The physical supply of the manufactured good equals its demand which consists of capitalists' consumption, investment and government expenditure (which purely for convenience is assumed not to be adding directly to capacity):

$$O^m = C^f + C^m + I^f + I^m + G \qquad (5)$$

where the consumption and investment expenditures of capitalists are denoted respectively by C and I with the superscripts showing the sectors to which they belong.

Investments in the short-run can be assumed to be given. Capitalists' consumptions are fixed fractions of profits:

$$p.C^f = Of^{(1 - w.l}f). c_1 \qquad (6)$$
$$C^m = O^m .\pi / (1+\pi). c_2 \qquad (7)$$

We have eight variables, O^f, O^m, p, Y, C^f, C^m, G, and w, whose values are to be determined. Given *either* G *or* w, the other seven are determined by these seven equations. Government expenditure and the level of real wage can be seen to be negatively related (which is another way of saying that deficit financing gives rise to forced savings through profit inflation). The government, I assume, fixes its expenditure at a level such that the real wage gets pegged to some minimum acceptable level, that is,

$$w = w^* \qquad (8)$$

gives us the eighth equation, w^* being the government's target real wage (which it believes to be the minimum acceptable one). Interestingly, however, the determination of the outputs in the two sectors occurs entirely through equations (1),(3), and (8). And from these it is obvious that the food output is autonomous while the manufactured good output adjusts to it. In fact using (8) we can rewrite (1) as:

$$O^m / O^f = (1-w^*.l^f) / w^*.l^m$$

and using (2) and (4) get

$$Y / O^f = 1+(1+\pi)(1-w^*.l^f)$$

which is a multiplier for this economy different from the Keynesian multiplier. The reason why this multiplier operates rather than the Keynesian multiplier is the following. There is no *generalised* demand deficiency in this economy because government expenditure invariably keeps the manufactured good output at the maximal level consistent with the 'acceptable' floor wage. Manufacturing alone is demand constrained, and that is because the food sector is supply constrained, that is, its output is given and cannot be augmented in response to demand.[1] An autonomous increase in the latter output would not only increase the demand for manufacturing (initially from the food sector capitalists, subsequently from within the manufacturing sector itself, and finally from the government) but also provide the wage goods necessary for increasing manufacturing output. Owing to our assumption about government behaviour, the different rounds of the multiplier would go on increasing manufacturing output until the additional employment in this sector exactly uses up at the given ('acceptable') wage the additional surplus (over its own wage bill) generated in the food sector as a result of the autonomous increase in its output.

Let us now investigate how the opening up of this economy to trade can have a retrogressive effect.

III. SINGLE PERIOD EQUILIBRIUM AFTER TRADE

Suppose trade takes the form of exporting food and importing a manufactured good from outside which substitutes for the domestic manufactured good. In this section, which deals with the simple case, I shall assume that the prices of the domestic and the imported manufactured goods are identical (which basically means that p is fixed at an appropriate level for this), but that at these identical prices there is an absolute preference for the imported good (maybe because it has prestige value).

Any trade of this kind, it is easy to see, would result in a shrinking of output and employment if real wages remain unchanged, or a shrinking of real wages if output and employment remain unchanged (through an appropriate increase in government expenditure). This can be put as follows: for any given level of domestic food availability there is an inverse relationship between the real wage rate and the level of manufactured good output, and economic *retrogression* can be defined as a shifting inward of this curve; opening up the economy to trade causes economic retrogression in this sense.

The reason for this is obvious. When exports of food take place, domestic food availability shrinks, which for any given real wage, reduces the output of the manufactured good. Equation (1) in other words gets altered to

$$O^f - X = w^* . l^f . O^f + w^* . l^m . O^m \qquad (1')$$

so that for any given O^f (and in the short run O^f is given), larger exports mean a smaller O^m. It follows that total output must be smaller than with lower exports or absence of trade. Alternatively, output and employment can be maintained only if real wages are reduced. In the rest of this study I shall discuss, for the sake of concreteness, only the case of unchanging real wages, so that I define retrogression exclusively in terms of output contraction.

Thus in an economy where the total level of activity is dependent upon the size of the wage goods sector, that is, where the existence of unutilised capacity in the non-wage goods sector and of unemployment in general is accompanied by full capacity output in the wage goods sector which is cleared at some given real wage rate, trade which results in an export of wage goods necessarily contracts output and employment at this real wage rate even if it is balanced.

It would be argued that we have got this result because we have ignored the possibility of capacity expansion in the wage goods sector. True, this expansion occurs over time, but then we should be looking at the matter in a dynamic setting; a demonstration of contraction in a single period really proves nothing.

While the dynamics of our simple case is examined in the next section, a heuristic argument can be given here to show why the results obtained for the single period would hold in a dynamic setting as well.

If the fact of larger exports could itself have a stimulating effect upon the wage goods output over time, then the above argument would cease to have validity in a dynamic context, since the contractionary effects of imports upon domestic manufacturing would be offset over time by the expansionary effects of exports upon the wage goods sector. But there are two factors which militate against this.

First, the very fact of contraction of the manufacturing sector in the face of rising wage goods exports, through cuts in government expenditure (for preventing inflation), releases the wage goods supplied for exports, so that there is no special stimulus for expanding the capacity of this sector.

Secondly, and more importantly, the expansion of this sector's capacity, as mentioned earlier, depends crucially upon larger public investment in this sector, since private investment is complementary to public investment. Now, a reduction in the size of the manufacturing sector would result in a *lower* level of public investment in so far as this investment was drawing in part upon the profits of the manufacturing sector (either through borrowing or through taxation), and lower output is associated with lower profits. This would entail, *ceteris paribus*, a lower level of public investment in the wage goods sector and hence a lower rate of expansion of this sector. We would thus have an immediate contraction in the level of manufacturing activity followed by a lower profile of activity in *both the sectors* than would otherwise have prevailed.

IV. DYNAMISING THE SIMPLE MODEL

For dynamising the model we shall introduce determinants for the levels of investment which we had taken to be fixed for the single period in the previous section, and put time subscripts for all the variables which figured there. In accordance with previous discussion I take investment in the food sector in time period $t+1$ to bear some fixed ratio to total government expenditure in period t: the implicit assumptions behind this formulation are, first, that the break up of government expenditure between consumption expenditure and productive expenditure which stimulates private investment in the food sector remains unchanged, and secondly, that any given level of productive expenditure in the current period brings forth a corresponding proportional amount of private investment in the next period. We thus have:

$$I^f_{(t+1)} = b.G_t \qquad (9)$$

For the manufacturing sector I assume that the rate of capital accumulation changes in response to the level of capacity utilisation, that is,

$$I^m_{(t+1)}/K^m_{(t+1)} = I_{mt}/K^m_t + d.(u_t - u_0) \qquad (10)$$

I ignore depreciation so that

$$K^f_{(t+1)} = K^f_t + I^f_t \qquad (11)$$

and

$$K^m_{(t+1)} = K^m_t + I^m_t \qquad (12)$$

and define u as

$$u_t = O^m_t / \beta^m . K^m_t \qquad (13)$$

In discussing the dynamic case it is convenient to start from a situation where the economy has already been open to trade and in such a case equation (1) of the previous section has to be replaced by (1'). Equation (5) too has to be replaced and in what follows, I shall, as mentioned earlier, begin by assuming that the price of the imported manufacture (in terms of food) is the same as that of domestically produced manufacture, the preference for the former being due to non-price considerations. The new equation which takes the place of (5) can then be written as follows:

$$O^m_t + M_t = C^f_t + I^f_t + C^m_{t + Imt} + G_t \qquad (5')$$

Since trade is balanced, we have

$$X_t = p.M_t \qquad (14)$$

Finally, I assume that proportion of exports to food output is some x; I take x as a parameter and vary it for examining the effects of trade upon the growth path of the economy. In other words,

$$X_t = x.O_{ft} \qquad (15)$$

Equations (1'), (2)–(4), (5') and (6)–(15) completely describe our universe. For any given x it can be seen that the system is capable of steady growth. We can visualise the determination of the steady growth rate as follows: from equation (9) it follows that along the steady state path, if one exists, the following relationship must hold between the growth rate g and G/K^f which I denote by h:

$$g(1+g) = b.h \qquad (16)$$

On the other hand from equation (13) we can derive the following relationship between g and h after making appropriate substitutions:

$$k.\beta^m.u_0 + x.\beta^{t/w} *1^m (1+\pi) - \beta^f (1-w*.1^f)c - k.\beta^m.u_0.c\pi/(1+\pi) - h$$

$$= g(1+k) \qquad (17)$$

where

$$k = \beta f(1-x- w*.1^f)/ \beta^m.u^0.w^{.1}m.$$

While (16) gives us an upward-sloping non-linear relation between g and h (in the positive quadrant), (17) gives us a downward-sloping linear relation between g and h (for given x). The intersection between the two gives us the steady-state values of g and h. I shall not discuss stability, though: since this is a model involving government intervention, the government can always be assumed to use discretionary means (that is, step outside of the rules within which we have bound its actions) to prevent any serious instability. I shall go straight into the question of what happens when x is varied.

Any variation in x has no effect upon equation (16) and hence upon the upward-sloping curve linking g (on the y-axis) with h (on the x-axis); it shifts the downward-sloping straight line, however, to the right or left. It turns out that if a very simple condition is satisfied then a rise in x has the effect of shifting the line to the left and hence of lowering the steady-state growth rate and the steady-state h.[2] And this condition is: *the savings per unit of capital stock at the desired level of capacity use in the manufacturing sector should be larger than the savings per unit of capital stock in the food sector.*

This condition is intuitively easy to understand. Any given steady state, associated with a particular value of x, entails a certain ratio between the capital stocks of the two sectors. As x rises, this ratio changes, against the manufacturing sector. Our condition merely ensures that the savings per unit of capital stock, being a weighted average of the corresponding figures of the two sectors, gets reduced as this happens, resulting in a lowering of the steady state growth rate. This condition can be stated in a different form, namely, that the savings per unit of capital stock of the manufacturing sector exceeds what is required for financing its own investment and its 'share' of government expenditure ('share' being equal to the ratio of its capital stock in total) in steady state.

This condition is likely to be easily satisfied. In the case where capitalists in both sectors save the same constant fraction of their profits (and workers do not save), this condition merely amounts to stating that the rate of profit at the desired level of capacity use in the manufacturing sector should be higher than the rate of profit in the food sector:

$$\beta^f(1-w^*.l^f) \, /p < \beta^m.u_0.\pi \, / \, (1+\pi)$$

Mark-up pricing in the manufacturing sector is based upon an oligopolistic structure. This would certainly ensure that the magnitude of mark-up is such as to yield a rate of profit in steady state, that is, at desired capacity use, which is higher than in food production, for otherwise the very *raison d'être* of oligopolistic pricing would have disappeared. Moreover, in our model we have, in the interests of simplicity, not introduced commodity taxation, the revenue from which has to be counted *in toto* as being on a par with savings generated by the sector.[3] Given this fact, the condition is likely to be even more easily satisfied, since the rate of taxation is higher on manufactures than on food. It follows then that a rise in the ratio of food exports to food output can well cause, for given real wages, not only a deindustrialisation of the economy in the short run but a lowering of the growth rate itself in the long run.

V. SOME MODIFICATIONS OF THE MODEL

So far I have been considering the simple case. I shall now introduce some modifications into the model to avoid accusations of excessive unrealism. I now assume that wages are spent partly on food and partly on manufactured goods; but, for simplicity, I take workers' expenditure on manufactures to be a residue after they have purchased a fixed amount of food. I also assume that the domestic price of food is lower than the world price at the prevailing exchange rate and money wages, which I take to remain unchanged, while the domestic price of manufactures is higher. The difference in the latter case is mopped up by a tariff imposed by the government on manufactured imports.

The view that agricultural goods are underpriced and manufactured goods are overpriced in the domestic markets of underdeveloped countries relative to the world market is a widely prevalent one. To what extent it retained validity in many of them (including India) at the end of the 1980s, but prior to liberalisation, remains however a moot point since the terms of trade moved sharply against agriculture in the 1980s in the world market while the insulated domestic markets did not see a corresponding shift.[4] None the less, deliberately to understate my case, I proceed with this assumption which is in line with the World Bank's view.

The equations constituting this general case, as well as the condition under which a rise in the proportion of exports to food output causes economic retrogression, are given in the Appendix. This condition has a fairly straightforward interpretation. It states that the *adjusted savings in the manufacturing sector, that is, the savings of this sector, less the sum of the loss in savings of the food sector and the loss in tariff revenue of the government on account of the fact that some food is consumed by the workers of this sector rather than being exported, exceed in steady state its investment requirement and its 'share' in government expenditure, 'share' being defined as the ratio of its capital stock to total.*

This condition can be alternatively stated: the 'adjusted' savings per unit of capital stock in the manufacturing sector in steady state should exceed the ratio of total private savings plus tariff revenue to total capital stock in the economy. Or, putting it differently, the ratio of adjusted savings to capital stock in the manufacturing sector should exceed the ratio of food sector savings plus tariff revenue plus this adjustment amount to the food sector capital stock in steady state.

This condition is analogous to the one we had derived for the simple case. There it amounted to saying that the manufacturing sector must make a net contribution to the rest of the economy from its savings, over above meeting its own investment requirement and due share of government expenditure in steady state. Here the condition is essentially the same, except that its savings now are reckoned after adjustment, that is, after deducting fom these savings the loss in savings that occurs elsewhere owing to its use of food which could be exported. The condition therefore is more stringent than the one we obtained in the simple case, and is collapsible to the latter when domestic and world prices coincide for both commodities (even when workers do not spend everything on food). But it is by no means a difficult condition to satisfy. Unlike in the simple case where *any* difference between savings per unit of capital stock in the two sectors was enough to associate lower steady state growth rates with higher food exports, what is required now for such a result is that this difference must exceed a certain threshold level. But this threshold is not prohibitively high, that is, for a range of plausible parameter values this condition is fulfilled.[5] It follows then that greater trade dependence of this kind would entail not only deindustrialisation in the short run but also a lower growth rate in the long run.

There is, however, a more basic point. Suppose our condition is not satisfied, that is, larger food exports do raise the staedy state growth rate (notwithstanding short run deindustrialisation which always occurs). The reason for that, *ceteris paribus*, is an insufficient saving ratio on manufacturing profits. But since this ratio can be raised through direct taxation of manufacturing profits without worrying about capitalists' subsistence, the non-fulfilment of our condition is tantamount in a sense to an inadequate fiscal effort *vis-à-vis* manufacturing profits (which is where the effort is most fruitfully made). An argument for food exports on *these* grounds amounts then to a *fiscal* argument for trade dependence which even neoclassical economists find unconvincing. In other words, in the case of non-fulfilment of our condition, it is better to change parameter values through a fiscal effort (and thereby fulfil the condition) than accept the parameter values and go in for food exports at the cost of short run deindustrialisation. This argument of course gets strengthened the moment we consider possible adverse movements in terms of trade and the threat to food security that larger food exports (or agricultural exports, as I argue below) entail.

VI. PRIMARY COMMODITY EXPORTS VERSUS MANUFACTURED GOODS EXPORTS

So far we have talked of food exports. But the argument retains its validity for exports of non-food crops as well, in so far as such exports entail a shift of acreage away from food crops. This brings about a reduction in domestic food availability (via a reduction in domestic food production) exactly in the same way as direct exports of food. In other words, to suggest that exports of non-food crops, even if they result in a decline in domestic food *poduction*, would not give rise to a fall in domestic food *availability*, since food can be imported with the foreign exchange earned from the export crops, is erroneous. And the reason is the following.

Let us assume that non-food crop production increases by 100 units, all of which are exported, by reducing food production by 100 units. Let us also assume that in the international market, these 100 units of non-food crops 'command' 125 units of food, that is, the country's 'comparative advantage' lies in producing non-food crops. None the less, if the profits from food production, say 50 units, were being used directly or indirectly for the purchase of domestic manufactures, while the profits from non-food exports, which would be the equivalent of 75 food units (125 minus 50 wage bill), are used for importing foreign manufactures (it is immaterial whether for consumption or for investment), the shift to export agiculture is still harmful for the country since it results in a decline in domestic food availability by 75 units and hence in deindustrialisation.[6]

All that has been said above does not of course mean that greater trade dependence *per se* is bad for an economy. But one must distinguish between manufacturing and primary sector exports. In a situation where greater trade dependence entails larger exports of primary commodities of agricultural origin, international trade becomes a substitute for domestic intersectoral trade and hence restricts the demand for domestic manufactured goods. This fact would necessarily produce immediate deindustrialisation; it may also produce lower long-term growth. But if greater trade dependence took the form of larger manufacturing exports, matters would be entirely different. Since the domestic manufacturing sector is normally demand-constrained, larger exports would *increase* employment and output immediately, and thereby also bring about higher long run growth rates. The virtues of export-led growth that Kaldor and other writers have talked about are virtues associated with manufacturing exports.[7]

Neo-classical economics, based as it is on the assumption of substitutability between commodities, cannot even in principle distinguish between agriculture and manufacturing in any essential way. This, together with its general assumptions of linearity and absence of demand constraints, makes neo-classical economics advocate the use of existing comparative advantage, and hence greater trade dependence in hitherto insulated economies, no matter what the commodity composition of exports and imports. While underdeveloped counties have been forced in recent years by institutions like the IMF and the World Bank to move towards greater trade dependence, and while the intellectual justification for it has been provided in terms of neo-classical theory, they do not, for a variety of reasons, succeed in becoming manufacturing exporters but get pushed instead into export agriculture. And the consequences of that may well turn out to be harmful for their economies, contrary to what the neoclassical advocacy of export-led gowth suggests.

VII. CONCLUDING OBSERVATIONS

The idea that it may be harmful for a country to get drawn into international trade as a primary commodity exporter is of course an old one in development economics, but the argument has focussed either on the demand side [*Seers*, 1962] or on market structures [*Singer*, 1950; *Prebisch*, 1950]. By contrast the argument of this paper concentrates exclusively on the supply side; to highlight this it even makes the neoclassical 'small country' assumption (unlimited ability to export or import at given world prices). And even within the supply side it does not invoke arguments based on scarcity of land or of natural resources, but assumes instead that supplies are augmentble through investment without any diminishing returns. In other words the perception of the crucial difference between agriculture and manufacturing underlying the present paper is different from what has been highlighted in the classics of development literature.

This perception is the following. In manufacturing an increase in demand calls forth not only larger output in the short run, but also larger investment following upon this larger output. There is what Kaldor, following Hicks, called a 'super multiplier' at work, stimulated by some autonomous increase in demand. Manufacturing output thus is demand constrained not only in the short run Keynesian sense, but in a more basic medium or long run sense. By the same token not only is agricultural output constrained on the supply side in the short run, and cannot be augmented if demand increases, but private investment in agriculture too does not increase merely through an increase in demand sustained over time. A necessary, though by no means a sufficient, condition for such investment to increase is the provision of complementary investment in overheads under the aegis of the state.

The *reason* for this difference has to do *inter alia* with the scale of operation in agriculture. Even capitalist agriculture, at any rate in Asian conditions, is operated on a scale that is much smaller than organised manufacturing. The large investments in overheads, required for instance for water management or for energy, can be undertaken neither on an individual basis, nor through cooperation among individuals (which becomes difficult as the economy makes a transition to capitalism), nor through the entry of some large capitalist extraneous to the agricultural sector (because such investments being 'feeder' investments, the private rate of return on them is completely unpredictable). They require either direct investment by the state or state guarantee of the private rate of return to be earned by some large capitalist from outside. In either case productive investment in agriculture proper becomes dependent upon the actions of the state and hence its ability to garner resources. It is because of this specificity of agriculture *inter alia* that the enactment of the 'liberal' paradigm in underdeveloped countries can be a harbinger of economic retrogression.

NOTES

1. This way of looking at the macroeconomics of an underdeveloped economy has been quite prevalent in India: see, for example, P. Patnaik [1972]; [1995], M. Rakshit [1989], Bagchi [1995] and Dutt [1995].
2. This condition is arrived at as follows: equation (17) is of the form A-Bh=g, where A and B are constants for any x. By differentiating the l.h.s., that is, A-Bh, with respect to x and setting the value of the derivative to be negative, we get the condition.
3. This is because within the price of the manufactured good what accrues as the profit component is partly consumed and partly saved, while what accrues as the commodity tax component is not availble for consumption to the capitalists of this sector. While the latter is thus analogous to the profit component, it differs from the latter in that it is saved, as it were, *in toto*.
4. For a discussion of this in the Indian context and for a comparison of Indian domestic prices with world prices in the case of a number of agricultural commodities, see Deepak Nayyar and Abhijit Sen [1994].
5. To give an illustration let us suppose that the domestic food price is 20 per cent lower than the world price and that the domestic manufactured good price is 20 percent higher. Let the other parameter values be as follows: wage share in food sector = .75; wage share in manufacturing = .40; savings propensity out of food profits = .25; savings propensity out of manufacturing profits = .60; proportion of wage bill devoted to food consumption in both sectors = .5; output-capital ratio in both sectors (that is, $\beta^m = \beta' . p/p^m$) = .4. Then compared to a steady state path with no food exports, a new steady state path involving food exports will have a lower growth rate associated with it. Our condition is satisfied in other words for x=0 and these other parameter values.
6. I am not going here again into the question of which path entails higher long-run (or steady state) growth.
7. A number of Kaldor's writings on the subject have been brought together in Kaldor [1978].

REFERENCES

Bagchi, A.K., 1976, 'De-industrilisation in India in the Nineteenth Century: Some Theoretical Implications', *Journal of Development Studies*, Vol.12, No.2.
Bagchi, A.K., 1995, 'Closed-economy Structuralist Models for Less Developed Economy', in P. Patnaik [1995].
Bukharin, N., 1972, 'Imperialism and the Accumulation of Capital', in Tarbuck [1972].
Dutt, A.K., 1995, 'Open Economy Macroeconomic Themes for India', in Patnaik [1995].
Kaldor, N., 1978, *Further Essays on Economic Theory*, London: Duckworth.
Kalecki, M., 1971, 'The Problem of Effective Demand with Tugan-Baranovski and Rosa Luxemburg', in *Selected Essays on the Dynamics of the Capitalist Economy 1933–1970*, Cambridge: Cambridge University Press.

Kalecki, M., 1976, 'The Difference Between Crucial Economic Problems of Developed and Underdeveloped Non-socialist Economies', in *Essays on Development Economics*, Hemel Hempstead: Harvester Press.

Nayyar, D. and A. Sen, 1994, 'International Trade and the Agricultural Sector in India', in G.S. Bhalla (ed.), *Economic Liberalisation and Indian Agriculture*, Delhi: FAO and ISID.

Patnaik, P., 1972, 'Disproportionality Crisis and Cyclical Growth', *Economic and Political Weekly*, Annual Number.

Patnaik, P. (ed.), 1995, *Macroeconomics*, Delhi: Oxford University Press.

Patnaik, U., 1991, 'Food Availability and Famine: A Longer View', *Journal of Peasant Studies*, Vol.19, No.1

Prebisch, R., 1950, *The Ecoomic Development of Latin America and its Principal Problems* (UN ECLA).

Rakshit, M., 1989, *Studies in the Macroeconomics of Developing Countries*, Delhi: Oxford University Press.

Seers, D., 1962, 'A Model of Comparative Growth of the World Economy', *Economic Journal*.

Singer, H., 1950, 'The Distribution of Gains Between Investing and Borrowing Countries', *American Economic Review*, May.

Tarbuck, K., 1972, *Imperialism and the Accumulation of Capital*, London: Allen Lane.

APPENDIX

The equations of the general case, where the domestic food price and the domestic manufctured good price are different from world prices (at the existing money wage and exchange rate which are assumed to remain unchanged), where a tariff equates the prices of imported and domestic manufactured goods in the home market, and where workers also buy the manufactured good but after buying a fixed amount of food per head, are set out in this Appendix.

Our equation (1) will now read:

$$O^f - X = \bar{w}.1.^fO^f + \bar{w}.1^m.O_m \quad ....(1'')$$

where w denotes the fixed food purchase per worker.

Since the money wage, donated by ω, is now assumed to be given, equation (2) becomes

$$p^m = \omega.1^m.(1+\pi) \quad ......(2')$$

Correspondingly, output is now expressed in money terms:

$$Y = p^f.O^f + p^m.O^m \quad ....(4')$$

Equation (5) changes to:

$$O^m + M = C^f + C^m + I^f + I^m + G + (\omega - \bar{w}.p^f)(O^f.1^f + O^m.1^m) \quad ....(5'')$$

where M denotes the physical amount of imported manufactures. Equation (6) becomes:

$$C^f = c_1. [X.\bar{p}^f + (O^f - X).p^f - \omega.1^f.O^f]/p^m \quad .....(6')$$

where p^f denotes the world price of food which remains unaffected by how much the country in question exports.

Our definition of economic retrogression remains as before, namely, a lowering of the output profile for a given real wage or the maintenance of the output profile only at the cost of lower real wages. As before, however, we shall assume that the government adjusts its expenditure to ensure that the real wages do not change, so that the entire effect of trade is felt upon output, so that the output profile becomes the exclusive focus of our attention. The assumption that the real wages are maintained can in the present context be stated (in lieu o equation (8)) as:

$$p^f = \hat{p}^f \qquad (8')$$

Equation (14) now becomes:

$$\overline{p}^f.X_t = .\overline{p}^m.M_t...(14')$$

where p^m denotes the world price of the manufactured good which again is assumed to remain unchanged by our country's imports.

Finally we have the tariff rate given by

$$\overline{p}^m (1+t) = p^m \qquad (18)$$

Equations (1''), (2'), (3), (4'), (5''), (6'),(7), (8'), (9)–(13), (14'), (15) and (18) completely describe our system. The steady state levels of the growth rate and government expenditure relative to capital stock in the food sector, that is, of g and h, are again given by the intersection of two curves, one of which is given by equation (16) as before, and the other by:

$$k.\beta^m.u_0 + x.\beta^f.\overline{p}^f / \overline{p}^m - c_1.\beta^f (1-x).$$
$$(\hat{p}^f - \omega.1^f) / p^m + c_1.x.\beta^f(\overline{p}^f.-\omega.1^f) / p^m - k.\beta^m.u_0.c_2.\pi / (1+\pi) - h - (\beta^f.1^f + k.\beta^m.u_0 1^m).$$
$$(\omega - \overline{w}.p^f) / p^m = g(1+k)....(17')$$

The condition under which a rise in the proportion of food output exported results in a lowering of the steady state growth-rate can be written as follows:

$$[(1-c_1+t) \overline{w}.\overline{p}^f - (1-c_1) \overline{w}.\hat{p}^f - (1-c_2)\omega.\pi].\beta^m.u_0.1^m/p^m + g + h/(1+k) < 0$$

whose interpretation is given in the text.

China's Rise, Russia's Fall

PETER NOLAN

INTRODUCTION

The contrast in outcomes from system reform in the former USSR and in China is one of the most important phenomena of the age. Systematic comparison of this experience is still its infancy [*Nolan*, 1995; *Sachs and Woo*, 1994]. It is, clearly, a process of the greatest importance for the citizens of both countries. Section 1 of this article outlines some of the key aspects of the changes in economic performance and their outcomes for the respective countries' populations.

The dramatic difference in results was predicted by no-one. It is now difficult to detach oneself from the benefit of hindsight. It is hard to imagine that the process could have proceeded in any other way than that which it actually took. A key issue of analysis in the ensuing years will be the degree to which the dramatic contrast in outcome was caused by fundamental differences in the inheritance from the pre-reformed system. At its crudest, an important, and already widely accepted, line of argument is that the difference in outcome owed nothing to the different policy choices made, and everything to the difference in systems bequeathed to the respective reform leaderships: 'It was neither gradualism nor experimentation, but rather China's economic structure, that proved so felicitous to reform. China began reform as a peasant agricultural society, EEFSU (Eastern Europe and the former Soviet Union) as urban and overindustrialised ... In Gerschenkron's famous phrase [China] had the "advantage of backwardness"' [*Sachs and Woo*,1994: 102–04]. Section II of this article examines this proposition and finds it wanting, arguing that policy choices were crucially important in determining the result. A principal difference between the Chinese and the former Soviet governments was their radically different approach towards the 'transitional orthodoxy' that emerged in the 1980s about the correct sequence of political and economic reform, the desirability of rapid versus incremental economic system change, and necessity of economic planning during the long transitional period.

Peter Nolan is at the Faculty of Economics and Politics, University of Cambridge.

1. ECONOMIC PERFORMANCE DURING THE REFORM PERIOD IN
   CHINA AND RUSSIA

The death of Mao Tsetung and the arrest of the 'Gang of Four' in the Autumn of 1976 ushered in a period of huge change in China's political economy. Although important changes occurred in the first two years after Mao's death, most observers date the beginning of reform as the Third Plenum of the Eleventh Central Committee of the Chinese Communist Party in December 1978. Gorbachev's election to the position of General Secretary of the Soviet Communist Party in March 1985 raised hopes that serious system reform would begin. However, it was not until the summer of 1986 that the distinctive features of the policy of *perestroika* could be seen. The subsequent period of 'reform', already much longer in China than in the former USSR, produced strikingly different results.

China

Output growth: China's economic growth record under reform policies placed it in the front rank of growth performances during the relevant period. In the 1980s and early 1990s it was one of only three economies whose growth rate of GDP was reported to have been over nine per cent per annum. It also attained one of the fastest growth rates of exports, with a real growth rate of almost 12 per cent per annum from 1980 to 1991 (Table 1) : the value of China's exports in US dollars rose from ten billion in 1978 to 92 billion in 1993 [*SSB*, ZGTJZY, 1994: 105]. Behind the growth of total output there was a massive accumulation process, with huge additions to the stock of capital goods. China's capital goods industries grew in leaps and bounds to feed the appetite of overall economic growth. The leading edge of Chinese industry was modernised rapidly with imports of high technology products, and the capital goods produced by modernising domestic factories.

Consumption: The improvement in economic performance was achieved through a sharp improvement in overall economic efficiency, reflected in the fact that the growth of output was accompanied by an extraordinary surge in living standards in the 1980s (Table 2). China's economic performance in the 1980s was much better than that in the most relevant comparator country, namely India, and was vastly better than virtually anyone in the late 1970s could have hoped. The level and composition of food intake greatly improved. Huge new consumer durable industries sprang up in the 1980s, with a 'first wave' of goods such as bicycles, watches, TV sets, fridges, and washing machines, followed by a more complex array of goods in the 'second wave', including products such as

TABLE 1

COMPARATIVE PERFORMANCE OF THE CHINESE ECONOMY,1980–91

	China	India	Low income countries (1)	Middle income countries
Av annual growth rate,1980/91(%):				
GDP	9.4	5.4	3.7	2.3
Agriculture	5.7	3.2	2.5	n.a.
Industry	11.0	6.3	4.0	n.a.
Services	11.2	6.7	4.8	n.a.
Av annual real growth rate of				
exports,1980/89 (%)	11.5	7.4	3.3	3.4
Av annual growth rate of population,				
1980/89 (%)	1.5	2.1	2.6	1.8
Av annual rate of inflation,1980/89(%)	5.8	8.2	23.4	67.1
Debt service as % of exports of				
goods and services				
:1980	4.4	9.3	11.6	23.9
:1980	12.1	30.7	25.0	20.3
Food production per capita				
(av annual growth rate, 1979–91)	3.0	1.6	–	–
-Daily calorie intake p.c				
:1965	1931	2103	1960	2482
:1988	2632	2104	2182	2834
Crude death rate(no/1000)				
:1970	8	18	19	11
:1991	7	10	13	8
Infant mortality rate(no/1000)				
:1981	71	121	124	81
:1991	38	90	91	38
Life expectancy at birth(years)				
:1981	67	52	50	60
:1991	69	60	55	68

Note: (1) excluding India and China.

Source: World Bank, WDR [1983, 1991, 1993].

motor cars, motor cycles, and video recorders (Table 2). A massive housebuilding boom took place over the reform years with space per person more than doubling.

TABLE 2
CHANGES IN THE MATERIAL STANDARD OF LIVING IN CHINA, 1978-92

	1978	1992
Index of real p.c. consumption	100	252
Consumption p.c. of :-		
grain(kgs)	196	236
edible oi(kgs)	1.6	6.3
pork(kgs)	7.7	18.2
fresh eggs(kgs)	2.0	7.8
sugar(kgs)	3.4	5.4
aquatic products(kgs)	3.5	7.3
cloth(metres)	8.0	10.7
Ownership of consumer durables(no/100 people) :-		
washing machines	–	10.0
refrigerators	–	3.4
tape recorders	0.2	12.2
cameras	0.5	2.3
TVs	0.3	19.5
sewing machines	3.5	12.8
bicycles	7.7	38.5
radios	7.8	18.4
watches	8.5	51.6
(1990)		
Retail outlets and food and drink establishments (no./10,000 people):-		
establishments	12	101
personnel	57	249
Health provision (no./10,000 people) :-		
hospital beds	19.3	23.4
physicians	10.7	15.4
Housing space p.c.(sq metres)		
cities	3.6	7.5
villages	8.1	20.8

Source: SSB, ZGTJZY [1991: 42]; SSB ,ZGTJZY [1994: 48, 51]; SSB, ZGTJNJ [1993: 279, 283–4].

Welfare indicators: China did well at raising the incomes of the poorest 40 per cent of the population. This was reflected in the improvement in already extremely favourable 'basic needs' indicators (see Table 1). Judith Banister, the most respected analyst of China's demography, concluded that between 1981 and 1990, there were 'real improvements in mortality ... especially for females above infancy and for children of both sexes' [*Banister*, 1992: 12]. She notes: 'it is impressive that the rural population of China has experienced measurably lower mortality in only nine years, especially since the Chinese countryside had already achieved rather advanced mortality conditions for a developing country rural area by 1981'[*ibid.*].

TABLE 3

POVERTY IN CHINA, 1978-90

	1978	1985	1990
Total population(m.)	963	1059	1143
Urban	172(17.9%)	251(23.7%)	302(26.4%)
Rural	790(82.1%)	808(76.3%)	841(73.6%)
Average per capita income(1978 yuan)			
Urban	–	557	685
Rural	134	324	319
Poverty line(current yuan/year)			
Urban	–	215	319
Rural	98	190	275
Incidence of poverty(million)			
Total	270(28.0%)	97(9.2%)	98(8.6%)
Urban	10(4.4%)	1(0.4%)	1(0.4%)
Rural	260(33.0%)	96(11.9%)	97(11.5%)

Source: World Bank [1992: v].

Notes: After three years of apparent stagnation in real rural per capita consumption, a substantial further growth occurred in 1991 [*SSB*, ZGTJZY, 1992: 42]. Had the 1991 data been made available to the World Bank, it is likely that there would have been some further reduction reported in rural poverty.

Poverty: In China on the eve of the reforms the worst concentrations of poverty were found in the countryside (Table 3). A variety of factors combined to produce a remarkable reduction in poverty in the reform period. These included trickle down from rich regions, explicit government policy to assist poor regions, rapid growth of non-farm employment, and fast income growth in the countryside at large. The World Bank constructed a constant poverty line for China from the later 1970s through to the late 1980s and estimated that the total number in poverty fell from around 270 million in the late 1970s to around 100 million only one decade later(Table 3).[1]

Inequality: Undoubtedly, the growth of market forces produced large new inequalities in China during the reform period. The absolute gap between regions widened. Inequality in some aspects of income distribution did increase substantially compared to the Maoist period. However, during the reform period, in contrast to most developing countries, China's rural population experienced faster growth of income than did the urban population.[2] During the reform period there occurred a massive, egalitarian land reform. Moreover, the vast bulk of national assets remained in some form of public ownership, with ownership rights residing in the hands of either the central state, the city, the county, or the village community, thereby severely limiting the possibility for wealth accumulation by private individuals. The government at different levels maintained a relatively effective tax system.

Psychology: China experienced around one hundred years of national humiliation, beginning in the 1840s with the Opium Wars, extending through to the chaotic period of the Warlords from 1911 to 1927. For a brief interlude of around ten years (1927–1936) there was some semblance of national progress under the Guomindang (KMT), but the modernisation effort was retarded by the Japanese occupation from 1936 to 1945. In 1949, there was enormous popular enthusiasm for the leadership of the CCP, under whom Mao Tsetung claimed the Chinese people would 'stand up' at last. Despite large achievements, the policies of the CCP produced the disaster of the Great Leap Forward in which as many as 30 million people may have died from starvation and related illness. The Cultural Revolution in the late 1960s and early 1970s brought anarchy to much of the country, damaged the economy and caused great suffering to a large number of people.

The massive success of the economic reforms since the late 1970s brought a renewed sense of national pride. The fact that the reform programme was carried out under the Communist Party, with only gradual change in ideology, produced only a limited sense of mass psychological disorientation.

Human rights: Throughout the reform period China remained a one party, authoritarian state. It also remained one with an extremely tough legal system, with several thousand executions in an average year [*Amnesty International*, 1987]. This presented profound ethical and philosophical dilemmas. There is a spectrum of 'human rights' and it may not be possible simultaneously to achieve improvements in all of them.

If one looks beyond the right to vote in an election to a wider range of human rights, then the situation in China improved drastically during the reform period [*Nolan*, 1994]. There was an explosion in the provision of a wide range of 'human rights', including improved health, education, freedom to migrate, huge increases in employment opportunities, better food, clothing, housing and a greatly increased range of cultural products. China's system of basic needs provision had enabled it also to achieve very low death rates for its level of income. By the early 1980s, China's death rate had fallen to an exceptionally low level for a poor country. The decade of economic reform in China saw no trend deterioration in China's exceptionally low death rates (Table 4). Indeed, careful analysis by Judith Banister shows that death rates fell for all age groups beyond the age of one (infant mortality rates rose for females for special reasons associated with the 'One Child Family Campaign'), a remarkable achievement for a country with such low death rates as China. Life expectancy rose from an already exceptionally high level for a poor country (Table 5).

TABLE 4

CRUDE DEATH RATES IN CHINA, RUSSIA, AND SELECTED
GROUPS OF COUNTRIES (NO/1000)

	1960	1970	1982	1991	1993	1994
China	10.0	7.6	6.6	6.7	–	–
Russia	7.4*	8.7*	10.5*	11.4	14.4	16.2***
Low income countries**	24	19	16	13	–	–
Middle income countries	17	11	10	8	–	–
High income countries	10	10	9	9	–	–

Sources: Bergson and Levine, [1983: Table 3, 4]; *SSB*, ZGTJNJ [1992: 78]; Ellman [1994]; World Bank [1984; 1993].

* RSFSR **Excluding China and India *** first quarter

TABLE 5

LIFE EXPECTANCY IN SELECTED COUNTRIES AND GROUPS OF COUNTRIES

		1970	1982	1991	1993
Low income countries					
	men	46	50	54	
	women	47	52	57	
Middle income countries					
	men	58	58	65	
	women	62	62	71	
High income countries					
	men	68	71	73	
	women	75	78	80	
China					
	men	61	65	66	
	women	63	69	71	
Russia					
	men	61(1979/80)	62	63	59
	women	73(1979/80)	74	74	73

Source: World Bank [1984: 1993]; Ellman [1994]; *Observer,* 13 March 1994.

Russia

Output: Soviet economic performance under Gorbachev was poor. After the collapse of the communist government in 1991 a poor performance turned into a disaster (Table 6). The disintegration of the USSR in the late 1980s led to a collapse also of proper statistical reporting. Any estimates are of only the roughest magnitude. Table 6 provides an extremely crude view of the picture as portrayed by standard sources. It shows a crisis of massive proportions, comparable in scale to the awful downturn in production in China after the Great Leap Forward.[3] Grigorii Khanin's meticulous estimates show a decline in national income of 34 per cent from 1989 to 1991, which was 'comparable to the decline in national income in the United States and Germany during the crisis of 1929–32, which was the worst in the history of capitalism' [*Khanin*, 1993a/1993b: 7]. However, much worse was in store with a decline in national income of a further 30 per cent in 1992 and 10 per cent or so in 1993 (Table 6). Moreover, 'utilised national income' fell by an estimated 40 per cent in 1992 [*ibid.*:17] as 'enormous inventories' accumulated, with enterprises producing unwanted

TABLE 6

SELECTED ECONOMIC INDICATORS FOR THE FORMER USSR

(all data are indices at constant prices, except where indication is to the contrary)

	1989	1990	1991	1992	1993*	1994*
Net Material product						
(i)	100	96.0	80.7	64.5*	58.1	48
(ii)**	100	–	66	47	–	–
Gross industrial output	100	98.9	90.9	77.3*	68.0	50
Gross agricultural output	100	97.7	87.9	80.0*	75.2	–
Retail trade turnover	100	110.4	99.4	59.6*	53.6	–
Gross fixed investment	100	101.0	89.2	49.1	–	–
Volume of foreign trade						
Exports	100	86.9	85.2	563.0*	–	–
Imports	100	98.6	90.8	70.8*		–
Foreign trade: index of value in current US$:						
Exports	100	95	72	54	54	47
Imports	–	100	64	58	47	47
Foreign debt(billion $)	60	61	65	76	–	
Consumer prices(% change on previous year)	5.0	8.0	150	2,500*	1,000	–

Notes: *estimates, for Russia only.

Sources: Economist Intelligence Unit, Country Report, CIS (formerly USSR), No.4, 1992; United Nations, Economic Commission for Europe [1993]
** Khanin,1993b,7,12; *Transition*, July-Aug.,1994; Smith New Court [1994].

output to keep afloat. Capital accumulation in Russia collapsed in the early 1990s (Table 6).

Furthermore, the decline gathered pace into 1994, with net national product estimated to fall a further 25–27 per cent in 1994 alone (*Transition*, July–Aug., 1994). Moreover, due to the disastrous foreign trade performance, the capital stock was unable to modernise quickly through importing foreign technology. While a huge new capital goods industry was growing in China, the capital goods industry in Russia in the early 1990s was simply disappearing. In the single year of 1994 alone it was estimated that output of the Russian machine building industry would fall by 42–45 per cent (*Transition*, July–Aug., 1994). Because the decline in output had been so large few people imagined that this rate of decline could continue much longer. However, there is no economic law which says it cannot be sustained for a substantial period even beyond this catastrophic fall.

Consumption: Bare statistics fail to capture the massive extent of the dislocation and suffering. Despite the paucity of hard data, it cannot seriously be disputed that for the vast bulk of the population real incomes fell significantly in the late 1980s and drastically in the early 1990s. It is true that every variety of foreign luxury suddenly was available in the shops, and, of course, one did not need to queue for most of these products. However, simultaneously large falls were taking place in the consumption of most foodstuffs, and consumption of basic non-food items fell even further. For example, physical output of textiles and shoes fell by around one half or more between 1991 and 1993. In the single year of 1992/93 cotton textile output (in square meters) fell by no less than 38 per cent [*IMF*, 1993: 87]. In the first half of 1994 output of textiles and shoes fell by a further 'one-third to one half' as the final *coup de grace* was delivered to Russian industry. Such devastating declines in output of basic industrial products cannot be consistent with anything other than a very large fall in income for a large proportion of the population. Khanin estimates that personal consumption in 1992 alone fell by over 30 per cent [*Khanin*, 1993a: 17].

Welfare indicators: One of the most important consequences of the economic collapse was the disintegration of the health service, which was already experiencing serious problems in the Gorbachev epoch. This, and the sharp rise in poverty were the factors that caused an 'explosion of morbidity' (Murray Feshbach, quoted in Ellman [1994]. In 1993 it was revealed that alarming increases were occurring in infectious diseases such as measles, whooping cough, tuberculosis, and syphilis (the rise from 1990 to 1993 was 142 per cent, 72 per cent, 34 per cent and 300 per cent respectively) [*Ellman,* 1994]. Large rises were reported also in diphtheria, dysentery and typhoid.

Moreover, the breakdown of government was accompanied by a very large increase in crime. Murders rose by a reported 42 per cent in 1992 and a further 60 per cent in the first half of 1993. Russia's murder rate for the first half of 1993 stood at 25/100,000 people placing it firmly in the category of 'high homicide' countries, with rates well above most other 'high homicide' countries such as Mexico (20/100,000) and Brazil (15/100,000) [*Ellman,* 1994].

Psychology: The consequences of the collapse are not just economic. It involved too, the deepest sense of national humiliation in this country which for most of the twentieth century considered itself to be the leader of the world's socialist nations. The sharpest change in social values occurred in a breathtakingly short time, away from collectivism and egalitarianism to rampant individualism. It was widely observed that for most ex-Soviet citizens their sense of 'social coherence' had been smashed. A nationwide condition of 'anomie' was brought into existence with a complete absence of reference points for the individual psyche. The sense of personal uncertainty greatly increased, especially because the changes since the mid-1980s occurred against a background of extremely high levels of security about most fundamentals, such as employment, personal safety, education, health and housing. The mood of national despondency and humiliation in the late 1980s and early 1990s was quite comparable to that of the 'three dark years' in China in the early 1960s.

Poverty: A mass of evidence supports the conclusion that for a large fraction of the population, probably well over one-half, the period since the late Gorbachev years saw a serious deterioration in living standards, alongside a large rise in income for a small fraction of the population. One serious, though extremely rough, estimate was carried out by the Russian Statistical Office (Goskomstat) together with the World Bank to estimate the level of poverty in Russia in 1992/93. In this study, 'poverty' was defined as an income which would allow a level of food consumption adequate to maintain a normal body weight at an average level of activity. It suggested that around 37 per cent of the Russian population was now living in poverty (quoted in Ellman [1994]). The situation was worse for children. In 1992 46–47 per cent of all children below the age of 15 were living in poverty [*Ellman,* 1994]. An estimate of poverty by the Living Standard Centre of the Russian Ministry of Labour, using a somewhat lower poverty line, calculated that 29.4 per cent of the population was living in poverty in the fourth quarter of 1993. However, it showed a frighteningly rapid deterioration of the situation in 1994, as the proportion of the population in poverty rose to 30.7 per cent and then again to 38.5 per cent in successive quarters (*Transition*, July–Aug., 1994).

An important aspect of the impoverishment was the deterioration in diet. In 1992, according to household budget surveys by Goskomstat, the consumption of meat and meat products fell by 11 per cent, of milk and milk products by 16 per cent, of fish by 19 per cent, of vegetables by 10 per cent and fruits and berries by 15 per cent. On the other hand, the consumption of bread rose by 3 per cent and potatoes by 9 per cent (quoted in Ellman [1994]).[4]

Inequality: Alongside the spiraling collapse there took place a massive redistribution of income and wealth. It is frequently the case that when disastrous collapses of output occur, such as in wartime, the hardship is shared relatively equally through rationing and direct state controls over production to ensure that basic needs are met for the poorest members of society. In the early 1990s in Russia the reverse happened. The dramatically declining average income was distributed grotesquely unequally.

In the chaotic economy of the early 1990s Soviet citizens had vastly different capacities, related to age, political position and connections, and initial capital endowments, to benefit from the 'privatisation' of assets : in just two years, the vast bulk of state assets was 'privatised' under lawless conditions. This was a process of 'primitive capital accumulation', which in the West took place over centuries, being conducted at the highest possible speed. A new 'aristocracy', often building on the old positions of power under the communist party, was created at high speed, rapidly accumulating a large share of the newly 'privatised' assets. The situation was analogous to a famine. Poorer people disposed of assets, however pathetic these might be, at a high rate in order to survive. This led to a decline in their real price, enabling those who possessed financial resources to accumulate resources at an especially fast rate.

Income distribution shifted at high speed. According to the journal *Trud*, the ratio of the income of the top decile to that of the bottom decile was in the order of 1:5.4 in 1991, and had risen to 1:8.0 by the end of 1992 (result quoted in Weir [1993: 2813]). The Russian Centre of Living Standards concluded that the growth rate of inequality was sharply accelerating in 1993/94 alongside the further stage of economic collapse. It concluded that there was a 'dramatic increase in the purchasing capacity of the wealthier strata of the population', alongside 'even further decline' in that of the poorer segments of the population. They estimated that the ratio of the income of the top decile to the bottom decile had risen at an alarmingly rapid pace, from 1:9.0 in the first quarter of 1994 to 1:13.0 in the second quarter (*Transition*, July–Aug., 1994).

Human rights: While China's economic prosperity and widening process of marketisation was steadily leading to the inexorable democratisation of daily life under the umbrella of one party rule, Russia's disastrous economic performance continued simultaneously with a slide back towards authoritarianism. If one constructs a balance sheet of 'human rights', then one has to offset the fact that Soviet citizens gained the right to vote and to speak freely, against the huge deterioration in other 'human rights' for most people, including the right to live safely, to employment, to decent food, to a decent education, housing and health service. Moreover, there was a hugely unequal capacity to benefit from the new 'negative' freedoms (for example, freedom of speech, freedom to accumulate capital), as were gained after the mid-1980s.

An alarming rise in death rates was a most powerful symbol of the deterioration in human rights under Soviet and post-Soviet reform. In the early 1960s the USSR stood proudly as a country with one of the lowest death rates in the world. By the late 1970s this had begun to rise ominously, reflecting mainly an increase in death rates among working age males. By the late 1980s, Russia's death rate had risen above the level for middle income countries. However, the most remarkable development was to occur in the post-Soviet period. By 1993 Russia's death rate had risen above even the level of low income countries (Table 4). Russia's death rate now stood on a par with that of such countries as Bangladesh, Nigeria, Sudan and Togo,[5] a dreadful testimony to the awful results of the reform process.

The human right to employment was eroded rapidly. Already in July 1994 the number of unemployed was estimated at around ten million, or 13 per cent of the economically active population (*Transition*, July–Aug., 1994). If bankruptcy provisions were strictly applied, then it is estimated that around five million more would become unemployed overnight (*Transition*, July–Aug., 1994). However, the concept of 'unemployment' was rapidly losing meaning. A large proportion of those 'employed' in the state sector were receiving no pay for long periods on end. The real value of government unemployment pay was falling rapidly alongside the collapse in real government expenditure. Fewer and fewer unemployed people were bothering to register as unemployed. As in the Third World, there was a rapidly rising 'informal' sector in which a large proportion of the 'self-employed' worked at any kind of 'business', however low the returns per hour. Far from heralding exciting new opportunities and signalling income growth, the explosion of these forms of informal sector 'service' activities reflected rapidly growing poverty and drastic shrinkage of full time employment opportunities in the formal sector.

Conclusion

The contrast in performance that accompanied the reforms in these two countries could not be greater. The impact on the daily life of the citizens of the two countries was dramatically different. The contrast is all the more striking because it was not predicted by anyone, least of all the leaders who initiated the reforms. Neither the speeches of Gorbachev in mid-1986, nor those of Deng Xiaoping in late 1978, when the two reform programmes began in earnest, anticipated this extraordinary outcome. Nor did any foreign social scientists predict this result.

What caused this dramatic and unpredicted contrast? The literature on the subject is still painfully thin, in part of course because the experience is so recent. In part also, however, this may be because of the discomfort caused by the role played by foreign advisors in each case. In the Soviet case, their influence was initially indirect, but still important. The direct influence rose steadily over time. In the Chinese case, foreign advice was accepted only selectively. China's reform programme was largely shaped despite, not because, of foreign advice.

The main line of argument that has been advanced to explain the contrast has been to suggest that the principal reason for the contrast lies not in the policies themselves, but, rather, in the different starting point from which the reforms proceeded. The main foreign advisers to the Russian government have exhibited no humility in respect to their contribution to the disaster that has befallen that country. One imagines that they would have been pleased to take the credit if their policies had brought success, rather than to attribute the success to the underlying conditions. Notable among the advisers is Anders Aslund, adviser to both Gorbachev and Yeltsin. He was asked in late 1992 as the disaster was unfolding, whether he 'would do anything different now'. He answered: 'Not really. I have been in favour all along of a very liberal solution for Russia. And the failures suggest that one has to go in a more liberal direction, as quickly as possible' (*Transition*, Nov., 1992, p.5).

The following section attempts to identify the degree to which the contrast in outcome was attributable to policy choice and how far to the underlying conditions of politics and economics inherited by the reforming governments.

CAUSES

The Transition Orthodoxy and Its Shortcomings

Until the reforms began in China, little was written on how to reform a communist system. The 'policy' content of the vast bulk of the writing on communist systems consisted simply of contrasting the shortcomings of these systems with the alleged advantages of capitalism. In other words, the implicit 'policy' recommendation was simply : 'establish a capitalist system and Western democratic institutions'. Even in the early 1980s the literature on the principles of reforming communist systems was small. Only in the late 1980s, and especially after the overthrow of communist systems in Eastern Europe in 1989, did a large 'transition' literature begin to emerge. This was relevant not only to the post-communist countries of Eastern Europe, but also to still communist countries of the USSR, China and, much less discussed, the smaller communist countries in Asia.[6]

A consensus quickly built up in the Western literature.[7] This 'transition orthodoxy' was constructed around a number of key propositions. It was held that serious economic reform was only possible after the communist party was overthrown. It was accepted as self-evident that the overthrow of communism was intrinsically desirable since it added to the welfare of the citizens of the communist countries by giving them political freedom. Moreover, it was 'twice blessed' since it was believed to be the only way in which 'serious' economic reform could be brought about. The belief in the intrinsic and functional virtues of democratisation was buttressed by the shift within the international institutions towards democratisation as a means to improve the situation in poorly performing developing countries, especially those of Africa.

'Transition' economists mostly believed that reforming communist countries could only achieve rapid improvement in their economic performance if they quickly moved towards a free market economy. The policies recommended were simply a more extreme version of the 'stabilisation and structural adjustment package' that had been implemented in so many developing countries under the supervision of the Bretton Woods insitutions. The intellectual lineage of the transition orthodoxy extends back to the economic liberalism of the utilitarian economists which underlay the economic policies of the British empire. It was 'laisssez-faire' in modern dress. Its key elements were tight monetary policy, price liberalisation, abolition of protection, and privatisation of state owned enterprises. These policies were closely linked with the proposition that a 'half-way house' solution of incremental system reform was a path to economic failure, worse perhaps even than the command economy. The notion that there was a 'Third Way' which combines the virtues of plan and market in some form of 'market socialism' was ridiculed by the most influential reform 'theorists', such as Kornai, and parroted by less influential figures.

The 'transition orthodoxy' was seriously flawed. It underestimated the capacity of communist governments to introduce serious market reforms. It underestimated the difficulty of producing a stable political environment in the wake of the anti-communist revolution. This problem was especially acute in large countries with wide regional diversities. It underestimated the importance of effective government of whatever political complexion for the conduct of economic life and for citizens' security: communist 'law' and communist administration usually is preferable to lawlessness and widespread criminality. The transition orthodoxy greatly underestimated the problems that would be caused by attempts to introduce rapid system change. It failed to anticipate the degree to which it would be necessary for the state to undertake a wide range of functions where the market 'failed' during the complex period of the transition away from the communist command system. These failures concerned both the achievement of growth and stability and also distribution of assets and income. Painfully little thought was given to the consequences for the resulting distribution of assets after a programme of rapid privatisation conducted under conditions of economic shock therapy.

The reforming leaderships in China and the former USSR adopted sharply different approaches towards the transition orthodoxy. These consensus views were held not only among social scientists in the advanced capitalist countries. They played a central role in the formal advice and informal influence of the powerful international insitutions, notably the IMF and the World Bank. They were important also in the approach adopted by domestic social scientists and policy 'think tanks' once they began to gain some independence of thought. Even in China the orthodoxy gained influence rapidly among policy advisors as contacts with the international community grew apace in the 1980s. It required enormous intellectual courage for a young Chinese economist sent for training at the World Bank, the IMF or in a Western university to resist the ideas presented by the vastly richer and more sophisticated teachers. Most of the teachers they encountered had contempt for socialism and planning. They considered the 'economics' of the Chinese reforms as primitive. They regarded the Chinese leaders as immoral in their approach to politics.

The Chinese leadership resisted these pressures and adopted policies that were quite contrary to those of the orthodoxy. Its economic policies were criticised widely as leading to a dead end, 'up the creek to nowhere'. Its political approach was condemned to the extent that an important part of the international community wished to punish China for not observing internationally acceptable norms of political behaviour. Gorbachev and his immediate advisers comprehensively embraced the central tenets of the mainstream reform consensus, intitially in their approach to political reform and latterly in their attempt to reform the economy. Under Yeltsin there was an even more explicit commitment to the transition orthodoxy in economic reform.

Political and Economic Conditions in the Two Countries at the Start of Reform

To what extent was the contrast in results caused by the large differences in the political and economic conditions in the two countries at the start of reform? There was, indeed, a wide range of differences between the two systems. These included geopolitical location, levels of per capita income, industrialisation and urbanisation, relative importance of small scale industry, the strength of the ancient roots of entrepreneurship, the availability of capital in the hands of overseas citizens, population pressure on farmland, relative size of the scientific community, cultural outlook, and relative size of ethnic minorities. However, there were many areas of fundamental similarity. These included the way the core of industry was organised; the relative importance of heavy industry within the industrial structure; the level of mass education relative to the country's income level; entrepreneurial capabilities as revealed in the modern period; the relatively large role of the military sector; and the huge common underachievement in relation to existing human and physical resources. In both cases there was a large potential for well designed institutional change to produce a substantial and continuing improvement in economic performance.

Many of the differences between the systems suggested a priori not that China would be likely to perform better than the USSR under a well designed reform programme, but rather the reverse. China's extraordinarily successful performance under reform was to a considerable degree despite, not because, of its legacy from pre- and post-revolutionary history. Its special handicaps for accelerated growth included the location of a large proportion of industry in remote inland areas; a low level of scientific personnel relative to both population size and level of income; a relatively large proportion of industrial output produced in small-scale, technologically backward plants; a miniscule amount of farmland per capita; and a high rate of population growth.

Many of the factors that are now identified as 'advantages' for China, such as the large amount of capital in the hands of overseas Chinese and the availability of a huge rural labour surplus, could only be taken advantage of because the policies adopted enabled them so to be. In the absence of policies that stimulated investment in the non-farm sector, the large and rapidly growing rural population would have been a huge liability, not an advantage, with ever-falling labour productivity in agriculture. Overseas Chinese capital would likewise have not been prepared to invest in China unless the policies chosen made it advantageous for them to do so. Had the Chinese system of political economy disintegrated in the way that the Soviet Union's did, investment by overseas Chinese would have been only a small fraction of that which actually occurred.

The Soviet Reform Path

By the mid-1980s the Soviet Union was in great economic difficulty. Fundamental system reform was necessary to improve the way the system operated. Tinkering within the traditional framework by applying more 'pressure' had aggravated rather than improved the situation. However, the system contained enormous unused productive capacities in both human abilities and capital stock. Moreover, the country possessed a huge domestic market, and massive natural resources. There was a high potential for rapid advance if the right set of political and economic policies could have been found. Under Gorbachev the leaders were groping towards an incremental economic reform strategy which would have eventually yielded good results. Within a few years the benefits of such an approach would have become manifestly clear from the Chinese experience, and the dangers of shock therapy equally clear from the Eastern European experience. This would have given added confidence to the leadership about the correctness of such a strategy.

The fundamental cause of the Soviet collapse lies in the destruction of the nation state and the state administrative apparatus under Gorbachev. This process was substantially the result of appalling policy error by the Soviet leadership. This in turn is explicable to some degree by deeper forces in modern Soviet history. However, the policy choice was attributable also to the massive pressure directed against the Soviet government, and Gorbachev in particular, in the final phase of the cold war. It was, moreover, influenced by the impact that contacts with Western, especially US, Sovietological institutions had upon key figures surrounding Gorbachev. The overthrow of the Soviet state was almost universally applauded in the Western media, by Western academics and, especially, by Western politicians. The overthrow of the communist state was the central building block of the 'transition orthodoxy'.

To be successful, an economic reform strategy requires political stability and effective government. These are necessary to maintain the government's fiscal capacity and to achieve financial stability. They are also necessary in order to enable the government to undertake the necessary planning functions in the transition away from the command economy. Moreover, they are necessary in order for the government to provide a sense of social coherence to minimise social dislocation likely to result from the transition.

The Gorbachev regime inherited a country that was politically stable. The 'revolutionary' dissident movement was confined to a small intellectual minority. Moreover, the regime possessed a powerful administrative apparatus in the shape of the Communist Party. The severity with which national minorities had been dealt with by previous governments meant that the nationalist movements had low expectations about the possibility for national independence. Gorbachev's policies of *perestroika* and *glasnost* turned the ideas of the dissident minority and a hostile international community into national policy. They resulted in the destruction of the Communist Party without substituting a stable, effective democratic system. They resulted also in the destruction of the nation state as it had existed basically since the eighteenth century.

The economic consequences of these changes were enormous. Their effects completely swamped the impact of the limited economic reforms that were tentatively begun in the 1987/88 reform wave. The bequest of the Gorbachev period to its successor was a government, a society and an economy in a catastrophic tail-spin. It is hard to imagine how any government which inherited power in the new Russian state in 1991, or indeed in any of the former republics, could have restored the situation even within many years. In fact, the polices adopted by the successor state made a bad situation much worse.

Once the state apparatus had collapsed, the range of options for any successor government was reduced greatly. The depth of the political and economic difficulties bequeathed to the Russian government in 1991 made it difficult to devise a successful economic strategy for the country in the early 1990s. The nature of the political problems after August 1991 was such that it was difficult for the government to pursue any kind of consistent policy. The composition of the new parliamentary institutions rendered it impossible to get agreement on a consistent economic policy. The state's fiscal capacity had been deeply undermined by the political changes, giving a high built-in propensity towards inflation. The framework of law and order had already begun to break down. This deeply undermined the security of property rights, and made it likely that the distributional consequences of any move towards privatisation would be heavily affected by criminal power. The government's confidence was shattered by the political disintegration of the USSR, the overthrow of the Communist Party of the Soviet Union, and by the swift collapse of communism in eastern Europe. Moreover, the government was desparate for international financial support. These events helped push it towards the international instititutions for advice on how to try to shape its economic programme.

The path that was adopted was one which produced the worst of all possible worlds. The shock therapy of instantaneous price liberalisation and wild, high-speed privatisation occurred without an effective framework of law and order, or government administrative strength. It occured in an economy with hyper-inflation and collapsed government fiscal capacity. The main purpose of the government in this period (1992/94) was not to minimise the human cost of the transition, but to maximise the speed with which capitalist insitutions were created. The most important such institution was regarded by the government as a capitalist class. There was the clearest view that the short term costs were worthwhile in the interests of creating the efficiency and growth promoting insititutions of capitalism. The result was a process of brutal and massively unequal primitive capitalist accumulation, the 'creation of markets in circumstances of total chaos', as Mr Soskovets, the deputy prime minister expressed it (*Financial Times*, 23 Aug., 1994). The policy of rapid privatisation was supported strongly by a large part of the circle of foreign advisors and by the international capitalists with whom government officals had contact.

Without a coherent, effective state apparatus no strategy for transition from the communist economy in Russia after August 1991 could succeed. In the absence of such an apparatus it was impossible to follow an 'East Asian' approach to the transition. However, the whole orientation of the Yeltsin government and the advice it received from the international insitutions was directed away from trying to reconstruct a strong state, destruction of which was regarded widely as the great achievement of the Gorbachev epoch.

China's Reform Path

During system reform the Chinese government was obsessed with maintaining social and political stability. This obsession arose from the long sweep of Chinese history, and the regular dynastic cycle: periods of stablity and prosperity alternated with dynastic decline into anarchy, chaos (*da luan*), famine and population decline. China had experienced just such an extended period of anarchy from the middle of the nineteenth century through to the revolution in 1949. All of the aged leaders after 1976 had lived through the latter part of this epoch of great national humiliation and widespread suferring.[8] Moreover, they had all witnessed the disaster of the Great Leap Forward of 1958–59 as a result of which as many as 30 million people died of famine. They had additionally witnessed, and mostly suffered from, the Cultural Revolution's anarchy, which caused a large economic recession but, more seriously, produced great personal suffering as political disorder spread over most of the country. Finally, China was still a very poor country, so that the leadership was acutely aware that a failed attempt to 'leap' into a better situation, could produce not just a decline in output but widespread famine.

The continued commitment to the old political insitutions allowed a great deal of official corruption to occur. However, the maintenance of a strong Communist Party enabled the state to remain comparatively effective fiscally. It meant that the rules governing the organisation of the economy were reasonably predictable and contractual arrrangements were reasonably secure. The Chinese government was unwavering in its commitment to experimentalism in reform, with priority to policies that would lead to growth of output and incomes. Economic agents were confronted by a reasonably stable set of parameters upon which to base their decisions. The government sustained a public commitment to key ethical values. The former collectivist values were not abandoned in favour of individualism. The interests of the individual and different social groups were subordinated to building a powerful country and common prosperity. The term 'socialism' was redefined gradually but not jettisoned. In 1994 the Chinese government still considered the country to be a socialist, rather than a capitalist, market economy. 'Socialism' came to be indentified, firstly, with planning through the use of markets. It was identified, secondly, with combining individual incentives with limitations on asset accumulation by individuals, and thirdly, with providing 'fair' opportunities to those in less advantageous socio-economic positions. These values, and the associated polices, helped ensure that during the reform period there was a reasonably effective trickle down of the benefits of growth. A sense of 'social coherence' was maintained during the reform period. This benefited popular welfare directly through its psychological impact. It helped also to cement social stability through giving citizens a sense of participation in a common endeavour.

The Chinese reforms aimed to improve the performance from publicly owned assets through the devolution of control over their 'use rights' (*shiyong quan*) in return for income sharing along contracted lines. Price liberalisation proceeded cautiously along dual track lines. Simultaneously, the material supply system was gradually liberalised. However, even in the early 1990s, domestic producers remained shielded from foreign competition. These gradually introduced, experimental, supply-side reforms improved labour productivity and incomes. Capital began to move towards those regions, sectors and enterprises that yielded higher returns. Not only did the returns from investment improve, but the rate of savings and investment was sustained at a high level. The 'Lewis model' of growth was able to operate with fast growth of non-farm employment generating large surpluses per worker for reinvestment, unhindered in much of the labour market by insitutional restrictions on conditions of employment. From extreme technical backwardness, China began to generate rapid technical progress. Fast growth of export earnings enabled rapid growth of imports of technology-enhancing products. The reforms provided domestic producers with increased incentives to achieve technical progress themselves.[9] Private direct foreign investment acted as an increasingly important channel for modernisation.

Throughout the reform period the Chinese economy remained highly protected. Domestic producers could be certain that for a long period ahead, their only serious competitors in most spheres were from within China itself. As domestic markets gradually liberalised, consumers of all products were able to chose more and more freely, and became progressively more discriminating purchasers. This applied most obviously in consumer goods markets. The quality of a wide range of consumer goods rose in obvious ways during the reforms, many of which could not be captured by statistics. The same processes began also to affect the production of capital goods. The enterprises that prospered and grew fastest tended to be those that produced products that were in some sense (whether price, design, durability or energy consumption) considered to be superior. The large increases in personal income caused a large increase in demand for consumer goods and services. An initial large rise in demand for food grain, shifted to increased demand for superior foodstuffs. Demand for housing was sustained at a high level throughout the reform period. In the early phase of the reforms the main source of increased demand for industrial consumer goods was relatively simple consumer durables, such as bicyles and sewing machines. As the reforms progressed, demand growth shifted to a new wave of industrial products, such as colour TVs, refrigerators, hi-fi equipment, and fashion clothing. Meeting this huge, fast growing demand mainly from domestic producers induced corresponding investment in the farm sector and in the light industries. In a substantially closed economy, meeting the demand for these products necessitated a large, corresponding rise in demand for capital goods and intermediate inputs. Demand from domestic producers for such products as steel, cement, a wide variety of machinery, and transport equipment, all grew by leaps and bounds.

A powerful symbiosis between supply and demand took place. Incremental insitutional changes released the latent productive potentialities embedded in the Chinese economy, as it was in all the communist economies. This allowed initial growth of income, which generated demand for both consumer and capital goods. This stimulated the growth of investment in these activities, which allowed modernisation of the capital stock and improvements in labour productivity. This in turn started the cycle again stimulating further rises in demand, investment and productivity. China was 'growing out of the plan' [*Wang*, 1993].

When Deng Xiaoping talked in the late 1970s and in the 1980s of the dangers of descent into political chaos in China if the Communist Party were overthrown, he was regarded by a large fraction of the intellectual democratic movement in China as at best foolish and at worst malign in whipping up an unreal danger in order to justify prolongation of a vile regime.[10] Political correctness and passionate rhetorical gestures are not a good basis for policy. It can now be seen the the communist system was extremely brittle, especially in the huge empires of Russia and China. There was no possibility of careful, controlled reform, gradually releasing the 'safety valve' of political control. The choice can now be seen all too clearly from the Russian case in a way that few imagined a decade or so ago. The only alternative to continued communist party rule in Russia and China during the transition to some form of market economy was indeed political chaos. The establishment of a stable democratic system was something that could only be accomplished after the market economy had made large progress and the habits of life necessary for stable democracy established. Unfortunately, political chaos creates the worst possible conditions for producing just such an advance in the market economy in a reforming Stalinist system.

CONCLUSION

After the late 1970s China slowly moved away from totalitarian, command economy communism. It moved towards a nationalistic, state guided, bureaucratic market economy, with a strong emphasis on harnessing individual entrepreneurial energies within a collectivist framework. The reforms harnessed the potential latent in the old system and set in motion a virtuous circle of growth out of the command economy. China became ever more powerful internationally. In Russia, the reforms quickly destroyed the old state apparatus, but failed to construct an effective successor state. They allowed the creation of a highly unequal and deeply disorienting process of primitive capitalist accumulation. The resulting inequalities in assset ownership will fix the parameters for economic life for many decades to come. The reforms caused a disastrous decline in investment and industrial output, setting in motion a vicious circle of economic collapse. Russia became ever weaker internationally, to the point that its policies were constructed at the direct instruction of the major international capitalist institutions. In the brief space of just a few years it had been humiliated and broken as a great power.

This article contains two implicit counter factual propositions. First, the selection of different policies in Russia could have produced rapid growth of output and a large improvement in popular living standards. Secondly, the selection of a different set of policies in China could easily have produced a political and economic disaster, with a large decline in popular living standards.

There is currently a great deal of interest in Russia in the 'Chinese solution' to Russia's deep problems. The analysis in this article does not lead logically to the easy conclusion that Russia ought now to follow 'the

Chinese path'. This was a path out of the communist command economic system, using the still extant insitutions of communism, working with a unified nation state, and reorganising an existing system of publicly owned assets. It began with the establishment of a virtuous circle of growth leading to a whole sequence of interconnected improvements in performance. The state apparatus in Russia is destroyed. The nation state is destroyed. There are few assets left in the public sector. The economy is in the deepest decline. It is a fantasy to imagine that one can simply reconstruct the old nation state, the old administrative apparatus, and the old publicly owned economy. Careful study of China's reform path would have been relevant to devising a reform strategy for the country in the late 1980s. It is not much relevant to Russia's current situation. This requires thinking afresh from the present conditions. The 'Chinese solution' is no more an answer to Russia's current disastrous situation than were 'free markets' and 'democracy' an answer to the problems of the communist command system.

Some commentators critical of the outcome of post-communist reform have argued expicitly or have implied that the most that was needed with the communist system was tinkering in order substantially to improve its performance. Others have argued that the command system served a useful function in the early stages of development, but had outlived it usefulness.[11] However, the basic concepts of the command economic system were fundamentally flawed from the outset. In both cases systemic problems were intensifying. However, neither system was on the verge of collapse. Dangerous reform experiments cannot be justified in hindsight as rescuing the systems from impending disaster. They needed system reform to rescue them from stagnation. The questions were: how fast, in what manner and towards what goal reform to proceed? Most importantly, what should be the relationship betweeen political and economic reform?

NOTES

1. Local studies such as Lyons' on Fujian province, confirm the huge achievement in the 1980s: 'Unless Fujian is grossly unrepresentative, China has indeed prosecuted a war on poverty of remarkable dimensions – and certainly one deserving of greater attention than it has received to date' [*Lyons*,1992: 64].
2. From 1978 to 1992, the reported average annual growth of real per capita consumption was 6.7 per cent for rural dwellers and 5.9 per cent for urban dwellers [*SSB*, ZGTJZY 1994: 49].
3. In fact, unofficial estimates of output suggest that the downturn began before 1989, and there may well have been negative growth of national product over the whole 1985–90 period [*Aslund*, 1991: 200].
4. The journal *Trud* estimates that from 1989 to 1992 consumption of meat fell by 21 per cent, dairy products by 34 per cent, sugar by 13 per cent, and fruits by 32 per cent. Consumption of bread rose by 22 per cent (reported in *Weir* [1993: 2812]).
5. A full comparison of death rates requires analysis of age specific death rates rather than overall death rates.

6. These 'smaller' countries were not all absolutely small. In the late 1980s the total population of Asian communist countries other than China was around 120 million, compared to 110 million for European communist countries (134 million if one includes Yugoslavia). Vietnam's population is almost twice that of Poland (65 million versus 38 million), and Burma's population (around 40 million)is larger than Poland's. In the applied literature on transforming economies, there is a massive dominance of books and articles on the east European countries, yet the communist countries of Asia other than China contain just as many people, and in the long run may well be more powerful economies than the former communist countries of east Europe.

7. Key components of this writing were Aslund [1990a, 1991]; Blanchard *et al.* [1991]; IMF, World Bank, EBRD, and OECD [1990]; Gomulka [1989]; Johnson [1990]; Kornai [1986; 1990]; Lipton and Sachs [1990a; 1990b]; Prybyla [1990; 1991]. Notable exceptions to the consensus were, from very different points of view, Galbraith [1990]; Macmillan and Naughton [1991]; Singh [1991]; and Walters [1991; 1992].

8. This is not inconsistent with considerable capitalist dynamism in the areas of political stability and secure property rights, notably the Treaty Ports.

9. In the same way as Japan at a comparable stage of development, this focused more on borrowing and adapting international technology rather than undertaking primary research.

10. In my own debates with members of the Chinese democratic movement I was attacked repeatedly for suggesting that the possibility of political chaos had to be taken very seriously indeed, and for suggesting that supporting policies that sound liberal but which lead to political chaos will have disastrous results for the lives of most ordinary Chinese people; for example, in debate with the 'Future of China Society' in New York in November 1990 (the proceedings were subsequently published in Chinese) (*Future of China Society*, New York, 1993), and in the debate at the Oxford Union on 4 May 1992, commemorating the 4 June massacre.

11. This view is effectively the same as that in the reformist 'joke'. Question : what is socialism? Answer: The transitional stage between feudalism and capitalism.

REFERENCES

Amnesty International, 1987, *China : Torture and Ill-treatment of Prisoners*, London: Amnesty International Publications.

Aslund, A., 1990, 'Gorbachev, Perestroika, and Economic Crisis,' *Problems of Communism*, Jan.–April, pp.13–41.

Aslund, A., 1991, *Gorbachev's Struggle for Economic Reform*, London: Pinter.

Banister, J., 1992, *Demographic Aspects of Poverty in China*, Washington, DC: World Bank, Working Paper.

Bergson, A. and D. Levine (eds.), 1983, *The Soviet Economy : Towards the Year 2000*, London: Allen & Unwin.

Blanchard, O., Dornbusch, R., Krugman, P., Layard, R. and L. Summers, 1991, *Reform in Eastern Europe*, Cambridge, MA: MIT Press.

Chakravarty, S.,1987, *Development Planning: The Indian Experience*, Oxford: Oxford University Press.

Clague, C. and G.C. Rausser, 1992, *The Emergence of Market Economies in Eastern Europe*, Oxford: Blackwell.

Ellman, M., 1994, 'The Increase in Death and Disease under *Katastroika*', Cambridge Journal of Economics, Vol.18, No.4.

Galbraith, J.K., 1990, 'The Rush to Capitalism', *New York Review of Books*, 25 Oct.

Gomulka, S., 1989, 'Shock Needed for the Polish Economy', *Guardian* (London), 19 Aug.

Hicks, G. (ed.), 1990, *The Broken Mirror*, Harlow: Longman.

IMF, World Bank, OECD and EBRD, 1990, *The Economy of the USSR: Summary and Recommendations*, Washington, DC: World Bank.

IMF, 1993, *Russian Federation*, Economic Review, No.8, Washington, DC, International Monetary Fund.

Johnson, C., 1990, 'Forward', in Hicks [1990].
Kenettt, D. and M. Lieberman (eds.), 1992, *The Road to Capitalism*, Orlando, FL: Dryden Press.
Khanin, G.I., 1993a, 'The Economic Crisis in Russia: Possible Ways Out', *Problems of Economic Transition*, Vol.36, No.2, pp.23–7.
Khanin, G.I., 1993b, 'Russia's Economic Situation in 1992', *Problems of Economic Transition*, Vol.36, No.7, pp.6–24.
Kornai, J., 1986, 'The Hungarian Reform Process: Visions, Hopes, and Realities', *Journal of Economic Literature*, Vol.24, pp.1687–737.
Kornai, J., 1990, *The Road to a Free Economy*, New York: Norton.
Lipton, D. and J. Sachs, 1990a, 'Creating a Market Economy in Eastern Europe: The Case of Poland', *Brookings Papers on Economic Activity*, Vol.1, 1990, reprinted in Kennett and Lieberman [1992].
Lipton, D. and J. Sachs, 1990b, 'Privatisation in Eastern Europe', *Brookings Papers on Economic Activity*, No.2, reprinted in Kennett and Lieberman [1992].
Lowe, A., 1965, *On Economic Knowledge*, New York: Harper & Row.
Lyons, B., 1992, *China's War on Poverty: A Case Study of Fujian Province, 1985–1990*, Hong Kong: Chinese University of Hong Kong, Institute of Asia-Pacific Studies.
Macmillan, J. and B.Naughton, 1991, 'How to Reform a Planned Economy', *Oxford Review of Economic Policy*, Vol.8, No.1, pp.130–43.
Nolan, P., 1994, 'Democratization, Human Rights and Economic Reform: The Case of China and Russia', *Democratisation*, Vol.1, No.1, Spring.
Nolan, P., 1995, *China's Rise Russia's Fall: Politics, Economics and Planning in the Transition from Stalinism*, Houndmills: Macmillan.
Popper, K., 1957, *The Poverty of Historicism*, London: Routledge & Kegan Paul.
Prybyla, J., 1990, 'A Broken System', in Hicks [1990].
Prybyla, J., 1991, 'The Road from Socialism: Why, Where, What and How', *Problems of Communism*, Vol.XL, Jan.–April.
Report of the Commission on Graduate Education in Economics, 1991, *Journal of Economic Literature*, Vol.29, Sept., pp.1035–53.
Reynolds, L.G., 1985, *Economic Growth in the Third World,1850–1980*, New Haven, CT: Yale University Press.
Sachs, J. and W.T. Woo, 1994, 'Structural Factors in the Economic Reforms of China, Eastern Europe, and the Former Soviet Union', *Economic Policy*, Vol.9, No.18, April.
Singh, I., 1991, 'Is There Schizophrenia about Socialist Reform?', *Transition*, July–Aug.
Smith New Court Securities, 1994, 'What Tune is Yeltsin Dancing To?', London, Feb.
State Statistical Bureau (SSB), (ZGTJNJ), 1984–93, *Chinese Economic Yearbook* (*Zhongguo tongji nianjian*), Beijng, Zhongguo tongji chubanshe.
State Statistical Bureau (SSB), (ZGTJZY), 1984–94, *Statistical Survey of China* (*Zhongguo tongji zhaiyao*), Beijing, Zhongguo tongji chubanshe.
Tinbergen, J, 1964, *Central Planning*, New Haven, CT and London: Yale University Press.
Transition, Washington , DC: World Bank. various issues.
United Nations, Economic Commision for Europe, 1993, *Economic Survey for Europe, 1992/3*, New York: United Nations.
Walters, A., 1991, 'Misapprehensions on Privatisation', *International Economic Insights*, Vol.2, No.1, reprinted in Kennet and Lieberman [1992].
Walters, A., 1992, 'The Transition to a Market Economy', in Clague and Rausser, 1992.
Wang, Xiaoqiang, 1993, *Groping for Stones to Cross the River: Chinese Price Reform against the"Big Bang"*, Cambridge University, Department of Applied Economics, Discussion Paper, No.DPET 9305.
Weir, F., 1993, 'Russia's Descent into Latin America', *Economic and Political Weekly*, Special Number, Vol.28, No.51.
World Bank, 1992, *China: Strategies for Reducing Poverty in the 1990s*, Washington, DC: World Bank.
World Bank, 1979–94, *World Development Reports* (WDR), Washington, DC: Oxford University Press.

Abstracts

Agrarian Questions Then and Now
HENRY BERNSTEIN

This essay is inspired by T.J. Byres' comparative political economy of agrarian transitions, which it tries to build on in the collective project of advancing the Marxist understanding of the agrarian question. Using as a basis the analytics and historical findings of Byres' work, it seeks to integrate them in the framework of the uneven and combined development of capitalism on a world scale. In doing so, it also interrogates the politics of the agrarian question, and two distinct conceptions of the end of the agrarian question.

Dynamic Economies and the Critique of Urban Bias
MASSOUD KARSHENAS

This essay investigates the theoretical foundations of the urban bias thesis and discusses new evidence on intersectoral resource flows. It is argued that the existence of dynamic economies makes a critical difference in the patterns of intersectoral resource flows at different stages of development. An appraisal of the five volume study by the World Bank of the 'political economy of agricultural pricing policy' is made in this context. This is followed by our own case studies where it is found that the nature of dynamic economies in the non-agricultural sectors, and the efficiency of resource use within agriculture, by and large neglected in the conventional urban bias literature, are the key elements in understanding the historical patterns of intersectoral resource flows.

Output Per Acre and Size of Holding: The Logic of Peasant Agriculture Under Semi-Feudalism
GRAHAM DYER

The inverse relationship between farm size and productivity is widely accepted as a 'stylised fact' of agriculture in developing countries, a generalised phenomenon observed in widely differing agro-climatic conditions and agrarian structures. Extensive debate over the inverse relationship is constituted by two distinct agendas: first, factors which give rise to and explain the inverse relationship in the static context; second, following the green revolution, a discussion of the breakdown of the inverse relationship in the dynamic context of changing technology. Byres [1972; 1974; 1977a; 1977b; 1981; 1986a; 1986b; 1990; 1991; Byres and Dyer, forthcoming] made the first serious attempt to integrate static and dynamic analyses into a rigorous and unified class theoretic framework in the context of agrarian transitions, to explain both the generation of the inverse relationship and its breakdown. Class relations in relatively backward agriculture exert economic compulsion on the poor peasantry to intensify cultivation, thus generating an inverse relationship. With the increasing development of capitalist relations of production and exchange, the inverse relationship breaks down as large farms capture the economies of scale associated with the new technology.

Communist Revolution and Peasant Mobilisation in the Hinterland of North China: The Early Years
R.G. TIEDEMANN

Much has been written on the significant contribution of wartime rural mobilisation in North China to the success of the Communist revolution. In contrast, far less is known about attempts at peasant mobilisation in this poor and disaster-prone region in the 1920s. The article provides a brief overview of this phase of radical rural work on the North China Plain, an area with a long tradition of organised competitive violence. It begins with an discussion of the complex setting, followed by a consideration of Communist incursions to gain control of existing militarised multi-class collectivities. Finally, the author examines the serious limitations of these mobilisation efforts and concludes that the unfavourable political situation, the revolutionaries' lack of coercive power, their inadequate ideological and organisational preparation, and above all the application of inappropriate policies contributed to the failure of the Chinese Communist Party to gain appreciable rural support in North China in the 1920s.

Popular Culture, Populist Fiction(s): The Agrarian Utopiates of A.V. Chayanov, Ignatius Donnelly and Frank Capra
TOM BRASS

Given the current resurgence amidst the capitalist crisis of attempts by non-Marxist social theory to construct an 'a-political' concept of 'community', this article examines previous attempts – also in the context of capitalist crisis – to construct an 'imaginary' alternative to capitalism and socialism, as projected in the 'community' constructed by agrarian populism in three literary/filmic texts: Caesar's Column (1890), The Journey of My Brother Alexei to the Land of Peasant Utopia (1920) and Lost Horizon (1933/1937). It is argued here that all three share a common utopic/dystopic vision based on a series of symptomatic oppositions. The discourse-against of agrarian populism identifies the dystopic (or absence of 'community') as dark, unnatural, and western, where large-scale technified production controlled by finance capital in an urban setting is linked discursively to the threat of socialism and chaos. Its discourse-for, by contrast, identifies utopia (= 'community') as a realm of light that is harmonious, natural and orientalist, in which neither finance capital nor proletariat exists, and which consists instead of small-scale artisan and peasant producers.

Globalisation and Restructuring in the Indian Food Industry
JAIRUS BANAJI

This article outlines the impact of global capitalist competition on the food industry in India, and in particular how subsidiaries of multinational corporations have from the early 1990s onwards restructured production in order to enhance, maintain or restore profitability worldwide. Following economic and financial deregulation, therefore, the principal effect of inward investment by agribusiness in search of cheap labour and new markets has been diversification into food processing, the rapid growth of contract farming, and the erosion of working-class unionisation as a consequence of deregulation.

Trade as a Mechanism of Economic Retrogression
PRABHAT PATNAIK

This essay theorises about a phenomenon whose prevalence would be recognised by many economic historians, namely, that an economy's being opened up for trade or engaging in larger trade can be a cause for its retrogression even when its trade is balanced, that is, that trade *per se*, not terms of trade shifts or plunder, 'drain' and other forms of unrequited exports, can have a short-term as well as a long-term contractionary effect on the economy. No strand of economic theory as it exists can explain this phenomenon. The basic distinction is between agricultural and manufacturing exports. If an economy is agriculture-constrained, in the sense that, while the agricultural sector produces to its capacity, its output is not larger enough in any period to permit full capacity use in manufacturing at some 'acceptable' real wage-rate, then agricultural exports, even if balanced by manufacturing imports, will result in immediate economic contraction, and, under certain conditions, lower long-term growth. A good export performance, far from being virtuous for growth, becomes a vice if it is based on agricultural exports, a conclusion which has obvious implications with regard to the Structural Adjustment policies being imposed on the Third World.

China's Rise, Russia's Fall
PETER NOLAN

One of the most profound events of the late twentieth century is the dramatic contrast of processes of 'reform' in China and the former USSR. This essay first illustrates that contrast in terms of available indicators of economic and social change in China since 1978 and the former USSR since 1989. It then considers explanations of this difference in fortunes. Criticising the 'transition orthodoxy' of neo-liberalism that emerged in the 1980s, the essay argues that China's success registers a rejection of that orthodoxy by careful movement towards a state guided market economy, harnessing individual entrepreneurial energies within a collectivist framework. Russia's acquiescence to the prescriptions of that orthodoxy, on the other hand, is a principal factor in explaining its rapid economic decline, with disastrous social consequences for the great majority of its citizens.

For Product Safety Concerns and Information please contact our EU
representative GPSR@taylorandfrancis.com
Taylor & Francis Verlag GmbH, Kaufingerstraße 24, 80331 München, Germany

www.ingramcontent.com/pod-product-compliance
Ingram Content Group UK Ltd.
Pitfield, Milton Keynes, MK11 3LW, UK
UKHW042200240425
457818UK00011B/318